Television at Work

T0323469

TELEVISION AT WORK

Industrial Media and American Labor

Kit Hughes

OXFORD
UNIVERSITY PRESS

Oxford University Press is a department of the University of Oxford. It furthers
the University's objective of excellence in research, scholarship, and education
by publishing worldwide. Oxford is a registered trade mark of Oxford University
Press in the UK and certain other countries.

Published in the United States of America by Oxford University Press
198 Madison Avenue, New York, NY 10016, United States of America.

Library of Congress Cataloging-in-Publication Data
Names: Hughes, Kit, author.
Title: Television at work : industrial media and American labor / Kit Hughes.
Description: New York, NY : Oxford University Press,
[2019. Identifiers: LCCN 2019021018 | ISBN 9780190855789 (hardback) |
ISBN 9780190855796 (paperback) | ISBN 9780190855819 (epub) |
ISBN 9780190855802 (updf)
Subjects: LCSH: Television in management—United States—History—20th century. |
Industrial television—United States—History—20th century. | Labor—United States—
History—20th century. | Industrial management—United States—History—20th century.
Classification: LCC HD30.34 .H74 2019 | DDC 651.7/9—dc23
LC record available at https://lccn.loc.gov/2019021018.

9 8 7 6 5 4 3 2 1

Paperback printed by Marquis, Canada
Hardback printed by Bridgeport National Bindery, Inc., United States of America

For Melvin "Harry" Hughes and Helen Taylor Hollingshead
who knew the power of asking
"Do you remember?"

CONTENTS

Introduction

Television and Work, Television at Work

The people you work with are people you were just thrown together with. I mean, you don't know them. It wasn't your choice. And yet you spend more time with them than you do your friends or your family. But probably all you have in common is the fact that you walk around on the same bit of carpet for eight hours a day.

—Tim Canterbury, *The Office* (UK)

Work structures our social relationships, experience of time, access to opportunity and material resources, domestic relations, mobility (whether crossing a carpet or a continent), and even our sense of self.[1] It is an engine of inequality and identity. While Tim muses he was "just thrown together" with his coworkers, this premise—extended to the nonfictional world—doesn't quite hold. Institutions filter people into laboring and class positions. Even in the fictional world of *The Office*, Tim shares more with his colleagues than he cares to admit. His much-performed disaffected pose in relation to work matches his coworkers' understanding of work as a crucial part (whether welcome or not) of their identities. David Brent's obsession with being the "cool boss" who seeks approval of his underlings is the most obvious example, but we might also think of Gareth's love of bureaucracy—an incessant rule-following that spans his leisure-time Territorial Army participation—or Dawn's dream of becoming a professional illustrator—a plot point that resolves one of the show's central tensions in its series finale. Work is central to who these people are and who they will ultimately care for and about.

Television at Work. Kit Hughes, Oxford University Press (2020) © Oxford University Press.
DOI: 10.1093/oso/9780190855789.001.0001

This book explores how work, television, and waged labor come to have meaning in our everyday lives. However, it is not an analysis of workplace sitcoms or quality dramas. Instead, it explores the forgotten history of how US American private sector workplaces used television in the twentieth century. It traces how, at the hands of employers, television physically and psychically managed workers and attempted to make work meaningful under the sign of capitalism. Returning to television's workaday past reveals a critical episode in the twinned rise of the technologically mediated corporation and a globalizing information economy. This book shows how the so-called domestic medium helped businesses shape labor relations and information architectures foundational to these transformations. Among other things, business and industry built extensive private television networks to distribute live and taped programming, leased satellite time for global "meetings" and program distribution, created complex closed-circuit television (CCTV) data search and retrieval systems, encouraged the use of videotape for worker self-evaluation, used videocassettes for training distributed workforces, and wired cantinas for employee entertainment and team-building. These disparate projects coalesce under what I call *television at work*. Referring to the use of televisual technologies within the specific social-spatial relations of the workplace, *television at work* also describes the myriad ways the medium served businesses' attempts to shape employees' relationships to their labor and the workplace in order to secure industrial efficiency, support corporate expansion, and inculcate preferred ideological orientations.

In short, I argue that industrial television sought to acclimate workers to the desires and conditions of post-Fordism. While industrial CCTV of the immediate post-war era pursued Fordist efficiencies by centralizing elements of manufacturing and office work, the applications of theater television, videotape, videocassettes, and satellite business television were more expansive. Targeting workers' emotions; will to self-regulate; ability to work at home and on their own time; identity; and identification with the boss, the firm, and the interests of capital, these uses of television engaged workers' most intimate capacities. By uncovering industrial television as a prolific sphere of media practice—one that continually sought to reshape the technology's cultural meanings, affordances, and uses—*Television at Work* positions the medium at the heart of corporate experiments into reconfiguring the American workplace and advancing understandings of labor that increasingly revolved around dehumanized technological systems and information flows.

TELEVISION AS ORIENTATION

Though rarely acknowledged, television has *always* been a multi-sited, multivalent technology worked over by a host of competing interests across hyper-local, regional, and national scales. Radically challenging traditional understandings of what television is, where it is located, and who (and what) it is for, this book examines the medium's use as an instrument of *orientation* engaged in cultural and logistical management in three interrelated senses. First, building on Lisa Parks's definition of television as an "epistemological system derived through the alternating discursive modalities of commercial entertainment, public education, military monitoring, and scientific observation," I see television as an interface that shapes viewers' understanding of their world and their place within it.[2] *Television at Work* adds corporate and workplace communications as a key discursive modality shaping this system (and I imagine that additional research—into medical television, for example—would expand this list further). Much like worker orientation introduces the uninitiated to cultural norms and expectations and provides the necessary tools for their success within the workplace, television has long been understood as a cultural resource that provides certain opportunities—and forecloses others—for orienting oneself to particular texts, viewing practices, and larger cultural and subcultural spheres. For a time and for some of the largest companies in the country, video programming became the chosen interface to mediate material, cultural, and social relationships among workers and with the firm. Exploiting employees' relationships with consumer entertainment technologies, television likewise sought to reorient expectations of mediated work, opening workers up to increased demands of corporate connection and cooperation. By looking at workplace television in this sense, we might pose one of the most important and vexing questions of our time: Why, in a country where one's job is so supposedly central to one's identity, do class-based solidarities hold so little appeal?

Second, I understand orientation as the logistical process of enabling action in space. Here I expand on Anna McCarthy's research into how television attempts to shape the activities and social relations of people in public spaces, whether this means directing the movement of travelers and female shoppers or pacifying those stuck and waiting. Although wary of definitional work, McCarthy suggests we can best understand television as a "site-specific cultural form," a slippery medium ultimately defined by "its *flexibility* as an environmental apparatus," that shapes the micro-politics of the TV set's immediate environment at the same time that it incorporates these relations into larger scales of institutional and even global power and movement.[3] Where I diverge from McCarthy is in my emphasis on television as a logistical tool that—due to its liveness and scaled connectivity capabilities—has been used to literally and materially shape action at a distance. This sense is closer to John Durham Peters's understanding of "logistical media" as devices that "arrange people and property into time and space" and that "do not necessarily have 'content'" but "establish the zero points of orientation, the convergence of the x and y axis."[4] In short, logistical media create the ground on which actions can take place. As I discuss in relation to satellite call-in programs as well as closed-circuit television systems that extend workers' abilities to control factory operations, television is a tool of logistical control that extends the power of the viewer to materially act in space, whether that means meeting with top brass at corporate headquarters 2,000 miles away, consulting a file in another building, or defusing a nuclear weapon from behind a blast shield. In these instances, television as a mechanism of orientation enables users both to understand their coordinate position within the building, institution, or country (if we think in increasing scale) and to act within those spatial relations. As a result, television works on employees' understanding of their own spatialized capabilities and their social, cultural, and political positions within spatialized hierarchies, e.g., headquarters versus branch offices (an orientation that works closer to the first sense mentioned earlier).

Third, I invoke orientation to describe the way television offered a productive site for diverse groups and institutions to engage in and orient themselves toward larger conceptual frameworks concerning the "problem" of electronic communication. Work on television—by inventors, manufacturers, marketers, private user companies, schools, the government, and other organizations—became an opportunity to experiment with different social, technological, cultural, and economic forms of connectivity, networking, action at a distance, and efficiency as they were important not only to commercial interests, but to institutional form writ large. In using an analytical frame trained on intermediality, I situate television's development in an extended trajectory of electronic communication, beginning with the telegraph and eventually running alongside (and at times anticipating) desktop and networked computing. By checking persistent business communication desires and beliefs against television as an always-in-transition, always-emerging set of technological attributes, affordances, exhibition sites, and discourses regarding connection and control, we can locate how powerful institutions oriented themselves to the problem of communication. The specialized circuits of information and control that flourished under business television helped crystallize an orientation to business communications increasingly invested in the pursuit of operational efficiencies and useful affective economies. These are the same ambitions that would increasingly recognize computer networks as the ideal (well, next) manifestation of the overlapping institutional desires served by television's consolidation of logistical systems control and cultural content distribution: massive data storage and retrieval, non-discrimination of content in transmission, ubiquitous access, liveness, and interactivity, to list just a few.

WORK'S TRANSFORMATIONS

When determining the context that supported the rise of television at work, distinguishing between "labor" and "work" trains our attention on how people produce commodifiable value for others' benefit *and* how groups and individuals struggle over the meaning of these productive activities. Historically, "labor" supports three interrelated meanings: (1) the act of melding human effort with capital to produce commodities for market exchange, (2) the class of people who perform this effort, and (3) reproduction.[5] In the first two uses, labor takes on the sense of an objectified input in capitalist figuring, or it can be used self-reflexively on the part of the class it names, e.g., the Labor Movement. The third sense refers to childbirth while invoking Marx's understanding of labor power as the activity a man [sic] performs to regenerate himself.[6] In contrast, the definition of work is itself a site of struggle. If we understand labor as the production of commodities (including labor power) under capitalist relations, work is better understood as the product of discursive processes. Following sociologists who understand "work" as a value label applied to privileged activities, we can see work as a historically variable category of activity constituted through power relations.[7] Who has the power to define what "counts" as work, who is included and excluded from the possibility of work, and what methods and discourses agents and institutions use to establish the meanings of work activities and identities become central questions in attempts to understand how "work" operates as a framework that shapes individuals' interpretations of certain types of experiences and the meaning-making that results from the hierarchical categorization of everyday practices.[8]

The organization of labor within the workplace—via technology and practice—has long been recognized as a mechanism to shape employees' relationships under capitalism. Automation, piecework, rewards systems, social and detailed divisions of labor, and workplace cultures have been credited with "generat[ing] consent" to the uneven social and economic relations of capitalism, thwarting worker solidarity, and "producing" workers themselves (e.g., shaping character traits, ambition, behavior).[9] In the mid- to late twentieth century (the period of this book), the organization of labor in late capitalism underwent something of a tectonic shift as many companies transitioned from Fordist to post-Fordist modes of production and employment. In the 1970s and 1980s, as manufacturers moved toward a production model based in niche markets, flexible specialization, and just-in-time manufacturing, the employment landscape accommodated. The Fordist bargain between employer and employee—relatively stable lifetime employment (for men) with raises and benefits in exchange for relinquishing autonomy and control over work—was revoked. In its place, employers embraced new staffing models that emphasized part-time, temporary, and contract work. Even "permanent" employees could no longer expect lifetime employment. Unionization likewise plummeted amid the high unemployment and inflation of the 1970s and early 1980s, as did any semblance of class-based politics. Discourses of entrepreneurialism and self-management arose to soften the hard edges of these changes via logics of empowerment and near-virtuous individualism. The terms of this transformation are detailed in Chapter 5.[10] Here, I want to focus on one particular vector of these changes that was a favored target of television: the diminishing boundaries between work and nonwork.

The fine distinction between work and nonwork time emerged alongside and supported industrial capitalism.[11] As described by Harry Braverman, "In a society where labor power is purchased and sold, working time becomes sharply and antagonistically divided from nonworking time, and the worker places an extraordinary value upon this 'free' time, while on-the-job time is regarded as lost or wasted."[12] While workers leased their time to employers, they often did so for a measured return: autonomy in the sphere of leisure and civic life. These distinctions between work and nonwork, however, were never so neat. Nowhere is this clearer than in the logic of the family wage, which set the remuneration for a male worker based on the assumption that he needed to support a wife and children; while the wife of this scenario did not *work*, she labored intensely, maintaining the household, reproducing the family, and regenerating the labor power of the husband. Even with the dissolution of the family wage and women's mass entry into the workforce, domestic and work spheres imbricated further via "work transfer," or the redistribution of once-paid work (e.g., filling grocery orders, ringing up retail transactions, directing phone calls) to unpaid, primarily women family members who were asked to navigate massive open-stock grocery stores and increasingly labyrinthine automated phone directories.[13] "Self-service" is labor, even if no one calls it work. Referring to similar phenomena via the concept of the "social factory," Autonomist

Marxists beginning in the 1960s pointed to the dissolution of physical and temporal boundaries around work and the dissemination of labor (but not employment) across all of society. When "the whole life experience of the worker is harnessed to capital," everyday activities erode distinctions between labor and "free" time.[14]

These boundaries deteriorated further via the internet-enabled extension of the workday and—under the sign of the knowledge/service economy—employers' increasing claims to workers' affective and communicative capacities. Mobile, consumer-grade technologies make people always-and-everywhere accessible to work, while our highly mediated environment enables a 24-hour workday that profitably exploits global labor pools and the international division of labor.[15] Meanwhile, self-quantification technologies and productivity apps that promise a perfected entrepreneurial subject grow popular as a guard against the precarity of advanced global capitalism.[16] Agnostic services like email materially bridge work and leisure time, providing coherence between the two that, for some, may be eroding any meaningful distinction between activities. In particular, the twenty-first-century knowledge worker is compelled to see her- or himself as a living engine of ideas and capacities (relational, linguistic/cognitive, corporeal/sensorial, and affective) to be worked on and over all the time.[17] As articulated by Andrew Ross's study of software engineers, "everything that employees do, think, or say in their waking moments is potential grist for the industrial mill . . . the work tempo is being recalibrated to incorporate activities, feelings, and ideas that are normally pursued during employees' free time."[18] Rather than merely the appropriation of cultural and affective labor to produce and sell consumer goods, digital media—and the workplace television that pioneered many of these practices—appropriates workers' social and cultural experiences in order to manage their labor.

The generalized acceptance of this intensification of work is surprising—or not. Capitalism has devised numerous ways to soften its edges. As John Tomlinson argues, the subjects of today's "culture of speed" are made an offer (that they can't refuse, yes, but) that appeals to real desires, including freedom from clock discipline and the ability to split one's attention among competing demands like work and childcare. As he puts it, "The reach of work into home life . . . is not generally experienced as a colonization, but more subtly as a yielding, a give and take, a flexible arrangement with either a direct or an indirect *quid pro quo*."[19] This is capitalism's accommodationist strategy, which sets forth renewed and intensified demands on workers alongside products and practices that make changes bearable. We might think of other contemporary examples like subscription box services, which save users time otherwise spent on quotidian cultural practice, from planning a meal (Blue Apron) to a wardrobe (Stitch Fix), and the growth of the sharing economy, which takes the edge off class inequality by making it easy to pool money for unaffordable goods and services (GoFundMe) or allowing aspirational shoppers to play dress-up as the wealthy for special occasions (Rent the Runway). Mediated workplace communication likewise accommodates by trading on people's existing, *pleasurable* social and cultural relations with domestic media practices. As we will see, companies routinely attempted to borrow the affective resonance of entertainment television—established by workers within the context of their leisure—to effect a more intimate, more entertaining, and ultimately, more tolerable mode of management that would be welcome outside the temporal and spatial bounds of the traditional workday. Business television's promise to extend workers' capacity to labor while simultaneously exhibiting corporate care and concern for workers was not secondary, but *central* to its appeal.

One of the foundational, but seemingly forgotten, lessons of cultural studies likewise understands the boundary between work and leisure as porous, and recognizes television's role in mediating between the two. Positing people's institutional affiliations as an *essential* site of critical analysis, David Morley's *The Nationwide Audience* revealed the extent to which work and nonwork are mutually constitutive with regard to people's everyday meaning-making practices. The *Nationwide* study—built around a popular news magazine program—indicated that audience members' interpretations of news items were not based in idiosyncratic interests but were shaped by their class positions, political affiliations, and, crucially, their social positions within institutions like unions and the workplace. In short, a given audience member's social position determined in large part the access that he or she had to various "cultural codes . . . the range of different decoding strategies and competencies" activated during interpretation.[20] Put otherwise, "individual readings will be framed by . . . shared '*orientations*'"—the very orientations that form the target of television at work.[21]

If, on the whole, workers and media consumers have long been one and the same, access to this doubled identity has changed significantly since World War II. Feminist and Civil Rights movements fought and won concessions for women and people of color seeking paid employment, especially in echelons of the firm that had previously been restricted to them. However, when diversity was welcomed (however tepidly) within private enterprise, it was often exploited as a cost-cutting strategy that supported a broader move to casual and poorly remunerated labor. The combination of intensified divisions of labor, "deskilled" work, and workers of marginalized identities continues to be a favorite recipe for lowering wages and legitimating part-time work.[22] Crucial to these efforts to profitably exploit a globally expanded labor force—particularly in the growing knowledge and service economies—was intense interest and investment in both skills and socialization training that buffered against high worker turnover and tensions caused by workplace norms that had long favored white men.[23] Delivered via seminars, handouts, activities, and television, this training sought to create both better workers and willing subjects of worsening labor conditions. As David Harvey writes,

> The socialization of the worker to conditions of capitalist production entails the social control of physical and mental powers on a very broad basis. Education, training, persuasion, the mobilization of certain social sentiments (the work ethic, company loyalty, national or local pride) and psychological propensities (the search for identity through work, individual initiative, or social solidarity) all play a role and are plainly mixed in with the formation of dominant ideologies cultivated by the mass media.[24]

Moving beyond the entertainment industries, tracing television at work provides a means to investigate how firms *directly* intervened in the building of employee minds, bodies, and hearts to manage cultural difference and acclimate workers to the conditions and expectations of post-Fordism.

THE AUDIENCE AT WORK

While television workers may be elusive, they are not completely unaccounted for. Indeed, popular culture research has often asked us to reconsider the boundaries between leisure and labor in the context of entertainment. Perhaps most famously, Dallas Smythe offers the "audience commodity" as a way of understanding viewers' time spent watching commercial mass media as commodified labor "produced, sold, purchased, and consumed" within and for the media industries.[25] Not only do commercial entertainment viewers (ostensibly) train themselves to participate as good capitalist subjects by watching ads alongside programming and generating positive associations that bolster their effectiveness, their aggregate viewing time can be packaged by the networks and sold to advertisers.[26] While Brett Caraway rightly critiques Smythe's characterization of audiences as "mind slaves" to capitalist mass media for ignoring the extent to which "use values [of messages] are not under sufficient control by the capitalist to warrant the reduction of audience subjectivity to the status of an owned commodity," the model is nevertheless useful for interrogating assumptions about audiences' function within the commercial media industry and the doubled utility of audiences' time.[27] Put simply, labor for the other overlays leisure for the self. The proximity of entertainment to labor becomes even clearer in the context of rating studies, wherein participants must channel significant effort into being watched (pushing buttons, completing surveys, training)—often for pay.[28] Physically and psychically managing time (in addition to spending it to benefit others) becomes the duty of the participant, who is additionally asked to see "see every activity, whether it's play, consuming goods or actual job activities, as a type of productive work benefiting corporations."[29]

Over the last 15 years, the scholarly shift in attention from active to interactive audiences renewed focus on distinctions between leisure and audience labor. Contemporary media render audience labor increasingly visible; conversations about television programming transform into online forums that sustain fan sites, opinions calcify into online ratings and suggestion systems for sites like Netflix or IMDB, and the sharing of fan texts becomes traceable through social networking sites. In turn, these activities also become more easily commodified—to the extent that they may become a valuable revenue source for media companies.[30] New forms of (free) audience labor are sometimes even strikingly similar to the (paid) labor previously undertaken by media and marketing professionals: managing consumer interaction, providing narrative input and paratextual production, corporate brand and reputation management, developing software content, and audience research via surveillance.[31] The growing creep of "playbour," which attempts to mask people's labor as play, likewise wears down boundaries between work and nonwork in order to appropriate increasing amounts of people's time in the generation of economic value for capital, pushing the spaces and times of labor into those once defined by leisure.[32]

Of course, these formulations tend to ignore the use value that leisure-time media engagement holds for individuals.[33] Although they may not be paid by the media industries that their labor benefits, many have non-monetary goals and needs that *are* met through their labor (richer media experiences, creative exploration and identity play, meaningful collaboration, strengthening skills, building status and social capital, influencing media production, navigating social situations, and even monetizing their own work).[34] To emphasize these dynamics, Ian Bogost describes the commodification of internet users' online "effort" by companies like Google and Twitter (whether for play or work) as "hyperemployment."[35] While underscoring the increasingly porous boundaries of leisure time made possible by agnostic devices and services, the term also invokes a sense of exchange whereby users consent to the commodification of their labor in return for some sort of compensation. Whatever value users might extract from their labor, however, it is not always (or ever) a fair trade between individuals and media conglomerates. What an equivalence of benefits would look like in the first place is difficult to determine, since users may see themselves as operating primarily within an affective economy, while media corporations are interested in directly monetizable behavior.

Facebook, though somewhat afield of television proper, is a case in point—and a useful example for exploring how, exactly, user-generated content platforms challenge boundaries between labor and leisure while accommodating the economic shifts already described. Some workplaces ban access to the site, acknowledging its threat to their control over employees' productive hours.[36] Increasingly, however, employers attempt to productively manage employees' Facebook activity for the firm's benefit through initiatives that transform their workers into online "brand ambassadors" or exploit workers' social relations as sales leads.[37] Invoking Smythe, Christian Fuchs argues more broadly that the platform transforms its users into the internet prosumer commodity, coercing its unpaid users into alienated and exploited labor, since users control neither the product nor the profits of their labors.[38] While evidently labor, it is unclear who using Facebook would consider it work. Indeed, research suggests that users understand Facebook, in part at least, as a means to *counter* poor working conditions and opportunities. As a "security blanket . . . a grounding mechanism and reassuring presence," Facebook enables users to maintain social relationships with friends and family that help them weather unstable and short-term employment situations.[39] Yet another example of capitalism's accommodationist strategies, these leisure-labor media practices based in pleasure and entertainment support the very same systems of exploitation they appear to protect against. They also represent an intensification of ambitions long linked to workplace television.

Tackling questions of work within the media industry itself, studies of production cultures have likewise paid special attention to how workplaces manage employee identity to destabilize boundaries between leisure and labor for the benefit of the firm. As is the case in other post-1970 workplaces, the commercial television industry exploits individuals' cultural identities to erase labor and skill, naturalizing underpayment and overwork. Vicki Mayer provides the example of casters, whose "feminine" interpersonal skills are positioned as inherent traits rather than skilled qualifications, with knock-on implications for how casters understand their everyday social relations as fodder for creating surplus value for media companies.[40] While other deteriorating employment conditions described earlier are replicated in the media industries, David Hesmondhalgh suggests that we must take special care to distinguish the culture industry as a site of symbol and knowledge creation that occupies "a central place in fantasies and beliefs about what 'good work' might involve in modern capitalism."[41] Alluding to precarious conditions, he suggests further, "because so few people are aware of cultural labor, believing it to be cushy and even glamorous, it is a particularly potent example of the way in which work is not recognized under capitalist commodity production."[42] However, despite careful attention to worker experience and textual production within the entertainment industries, mapping the audiovisual industries explicitly and uniquely tasked with making work meaningful to employees remains elusive.[43]

MEDIA AT WORK

Media analysis centered on commercial entertainment cannot fully account for the appeals of capitalism. How consumer systems win subjects' support for a vastly inequitable system is undoubtedly crucial to our understanding of capitalism's hegemony. However, a near-exclusive focus on how consent is generated (or resistance is performed) at the point of consumption ignores strategies used by workplaces to generate consent to capitalist systems at the point of production. The common disregard of workplace media (beyond production cultures analyses) is likewise convenient for capitalism, since it can lead to a scholarly emphasis on the politics of consumption, choice, and empowerment rather than examinations of quotidian exploitation and control.

Fortunately, recent years have seen a groundswell of attention devoted to media use within institutional settings such as schools, factories, and the military, interested in how "cameras, films, and projectors have been taken up and deployed variously—beyond questions of art and entertainment—in order to satisfy organizational demands and objectives, that is, *to do something* in particular."[44] In examining how film, television, and sound are used for projects like employee and member training, presenting new programs to various publics, or streamlining work processes through increased communication, "useful" media and nontheatrical film studies offers an opportunity to trace the output of the United States' largest non-entertainment institutions while disturbing canons and traditional paradigms based on entertainment media production, distribution, exhibition, and reception. As is becoming increasingly clear, the commercial media products at the center of our histories represent the minority of media texts produced in the twentieth century. A cultural studies project investigating how these "marginal majority" media shape social relations beyond the theater, leisure, and the home enables us, finally, to more fully account for "culture as a whole way of life."[45]

This accounting requires the study of complex power relations often overshadowed in the analysis of commercial media. Thinking of industrial media as interfaces, "translation devices," and "theory machines" foregrounds the extent to which heterogeneous social relations, knowledge projects, and power/governance systems influence the construction and reception of institutional texts and technologies.[46] We might consider how institutional films—for example, those on skills training or interpersonal dynamics—may be the product of combined theories about social relations, psychology, learning, communication, identity, race, and organizational management.[47] Or how struggles between institutions and agents—government bodies, museums and libraries, funders, experts, filmmakers, and corporations—shape textuality and institutional media cultures.[48] We might likewise attend to how film carved out a path for television at work by making the mediated corporation appealing to multiple constituencies. For example, though ostensibly designed to market their consultation services to company owners, the Gilbreths' micromanagement study films were simultaneously tailored to workers (as nonthreatening and exciting), the general public (via spectacle and pro-worker discourse), and international audiences (with emphasis on their unique contribution to the field). Tracing these interwoven vectors of power and influence provides a basis for understanding the orientation work of industrial media as they attempt to coerce emotions, direct perception, build knowledge, and shape attitudes in ways fitting to the needs and desires of private companies.

Embedded within the spaces of work, school, travel, commerce, and leisure, institutional media also ask us to consider how technologies position audiences in relation to both texts and each other (whether separated by an ocean or occupying the same space and different positions of power).[49] Stephen Groening, for example, showed how training films targeting female telegraph operators collapsed the habits of "good spectatorship" (silence and individual concentration) with proper work comportment (self-isolation from coworkers).[50] Media projects based in social interaction theories and models (small-group, role-playing) likewise worked intently on participants' relationships with each other and their organizations.[51] In the following chapters, television's role in these same process will become clear as case studies describe its application to physically extend the capacities of workers, bind spaces, and create intimacies among employees.

In the interests of analyzing and combating the unequal distribution of resources necessitated and facilitated by late capitalism, a focus on business media also enables an exploration of the rise of corporate speech inside and outside of the corporation, as well as its role in developing and maintaining these conditions. Beginning in the 1930s, institutionally sponsored broadcasts provided companies an outlet for their self-positioning as public benefactor, in direct opposition to the government.[52] Directed internally, corporations used media to manage expansion, record activities, rationalize practices, and provide sustaining rhetoric to insiders; "organizational practice is always already media practice."[53] Attending to these mutually constitutive practices via workplace television charts new territory within major debates regarding organizational life, corporate personhood, and the centrality of business interests in American culture.

Due to television's prominence in post-war era workplaces—especially following the introduction of the U-matic in 1961—the medium allows for exploration of a key period in labor reorganization in the US not documented fully in film. Certainly, the Orphan films movement that began in 1999 to raise awareness of the serious threat posed to non-commercial, amateur, and underground films by lack of preservation and scholarly attention, and the turn to useful cinema have developed vital theoretical and methodological approaches to vast fields of media practice. However, despite these twin movements' shared interest in challenging the marginalized position of non-commercial texts within the field of media studies, they focus primarily on film. While reinforcing medium-specific hierarchies, this emphasis leads to a lack of attention given the post-Sputnik era, when videotape ascended as the medium of choice in institutional communication. Similarly, otherwise excellent work about video—which has drastically expanded understandings of the spaces, places, and uses of television for diverse audiences—focuses on a limited set of home video-related topics: Hollywood content, adult films, and home users; agents of the format wars; and bootlegging, piracy, and democratization of culture.[54] Notable exceptions to these trends reveal the productivity of tracing television's institutional paths. Anna McCarthy and Joy Fuqua have shown how television has been routinely implicated in shaping institutional space and social relations, governing and educating citizens, and managing the sick.[55] Despite these interventions, however, media scholars have yet to seriously account for how television at work supported the needs of capitalism in the transition to post-Fordism.

Ultimately, workplace television's utility for employers must be measured in its ability to organize information systems as well as its capacity for cultural management. Although JoAnne Yates, Paul A. Argenti,

Paul M. Leonardi and other business communication scholars have investigated how technologies impact industrial organization and expansion, television—with the exception of its use to reach consumers—remains conspicuously absent in their analyses.[56] Using Yates's landmark research as an example, *Control through Communication* addresses how organizational technologies like vertical files enabled networks of communication that extended companies' management capacities, facilitating their expansion from 1850 to 1920.[57] Yates's *Structuring the Information Age*, which traces the prehistory of business computing, draws extensively on tabulator technology but excludes television (and film), even though, as will become clear, television was an important predecessor to desktop computing.[58] In both instances, Yates's focus on *logistical* mechanisms of organization elides the important role that organizational technologies *as cultural systems* play in the management of the firm.

While connected to broader processes of subject formation, workplace culture has likewise been recognized within business theory and practice as a fulcrum of stability, social control, and problem-solving; norms, for example, transmit knowledge and ways of working that maintain consistency in production and accommodate change.[59] Organizational attempts to develop work cultures are often most visible in new employee orientation and training—two practices in which television plays a starring role. Indeed, the "artifacts" that transmit workplace culture—stories, jargon, symbols, jokes—are the very substance of media technologies based in physical and affective connectivity.[60] And yet, television has yet to be taken seriously as a medium of American labor relations. This is all the more curious given researchers' acknowledgement of the "cultural imprint" of popular representations on workplace ideologies, as well as the increasing emphasis on identity as a crucial mechanism of management beginning in the 1980s.[61] Taking a critical rather than technocratic stance, *Television at Work* fills in these gaps using an interdisciplinary understanding of everyday culture, technology, and the workplace.

CHANNELING THE UTILITY OF TELEVISION

This book examines television as an emergent medium—several times over. Since, as Raymond Williams suggests, "the moment of any new technology is a moment of choice," attending to the earliest periods of television's life as it is continually "reborn" in new instantiations (ITV, CCTV, videocassettes, satellite) allows us to trace how decisions regarding its cultural meaning and potential uses were negotiated and contested—as well as what groups and institutions gathered and maintained the most power to enforce their visions.[62] While I touch on the ways workplace television fits into common discursive tropes, including utopian and dystopian strains of technological determinism and remediation, I am most interested in the practical development of television via a series of inter-institutional decisions made about the technology's aesthetics, affordances, economics, and uses in struggles over meaning in the American workplace.[63] Close analysis of these early moments of media in flux provides insight into the development, destruction, and persistence of interpretive frameworks; battles over cultural legitimacy and institutional authority; and users' changing relationships with media technologies.[64] Attending to moments of emergence in this way builds on traditional cultural studies questions of power, politics, and identity.

Treatments of emergent media that focus on their adoption by popular audiences tend to ignore or swiftly pass over the development of media to meet (non-entertainment) industrial needs as well as the complicated relationship between the two sectors (populated, we often forget, by the same viewers and users). I emphasize connections between the development of television within the corporate sector and the later proliferation of televisual technologies in the home, as well as implications regarding shared pools of television labor, aesthetic strategies, gendered discourse, and affective practice. This focus on the early institutional development of television expands our broader understanding of the relationships between the American corporate sector, the entertainment industries, and popular users.

On a practical level, I emphasize intermediality and the continuities that bind workplace television and video to previous media forms, especially as they have been used in other institutional settings. Though emergent media are often swept up in utopian revolutionary discourses, they tend to be rooted in older forms—whether by drawing on similar research and understandings about communication—or by becoming meaningful through comparison to older media.[65] As noted by Jonathan Sterne, Lisa Gitelman, Janet Abbate, and others using social constructionist-inflected models of media research, what often appear to be the socially neutral or even ontological attributes of technologies are actually the results of contingency, conscious decisions, and aggregated custom.[66] In the following chapters, I look to standards, protocols, television workers' practices of professionalism, and the development of formats as manifestations of these struggles over control, social relationships, economic forces, and material experience.[67]

Ultimately, I pursue an analysis of television "not as a collection of wires, transmitters, and electrons but as a social practice grounded in culture, rather than electricity."[68] The routine transmogrification of television attests to Sterne's and Gitelman's assertions that any given medium is a temporarily congealed manifestation of a complex set of social, cultural, economic, and material relations.[69] Asking why business television emerged in one form rather than another, this book is interested in how equipment manufacturers, corporate leadership, audiovisual professionals and others developed possibilities for the shape of television, and how these possibilities were taken up (or not) as television use evolved in the corporation following World War II. In other words, this is a history of shifting understandings of how technology could improve, and render more profitable, the business that integrated it into its workflows. As such, I relinquish other narratives—notably the responses of workers and labor unions—to future scholarship.

Accounting for possibilities as they arise and recede moves beyond mapping the easily identifiable roots of existing phenomena in order to disrupt understandings of television in its most "successful" or stable form: commercial broadcasting in the home. Michel Foucault's genealogical approach is especially helpful here, since it does not attempt to reinforce the singular foundations of our received past, but disturbs and disrupts by focusing on "the accidents, the minute deviations—or conversely, the complete reversals—the errors, the false appraisals, and the faulty calculations that gave birth to those things that continue to exist and have value for us."[70] This approach is well suited to mapping the messy heterogeneity of standardization battles and the diverse but connected experiments across different industries including business, education, and commercial entertainment.[71] The development of television left a slew of failures in its wake—of technologies, aesthetics, programming practices, and communication strategies. These failures—knowledge projects that nevertheless circulated discourses on the utility of television—helped establish the "conditions of possibility" in which business television became legible as a technology and practice.[72] As Sterne notes, "possibility is both a conceptual problem and a material issue: a practice or an event must be both thinkable and potentially able to be accomplished."[73] Attending to possibility thus configured, the following chapters trace the ongoing imbrication of televisual affordances and intensifying management ambitions as they were pursued by employers.

Historiography, too, is both a conceptual and material problem.[74] As will become clear, industrial television can be a particularly difficult historical subject due to the material fragility of its sources (videotape and its requisite hardware), the lack of recognition of its cultural, historical, and economic value, and a common (but by no means universal) unwillingness of private corporate archives to grant access to outside researchers. Indeed, I am indebted to those archives and archivists that did open their doors to me. Following the work of scholar-archivists, I recognize the "personal, structural, and political pressures which the archives places on the histories [historians] end up writing—as well as those they do not."[75] While I remain mindful of these dynamics throughout the next five chapters, my conclusion addresses these questions in greater detail.

Archives, of course, are only one site in which we can locate traces of the past. Those invested in the development of business television created extensive materials to prove the medium's value and to carve out professional identities as audiovisual workers. Many of these traces—legends, memories, personal papers—continue to exist. I pair industrial and educational media trades (e.g., *Business Screen, BusinessTV*) with trade journals in fields as diverse as banking, steel, and agriculture to trace the multifarious but often distinctly patterned discursive positioning of television and its use in practice.[76] Equipment handbooks and production manuals, industry market reports, popular news coverage, and extant corporate video and film texts likewise help describe the ambitions that animated television at work. Borrowing production cultures frameworks, I also interviewed several former television professionals—most of whom worked in market research or production—to understand how they contributed to the proliferation of the medium and the building of corporate media empires. In particular, I asked after how they understood television at work's value in meeting their own personal and professional goals as well as serving the needs of their employers. Turning to these stakeholders, often unrecorded in corporate archives, enables greater consideration of the meaning of business television for those who used it.[77]

REVISIONIST HISTORY

Some twenty-first-century onlookers mourn the death of the domestic medium. No longer the electronic hearth around which countless imagined American families gather to partake in the country's preeminent cultural forum, post-network television is mobile, fragmented, and on-demand. It is a medium, so critics say, that has become unrecognizable in its temporal and spatial flexibility. These fateful discourses demand an unquestioned articulation between television and the home. However, television's eulogists never knew their dear friend as well as they thought. Television was born a wanderer, stealing away from the living room antics of the Goldbergs and

Uncle Miltie to hole up in local taverns, go shopping, and visit sick friends at the hospital. Following television as it sought employment in factories, boardrooms, and office cantinas, this book proceeds chronologically, using an episodic approach that dwells on key moments in television's emergence and continual refashioning at the hands of American business. Overlaid on this structure is a re-examination of several "keywords" of television—terms and concepts understood to be central to television's technological and cultural functions. Designed to emphasize the stakes of tracking television outside of the home, this organization refashions some of our longest-held understandings of the medium.

Forgoing an examination of the *media* industries, Chapter 1 focuses instead on the rise of what we might call the *mediated* industries. A prehistory of television at work, this chapter traces an intensifying relationship between electronic media and the workplace, beginning with the telegraph. Situating this discussion in the context of scholars' treatment of communication and empire, I argue that television occupies a key transitional position for the mediated corporation in which electronic communication's dual uses as a logistical tool and as a conduit for cultural production converge. These processes illustrate the development of an alternative media sector and the symbiotic relationship between the "knowledge industries" and corporate expansion, as well as the specificities of how media infrastructures are created at scale.

Remaining chapters examine how television's meanings and uses underwent revision as its technological affordances shifted over the course of the twentieth century. Chapter 2 (keyword: flow) explores how live, two-way closed-circuit television systems provided employers an opportunity to reconfigure workers' physical and mental capacities. A widely used synonym for closed-circuit television in the United States, "industrial television" (ITV) represents the first major attempt of business and industry to bend television to its needs. Although ITV shares with CCTV surveillance a desire to regulate people in space, ITV was used not to limit movement, but to extend bodies; it adapted workers to the increased physical demands of expanding industrial and informational architectures. Businesses promoted ITV as a prosthesis that could make working bodies stronger, bigger, and more tightly bound into automated information systems. Faster than a speeding assembly line, more powerful than a six-story furnace, able to retrieve dispersed data with a single command, these supermen appealed to industries seeking production and workforce efficiencies. This chapter interrogates ITV's utopian promises of cyborgian human-machine networks and the consequences of these "transformations" for embodied experiences of work.

Using AT&T as a case study, Chapter 3 (keyword: immediacy) follows a series of somewhat halting experiments surrounding live and near-live television that attended the medium's move from the factory to the office. First, I describe how, in the early to mid-1950s, companies adopted theater television (television signals distributed to movie theaters) for live, city-spanning business meetings. Until now understood as a short-lived site of tension between film and broadcasting interests invested in commercial entertainment, theater television reached its apotheosis as a site of business experimentation with efficient and affective management. Workplace television's promoters also transformed the medium's limitations into virtues. Working with early videotape systems—bulky, hard-to-move, and overcome with compatibility issues—companies promoted taped self-observation for hyper-local training. Borrowing legitimacy from psychology's use of "encounter groups" and therapeutic confrontation exercises, self-observation required workers to tape themselves in various situations for immediate playback. Encouraging a narcissistic engagement with one's video image—like much early video art—this use of television drastically intensified demands on workers' self-regulation. Detailing how these early enthusiasms set the stage for television's induction into the corporation, the second half of this chapter traces AT&T's installation of in-house (but increasingly geographically expansive) CCTV systems as a mechanism of cultivation and coordination. In addition to distributing content, CCTV systems supported corporate imaginaries in which geographies were themselves subject to executive control and reorganization. Ultimately, pursuing the capitalist "mantra of efficiency," CCTV extended the power of the corporation to direct its actors in space and time, and, indeed—through discursive understandings of immediacy—reconfigure the meaning of distance itself.[78]

Chapter 4 (keyword: time-shifting) addresses a persistent gap in understandings of videocassettes: their development in industrial (and educational) contexts prior to their success in the home market. Drawing on trade journals in business and education, popular histories of videotape, archival materials, and interviews with audiovisual professionals, I outline how industrial users contributed to the development of media cassettes, their cultural meanings, and practical applications well before "the" format wars between VHS and Betamax. Via three case studies of pre-VHS era cassettes and cartridges (8mm film cartridge projectors, CBS's EVR, and Sony's U-matic), I demonstrate how the home—as a guarantee of comfort, intimacy, and pleasure—figures in marketing campaigns introducing video cartridges to the workplace as a replacement for training film. While the "whatever whenever" affordances of cartridges promised flexibility in managing the training of dispersed workforces, television's status as a domestic entertainment medium promised employers a new tool to entice workers to engage with workplace communications wherever and whenever. Further, as a technology ultimately aimed at the mass market, video cassettes also promised usability for whomever—a crucial claim in an era of a rapidly diversifying workforce. In effect, the marketing of video cartridges to the workplace blurred distinctions between work and home, promising that television could make the workplace more homelike by drawing on the meanings of television workers produced in their leisure time. Taking work home—in the form of a cassette—also (ostensibly) became more bearable. This episode in the ever-increasing colonization of employees' nonworking time reveals how the affective resonance of the home—and its technologies—can be translated to corporate productivity and profit. This anticipates the proliferation of agnostic technologies (personal computers, mobile devices) that disrupt barriers between work and leisure, intensifying workers' contact with and capacity to labor.

Chapter 5 (keyword: narrowcasting) explores the development of private satellite networks to manage distributed workforces in the context of globalization and a "cultural turn" in popular management theories. Following a series of early international experiments undertaken by governments and educational organizations that promoted expansive notions of learning by satellite, the late 1980s saw the proliferation of industry-focused subscription channels (e.g., geared toward insurers and automotive companies) as well as internal "networks" housed by a single company like JC Penney or Hewlett Packard. To show how businesses targeted worker identity or attempted to supplant other modes of affiliation (including, of course, class-based solidarity) within the unstable employment environment of the 1980s and 1990s, I turn to two case studies built from analyses of satellite programming and interviews with key communications personnel. In exploring Johnson Controls' hybrid house organ/cable-style news program and a series of Steelcase programs that comment explicitly on the potentials of television, I describe the narrowcast "edge" aesthetics of entertainment, sincerity, and interactivity that bolstered these companies' claims to liveness, connection, and instantaneous global (but perfectly targeted) reach. Ultimately, this iteration of corporate narrowcasting would seek to reinforce viewers' position within increasingly niche interest groups for the benefit of capital.

I end where many books begin, with my acknowledgments. The Conclusion addresses the conditions of possibility that enabled this research—both the individuals who shared their time and resources with me, and the institutions, especially archives, that weighed on my ability do to this work. In particular, I describe a series of interviews and interactions I had over the course of several years with corporate communications consultants, television directors and producers, trade organization leadership, authors, teachers, and market researchers who guided my investigations into corporate television. Although I am often critical of the practices I discuss in the following pages, I also argue that we must distinguish between the desires of multinational capital and the aims of the people who devoted their lives to television at work, many of whom were (and are) sincerely invested in making the workplace more humane. It is in following this latter ambition—the workplace as an opportunity to build community, as a locus of personal connection and self-actualization—that we might renew attempts to build broad-based worker solidarity, developing the conditions of possibility for just labor.

CHAPTER 1

The Persistence of [a] Vision: The Electronically Mediated Corporation

Prehistory

Television at work is a messy magpie technology that recombined the affordances and ambitions of its predecessors in the service of on-going experiments in management, organizational structure, production methods, and worker engagement. Each of the technologies described herein (as well as those excluded for space) can lay claim to a Proustian biography replete with adolescent episodes long forgotten in the flowering of dominant uses and applications. This chapter operates as a "Previously on . . ." truncating a wildly unspooling narrative into hard bits of continuity crucial to later plots. To navigate the inevitable redundancies and dead-ends of industrial media experimentation spanning the telegraph to the television, I focus on the persistence of a vision: the mediated corporation as efficient, economical, and expansive, with tractable employees and contented publics.

Scholars have long coupled the terms "media" and "industry" to describe the formal organization of production, distribution, and exhibition of time-based audiovisual texts. Radio programs, television series, films, soundtracks, and even ancillary products are often situated as these industries' principal products. To this litany, advertiser-supported media add yet another output, the "audience commodity." Coined by Dallas Smythe to describe viewers' attention as it is quantified, packaged, and sold to advertisers and their clients, the audience commodity begets its

Television at Work. Kit Hughes, Oxford University Press (2020) © Oxford University Press.
DOI: 10.1093/oso/9780190855789.001.0001

own subseries of manufactured and marketed products (psychographics, demographics, People Meters, and other ratings technologies).[1] While Smythe's positioning of viewers' watching as labor oversteps the bounds of how most people would define a second shift, the concept nevertheless points to how common understandings of both the products and producers of media have long been circumscribed.[2] It makes legible the second order of consumption that media industries hope to foster in their viewers— suds as well as soap operas—as well as the value that viewers create for networks and other interests.

The audience commodity also offers a lever to pry open the long-standing relationship between industrial production and broadcast programming, or how material shifts in goods manufacture support changes in desired audience composition and the media industry's own strategies of textual production. It is no coincidence, in other words, that the network era (from the early 1950s to the early 1980s) was underwritten by Fordist mass-production processes interested in advertising to a relatively undifferentiated broadcast audience—or that the multichannel transition and post-network era sought small, homogenous narrowcast audiences targeted by goods companies investing in new manufacturing processes (e.g., flexible specialization, small-batch production).[3] While these overlapping levels of production and consumption within the "media industries" thus defined have been relatively well accounted for, scholars have devoted far less attention to the *mediated* industries end of this equation.

This chapter moves beyond media's role in the marketing and consumption of goods—or as a consumable in and of itself—to detail how electronic media sit at the very heart of industrial production and organization. Following the lead of work on the culture industries, I am interested in how media produce things (whether television series or cars), as well as in how they produce people (citizens, consumers, employees). To fully account for these overlapping levels and modes of production, I offer the notion of *expanded vertical integration*.[4] Well familiar to those studying the media industries, vertical integration represents the process whereby a firm specializing in a particular good (e.g., feature films, steel) absorbs additional industrial stages in its manufacture or distribution (e.g., by controlling exhibition and distribution in the case of the Hollywood studio system, or by owning the coal mines needed to power steel mills). Certainly, the many technologies discussed in the following were central to firms' ability to develop and manage increasingly complex supply chains. However, I use *expanded* vertical integration to draw similar attention to an "input" often overlooked in traditional uses of the term: labor.[5] Put another way, this broader view attends to how media helped manufacture goods *and* the employees needed to manufacture, sell, and distribute those goods. Situated at the intersection of overlapping institutional communication desires, television found success via its resolution of logistical systems control with the distribution of cultural content designed to manage workers' capacities, emotions, and relationships.

Both entertainment and industrial media find themselves party to a larger project of creating objects and subjects in the service of advanced capitalism. No less complex than the products of media industries, the "products" of mediation within industry run the gamut from national markets, integrated firms, new processing methods, divisions of labor, skills, ideologies, affect, and, of course, more than a few film, television, and radio programs. To achieve some specificity in tracing how particular technologies contribute to these ends, I distinguish between *coordination* functions and *cultivation* functions. Coordination functions comprise telemetry signals, correspondence, and dispatching alerts that serve chiefly to exchange intelligence or direct workers' mobility and action in real time (subject to the delays of inherent technological constraints). Cultivation functions, on the other hand, work directly on workers' affective, intellectual, and physiological faculties to develop "better" employees. Put otherwise, whereas coordination messages help produce goods and services, cultivation messages seek to produce people. (As we will see in Chapter 2, some uses of television collapse these differences.) Both aim to secure greater profits. While the terminology of cultivation invokes George Gerbner and Larry Gross's well-known network era theory of viewer socialization, here I am interested in cultivation not as the *effect* of long-term exposure to omnipresent representational patterns (e.g., of violence), but as the overarching *ambition* of many corporate communications projects. Further, the purposeful deployment of cultivation messages within organizations seeks narrowly to build subjects to meet the mission of the institution. The terminology of coordination versus cultivation recognizes the dual modalities of television while acknowledging its continuity with dominant applications of earlier technologies (telegraphy-as-coordination versus film-as-cultivation, for example). And while extensive experimentation with new industrial media meant that any given technology would likely cross these categories' borders, none would do so as successfully as television. Although early telecommunications (telegraph, telephone, phonograph, radio) focused most heavily on coordination as control, industrial film's emphasis on employee cultivation became increasingly important to discussions of television as the twentieth century wore on. By the time television was ready for mass employment in the 1970s, this latter capability dominated its perceived value (though, of course, it soldiered on in the surveillance stations and observational posts of many a factory). To follow television's dual lives requires a turn back to the many relatives that contributed to its twin nature.

BUSINESS BY WIRE: BIGGER MARKETS, BIGGER FIRMS

The reciprocal relationship between technology and business has long been a topic of scholarly and popular interest, with many analyses focusing on machines that replicate or transform the labor activities of human workers (the mechanical loom, Fordist assembly lines, computers).[6] Less focus has been given to how electronic communication technologies shaped and were shaped by business. (And while the railroad may be an exceptional technology that significantly changed patterns of both manual labor and communication, analyses of its relevance to business often focus on product distribution.)[7] Although a discussion of communication technologies enmeshed in business development could worm its way back to the printing press by linking its invention to the eventual rise of urban dailies and other publications that supplied information to commercial interests around the turn of the nineteenth century—or, following Harold Innis, back even to the clay and papyrus that coordinated the Mesopotamian and Egyptian empires—such an origin does little to elucidate the industrial utility of television.[8] Instead, to follow how television inherited the fortunes of both business telecommunications and publishing, this chapter begins with the telegraph.

Six years before Samuel Morse famously announced the opening of a Washington-Baltimore route by telegraphing, "What hath God Wrought?" to his partner Alfred Vail, the pair made a more modest demonstration in Speedwell, New Jersey. Vail's father—who supplied lab space and funding for their early experiments—was summoned in January 1838 to see the fruits of his investment. In a room wound with some three miles of wire, Vail-the-junior tapped out the message of his father's choosing, "A patient waiter is no loser." Read in hindsight, the first telegraph message contains some irony. (And, perhaps, passive aggression; the senior Vail was reportedly highly "discouraged" prior to the delayed demonstration.)[9] While a fitting tribute to the temporalities of investment in industrial research and development, it belies the extent to which speed—"the outcome of the pursuit of the maximization of profit"—would prove to be one of the telegraph's chief assets as a coordination medium.[10] The first electronic communication technology to drastically change the course of business in the United States and abroad, the telegraph used this capability to enlarge markets, grow the scale of firms, and even birth whole industries. (It also has the dubious honor of providing the basis of the nation's first business monopoly in Western Union.) Throughout the nineteenth and twentieth centuries, the telegraph's foundational promises of spatiotemporal connection and control would continue to excite entrepreneurs and business executives via an ever-expanding series of tele-technologies, including, of course, television.

Business's intense interest in the coordination capabilities of the telegraph dramatically shaped (and constrained) the technology's development in the United States. In lieu of financial support from technology manufacturers, rights holders, or the government, the American telegraph's earliest users—small enterprises, independent merchants, and wholesalers in the fields of retail, finance, and news—funded the expansion of telegraph lines.[11] This reliance on business capital encouraged patterns of use and technological dispersion that were largely unique to the United States. For example, it was these business interests who demanded the telegraph's national expansion (particularly westward), encouraging the development of monopolistic practices within the telegraphy industry.[12] Furthermore, unlike in Europe, where "social uses" of telegraphy predominated—and where telegraphy was almost exclusively a nationalized industry—some 70% of messages sent over the "lightning wires" in the United States were commercial in nature.[13]

Several factors explain the dominance of business uses in the United States, including high rates, emphasis on urban infrastructural development, and traffic prioritization practices. In 1869, sending a couple of sentences via telegraph could cost 68 times more than sending a letter through the post. These prices were far more acceptable to business users who were willing to pay for "almost interactive" communication.[14] Telegraphy offered a facsimile of the in-person meeting, a proposition becoming increasingly expensive as industry spread across the nation.[15] Rates were thus structured in the United States to meet the profit desires of the private telegraphy industry and to take advantage of businesses' willingness to pay top dollar for rapid communication. Likewise, though the telegraph held the promise of nation-spanning universal connection—making Lewistown, Pennsylvania, as accessible as New York City—the system developed unevenly. Lines favored larger cities with more extensive communication infrastructure—infrastructure that was developed, in part, to suit the needs of industry. Even when smaller towns were wired for telegraphy, it was common for a person wishing to send a message to wait hours until the traffic between or within major industrial cities (New York, Philadelphia, Boston, Washington, New Orleans, St. Louis) momentarily ceased. This was not simply an issue of heavy use of the lines (though businesses' needs for exact, verified information did generate extensive traffic). In a practice that recalls the warnings of net neutrality proponents, a hierarchy of users—which placed individuals firmly at the bottom—was built into the use of telegraphy wires. Government, police, and (occasionally) the press were given top priority, with "higher order" (busier) stations close behind. These busy urban stations used their privileged spot in the hierarchy to better serve their biggest customers, allowing large commercial interests right of way on the nation's wires.[16]

Western Union's expansion strategies substantiate businesses' heavy influence on the national development of telegraphy—and telephony. In 1877, Western Union declined the opportunity to purchase Alexander Graham Bell's phone patents. The decision arose from the uncertainty of the new technology's utility for industry and commerce. Unlike the telegraph, the telephone did not leave a material record "in an era when written communications"—for business, at least—"was essential."[17] Shortly thereafter, as the phone increasingly seemed like a viable threat, Western Union began experimenting with telephone applications. After being sued for patent infringement by the Bell Company, Western Union agreed to a settlement in 1879. The terms of the agreement reinforce the latter company's keen pursuit of business communications. Western Union dropped all interests and patent claims relating to telephony in exchange for Bell's extraction from telegraphy, and more explicitly, the business message trade. During the 17 years of the settlement, for example, local telephone exchanges were limited to hosting personal conversation and prohibited from serving business purposes (or commercial news).[18] While this decision proved disastrous in the long term, it safeguarded Western Union's immediate interests in what it saw as its primary market. In 1884, after Western Union found success leasing private wires to businesses, the firm briefly considered eliminating its message-sending service wholesale and moving into the leasing of wires for private use.[19] Since Western Union was a well-established monopoly by this time, we might speculate that the implications for "social" uses of telegraphy would have been dire. Though Western Union ultimately maintained its message-sending service, the incident—and the firm's dealings with Bell—reveals the primacy of business applications in the development of telegraphy.

If the preceding indicates a few ways in which business shaped the ultimate form of telegraphy in the United States, it provides little to indicate how telegraphy, in turn, shaped business. Perhaps most fundamentally, the telegraph provided a template for how electronic coordination media could abet the development and management of national markets and corporate empires. A space-binding medium, it "freed communication from the constraints of geography," making fast, frequent, and distant communication possible.[20] As a means of controlling growing railroad and steamship operations, telegraphy enabled the expansion of markets, reducing costs associated with coordinating inventory across large geographical expanses and making such oversight "tenable" in the first place.[21] Via the telegraph, companies became capable of managing the distribution of goods to meet the changing needs of diverse and ever-expanding markets through precise logistical control.[22] This was particularly important to industries that required rapid, near-constant communication: the railroad (to avoid crashes), the meatpacking industry and agriculture (to avoid spoilage), and even department stores (to avoid bare shelves resulting from the fast turnover of seasonal goods).[23] In short, for the first time, the United States could be imagined by industry as a national mass of consumers.

In addition to magnifying the scale at which business understood its consumer base—which would have its own outsize impact on mass-market commercial entertainment—the telegraph encouraged the development of large-scale firms. The transformation of local and regional markets into national markets led to expanded production practices and "a whole new framework for entrepreneurial decision making" that required greater communication based on remote markets and the growing anonymity among buyers and sellers.[24] In some instances, the scale of business operations increased 10-fold.[25] These particular effects of the telegraph were heterogeneous, depending on varied factors, including the communication needs of a given commodity. The more complicated a product—a specialty piece of farm equipment, for example, that required detailed user instructions and an ongoing service relationship—the greater the benefit from increased communication.[26] Firms bolstered by the new capabilities of the telegraph began trending toward varying degrees of (expanded) vertical integration; to realize economies of scale through tight coordination of goods and services over large, even national, markets, firms absorbed functions that previously occurred as (inefficient and undependable) market transactions (e.g., purchasing raw materials and product distribution).[27] For some companies, like those in the steel industry, the telegraph supported continuous flow processing that sped up and regulated production.[28] The telegraph also enabled firms to exert greater control over expanding operations via intelligence communications, such as surveillance over dispersed company agents or the rapid transmission of strategic price and quantity information (secret codes shielded proprietary information from prying ears).[29] Those who had access to wired intelligence could act more quickly and more assuredly than their counterparts, giving them a keen advantage over competitors and leading to greater concentration of power in larger, integrated firms.[30] Private lines, which might connect a head office with the shop floor or link a law firm to the courthouse, enabled even faster and more direct intra-firm and intra-industry communications and oversight.[31] Switchboards, like those connecting major New York banks, further supported industrial coordination by enabling "intercommunication" between subscribers.[32] As mentioned earlier, because telegraphy was practically engineered to serve urban markets that headquartered large firms, these companies were again advantaged by the telegraph when they became its preferred users.[33]

In some instances, the telegraph's coordination capabilities radically reshaped existing industries—with consequences for how participants understood the value and function of communication writ large. In finance, for example, the 1867 invention of the ticker (a printing telegraph that broadcast real-time exchange information to subscribers) alongside a shift to continuous trading drastically expanded participation, altered trading opportunities, and reconfigured the material and psychological geography of trading. On the first count, the wide accessibility of tickers not only enabled brokers to participate in trading beyond the floor proper, but also gave rise to betting parlors (bucket shops) that took wagers on price movements. While not intervening directly in exchanges, bucket shops nevertheless provided the opportunity for average people (at that time dissuaded from formal participation in exchanges) to tie their fortunes to the movement of the markets. On the second count, the speed of the ticker—and brokers' adoption of private lines—enabled parties to place orders in direct response to ongoing conditions.[34] This (relatively) homogeneous distribution of accurate quotations, in turn, did away with certain modes of arbitrage that relied on discrepancies between exchanges. Furthermore, the anonymity afforded by distant trading vastly expanded the possibility of covert corners (buying enough of a particular stock to manipulate its price). Finally, the disarticulation of trading from local exchanges transformed the cities of New York and Chicago into centers of finance.[35] According to David Hochfelder, the combined result of these changes was the abstraction of markets into information as "participants came to regard markets less as places to trade tangible things and more as the flow of quotations printed by the ticker and posted on distant blackboards."[36] This reconfiguration is not inconsequential. As James Carey notes, "the telegraph was not only a new tool of commerce but also a thing to think with, an agency for the alteration of ideas."[37] The telegraph promoted understandings of communication as a tool for "the control of distance and people," "a network of power, administration, decision, and control—as a political order."[38] In a McLuhanesque turn, the "meaning" of electronic communications became the possibility of domination and competition.[39] Although Carey is primarily interested in political agencies, these same logics were adopted by private industry—and those who eventually succeeded in selling television as a business communications technology.

The telegraph's reorganization of space and time promoted the concentration of monopolistic power within integrated firms, an organizational arrangement that did not exist before the introduction of electronic communication.[40] Firms grew to ever-larger proportions, with their needs for internal coordination and communication growing in kind. Historian Glen Porter remarked, "it was the telegraph which first brought the speed of electronic communication within reach of the potential empire builder."[41] As we will see, while the forms of electronic communication used to build and maintain these empires have shifted over time, the basic need for wide-scale coordination (between suppliers, workers, trustees, distributors, and consumers) in these giant firms remains—and accelerates. Nowhere is this continuity clearer, perhaps, than in the adoption and use patterns of an invention that followed close on the heels of the telegraph, Alexander Graham Bell's "electric speaking telephone."

... AND A BIGGER USER BASE

In the year following its presentation to the American Academy of Arts and Sciences in 1876, the telephone was understood as an analog to the telegraph. Like privately leased telegraph lines, the telephone could connect (wealthy) homes and businesses.[42] Given its short range, the phone could also operate as an adjunct to telegraphy; centralized (often urban) message offices used the telephone to route long-distance telegraph communiqués to local receivers.[43] It was suggested that this practice could benefit smaller communities that couldn't support the wages of a skilled, full-time telegrapher.[44] Indeed, according to its inventor, the young telephone's "great advantage" over the telegraph was "that it require[d] no skill to operate . . . the telephone actually speaks, and for this reason it can be utilized for nearly every purpose for which speech is employed."[45] In addition to expanding the potential users and applications of electronic communication, the telephone's circumvention of trained operators offered privacy, doing away with the need for coded messaging.[46] Given the primacy of the human voice in these communications, the telephone also offered the opportunity of more intimate (but still masculine) communication between the office, factory, and warehouse.[47] The telephone thus presented a doubled incentive to employers who could take advantage of cheaper deskilled labor and manage workers' commitments via personal connection.

Despite these differences, it was not until the invention of the switchboard that the telephone distinguished itself as a significant tool of business. Building on the precedent of telegraph exchanges, switchboards connected any user to any other user within an established network.[48] After the technology became publicly available in the United States in 1878, the speed and convenience of this "central office system" quickly came to define telephone service and drive adoption rates.[49] By the first decade of the 1900s, internal switchboards connecting intra-organizational users further speeded business's embrace of telephones.[50] In its mission to build a dense network of telephone users, the switchboard found a counterpart in an AT&T corporate strategy, promoted most famously by president Theodore Newton Vail as "One System, One Policy, Universal Service."[51] Drawing on his experience as general superintendent of the federal Railway Mail Service, Vail (cousin to Alfred) sought a network that bound together everyone in the country—even in unprofitable (often rural) areas. While this would dramatically increase the utility of the network for any given user who could then reach any other user, this imperial vision also legitimated AT&T's claim to a natural monopoly.

Although the promise of being able to access anyone, (just about) anywhere, would become a centerpiece of business telecommunications promotions, anything resembling "universal" service would take decades to realize. In the early years of its commercial development, the telephone followed the strategy of its immediate predecessor, focusing primarily on business users who were already paying for telegraph services.[52] Again, high costs limited the technology's use almost entirely to these subscribers.[53] Indeed, although Bell, in his 1878 letter cited earlier, offers an expansive vision of telephone use that includes the home, his final remarks are far more circumscribed, leaving little doubt as to the chief applications he sought to promote:

> In conclusion, I would say that it seems to me that the telephone should immediately be brought prominently before the public, as a means of communication between bankers, merchants, manufacturers, wholesale and retail dealers, dock companies, water companies, police offices, fire stations, newspaper offices, hospitals and public buildings and for use in railway offices, in mines and other operations.[54]

Bell built its market accordingly, using advertising that—up until the mid-1920s—focused almost exclusively on "instrumental" uses of the phone and ignored its capacity for sociability.[55] Likewise, early representatives of the Bell Company and its independent competitors in the United States and Canada cultivated subscribers across the fields of manufacturing, distribution, finance, and sales.[56] While territories outside of the Northeast adopted the telephone more slowly and in more diverse arrangements, these differences resulted largely from alternative commercial patterns endemic to the South and the Midwest.[57] Sidney H. Aronson concludes, "The early history of telephone usage, then, is largely the story of how commercial and professional communities adopted the new means of communication."[58]

The utility of the telephone's coordination capacities varied according to industry. For firms already using the telegraph, the telephone accelerated current practices of connection and control. As companies increasingly sought new means to manage their increasing scale, the telephone—"perhaps the most important new instrument of communication to become widely available to managers"—enabled oversight of newly multi-divisional and decentralized organizational forms.[59] Phones became a crucial facet of the increasingly rationalized, automated, and efficient office—and a primary mechanism of experimentation with management control systems.[60] The telephone's ability to supersede distance also enabled companies to secure economic efficiencies by geographically disarticulating the head office from factory operations, moving parts of the organization to cheaper locales.[61] Its space-binding properties were useful for orchestrating tasks specific to a number of industries, including construction (linking architect to foreman in large-scale projects like skyscrapers and canals), utilities (managing far-flung operations), mining (enabling contact with the surface in cases of emergency), medicine (connecting doctors to pharmacists), retail (coupling grocer to wholesaler) and finance (again, allowing intercommunication among banks).[62] The telephone was particularly useful for linking members of industries based outside of communications-rich city centers. Across the South, the Midwest, and southern California, farmers and independent phone companies developed systems for linking rural and regional residents and professionals.[63] These circuits became crucial for industries like agriculture, which demanded accurate local information (on frost conditions, for example). Like the telegraph, the telephone supported the further growth of communications-intensive professions, from legal services to hospitality.[64] Its fast adoption within Los Angeles hotels, for example—to enable vacationing managers to keep in touch with the home office—is credited, in part, for the city's premier ranking in phones-per-capita in 1885.[65] Like the telegraph before it, the telephone enabled businesses to reconfigure space and geography to suit their aims, whether to build nation-spanning multi-divisional organizations, connect people within an architecturally complex job site, or support local hubs of commerce.

While the preceding rehashes many of the acclaimed affordances of the telegraph, the telephone's wide usability for diverse, (relatively) untrained constituencies vastly increased the number and scope of workers and institutions engaging in electronic communication. Furthermore, the telephone's eventual take-up as a leisure technology would mark it as one of the first electronic business communication technologies to bear the affective resonance of entertainment. Although sociability uses for the telephone were not substantially promoted by Bell in its first few decades, "pleasure telephone" services providing music, election results, and other entertainments existed in Europe as a early as the 1880s.[66] When Bell began promoting the social value of the telephone in the pre–World War I era, advertisements promised personal connection and presence, e.g., in the form of "visiting" via telephone. As sociability advertisements proliferated in the late 1920s and 1930s, "comfort and convenience" became the watchwords for copy that emphasized the themes of family and friendship.[67] Because the telephone was ultimately positioned as an agnostic technology—one adapted just as easily for labor as for leisure—it represented a novel opportunity for companies to harness the positive associations workers built with the technology in their leisure time. Although it is unclear if businesses used telephones to this effect, reports of workers using the telephone socially while on the clock point to (ongoing) tensions between workers and employers introduced by agnostic technologies and the "productive" use of time.[68] More significantly, the sense of "symbolic proximity" built by social phone practices— a psychosocial property combining "imminent connectedness" to others with the possibility of "immediate interaction"—laid a foundation for later business technologies, including radio, that would more explicitly draw on the connective and affective capabilities of telecommunications.[69] (Where the telephone also distinguishes itself from telegraphy is in AT&T's pride of place as one of the country's most significant users of business media for training, human relations, and management. This, however, is a story for Chapter 3.)

Over the course of the twentieth century, the telephone would be conscripted by a host of agents and institutions to serve a wide variety of coordination—and even cultivation—purposes. Some of these applications are scarcely legible to contemporary readers as suited to the technology, while others were not technically telephony, but radio masquerading as such.[70] In the pre-war era and into the 1960s, experiments with "teleteaching" used telephones to connect homebound, hospitalized, or otherwise isolated students to a skilled instructor. Much like industrial telephone systems, these transmissions hoped to achieve economies by managing activities over extensive space and by extending the presence of experts within districts via relatively cheap, accessible equipment.[71] In the post-war era, the telephone would also be incorporated into industrial monitoring and remote control systems that likewise made use of the telephone's space-binding properties to increase productivity and save labor costs.[72] These diverse uses (remote control, broadcasting, narrowly directed two-way wireless contact) all became the object of extensive industrial experimentation—with radio. However, before turning the dial to more fully explore the ether, another audio technology warrants discussion for its pursuit of industrial efficiency—not via connection, but through reproduction.

RECORDING AND REORGANIZATION

Much like the telephone, before the phonograph built strong associations with popular amusements, it was imagined as a business technology that could modernize corporate administration. It offered a flashpoint for experiments in media, labor, automation, and rationalization, and bore witness to the increasing decentralization of electronic business communication via "office systems" installed within the architecture of individual firms. Furthermore, visions of the mass adoption of business communication technologies fueled the pursuit of usability for a diverse, untrained user-base—one of the chief strategies employed in expanded vertical integration. While the phonograph could not offer the resource-stretching or space-binding capabilities of radio, its reorganization of office labor promised efficiencies in coordination that were just as valuable.

Despite Thomas Edison's popular association with entertainment technologies like the kinetoscope, he devoted considerable resources to working on business technologies. His success with the electric light for offices and the growing market for business technologies like the telephone fed his pursuit of industrial applications for the phonograph.[73] Although Edison patented a rudimentary tinfoil phonograph in 1877, commercial development of the device languished for almost a decade as he pursued other inventions. Allegedly, it was the successes of the Volta Laboratory Association and Alexander Graham Bell in developing their own sound recording device, the gramophone (often marketed as the Dictaphone), that spurred Edison to return to his invention.[74] By the mid-1880s, two interests vied for the lead position in the recorded sound market, and both pursued "practical purposes."[75] They imagined a market comprised of "[b]ankers, merchants, lawyers, and editors" in want of a dictation device that could record their correspondences on a wax cylinder for speedy transcription by an "office boy" (or woman).[76] Early promotions of such dictation and transcription systems promised cheaper communication and administration (compared, as usual, with in-person meetings), greater flexibility in the use of employee time, and (largely as a result) increased efficiency in the coordination of operations. However, as the technology matured, its value was increasingly made legible as a mechanism of tighter control over employee labor according to the principles of scientific management.

It would take some time, however, before even the machine's early promises of cost-effectiveness were to be realized. Many of the phonograph's most trenchant problems resulted from Edison's decision to mass-produce his device to match the increasing size of American industry. At West Orange, Edison devoted the expertise of his inventors and craftsmen to the design of interchangeable parts and the precision machines with which to make them.[77] As a result, he hoped to staff his factory—the Phonograph Works—with unskilled labor, doing for his factory what he hoped the phonograph would accomplish for the office. However, the precision machines themselves were difficult to operate and required constant adjustment and intensive training for their operators.[78] In conjunction with research setbacks in the lab, production of the phonograph stalled. At the end of the decade, it was still too delicate a device for the methods of mass production necessary to profitably reach the expanding business market (or, indeed, its entertainment counterpart).[79]

The second major problem caused by the intended scale of Edison's operations was the breadth and diversity of users that he imagined for each machine. The phonograph was a far cry from the telegraph, barred from lay users by a system of use that demanded expert operation. Much like the telephone, in the normal scope of use a phonograph could be employed by an executive, a typist, and an office manager working on its upkeep and care. Dust, vibration, and anything less than gentle treatment of the device as it moved between users "brought this technological revolution in the workplace to a halt."[80] Further, evidence indicates that workers didn't welcome even fully functioning devices with open arms—and experienced significant difficulty making intelligible recordings.[81] When the machine was redesigned in the 1910s, the primary criterion for the new device was ease of use and the ability to withstand careless, casual use.[82] As the twentieth century dragged on, the need to appeal to non-expert users became increasingly important for an office workforce that was often engaging directly with media communications technologies.

The eventual establishment of dictating machines as indispensable tools of the "modern office" following World War I resulted from at least three major shifts related to the machines' capacity to manage a changing workforce. First, the turn of the century saw waves of women entering the workforce as low-wage labor. Dictating machines enabled firms to replace expensive, skilled stenographers with women (and boys), vastly reducing the cost of administrative labor. Simultaneously, the devices promised an additional method for managing risk, since their inventors promoted them as far more reliable than human capital who might get drunk, tired, or demand a raise. Whether there was a concurrent epidemic of inebriated stenographers is unclear; whatever the case, the bodily and individualized nature of the "risks" outlined by the promotion of the dictation machine emphasizes the easy "manageability" of a standardized, mechanized worker. (Discourses concerning the value of the mechanically enhanced worker are explored further in the next chapter.)

Closely tied to the preceding developments, the first two decades of the twentieth century witnessed the rise and popularization of Taylorism and scientific management as a set of theories and practices aiming to reduce costs by increasing efficiency and ease of management through rigid hierarchy and division of labor. Before the technological transformation of the phonograph into the more user-friendly 1916 Ediphone, Edison's laboratories developed a Taylorist solution to its problems that helped manage problems of scale—both in regard to the complexity of machines for mass production and the need to serve diverse and careless users. Instead of a single device that could fulfill multiple functions, he developed a total office system, wherein even the technology was subject to an efficient division of labor. The complete Edison dictation system comprised three different devices calibrated to gendered hierarchical roles—a dictating machine (male executives), a transcribing machine for playback and typing (female typists), and a cylinder shaver that did the dirty work of erasing messages for reuse (office boys). By dividing the labor of dictation into three specialized machines, each became easier to mass manufacture.[83] Furthermore, the interactions between machines and their intended users also became simplified, since a particular class of users would generally only interact with a single machine and its smaller cluster of affordances. Dividing, simplifying, and distributing the diverse tasks of a stenographer to unskilled workers also increased the manageability of the workforce, since menial workers could be quickly replaced if their work was unsatisfactory.[84] Just as phonographs and Dictaphones cut down on the potentially "wasteful" flexibility of the stenographer who often organized his own time and tasks, they introduced greater flexibility for executives who could record their correspondences at their convenience rather than attempt to collaborate with a stenographer who might be otherwise engaged.[85] In addition to ensuring good scientific management practices, such a system also maintained gendered and classed labor hierarchies based on assumed capabilities and affinities. While Andre Millard offers the Edison system as an example of how communication technologies can directly restructure office work, we can also understand the episode as yet another beat in the mediated company's ongoing efficiency march to reorganize the temporality of labor and exploitation of resources through interconnected systems and new manufacturing processes. On the whole, the machine stands as a useful example of how *both* communications messages and their technologies of transmission could be bent to the efficient coordination of resources.

Although phonographic dictation machines eventually became manageable for mass production, successful mass *re*production of content for business would remain out of reach for the wax cylinder.[86] Unlike the gramophone developed by Emile Berliner (available to the public in 1895) that used flat disks easily stamped in a mass production process, any duplication of content on wax cylinders proceeded only through two cumbersome techniques. Either performers repeated their work ad nauseum for multiple machines recording simultaneously, or cut cylinders were copied through a difficult pantograph process that produced inferior sound.[87] Despite duplication difficulties, Edison pursued reproduction—for coin-in-the-slot machines growing in popularity as entertainment novelties.[88] The business phonograph, however, remained a device substituting for interpersonal communication; any sort of publishing industry for business communications would have to look to radio and, far more extensively, film.

MANAGING TIME AND SPACE

While radio eventually distributed reproduced material for the workplace following the start of World War II, the balance of its use tends toward coordination applications similar to those of telegraphy and telephony. Through its broadcast affordances, which freed communications from wired infrastructure, radio offered an intensified means of engaging workers and managing dispersed facilities across large, and often challengingly complex territories (oceans, cities, mountainous forests). By 1957, analysts estimated that businesses invested over 4.6 billion dollars in radio for private communications—pursuing the same goals of increased efficiency, expansion, and control promised by its forebears.[89] However, it would take some time after radio's turn-of-the-century debut before businesses understood the full utility of these "Work-Horse" capabilities.[90] When dots and dashes still ruled the ether, many inventor-entrepreneurs used wire telegraphy as the structuring logic to promote their systems and identify key markets. (Crucially, in the late 1890s, telephone systems would not yet match the transcontinental scope of the telegraph—and had been prevented from engaging in the lucrative business message trade for much of the 1890s due to their patent settlement with Western Union.) The man credited with first introducing wireless to the public, Guglielmo Marconi, thus sought a Western Union–style monopoly across the British Empire that would compete directly with wired telegraphy. He focused his early efforts on commercial and naval ship-to-ship and ship-to-shore communication and the establishment of a transatlantic channel.[91] Likewise, inventor Reginald Fessenden promoted government and maritime uses for his radio technologies, targeting the US Signal Corps, the navy, and other governments.[92] In 1904, yet another of radio's inventors, Lee De Forest, contracted with the United Fruit Company. The first major American corporation to heavily invest in wireless technology, the firm hoped to better coordinate global shipping operations of highly perishable goods.[93] These formulations often imagined wireless as a point-to-point system of communication between known interlocutors. The indiscriminate spread of wireless signals was understood as a nuisance to those seeking the same affordances of the business telegraph or telephone. While a number of early technological and practical strategies attempted to rein in its broadcast capabilities—from advanced tuning to coded messages—the ability of communications to saturate a field would eventually be recognized as one of radio's virtues.

Before being slowly pulled into post–World War I industrial projects, radio became the object of experimentation for a variety of constituencies hoping to better coordinate (and even sell) timely information. We might think, for example, of an oft-repeated origin story, Marconi's public demonstration of broadcasting at the America's Cup Yacht races in October 1899. While the race's emphasis on ship-to-shore communication supported Marconi's interests in establishing wireless as a tool for shipping and trade, it was a pair of newspapers, the *New York Herald* and the *San Francisco Call*, that orchestrated the wireless demonstration for their own commercial interests. Promoting near-instantaneous reports from Marconi's wireless as the "crowning glory of journalism," the *Call* (much like the *Herald*) used the event to further its position within a crowded news media landscape.[94]

Positing the races as a multifaceted battle (between countries, yachts, wireless and wired telegraphy, and between papers seeking accurate, up-to-date information), the *Call* declared wireless—and the papers that used it—the victors of the day. Indeed, while the paper spared a few inches to report race results, most of the coverage that spilled across its pages emphasized the triumph of wireless and criticized other papers' slow, unreliable, and intentionally fake race reportage.[95] While foreshadowing the tight articulations between radio, commercial news, sports, and entertainment that followed the advent of voice transmission in the mid-1900s, the papers' strategic use of wireless to secure temporal efficiencies in information distribution continued preexisting mediated business practices.

Of course, the commercial broadcasting industry represents the best-understood means by which radio proved its utility for business. Following an unusual path, the US government actively developed a broadcasting system heavily favoring private commercial use. During World War I, under the rubric of national security concerns, the government commandeered existing wireless systems and banned amateur transmissions (at that point the largest group of users). As has been well documented, when the government realized it could not maintain command of wireless following the war, it helped engineer American control over US systems by aiding the formation of the Radio Corporation of America (RCA), an oligopoly (General Electric, American Telegraph and Telephone, Westinghouse, United Fruit) that together held important radio patents. Likewise, by 1922 the regulatory tide increasingly favored commercial ownership (over, for example, that of educational institutions, churches, city government, and other nonprofits) through a series of policy decisions regarding licensing, frequency assignments, station power allowances, and content restrictions.[96] By exploiting the medium's publishing capacities, the commercial model of radio—and, in turn, television—provided a powerful resource for industrial concerns seeking to engender the public's support, manage audiences' consumption, and promote economically advantageous political systems across the twentieth century. Beyond product advertisements, corporate speech could be found in the form of institutional advertising, which burnished the company image in the hopes of engendering listeners' goodwill. Companies' advocacy advertising more ambitiously hoped to intervene in political policy by managing the opinions and actions of listening voters. Both modes took varied forms, including sponsored newscasters, concert programs laden with promotional speeches, and fictionalized series following small-town American everymen.[97] And, certainly, broadcast networks, local stations, advertisers, set manufacturers, and program producers represented a significant industry in their own right. While the broad contours of this particular commercial use of the American airwaves are well established, less understood is a smaller, heterogeneous field of broadcasting practice likewise bent to the will of industry. To avoid confusion with commercial entertainment, I refer to these uses as "applied radio."

The same licensing system that ceded control to RCA, eventually and with some cajoling, carved out space for a range of industrial, emergency, and public service applications. Some, like radio compasses for marine and airplane navigation, built on wireless's existing reputation as a tool of trade.[98] Others were more interested in repurposing commercial broadcasting. An early entrant into workplace radio, the Detroit Police Department obtained a station license in 1923 to broadcast dispatch calls to on-duty patrol officers. However, appropriating entertainment broadcasting's infrastructure proved challenging. Due to license stipulations requiring entertainment programming, station KOP prefaced each call to officers with "Yankee Doodle"—a nightmarish scenario for those not fond of jingoistic earworms. Further, officers reportedly tuned their dials beyond KOP to catch up on the latest sports scores.[99] Radio's erosion of the boundaries between business and pleasure—eventually championed by those promoting industrial television—was then understood as a drawback. As the 1920s transitioned into the 1930s, experimentation widened to include workers in marine patrolling and fire fighting, forestry, utilities, and emergency response.[100] World War II marked a watershed moment for applied radio in North America. While the US Army experimented with two-way radios in tanks, water and power companies on the home front used "the unlimited national emergency" to gather support for expanding their permitted use of radio services.[101] After the war, with applied radio's utility proven, the Federal Communications Commission (FCC) established a Radio Technical Planning Board (RTPB) to oversee the development of functional radio services. Following the work of the RTPB, licensed operators gained the ability to use radio for routine uses, including dispatching.[102] This represented a dramatic loosening of restrictions, which previously confined broadcasts to emergencies when existing communication infrastructures failed. As a result, radio use grew significantly. In the utilities industries alone, licensees jumped from 250 in 1947 to over 2,000 about 10 years later.[103]

Applied radio found its appeal in its ability to precisely manage operations over vast and inhospitable territories. Ships' reliance on radio for navigation and information offers a paradigmatic example. On land, the ability to render dispersed and mobile workforces more manageable was routinely cited as radio's chief asset for industries that employed "field forces."[104] Police radio, for example, extended preexisting strategies that cut municipal space into smaller, more manageable districts and beats. While territorial divisions made individual cops easier for dispatchers to locate, radio-equipped cars increased the speed and ease of this task by making all space (and people) within the remit of broadcast signals immediately accessible.[105] Later paging systems worn directly on the body enabled firms to target workers even more precisely.[106] For their part, utilities companies championed radio as a means to coordinate stable infrastructure (stations, plants, control centers) with flexibly circulating field crews (engineers, supervisors).[107] Often, these capabilities were framed as essential to the careful distribution of precious resources across otherwise unmanaged territories. Prophesying in 1957 that "the time is not too far distant when every commercial vehicle will be radio-equipped," mobile radio boosters Jeremiah Courtney and Arthur Blooston reasoned that "the high cost of labor and vehicular equipment makes it imperative for every enterprise to have *as close control as possible* over the vehicles operated out of the sight of management."[108] Put another way, radio enabled managers to realize their "primary function": "the projection of themselves to the greatest extent possible into every important part of the industrial or commercial process."[109]

In addition to intensifying the control management held over distributed workforces, applied radio enabled the navigation of expansive territories difficult (if not impossible) to wire permanently. These applications sought to tame geography itself, rendering all space *manageable*. Before the loosening of licensing regulations, the bulk of these services operated as temporary emergency measures.[110] Some of the most sophisticated of these systems belonged to the forestry industry, which used heavy long-range and lightweight portables, walkie talkies, and even aircraft radio to coordinate fire-fighting crews responding to live fires spreading across vast, rugged, and undomesticated terrain.[111] During the war, radio enabled Allied forces to maintain communications while invading what literally constituted enemy territory (Occupied France).[112] In the late 1950s and beyond, Citizens Band (CB) radio allowed American truckers to learn *in transit* about upcoming traffic and weather conditions, locate cheap fuel, and— especially during the lower mandated speed limits of the 1970s oil crisis— avoid traffic cops.[113] For more stable, but still significant expanses, radio telemetering—"the science of transmitting information [often encoded audio signals rather than voice transmissions] detected at one point to another point a distance away"—enabled firms to manage and even remotely control otherwise empty or isolated plants.[114] Ranging from checking equipment functionality to measuring mountain snow levels, radio telemetry represented yet another means of securing labor efficiencies through mediated coordination.[115] Ultimately these deployments of applied radio understood the medium as a means of preparing the ground over which companies hoped to operate. They transformed expansive "fields" into knowable, manageable territories no matter their physical and—in the case of war—political properties. Combined with the ability to precisely target workers within these territories, applied radio intensified firms' capacity to manage across space. Television (via satellite) would offer much the same—on a potentially global scale.

As a function of these spatial affordances, applied radio also offered temporal efficiencies in coordination and control. Users emphasized the speed at which radio could reach dispersed listeners in the "shortest possible space of time," rendering them "instantly available."[116] In addition to enabling quick responses to shifting conditions, radio made time itself more productive. With radio-equipped cars, workers no longer needed to wait at headquarters for instructions. Instead, they could complete other tasks until called back by their supervisors (and supervisors no longer wasted time looking for their employees).[117] While early radio-based paging systems might simply signal to a car or worker that they were wanted, two-way radio saved field workers additional time spent searching for the parking spaces and pay phones needed to contact their dispatchers for further instructions.[118] Across fields ranging from contracting, trucking, heavy equipment sales, and utilities, firms translated this "substantial conservation of machine-hours, man-hours, and vehicle-hours" into relatively precise increases in efficiency, productivity, and cost savings ranging from 10% to 40%.[119]

The temporal efficiency promised by radio reached its zenith in materials processing. Another example of the linkages between media systems and commodity production, radio telemetry—as part of a larger system of coordinated process control—supported industrial interest in continuous processing. Unlike batch processing, during which machinery completes a single production cycle before being powered down, checked for faults, and turned back on for the next cycle, continuous processing is characterized by machinery that runs constantly and outputs at a regular, unceasing rate. One entry in a long line of twentieth-century experiments in time, work, and manufacture, continuous processing became increasingly appealing to industrial producers (especially in petroleum and chemicals) due to its promises of increased output, savings on labor during down time, and preservation of machines and materials that did not weather stop-start of cycles well.[120] However, because of the increased complexity of coordinating always-on systems, workers needed access to updated information concerning activities that might span an entire plant, several miles, or include otherwise hard-to-reach spaces. While continuous processing might operate at impressive scales, precision oversight was the linchpin that made it work; as one engineer suggested, "*time* is the governing factor in coordinated control."[121] Radio telemetery ensured that the workers tasked with overseeing such time-sensitive activities had immediate access to accurate information across industrial operations.

MANAGING BODIES AND MINDS

While the impact of radio's temporal or spatial efficiencies might be reported with an engineer's precision, more difficult to account for was the affective value of "presence" provided by telecommunications. Though the previously mentioned applications were designed to fulfill coordination purposes, some nevertheless offered employers a simultaneous means of cultivating their employees. Cited as "the end of . . . isolation," the constant contact enabled by applied radio promised to work on listeners' relationships with the firm by improving morale, promoting teamwork, and tightening bonds among workers and with supervisors.[122] The emphasis on the virtues of collectively experienced radio broadcasts would find a corollary in the contemporaneous promotion of "group listening"—by women's homemaker clubs, for example—to build economically productive bonds among audience members that provided affective support and information exchange.[123] This "presence"—the special province of telecommunications' connection and broadcasting's "liveness"—would become increasingly important to employers, as detailed in Chapters 3 and 5.

Despite cultivation messages' interest in developing audience member capacities rather than logistically coordinating resources, they often likewise pursued efficiencies, expansion, and control. Although businesses were slow to explore these affordances, universities, museums, newspapers, and schools used radio cultivation to meet their missions. Public universities, for example, used radio to efficiently expand extension programs, distributing agricultural research, market information, and home economics guidelines to improve rural economies and listeners' material wealth.[124] Radio's ability to stretch scarce resources also found forceful proponents in primary and secondary classrooms struggling to manage the funding inequities of American public schooling. Much like teleteaching, radio was hailed for its ability to transmit the expertise of a single skilled teacher and provide a more diversified curriculum to students who would otherwise lack access.[125] At all levels of schooling, radio made it possible to overcome the vagaries of geography, bringing far-flung listeners into the remit of public education. This was particularly important for institutions whose territorial interests were dictated not by market profitability, but by a democratic mission to serve all of its constituencies regardless of their personal resources.[126] While little evidence suggests that businesses used radio similarly for training purposes, broadcasting's economies of scale would eventually appeal to companies pursing workplace television.

Workplace radio, when finally taken up by employers, provided a resource far afield from the lessons of classroom instructors. In the 1930s, researchers began exploring music's ability to increase workers' productivity—by regulating their stamina, attention, and muscular energy on a physiological level. Indebted to the Hawthorne School of Human Relations, these trials hoped to both improve factory workers' experience of laboring in repetitive, tedious jobs and (often more importantly) increase their output.[127] As it did for other "useful" media, World War II provided an opportunity to test technologies, theories, and practices. In the summer of 1940, the British Broadcasting Corporation began airing *Music While You Work* at 10:30 a.m. and 3:00 p.m. for workers in UK armament factories. Comprised of upbeat, regimented music consistent in rhythm, tempo, and volume, the program hoped to adapt workers to de-skilled repetitive work during their (statistically determined) least productive hours.[128] Quickly following the example set by the British, the US War Production board and RCA researched the use of music in war plants and shipyards (often filling the void of a national public service network with gramophone records).[129] In the immediate post-war era, managerial interest in "functional music" coalesced in the rise of Muzak.[130] Initially conceived of as an entertainment company targeting the home, by the mid-1930s the firm had entered commercial service, transmitting functional music—via telephone lines—to hotels and restaurants.[131] During the war, Muzak collaborated with the Office of War Information and several military branches to conduct their own studies of work productivity.[132] Having successfully drawn the attention of businesses, Muzak's subscriber base grew to include a wide range of factories and offices by 1946.[133]

Muzak's approach to increasing worker productivity manifested in a technique called "stimulus progression." A carefully regulated system that matched the rationalization of the work it accompanied, stimulus progression carefully rated songs according to the mood they were assumed to induce in the listener. The numerical score of each song considered tempo, instrumentation, rhythm, orchestra size, and other characteristics (vocals were often forbidden). Scored songs were then modularly recombined in 15-minute blocks to match fatigue cycles of workers in different settings, with different programs, for example, geared toward offices and factories.

The most "stimulating" music would play during points in the day when workers were most likely to be bored, tired, and unproductive. Each quarter hour of programming was paired with a quarter hour of silence to provide listeners an indication of the passage of time as music blocks began and ended.[134] While Muzak thus shares with other technologies an interest in reorganizing the "time" of labor, it distinguished itself by attempting to cultivate individual workers' endurance within Fordist production processes.[135]

This "cultivation" reached beyond physiological response. As a means of "cultural adjustment" to the unrelenting tempo of the assembly line, Muzak strove to make employees more comfortable and content—and therefore, more tractable.[136] Before the managerial introduction of functional music in factories, song had previously manifested as a tactic to soften the challenging tedium of work. However, because music under the control of workers might express criticisms of hard labor or operate at tempos that interfered with the consistency desired by employers, it was often banned outright.[137] The reintroduction of music was careful to modulate its affective resonance to create the "optimum [sonic] work womb."[138] Selections drew from popular music laden with themes of fantasy, romance, and nostalgia to "produc[e] an overall feeling of pleasantness."[139] The emphasis on commercial entertainment—music that workers would otherwise encounter in their leisure hours—helped "blur the distinction between work and leisure, factory and home."[140] Media's ability to disrupt these boundaries would become increasingly important to employers hoping to productively manage workers' feelings and emotional commitment to the firm. This particular strategy—termed "deinstitutionalization" by Joy Fuqua in their analysis of hospitals' use of television to shed their overly clinical reputations—seeks atmospheric remedy to make institutional spaces more appealing.[141] Unlike more controversial uses of "forced" listening (advertiser-supported music on city transit; loudspeaker trucks to campaign, proselytize, and sell), Muzak's primary message was one of employer concern for the listener and their well-being.[142] This emphasis on "care" and relationship development fit well within Human Relations models of employee management that hoped to consolidate the twin goals of increased productivity and a more humane workplace. Eventually, however, workers ceased to be the primary audience for functional music. By the mid-1980s, "foreground" music distributed to malls, supermarkets, offices, and restaurants overtook factories as Muzak's top patrons.[143] While these services continued to focus on the atmospheric qualities of functional music, they targeted the affective and behavioral attributes of consumers—often outright ignoring the experiences of workers.[144]

COORDINATION AS CULTIVATION

Just as television was not the first technology to combine cultivation and coordination, it was not the first to link speedy long-distance information distribution with the reproduction of images. Beginning in the 1920s, "illustrated radio," for example, placed images in newspapers to accompany educational radio broadcasts.[145] In the context of business, the most significant experiments with image transmission prior to (and running alongside) television concerned the facsimile (fax) machine. Although invented in rough form in the 1840s, the technology would not find commercial success until after World War I. A striking example of how a given technology might be bent toward varied applications, the fax first sought to compete with the telegraph as an improvement (on cost, speed, or ease) of an existing service, rather than make claims to a new mode of visual communication.[146] In the late 1930s and again in the mid-1940s, the fax was linked to broadcasting and the press as a means to distribute newspapers to homes and businesses.[147] The fax also found its fortunes tied up with television, with which it shared "researchers, patrons, and bureaucratic classification" (courtesy of the FCC).[148] While some believed that fax technology was a stepping stone to television's video transmission, others conflated the two technologies outright. Their respective associations with business and entertainment, however, became a key means of distinguishing their separate utilities. Television provided personalized access to (fleeting) moving picture entertainment; fax—like the telegraph before it—provided a hardcopy duplicate of the images it transmitted (copies that eventually gained legal contractual and evidential status).[149] Ultimately, the facsimile found success in these latter purposes, as an aid to business and the government.

The value of faxing for these interests was varied, though they tended toward speed, thrift, and accuracy in the transmission of coordination information. Early in its career, facsimile became important as a means to send still images when fidelity was important (signature verification for banks, maps for military purposes, fingerprints for police investigations, X-rays for hospitals, images for teleconferences). However, faxing's ability to quickly send documents and information led to its rapid and far-reaching post-war adoption. Compared to airmail letters and trains, the fax "accelerated the work cycle from weeks or days to hours or minutes."[150] In the 1970s, the fax moved companies closer to the increasingly popular vision of office automation that sought perfectly instant flows of information across technologies and around the world.

Combined with its user-friendly lack of a keyboard, the speed of faxing bore knock-on effects for the organization of labor. On the first count, a wide range of workers could be made responsible for their own messaging, saving labor costs. On the second—and with implications for understanding the cultivation capacities of telecommunications—faxing shifted the temporality of work for certain office workers. By disrupting the boundaries between work and nonwork time, the fax machine intensified management's demands on workers' hours—and stretched workers' thresholds for working in off-hours. According to Jonathan Coopersmith, "For workaholics, fax machines enabled them to take their work anywhere. For everyone, deadlines never ended. Instead of meeting a Friday deadline by readying a package for Thursday overnight pickup, faxing encouraged—or demanded—working up to the deadline as well as procrastination."[151]

While the cultivation of worker habits and beliefs offered an unintended bonus to firms primarily interested in exploiting the fax machine's coordination capacities, television would provide a full-throated embrace of these "virtues"—speed, economy, efficiency, productivity, usability, permeable barriers between work and leisure—by marrying the connective and directive capabilities of telecommunications with a vast empire of moving image practice: industrial film.

Before television entered the boardroom and stood on the shop floor, the nontheatrical film industry represented the largest sustained attempt to develop cultivation media for business. Screenings focused on workers' skills, knowledge, beliefs, affective states, and relationships to their work and each other. More than any of the fields spawned by telecommunications technologies, industrial film provided an opportunity for media workers to develop infrastructures (corporate media theory, magazines, awards, professional organizations) that would shape the adoption of television within the workplace.

FILM THAT SELLS, WORKS, CULTIVATES

While television draws extensively on the corporate techno-imaginaries of telecommunications, nontheatrical film provided a proving ground for textual cultivation strategies and a model for building a media profession outside of (but often imbricated into) the entertainment industries. Although workplace television professionals boasted varied training (nontheatrical film as well as commercial broadcasting, office communications and data management, and, eventually, film school), the film industry founded key sector supports for business media workers, including trade journals, professional organizations, awards, and market research. While these would expand and transform with the rise of workplace television, they helped sketch the initial contours of its media practitioner communities. Furthermore, sponsored film—distributed via television in the late 1940s and 1950s—provided many companies an early opportunity to bend the domestic small screen to their varied purposes.

Business's first use of film came when Edwin S. Porter, six years away from making *The Great Train Robbery*, perched in a small coop on the roof of the Pepper Building to project a film in New York's Herald Square. Displayed on a painted café backdrop declaring "Dewar's Scotch Whiskey," the film depicted four men attempting a frenetic approximation of the Highland fling.[152] Or, it was 1893 when denizens of the Garment District happened upon the spirited dancers projected on the back of a Broadway building.[153] Or, maybe the year was 1894, and the decisive occasion was not the projection of the film, but the moment a Dewar's distributor was disposed to inspiration when he noticed prolific lines of "giddy menfolk" waiting outside Kinetoscope parlors and the idea struck: "Why not run a peep show to advertise Dewar's Scotch whisky?"[154] (Strictly speaking, the first advertising film might not have been about Dewar's at all. The whisky advertised by Porter's projection could have been Haig & Haig. It's also possible that less-remembered beer and chocolate ads ran first. Or an entirely different set of films—for Columbia bicycles, Admiral cigarettes, Piel's beer, and the Southern Pacific railroad—deserve to duke it out for the mantle of the first advertising film.[155] And, N.B., a more accurate accounting of the inspiration for *Dewar's* would include outdoor electrical advertising and slide projections that were then popular.[156])

Although the identity of the first advertising film remains hazy, the stories told about the origins of "commercial" cinema are nevertheless instructive.[157] The primary source material for the preceding is Terry Ramsaye's historical serial "The Romantic History of the Motion Picture," commissioned by *Photoplay* and eventually revised and repackaged as his landmark (if sometimes faulty) *A Million and One Nights*. For Ramsaye, the first advertising film marks a shift in the development of cinema, from technological wonder to self-conscious commercial industry and art form. It likewise delivers on the romance promised to *Photoplay* readers in its introduction of Porter, one of the "men of destiny of the motion picture" whose biography spans the West Indies and Manhattan, and involves not one, but two separate tales of adventure and arrest brought on by flaunting the protocols of projection at the service of expanding moving image exhibition.[158] Recounting the origins of advertising motion pictures served far different purposes for *Business Screen*, the lead publication for industrial film producers and sponsors. In 1938, still in its first year of operation, the trade journal needed to establish the field it hoped would serve as its market. Using cinematic heritage discourses, *Business Screen* traced its lineage to figures like Porter and Edison, situating itself as yet another visionary player experimenting with the power and possibilities of cinema.[159] Invoking Ramsaye's canonical chronicle as its source material evinces *Business Screen*'s historiographical authority and profits from romantic associations with the glamour, success, and prestige of the entertainment film industry—all while flattering its readership that "the business movie has a historical edge on the entertainment product."[160] Different motivations animate *Business Week*'s 1939 message to executives, where the story serves as a brief prologue to a rebuke that decries the lack of acceptance for industrial films and instructs readers on how to adopt film as a crucial element of company communications. Exhibiting a sportsmanlike appreciation for the utility of an agreed-upon origin story, *Business Week* notes that *Dewar's—It's Scotch!* is "a matter of record"—and not one they care to challenge. As the editors so delicately put it, "The point is, commercial motion pictures are at least 45 years old; yet advertisers still think of them as a new medium."[161] Combined, these retellings reflect the diverse interests served by reshaping the significance of the first advertising film. *Dewar's—It's Scotch!* becomes a means to characterize a lead player in a romantic historical epic, legitimize a fledgling industry, and chastise the hesitation of businessmen to modernize their advertising techniques. The different shapes of these retellings allude to the diversity of interests pulled into the remit of the film industry, as well as the complex circuits of capitalist production and consumption (advertising, entertainment, art, worker training, intra-firm product sales, sponsored film) in which media would become implicated across the twentieth century.

According to its many biographers, business film entered a latent period following its debut on the Great White Way. The fledgling industry passed its next milestone in the early 1910s with the release of International Harvester's *Back to the Old Farm* (c. 1911).[162] As Gregory Waller notes, although the film was initially distributed and exhibited as an Essanay release—without International Harvester (IHC) as a named sponsor— *Business Screen* nevertheless pulled the film into its 1938 efforts to legitimize the nascent field it hoped to serve.[163] Featured twice in *Business Screen*'s first four issues, the film supported the trade journal's efforts to establish the field's forward momentum and future trajectory through historical self-definition. (In a self-mythologizing Ouroboros feeding frenzy, *Business Screen* would later invoke one of these articles on *Old Farm* in the journal's own thirtieth anniversary issue.[164]) Labeled the industry's pioneering "organized creative effort" and "the first motion picture to apply showmanship to selling," the film follows George Randall, a young urban real-estate agent who accepts an invitation to visit the farm he grew up on as a child.[165] Upon seeing the miracle of modern electric (International Harvester) farm machinery, he falls in love anew with agriculture—and his childhood sweetheart.

Despite the heritage treatment given *Back to the Old Farm*, it was likely not the first narrative sales film.[166] (Though *Old Farm* made for good copy in an issue that included a lengthy profile on International Harvester's film program.[167]) Indeed, it was not even the first time IHC used motion pictures. The manufacturer began using film under the auspices of its Service Bureau two years earlier with its first feature, *The Romance of the Reaper*, an illustrated lecture that combined about 200 color slides with 5,000 feet of film showcasing the operation of IHC machines and plants; the manufacture of binders, twine, and farm implements; and scenes of global harvest.[168] Touring fairs, Chautauquas, schools, dealerships, and rural communities, the feature was screened to hundreds of thousands of viewers across the United States over the course of several years. Quickly followed up with other lectures and an industrialog series, *Reaper* cemented the strategic role film played within the larger operations of the Service Bureau. After the later success of *Back to the Old Farm*, IHC's advertising department permanently installed motion pictures—such as *Making Hay with New Machines* and *Evolution of Harvesting* (both 1913)—as a regular part of their customer outreach campaigns.[169]

IHC's entry into motion pictures can be considered representative of other major companies. Ford, for example, also experimented intermittently with film in the first decade of the twentieth century (particularly for motion studies and filming production processes—that is, coordination applications), but waited until 1914 to regularly target worker, student, and public audiences with films that promoted utile modes of industrial and liberal capitalist citizenship.[170] While the illustrious lineage of *Dewar's* and *Old Farm* may seem a happy accident, the films' connections with commercial film production indicate the extent to which industrial film made use of preexisting infrastructure before developing its own dedicated sector. Other storied firms such as Vitograph, Universal, and Pathé also played significant roles in this early, chaotic history of industrials.[171] This parasitical relationship continued into the 1920s and 1930s as independent producers borrowed equipment and salvaged footage from Hollywood productions for their ad hoc nontheatrical ventures.[172] Although the infrastructure necessary to support a robust nontheatrical field would not fully manifest until World War II, interest in film's potential as a means of management and persuasion fermented well before the war. Indeed, when Lee Grieveson posits the interwar period as marking a transition toward a US-led liberal political economic order based in economic growth maximization strategies that forgo regulation to preserve corporate interests, plus a state limited to the protection of private property rights, he situates cinema (and radio) as key instruments used to govern populations and gain acceptance for privatized resource extraction and other exploitative practices.[173]

While Grieveson points to cinema's role in developing a new world system, the quotidian hopes that business interests harbored for film ranged widely. Directed toward workers, film promised to provide yet another machine to automate work. Early champions of film for such purposes were Frank and Lillian Gilbreth, leaders in the Progressive Era scientific management movement. As a means to document, study, and improve work processes, the Gilbreths believed film could rid firms of waste by determining "the one best way" to complete a task.[174] More ambitiously, film was employed to reorganize worker relations with the firm and with each other. In response to threats of unionization, for example, Western Union fired experienced employees and (among other things) developed a film program designed for a newly deskilled—and newly feminine— workforce. As noted in this book's introduction, Western Union employed gendered understandings of absorptive female spectatorship to appeal to their new workers and encourage a mode of self-regulation amenable to producing more tractable employees.[175] Other advocates of industrial film devised extensive application taxonomies to promote the flexibility and pervasive utility of the medium (Figure 1.1). Suggested uses ranged from training workers in specialized selling techniques to documenting job applicant information and "making each employee feel that he is important to his company and that his work makes him an important member of society as well" (employee relations).[176]

Beliefs about film's efficacy were undoubtedly influenced by persistent Progressive era discourses about the influence and power of motion pictures for education. In the presentation of training information, film could allegedly show complicated processes more quickly and clearly than other methods, overcome language and literacy barriers, and even make workers more serious about their jobs.[177] Pointing to scientific research, industrial film advocates went on to claim that—like vitamin D—information is best absorbed through the eye, the strongest "pathway to the brain."[178] And unlike print, film "defies non-attention on the part of audiences" given the ability of a darkened room to eliminate extraneous stimuli and the time-based nature of the message, which ostensibly prevented superficial scanning or outright avoidance.[179] The perceived capability of training film to work on employees' psyches as well as their skills endeared it to industries of all stripes, paving the way for ongoing

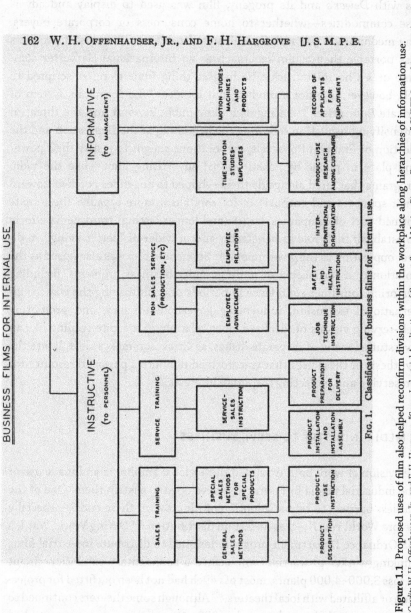

Fig. 1.   Classification of business films for internal use.

Figure 1.1 Proposed uses of film also helped reconfirm divisions within the workplace along hierarchies of information use.
Credit: W. H. Offenhauser, Jr., and F. H. Hargrove, "Some Industrial Applications of Current Sound Motion Picture Equipment," *SMPTE Journal* 34, no. 2 (1940): 162.

engagements between social science research and managerial interests within applied communications.[180]

Industrial film also became a significant means of communication with consumers, citizens, stockholders, and other external audiences. As with *Dewar's* and its progeny, film was used to display and advertise commodities—whether to home consumers or corporate buyers. The medium was particularly well suited to demonstrations of products less portable than a film reel, such as an International Harvester combine or a Chevrolet truck. The biggest thing films were conscripted to sell, however, was not a product, but an idea: "The American System of Private Enterprise."[181] Facing dwindling public support and the threat of intensifying regulation following the beginning of the Depression and the election of Franklin Roosevelt, corporations sought to justify their power and place in public life. Institutional advertising films—like the radio programs that aired alongside them—hoped to engender goodwill toward their sponsors and enthusiasm for capitalism more broadly. These texts formed part of companies' larger (and longer-lasting) transmedia efforts to establish their role as benefactor and provider of "better living," in direct opposition to the government.[182] Sponsored film was also posed as the solution to a cornucopia of more granular business problems, including restoring consumer confidence in periods of crisis, paving the way for international expansion, influencing government policy, and promoting self-serving visions of idealized labor relations.[183] Despite reading like an overstuffed menu of disparate dishes, as Grieveson makes clear, it was the synthesis of these uses that transformed film into a powerful resource for preserving and projecting corporate interests.

A MEDIA INDUSTRY TO SERVE BUSINESS

Television at work both extended these global ambitions and made use of the industrial media infrastructure developed to sustain them. One of the earliest barriers to robust adoption of film toward these ends—especially before World War II—was uncertain distribution.[184] During World War I, a US Ordnance Department program designed to distribute industrial films "linking worker to warrior" established a rudimentary exhibition circuit across 3,000–4,000 plants, most of which had not been outfitted for projection or affiliated with local theaters.[185] Although some theaters continued to show sponsored films as late as the 1920s, these exhibition agreements had to be negotiated on a costly theater-by-theater basis.[186] Some companies created their own distribution networks with nodes in showrooms, at fairs, and elsewhere. International Harvester, for example, developed a fairly formal distribution protocol in the 1920s whereby films spent their first year at the company's branch houses so that dealers maintained the privilege of debuting the features at annual events. In their second year, films were distributed far and wide to schools, civic organizations, and other institutions.[187] Sponsors lacking IHC's massive infrastructure were served by slowly developing circuits helmed by a range of institutions in the teens and early twenties, including the Y.M.C.A.'s Motion Picture Bureau, the nongovernmental Bureau of Commercial Economics, and National Non-Theatrical Motion Pictures, Inc., the last a film exchange created in 1921 by Harry Levey—"The Griffith of the Industrial Picture."[188] Modern Talking Picture Service (originally ERPI, a subdivision of Western Electric) helped formalize exhibition practices by creating the road show license for itinerant exhibitors, an invention that provided the field with its guiding business model.[189] The state's interest in developing an economically productive citizenry also led to the incorporation of industrials within larger networks of visual instruction anchored by extension services and educational institutions.[190] However, despite the emergence of these overlapping distribution and exhibition networks, as late as 1938 it could be said that "well-organized, standardized channels of [industrial film] circulation do not exist."[191]

The 1910s and 1920s also saw the fledgling formation of a dedicated industrial film production sector as several studios began to identify industrials as part or all of their focus. One of the earliest nontheatrical producers devoted specifically to business films, Industrial Moving Picture Company, became Rothacker Film Manufacturing Company in 1916. Burton Homes Films, C. L. Venard Productions, Wilding Productions, Leggett-Gruen Corporation, Altas Film Company, and Films-of-Business also devoted resources to industrial film production in the 1910s. While entertainment outfits like Universal and Paramount continued to create films for businesses, the 1920s also saw more New York- and Chicago-based studios, including Caravel Films, William J. Ganz, and the Chicago Film Laboratory, add their names to the industrial film roster. As with the establishment of distribution circuits, the development of an industrial film production sector was beset with difficulties. While some sponsors and producers developed strong symbiotic relationships leading to prolific output (e.g., Jam Handy and the Detroit automotive industry), this was the exception. More often came complaints of "[i]rresponsibles, 'fly-by-nights' and plain ordinary crooks"—small, often one-man outfits that delivered unwatchable films or disappeared once it came time for the hard work of distribution.[192] Although some marked the mid- to late 1930s as a turning point, when film was beginning to be understood by advertisers and businessmen as "an important part of their armamentarium," estimates suggest only 18–20 "producers of consequence" serving fewer than 200 "consistent users" of business film operated in the period.[193]

Recognition for industrial film's potential further coalesced in the late 1930s with the establishment of *Business Screen*.[194] As Eric Hoyt notes, trade presses provide the opportunity for a confluence of actors (manufacturers, producers, distributors, exhibitors and, in this case, sponsors) to stake their claim to industry knowledge and oversight.[195] *Business Screen* focused much of its early years on successful film campaigns, news briefs, production and marketing advice, advertisements, and historicizing and legitimating the field.[196] Surveys and yearly reviews attempted to stabilize information and communication flows by offering extensive coverage of industrial production companies, labs, and relevant equipment.[197] *Business Screen* also regularly published profiles that featured workers' labor history, expertise, and future plans. By defining achievement, demarcating specific paths to success, and making geographically dispersed individuals "known" to each other, these profiles helped strengthen the "imagined community" of industrial film workers.[198] In addition to acting as the industry's booster, *Business Screen* policed its membership by promoting community standards (e.g., publishing checklists delineating producer and sponsor responsibility) and "weeding out" (striking from annual reviews) or otherwise discouraging less-established producers from endangering the lucrative contracts already held by senior companies (and presumably, the major financial backers of the magazine).[199] Combined, these sources not only served as marketing for the companies and individuals involved, they fostered stability by establishing a community based on trust and relatively open circuits of information exchange.

Soon after the founding of *Business Screen*, World War II—marked by the government's need to coordinate resources and cultivate workers, soldiers, and cooperative citizens—facilitated the strengthening of industrial networks of communication.[200] On the home front, the wholesale mobilization of screening resources—for indoctrination, Treasury Drives and other initiatives—drew together projectors, prints, and exhibition spaces that would be vital to the continuing success of the nontheatrical sector.[201] The war also saw extensive use of film for coordination applications like combat photography that would continue well into the Cold War (notably in atomic weapons research).[202] Although the war was a boon to distribution networks, the early 1940s were lean years for many in the industrial film sector due to wartime manufacturing restrictions and a War Production Board that redirected producers' efforts to war films.[203] Indeed, it wasn't until 1947 that the industrial film sector got its first trade association—the Industrial Audio-Visual Association (IAVA).[204] Led in its early years by employees of industrial giants such as Swift and Company, Kraft Food Company, General Motors, Santa Fe Lines, and Standard Oil Company, IAVA's membership was designated by company rather than individuals.[205] Like other film industry trade meetings, their conferences featured panel discussions, demonstrations of new equipment, and group activities (e.g., hypothetical media assignments) that recall the special events (bake-offs, shoot-outs) contemporary trade shows use to induce cohesion among members.[206] IAVA featured other social and ritualistic events, such as luncheons and dinners, tours, new member inductions, and votes on leadership that enabled members to confirm alliances and build the trust that could facilitate the ongoing development of industrial film sector across diverse and distant interests.

Also supporting the sector's growth and stabilization in the post-war era were film festivals that provided legitimacy and eased distribution difficulties. While industrial films showed occasionally at the margins of young festivals, including Edinburgh's International Film Festival and Venice's International Exhibit of Cinematographic Arts, the Cleveland Film Festival (1949) became the first widely reported festival dedicated to educational and industrial films.[207] Other festivals—in cities ranging from Boston to Antwerp—followed close behind.[208] High festival activity—and the US State Department's desire to use nontheatrical film in support of its foreign policy—led to the 1957 creation of the Committee on International Non-theatrical Events (CINE). A coordinating body staffed by United States Information Agency officials and other governmental and non-government members, CINE spent its early years as a cultural gatekeeper helping American outfits submit to international festivals.[209] The energy surrounding these festivals following World War II responded to evergreen concerns regarding nontheatrical distribution; networking and foreign press marketing were valuable means of opening up international distribution markets.[210] At home, this period also saw rapid growth in 16mm film libraries that handled industrials (among other genres) and the mass exhibition of sponsored film as free filler on local television stations.[211]

Extensive effort on the part of diverse participants over several decades finally pulled the audiovisual (AV) sector (dominated by nontheatrical film, but including early open reel video, slides, and other formats) into the start of a golden era in the 1950s and 1960s.[212] By the end of the 1960s, some 75,000 people were estimated to work in the AV industry, with 600 companies producing hardware or software for a range of institutions.[213]

Figure 1.2A and 1.2B RCA's vaunted facilities. Television is given pride of place in the lower left-hand image and stuffed off in the wings in the top and bottom images on the second page.
Credit: "Business Theaters: RCA's Plant Center," *Business Screen* 8, no. 7 (1947): 28–29.

In 1969 alone, business and industry invested \$3.7 billion on audiovisuals, making it the largest spender among institutional subsectors.[214] In addition to equipment and other purchases, this money funded the production of 9,400 film titles intended for the 240,000 projectors that then populated company screening facilities.[215]

(b)

Left: Frank M. Folsom, Executive Vice President in charge of the RCA Victor Division, addresses a group of broadcast engineers from the stage of the little theatre.

sound motion picture projector. In addition, there is equipment for using slidefilms, glass slides and transcriptions.

The front of the theatre has a stage that more often presents equipment than people. The screen is interchangeable with a blackboard of the new dark green non-reflective type. A sound-absorbent dropped panel above the stage carries spotlights. General indirect light by incandescent bulbs on a hung soffit is controlled by an electronic dimmer. Below the screen is an RCA emblem concealing a built-in 10-inch loudspeaker which connects under floor level with the sound-film projector at the rear.

Side walls are dramatically treated with natural birch paneling arranged in zig-zag patterns to break up sound reflections, aided by large applied figures which lend a highly-modern note.

The color scheme is at once restful and dramatic. Floor carpet and walls are deep green, the ceiling is green and deep grayish pink, seats are covered by light green upholstery, and stage curtains are brilliant red.

Connected with the theatre is an installation of a central plant broadcast system, glass-enclosed and high-lighted by special illumination. Adjoining is a small "announce" room and offices of the program director.

The RCA console, centrally placed in the control room, distributes sound and inter-plant broadcasting to 22 areas in 19 buildings, some of them several miles from the plant. Over this system, employees receive music programs, addresses by management, announcements, and paging service.

Another important part of the showroom is a special sales display and conference room equipped for motion pictures, slides, and blackboard demonstrations. Executive conferences and sales meetings are held here against a background which itself exemplifies creative merchandising. One wall is of birch paneling, one pink marble, another deep blue-gray painted plaster, and the other wall curtained. Light is from cold cathode tubes in ceiling troughs and incandescent down light in the central hanging soffit. A sliding panel provides at a touch blackboard facilities, motion picture screen, or an attractive decorative panel.

Projected sight and sound in its most modern form—television—is provided for by RCA Victor in a special television viewing room. Here customers, dealers, distributors, and special guests see television in operation in an air-conditioned, modernistically furnished setting of living-room proportions.

On another floor, a meeting room and film workshop is set up for preview of product developments, splicing and editing of films for product meetings, studying of industrial engineering techniques based on 16mm loops of job operations, previewing of films by small groups, and similar activities.

From this workshop, too, motion and slide films are made available through a Central Film Library to the ten RCA Victor plants, regional offices, distributors—wherever there is need for films in training activities. More than 250 films are maintained in this library.

From the vantage point of this sound control room, the "announce" room (left) and theatre can be viewed through sound-proof glass.

Technical sessions, sometimes involving use of the chalkboard mounted in the screen area, can be held with comfort and convenience in the well-appointed little theatre.

Figure 1.2A and 1.2B Continued.

TELEVISION AT WORK

The promotion of television for business did not come quickly to the industry that had worked for so long to establish its identity in film. Often figured as an extension of broadcast radio, most early discussions of television understood it not as a tool for internal industrial communication, but as a commercial medium for reaching the public. The potential disruptive force of the new medium was diffused through articles that oscillated between positioning the "ballyhoo" around television as overly eager—suggesting that television should be considered a viable but "'future' interest"—and painting the new medium as one with a big problem (not enough content) that only business film could solve (via sponsored films).[216]

Even RCA, which had a clear stake in the proliferation of television equipment, promoted its product as a commercial medium for the home. Evidence of this stance appears in a 1947 two-page spread that toured RCA's audio-visual communication facilities for the readers of *Business Screen* (Figure 1.2).[217] Throughout a lengthy description of the company's lavish facilities—which even fussed over its company theater's "restful and dramatic" color scheme of deep greens and greyish pinks—television makes it into the article's copy just once. Despite appearing at the margins of two other images, readers are directed to focus on television's placement only in a small mock living room space—complete with flowing drapes and an ambitious mid-century wallpaper—designed for the limited purpose of showing "video programs" and holding sales merchandising meetings. Rather than promote television for meetings and trainings, the technology is articulated to the feminine domestic sphere through the architecture the firm built to house it, its promoted uses, and the inclusion of a predominantly female audience in its depiction. Although the technical limitations of television for large audiences might suggest itself as the reason 16mm was the gold standard in RCA's other screening facilities, this was the same year RCA introduced its "Large Screen Theatre Television" which magnified a 15-inch screen to 18 x 24 feet.[218] Furthermore, boardroom areas, which held only a limited number of participants, could easily be served by a television's small screen. The narrow range of uses for television promoted by RCA—a firm that already boasted *a local broadcasting system* sonically linking 19 buildings over 92 acres—suggests the persistence of larger cultural frameworks promoted by the nontheatrical industry for distinguishing between television—a feminine, domestic medium operating as an extension of commercial radio—and film—a versatile technology, often used as a masculinized instrument of labor, that could operate as effectively on the sales desk as it could to train employees.

While these divisions between film and television continued as film professionals attempted to protect their industry from competition, television made its way to the company grounds through an avenue far more familiar to those working in telecommunications—and manufacturing. The earliest sustained uses of workplace television, CCTV to monitor industrial production, had more in common with radio telemetry's distant surveillance of factory operations than it did with the visually appealing products of the industrial film sector. However, as we will see in the next chapter, despite CCTV's lack of pretty pictures—and its emphasis on coordinating labor—this mode of television became intimately invested in cultivating the capacities of its employees.

CHAPTER 2

To Extend Vision Beyond the Horizon, to See the Unseen: Industrial Television in the Post-War Era

Flow

Modern Times' (1936) most famous scene depicts the automated factory bending the worker to its will. Charlie Chaplin's Tramp is literalized as an errant cog in a massive industrial machine, his body curving wildly to fit a dizzying array of gears and sprockets. The scene spectacularly realizes one of the film's chief concerns, the effect of mechanized labor on the body. Elsewhere, tasked with tightening nuts on an endless stream of metal sheets stripped of any relation to a finished object, the Tramp's movement becomes regulated by the assembly line. Even on break, his body tweaks with the memory of repetitive motion. Everywhere he looks—women's clothes, coworkers' noses, and the very machine that swallowed him— he sees bolts that need tightening. This mechanical monotony leads to a nervous breakdown, but not before the Tramp becomes a guinea pig for a feeding machine that regulates the most organic of functions to prevent workers from breaking the rhythm of the factory. The film's satirical bite zeroes in on anxieties surrounding workers' loss of humanity in a world where they are asked to work intimately and extensively with machines.

The film also tackles the increasing alienation of workers from their labor. Even the engineer, who ostensibly creates the mechanical monstrosities of the factory, is not free from its adverse effects; he becomes imprisoned in his own creation after the electricity is cut. Indeed, the only person not

Television at Work. Kit Hughes, Oxford University Press (2020) © Oxford University Press.
DOI: 10.1093/oso/9780190855789.001.0001

alienated from work in the Marxist sense is the owner, who oversees the entire production process and sets the pace of work. His mechanism for accomplishing all of this is, of course, television. Using a two-way screen machine that connects him live to anywhere in the factory—including the bathroom—the owner watches and controls work (and leisure) from his desk. Anxieties over the incorporation of electronic communication technologies within factory automation surface on the film's audio track. The only (legible) voices in the film originate from the two-way television and an audio recording describing the feeding machine. Both the booming voice of the factory owner and the crisp manual-like description of the feeding machine's functionalities contrast with the aural landscape of the rest of the film, reinforcing the mediated factory as a space of sensory onslaught and danger.

Modern Times joined a small but growing cohort of films coming to terms with the potential implications of a new and unknown technology. As Richard Koszarski and Doron Galili note, film had been imagining television's future since at least 1908.[1] Like Chaplin's film, many of these thought experiments positioned television as an adjunct to telephony that enabled one- or two-way visual communication (*Up the Ladder*, 1925; *Metropolis*, 1927).[2] Several films placed television as radio's heir, a means of distributing news and entertainment (*L'inhumaine*, 1924; *Thought for Food*, 1933). Still others shared *Modern Times*' uneasiness about the possibility of television-turned surveillance technology, serving at the pleasure of governments, criminal organizations, and murderous pet-owners (*For the Secret Service*, 1914; *Shadow of Chinatown*, 1936; *The Thirteenth Hour*, 1927). The most imaginative of these films—many of them war films like *The Flying Torpedo* (1916) and *Bombs over London* (1937)—incorporated television within logistical control systems that enabled users to act—not merely communicate—at a distance. Together, these films helped generate a rich vision of what television could be. Indeed, the medium would take many of these paths—two-way communication, content distribution, surveillance, logistical control—over the ensuing decades.

In accounting for the heady exuberance of television's first years, this chapter returns to the near future that so concerned Chaplin—the incorporation of screens into factory workspaces as mechanisms of efficiency and regulation—to trace the development of "industrial television" (ITV). A widely used synonym for closed-circuit television in the United States, ITV was the first sustained initiative backed by the research programs and funding capabilities of major media and technology institutions such as RCA and DuMont to recognize the potential of television tailored specifically to the needs of industry, science, medicine, education, and the military. Many—Vladimir Zworykin among them—claimed that ITV's capacities for industrial use and "pure research" were always the primary target of their invention, and commercial broadcasting discouragingly and bewilderingly overshadowed and limited these possibilities.[3]

Bewildering or not, commercial broadcasting has also overshadowed our retrospective accounting of the medium, its uses, meanings, and even our understanding of its ostensibly "defining characteristic"—flow.[4] Television scholars tend to think of flow in the terms set forth by Raymond Williams—broadcast programming's streaming "series of differently related units" in which the discrete contours of presentations (news, sports, dramas) are disrupted and reorganized with commercials and trailers to serve broadcasters' need to maintain viewership throughout the course of an evening.[5] Although Williams's concern is late network-era television, I follow William Uricchio in adapting flow—as "an element of discursive continuity" for television studies—to the context of industrial, non-broadcast television.[6] Given the young state of research into industrial television, it makes little sense to abandon theoretical frameworks that have proved useful for describing the technology and its forms—if for nothing else than to open up a space of reflection regarding the way our object of study has heretofore been circumscribed. In this spirit, how might we understand the relationship between the flow of broadcast television and television as a technology of industrial flow? How does televisual flow coincide with other forms of everyday flow, such as materials handling, and how might we understand workers' experiences of watching the flow of ITV commodities like steel billets or freight trains? In tackling the first of this book's four "keywords" of television studies, I take an expansive view of flow that extends beyond questions of textuality to consider television's position within circuits of commodity production and consumption, as well as its use within the temporalities of labor management.

By consulting a wide range of sources created alongside the development of CCTV—technical reports, trade journals, handbooks and manuals, archival documents, and newspaper coverage—I will address the preceding questions and offer a corrective to common understandings of CCTV as a surveillance technology primarily designed to police behavior. Instead, this chapter will show how CCTV was positioned by its creators, promoters, and early users as a mechanism not to constrain bodies, but to extend them. As we increasingly recognize the complicated relationship between capacity building and surveillance built into digital technologies like GPS and wearable computers, CCTV, as an antecedent, offers an opportunity to better understand this tension. This chapter demonstrates how CCTV was hailed for its promise of remote viewing and augmented sight. It argues that the technology provided employers an opportunity to reconfigure the ideal working body, adapting it to meet the shifting demands of post-war industrial and informational architectures. Ultimately, workplaces sought to make the body *elastic*: reshaped to tackle inhuman feats, expanded to cover the duties of several men, or even compressed until it disappeared from the payroll. This televisual reformation of the body, in turn, was central to managing flows of industrial production and worker experience—an exemplar of expanded vertical integration. In pursuing this line, I illustrate how "work systems" produce people, socializing them to the conditions and expectations of capitalism, and investigate how technologies—whether media, maps, clocks, or factory automation—alter workers' relationship to their labor.[7]

This chapter addresses the specific shape of these electronic transformations in two parts. First, I discuss the myriad ways television promised to make the industrial worker's body bigger and stronger, building its capacities to toil among heavy machinery. Second, I examine how CCTV targeted clerical workers, physically embedding them within increasingly complex information architectures. Although workers' transformations may seem empowering—expanding agential abilities via the cyborgian sublime—practical results were bleak. The expansion of workers' physical capacities via televisual appendages ensured, somewhat ironically, that their bodies remained immobile and dormant, anchored even more deeply within automated systems over which they had little control.

Although ITV got its start in the late 1940s and is still in use some 70 years later, the 1950s were the liveliest period—in the American industrial context—of negotiations over the varied forms industrial television could take. Contemporary analyses of CCTV tend to focus primarily, if not exclusively, on issues of surveillance and surveillance culture.[8] This may stem, in part, from how industry positioned CCTV—as a law-and-order "spy" and "hero"—to capture public imagination.[9] Furthermore, increasing concerns with privacy, security, and the public nature of surveillance operations help obscure the technology's origins, making its ongoing operations less visible to everyday life. While this chapter focuses primarily on industrial users of ITV, I occasionally touch on other users and uses to acknowledge the motivations of CCTV's developers and to account for mundane but omnipresent uses of television (e.g., the transmission of water gauge levels).[10]

Although some stories regarding the potentials of industrial television appeared in major newspapers and popular magazines like *Popular Mechanics* and *The Rotarian*, the vast majority of ITV coverage existed in specialized trade papers and manuals. These articles tended to focus on specialized applications within specific industries (rail, steel, sewage, commerce) or technical innovations (color, greater light sensitivity).[11] When invoked in broadcasting industry magazines, ITV's industrial applications might provide only a brief preamble to discussions of its utility for merchandising and commercial sales.[12] A series of books published in the second half of the 1950s attempted to describe and market the young industry. Written by engineers for RCA, DuMont, and Pye, they are remarkably similar, often using the same examples and even occasionally the same photograph illustrations, though the biases of the authors toward their home institutions reveal themselves.[13] While these books and trade journal articles developed a sense of what ITV could mean for American business and industry, they are not neutral.

Coalescing as an academic discipline in the 1920s with the publication of textbooks and the formation of professional societies, technical communication was well established as a professional practice by the end of World War II.[14] The materials cited here follow a traditional instrumentalist approach that attempts to integrate technology into users' lives "invisibly" and "unobtrusively."[15] Insofar as this mode seeks to naturalize relationships between users and machines, this chapter denaturalizes these same relationships in order to expose the workings of power behind the dry and certain discourse of technical writing. These trade publications are a literature of optimism that belied the hopes of business far better than it demonstrated the substantial success of ITV.

This chapter will not address all of the divergent uses enabled by the flexibility and local adaptability of CCTV. Anna McCarthy has already discussed the topic of closed-circuit television as a technology of sales display, and those practices will not reappear here.[16] The next chapter touches on the use of CCTV for two-way communications and telecasting at meetings to geographically dispersed employees, as well as its use as a distribution mechanism for videotape programming in the pre-cassette era. Although these uses were part of early conversations regarding the capabilities of CCTV, they stood apart from developers' focus on ITV as an extension of human sight rather than a content-delivery system or a mechanism of co-presence.

DEVELOPING THE SYSTEM

Many histories position World War II missile guidance systems as the inaugural use of CCTV.[17] The first post-war demonstration of ITV—according to a DuMont CCTV manual—was a 1946 contract closing between DuMont and Chevrolet. To avoid the expense and hassle of travel—and to demonstrate the technical savvy and inventiveness of both companies—the president of DuMont and the general manager of Chevrolet each signed a copy of their contract under the watch of a television camera. With the signatories "separated by 250 miles," the camera feeds were superimposed to display both signatures on the same document. To establish a permanent record of the occasion, the companies took a photograph of the "signed" contract. After this splashy beginning—complete with predictions for its forthcoming wide-scale adoption—several years lapsed before ITV grew from its "fumbling adolescence" to "vigorous maturity."[18]

Although British engineers may have been working on ITV proper as early as 1936—and continued to be instrumental in the technology's development—American magazines and trades began covering industrial television in the mid-1940s with stories heavy on its potentials but light on concrete manifestations.[19] Figures suggest that despite industry enthusiasm and the marketing efforts of manufacturers, adoption of television was slow before increasing steadily around mid-decade.[20] Numbers varied wildly from source to source, however, with industry-wide estimates of sales volume for 1956 ranging from $23 million to $65 million even a full nine months after the year's official close.[21] Another set of numbers circulated by the Electronic Industry Association claims sales of industrial television increased tenfold between 1954 and 1958, quickly jumping to a 89 million-dollar industry.[22] Still others located a 500% increase in ITV use among industrial, military, and scientific groups between 1956 and 1961.[23] Whatever the veracity of these figures, together they point to rising adoption of ITV by a range of users. Suggesting "the period of experimentation [came] to a close" in 1956, industry insiders claimed that ITV was "generally accepted" by 1961.[24]

Early systems were simple. At its most basic, an ITV circuit needs a camera, power source, video amplifier, and monitor. The image picked up by the camera travels directly via coaxial cable to a monitor where users can make a permanent record of the telecast using a kinescope (later, videotape). This system is easily modified by the addition of monitors or cameras (for two-way communication), as well as speakers and sound amplification. To expand distribution of the television signal, users might supplement the coaxial cable with microwave relays, telephone lines, or some combination therein.[25] Within these boundaries, users could create modular systems geared toward highly localized specific uses, all of which sought perfectly targeted subjects and audiences. As with many of the eventual applications of television in the workplace, ITV enabled a particular form of narrowcasting, one enforced by technology rather than taste.

The identity of the first permanent ITV system is unclear, though many point to the New York Edison Company's 1946 installation of television to monitor the water levels of giant boilers.[26] Due to a number of factors, including the massive scale of their operations and the relative cost-effectiveness of ITV monitoring, power stations and utilities companies represented the swiftest and most enthusiastic adopters of early industrial systems.[27] "Big Steel" quickly followed, reacting to surging demands for increased production in the post-war era that required factories to find new methods to expand output.[28] According to RCA's R. F. Schneider in 1955, following the installation of ITV for "essential applications" such as safety uses in ordnance factories and nuclear facilities, "cost-reduction applications" became a major site of interest for industrial users, with "luxury applications"—for example, shopping by television—as the final trend completing the cycle of experimentation and use.[29] Adoption of ITV appears to have been faster on the East Coast than in the West, and the military continued to be an important user of ITV throughout its early years and beyond.[30] By the late 1950s, what began as a closed industry with a few manufacturers grew to encompass a dozen companies; in the lingo of the era, the industry was described as "mushrooming" by mid-decade.[31] RCA, Diamond Power Specialty Corporation, and Remington Rand all marketed their own ITV camera tubes by 1950.[32] By 1955, RCA, Diamond, the Dage Division of Thomas Products, Inc., and Kay Labs shared most of the American market, though several others hoped to challenge their dominance (including DuMont, GE, Philco, GE, CBS, Farnsworth Electronics, and General Precision Laboratory).[33] Pye and Marconi, meanwhile, hoped to secure the British market.

Equipment costs slowed wide-scale adoption, though exact figures are as muddy as volume sales reports.[34] Between 1950 and 1952, a user could spend little as $32,500 or as much as $216,907, though most prices ranged from $43,000 to $87,000.[35] As ITV research targeted cost reduction, average prices fell to $17,000–$30,500, leading to increased sales.[36] However, even given reduced prices, justifying any costs for a product that did not yet have a very defined set of applications was difficult. On the brink of "commercialability," in 1951, an RCA technical memo suggested a straightforward strategy: sell 100 systems to "selected customers" and "[b]y working closely with these customers [. . .] find and develop applications for the equipment and, in addition, obtain additional market information."[37] Anxieties over "finding" applications for ITV appeared in routine disclaimers that "the full burden of identifying practical applications of remote viewing cannot fall on the manufacturers of industrial television equipment" and appeals to industry insiders to devise uses for ITV, since, as potential users, they were the "best equipped to point out those problems to which television offers better solutions than any yet found."[38] This may explain the tendency of early CCTV technical guides to devote almost as much space to potential applications as they do to technical specifications; developing new needs and uses was as important as improving technology.[39]

These publications also enabled manufacturers to position ITV not as a narrow technical product, but as a "service" to industry, science, and education and a harbinger of broad social, economic, and political change. According to RCA, for example, industrial television bore the disruptive potential of the automobile, radio, and broadcast television and their "profound effects" on personal habits, community development, customs, and family life.[40] In establishing the qualities and conditions of this transformative "service," early applications of ITV laid the groundwork for reimagining the ideal relationship between industrial employees and their physical and visual capacities in the context of labor. Television became enmeshed in a series of experiments in cyborgian sight at the service of industrial coordination, labor, and communication needs. An aphorism that circulated in the ITV industry summarized the technology's value thus: "Whenever it is too dangerous; too difficult; too expensive; too inconvenient; too inaccessible; too tiring; too far; too hot; too cold; too high; too low; too dark; too small to observe directly, use television."[41] In a world populated by Goldilockses limited by their physical stature and abilities, industrial television became a prosthesis that made men bigger, stronger, faster, and smarter to meet the demands of their material environments and the desires of their employers to maximize production flows and workforce efficiencies.

BODYBUILDERS

Using machines to manage men was not new to the 1940s. The industrial revolution introduced new technologies for organizing worker production that coalesced and expanded in the assembly lines of the early twentieth century. A process technology, the assembly line naturalized acceleration as an agent of progress while promoting hybrid human-machine systems populated by unskilled laborers and tightly regulated by management as the key to increased productivity. This arrangement, in turn, was situated as the precondition of increased consumption and higher standards of living.[42] Also commonplace by the 1940s were beliefs in efficiency as a moral good and industrial imperative. Early nineteenth-century understandings of machine efficiency, however, were not divorced from concerns with the well-being of machine operators and their qualitative experience of laboring; perfected machines provided workers freedom to move and think in complex ways. In the Progressive Era, efficiency maintained its valued status while transforming into a generalizable principle of regulation and social planning. As efficiency became more aligned with control and managerial mastery over material inputs (including labor), workers increasingly found themselves subject to the same rigid discipline—and constricted movement—as machines.[43] These are the conditions in which television emerged as a mechanism to transform workers' physical capacities.

By affixing monitors, cameras, and wires to employee bodies, many industrial television users sought to develop stronger workers who could withstand deathly forces, adapt to inhuman climates, and see with superhuman sight. These applications attempted to "extend the limits of normal vision and to overcome or compensate for limitations of biological factors of the human physique and its capabilities to withstand hostile environments."[44] Invoking television's capacity for material mediation, these installations reconfigured the relationship between employees, their capacity for sight, and the observation of processes that formed the bulk of their work.

Stronger

One of the most widely accepted early applications of industrial television was remote observation of hazardous operations.[45] Although public utilities companies comprised the majority of these users in the 1950s, ITV proved valuable for a range of companies in chemistry, transportation, and manufacturing.[46] In such cases, a protective barrier separated cameras trained on dangerous industrial processes from a human observer who monitored activity on a TV screen in a safe, climate-controlled space. Prior to the development of CCTV, companies employed a range of cumbersome sighting tools: manual bell and light signaling systems, thick, anti-radiation zinc bromide windows, potentially faulty remote indicators, and, most commonly, periscopes or intricate, expensive mirror systems that required extensive duct networks to ensure a clear line of sight from the process being observed to the technician.[47] ITV offered a more economical and efficient solution to these systems, often allowing faster readings of distant information and reconfiguring industrial architectures by removing the need for an unobstructed light corridor connecting worker and object.[48]

"Protecting human life" was the primary goal of many of these installations in factories dealing with explosives, radioactive materials, and chemicals; nuclear power and weapons facilities; wrecking and blasting operations; and research laboratories that held the possibility of explosion or other harm.[49] ITV became a "lifeline" for industrial workers, depicted as a physical extension of the human body that could be harmlessly sacrificed to protect workers' lives.[50] As described by one ITV manual, "should a mishap occur, the only loss among the personnel is the loss of the 'eyes,' the TV camera."[51] Descriptions of protective ITV camera housings—via weatherproofing, climate control, and pressurization—further emphasized the camera's superhuman capacity. As one author explained, "it may be correctly said that television systems can be designed to operate under what would appear to be the most adverse conditions"—conditions that reveal the limitations of the human body.[52]

A widely distributed advertisement for RCA's Vidicon system (Figure 2.1) visualizes the protective powers of ITV systems. A lab coat–clad engineer stands amid flames that lick his legs and reach above his head but do not consume him. Calmly, with clipboard and pencil, he stands on rough rock, peering into the source of the fire. The caption reads, "*Eye-witness reports from a fiery furnace!*"[53] The body of the advertisement continues, "Something's gone wrong inside a big blast furnace, and heat is too high for engineers to approach in safety. Focus the Vidicon camera of an RCA Industrial Television System on the flames and the fiery furnace can be studied in comfort on a television receiver." Rather than portray a realistic scene depicting an engineer watching from the safety of the control room, RCA represents the ITV system as a mechanism for transforming the human body, building its capabilities for previously impossible feats. Although the copy acknowledges the body's need for physical accommodation, the tag line's invocation of "eye-witness reports" reinforces the system's claims to enable human presence where physically impossible.

ITV was also promoted as an apparatus that enabled the exploration of inhospitable and as-yet unexplored environments, whether high altitudes, sea depths, or previously inaccessible spaces.[54] Again, ITV promises to enable workers to "*see* even where we can't *look*," with the critical difference between "see" (perception) and "look" (directing one's perception) resting on the more obviously embodied nature of looking.[55] The camera remains a prosthesis, "an 'eye' that sees better many things that would otherwise be imperfectly viewed or not seen at all."[56] Aviation researchers, for example, used industrial television to observe previously inaccessible areas of a plane while in flight, while astronomers sent televisions aloft in balloons to collect data free of atmospheric disturbances.[57] Television was promoted as "of course, a necessity" for observing guided missiles and flying pilotless

Compact industrial television system—developed at RCA Laboratories—lets us see the unseeable in safety!

Eye-witness reports from a _fiery furnace!_

Something's gone wrong inside a big blast furnace, and heat is too high for engineers to approach in safety. Focus the Vidicon camera of an RCA Industrial Television System on the flames and the fiery furnace can be studied in comfort on a television receiver.

This is only one suggested use out of many, for RCA's compact industrial television system is as flexible as its user's ingenuity. "Eye" of the tiny camera—small enough to be held in one hand—is the sensitive Vidicon tube. Extremely simple, the only other equipment needed is the Vidicon camera's suitcase-size control cabinet, which operates anywhere on ordinary household current.

The Vidicon camera could be lowered under water where divers might be endangered—or stand watch on atomic chain reactions, secure from deadly radiations. And it is entirely practical to arrange the RCA Industrial Television system in such a way that observers can see a *3-dimensional picture . . . sharp, clear and real as life!*

See the latest wonders of radio, television, and electronics in action at RCA Exhibition Hall, 36 West 49th Street, N. Y. Admission is free. Radio Corporation of America, Radio City, New York.

Here's RCA's Vidicon system at work beside a steaming vat. Note how the compact television camera is getting a safe "close-up" of the action.

RADIO CORPORATION of AMERICA
World Leader in Radio — First in Television

Figure 2.1 RCA Advertisement for the Vidicon system.
Credit: *Broadcasting* Oct. 2, 1950, back cover.

planes.[58] At sea, late 1950s television cameras could reach depths of up to 3,000 feet—nine times deeper than an unaided human diver—allowing for a dramatic extension of the range of scavenging and other deep-sea ventures.[59] Television economized on the ground by providing sight in previously inaccessible wind tunnels and sewer, water, and gas pipes.[60] In describing the implications of this shift, Zworykin et al. argued, "In certain industries television does not merely make it possible to do things better and more cheaply, but opens up entirely new possibilities."[61]

More Comfortable

In addition to saving lives and adapting humans to new environments, ITV systems pursued the more modest goal of making workers comfortable.[62] Pointing to "excessive heat, high noise level, excessive cold, or unhealthy atmosphere," proponents of ITV argued, "[i]n such instances the worker can almost invariably be replaced to advantage by a television camera, which is immune to factors annoying and painful to the human observer."[63] They also suggested that television systems could eliminate "undesirable occupations" altogether.[64] Significantly, the key terms of these discussions are "discomfort," "annoyance," "undesirable," "drudgery," "inconvenience," "exertion," and "tiring."[65] Although some jobs proposed for the television comfort treatment were undersold in terms of their adverse effects on human health (e.g., observation of sulfite pulp digesters), these discussions promoted television as a means to make non-life-threatening work more physically agreeable to laborers—by terminating them, if need be.

Several applications attempted to transform the specialized, physically demanding viewing of the technician into the common, comfortable experience of watching TV—by then overdetermined as a leisure technology. Eyestrain induced by small viewfinders and dim X-rays were a common target of ITV screens, which promised larger, brighter, more detailed images and thus visual "comfort" and "less tiring working conditions."[66] ITV engineers similarly extolled television's capacity to shoulder unpleasant viewing experiences by praising its ability "to stare into a flaming furnace for hours without blinking."[67] While watching remotely enabled employees to work in environments tailored to the sensory thresholds of humans, the TV screen allegedly offered relief to the senses via material properties (illumination, picture quality, image size) and modes of embodiment associated with leisure:

> an observer can sit comfortably in front of a television monitor, yet watch the interior of an industrial furnace, observe closely the launch of an untested space booster from every angle, explore the bottom of the ocean, view objects under infrared or ultraviolet light, or look for defects in a sewer.[68]

The experience of watching television contrasts with a panoply of physically demanding—if not inhuman—viewing jobs. In the decades following, industrial television would continue to draw on associations with entertainment television to boost its efficacy.

A hypothetical application of ITV literalized these tensions between television as a leisure and labor technology while reinforcing television's role as a human comfort machine protecting the body from wear. This system enabled a small business owner to survey and communicate with his shop via a closed-circuit camera linked to his home television set.[69] Freed from attending to his store in person, the owner could undertake other business in the comfort of his living room, saving him "much time and exertion."[70] Again, this "sell at home" system concerned itself with the capacities of human workers and the (embodied and economic) labor-saving capabilities of television.[71]

Bigger

Yet another way ITV expanded the worker's body was by turning men into giants that could see at incredible distances and around massive obstacles, often with the goal of enabling a single man to do the work of two or more. While David Morley, Lisa Parks, Harold Innis, James Carey, and others have already established the capabilities of media to bind spaces, disrupt geographies, and enable viewer mobility, ITV extension and connection occur at far more local scales and within particular institutional contexts.[72] Building the body "bigger" became tantamount to adapting human workers to expanding industrial architectures. In these instances, television functions as an "extension of human sight" that enables individual workers to observe and control the complex, spatially distant processes particularly germane to the fields of manufacturing, energy production, product distribution, and security.[73] Scaled sight might enable an operator to survey the batch processing of pulp in giant vats, to manage the smooth flow of an entire yard of freight cars, or to ensure the safety and security of a department store warehouse. These uses were sometimes described as the "principal objective" of ITV and continue to be, under the guise of surveillance, the primary function ascribed to CCTV.[74] In the late 1940s and early 1950s, these activities were being corralled under the umbrella of what was coming to be known as materials handling.

Materials handling was part of the post-war fantasy of the fully automated factory that functioned through "the substitution of mechanical, hydraulic, pneumatic, electrical and electronic devices for human organs of observation, decision and effort, so as to increase productivity, control quality and reduce costs."[75] Recalling the ITV camera as an electronic replacement for the frail human body, automation and materials handling descriptions repeatedly emphasized the substitution of machines for "human hands" and even "human reasoning, responses, and reactions." Electronics, adopting human form, served as automation's "intricate nerve center and sensory system."[76] Reportedly a 9.8 billion-dollar industry in 1951, the specific aim of materials handling was to maximize the efficiency with which resources, products, and workers were distributed across industrial operations—most commonly in steel mills; machine shops; chemical, nuclear, and power plants; coal mines; and automotive and consumer goods factories.[77] According to one report, "picking things up, moving them around and putting them down again cost the average American factory 25% of its production payroll."[78] By automating these processes, factories hoped to save both time and money, securing economies that included "greater output from a given floor space, elimination of bottlenecks, reduction in damage to products, increased safety, better labour and capital productivity, upgrading of personnel, increased speed of handling materials, and resulting from these and other benefits, reduced costs."[79] While a glut of materials handling conventions in the early 1950s featured a variety of devices "for guiding, testing, weighing, sorting," they also featured feedback and communication technologies for monitoring automated processes.[80] Alongside two-way mobile radio, facsimile, computers, memory devices, and telemetering, ITV was promoted for its particular ability to observe dangerous processes and manage massive, far-flung operations, conserving money and "man-power" in the process.[81]

Engineers and manufacturers emphasized the superhuman scale of ITV sight via schematics and discursive strategies contrasting human capability with the sight range of television cameras. In one illustration of an installation at United States Steel's Geneva, Utah, plant (Figure 2.2), three furnaces for reheating steel slabs sit opposite two pairs of cameras (facing the outer two furnaces) and a viewing booth (directed at the middle furnace).[82] The cameras angle downward, emitting a three-dimensional ray covering the entrances of the outer furnaces and the massive slabs intended for reheating.[83] Clearly, the booth and the tiny worker inside cannot possibly see the spaces covered by the cameras given the distance between furnaces; they are "blind" spots. ITV's angled rays highlight newly visible space, demonstrating the potential of television to increase the output of a single worker by replicating the worker's vision across multiple installations. Despite visual gaps embedded in industrial architectures built for larger workforces, ITV promises perfect sight at a distance, i.e., *total coverage*, of anything trapped within its scope.[84]

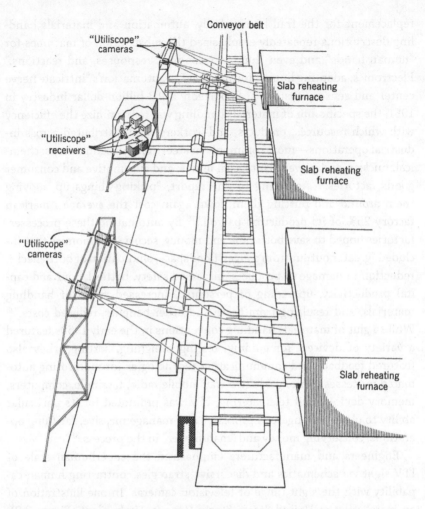

Conveyor belt

"Utiliscope" cameras

Slab reheating furnace

"Utiliscope" receivers

Slab reheating furnace

"Utiliscope" cameras

Slab reheating furnace

Figure 2.2 A single worker oversees three gigantic steel furnaces.
Credit: V. K. Zworykin, E. G. Ramberg, and L. E. Flory, *Television in Science and Industry* (New York: John Wiley & Sons, 1958): 164.

Other schematics emphasized ITV's ability to match the increasingly in-human scale of industrial manufacture. Figure 2.3 details a Long Island Lighting Company power station installation showing a coal furnace dominating the right half of the image. A monstrous Pompidou Center-esque skyscraper with its mechanical innards and control systems on display, the furnace dwarfs a tiny figure drawn into the bottom-right corner of the schematic. A camera sits at the top of the furnace, with the scope of its sight indicated by the requisite dotted-line rays reaching their pin-nacle at the camera's lens. Safely tucked within its range are the furnace's

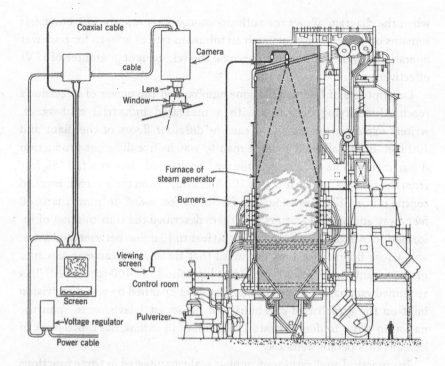

Figure 2.3 A diminutive human worker demonstrates the power of scaled sight.
Credit: V. K. Zworykin, E. G. Ramberg, and L. E. Flory, *Television in Science and Industry* (New York: John Wiley & Sons, 1958): 159.

giant flames. Connected to the camera by a topological wire is the viewing screen, a tiny square floating near a "control room" label that designates distance from the furnace rather than a material location. Were the male figure a part of imagining the ongoing operation of the system, he would occupy a position near the control room. Instead, he stands at the corner of the image—at less than one-tenth the height of the furnace—simply as an indication of the scale of the machine and, consequently, the sight of the camera. The "close-up" diagram of the camera-screen-power system to the left of the furnace further decreases the proportion of the image occupied by the figure, intensifying the diminutive nature of anthropomorphic scale. The position and function of this nonworker figure offer a reminder that schematics are "convenient conceits . . . conventions grounded in historical and cultural exigencies."[85] The line drawings circulated by CCTV developers often exclude the perspective and representation of workers to focus instead on the technological qualities of connection across industrial space. As a result, ITV becomes a neutral managerial tool, sidestepping questions about workers' numbers and conditions. Even in this instance, when the diagram allows for anthropomorphic representation, emphasis remains on ITV's ability to match an inhuman rate of growth for post-war operations. Work architectures become the self-evident guarantee of ITVs effectiveness.

Descriptions of ITV installations emphasized the power of television's reach. Quantifying distances with a measured industrial exuberance, writers explained systems that sat on "different floors of the plant and 100 feet apart," allowed a single man to watch "five different production departments in its four-story building," positioned viewers a full "80 feet from the furnace" or "as much as 100 feet away" from their target, reached central offices "12 miles away," saw "about 60 feet away" or "more than 600 feet away and around corners."[86] Others described the transmission of information over distances spanning 450 feet to 10 miles, between buildings, and across floors.[87] Authors enthused that these same cameras saw into machines anywhere from 6 to 100 feet high and 15 to 400 feet wide.[88] This sustained emphasis on the specific distances spanned by wired television built on the established capabilities of broadcast television to span the nation in order to demonstrate ITV's ability to extend the capabilities of humans to "operate" remotely.

The practical applications of sight at scale manifested in three functions appealing to business and industry: enhancing security, centralizing operations, and controlling the flow of production and distribution. The first of these, security applications, situated ITV as a mechanism to prevent theft and disruption, downsize workforces, and streamline authority structures.[89] Systems designed to extend the surveying eye of guards collapsed the physical space of the control room and the warehouse floor to grant officers superhuman size and speed; "Seated in his office [a guard] can turn in any direction to observe the area of his choice, covering his entire 'beat' in a matter of seconds."[90] In shipping and manufacturing facilities, removing men from gatehouses to install minimally staffed control centers created a more direct link between the process of granting access—the guard's job—and the "higher authorities" who could provide guidance in "doubtful cases."[91] Replacing a diverse, distributed workforce with centralized operations reduced liabilities and increased control, first by limiting the people participating in the labor force, and second by strengthening lines of communication. Television enabled companies to remove links in a chain of command where authority had been delegated widely. Surveillance by television promised a self-sustaining system whereby workers, prisoners, and customers not only monitored their own behavior; what remained of the job was carried out by a mere handful of workers with close access to (and closely monitored themselves by) the "authorities."

This emphasis on reconfiguring work architectures by centralizing operations was itself a key promise of televisual sight at scale. For in-plant surveillance and communication, television was imagined as a solution to time lost to the "continuous parade of personnel" "taking excursion trips around the plant" to gather information and deliver messages.[92] Consolidating the coordination of operations at central control points, ITV promised to secure workforce efficiencies by downsizing while reducing confusion brought about by the delegation of sight to a chain of imperfect human communicators.[93] Indeed, engineers often suggested that television systems could develop an improved workforce by replacing costly human labor with technologies of perfect perception. Eliding both the mediation of the television and the need for human interpretation of screen images, writers boasted that the television's "unblinking eye" offered a "fail-safe picture" and "zero error in communication," making incorrect readings an "impossibility."[94] Television was just as good or better than physically being there. Televisual sight became equivalent to first-hand knowledge. Communication—riddled with potential misunderstandings and (ironically) transmission errors—could be avoided. Again, ITV promised to match bodies to growing industrial architectures through the space-collapsing capabilities of television as superhuman visual prosthesis.

More Perceptive: Flow and Worker Experience

Managing flow, the third goal of ITV's "bigger" bodies, promised additional changes to industrial organization and work processes. Using television's capacity for scaled sight, workers with a "complete and continuing story of plant-operating conditions" could speed up or slow down conveyor belts filled with logs, scrap metal, and roller bearings; switch out filled containers and freight cars at exactly the right moment; time processes, such as the reheating of steel slab mentioned earlier; and avoid bottlenecks at trouble spots.[95] (Tele)vision became the key to perfect timing, which aided efficiency and the prevention of costly mistakes.[96] Workers could also use television to manage massive machinery—boilers, furnaces, processing vats—that grew under the expansion of mid-century American manufacturing and technological advancements.[97] In some instances, sight at scale was identified as a means for workers to collect and correlate new information, such as the relationship between flame consistency inside a furnace and the output of smokestacks atop the plant.[98]

Television also promised to smooth traffic and travel in distribution. By situating cameras along vast spans of travel routes, shippers could analyze route efficiency, railways could search for competitive advantage against the expanding highway system, and officials could regulate traffic—avoiding stoppages and managing accidents and construction—through the strategic deployment of lighting and police "to meet hour-by-hour changes throughout the area."[99] Railroads—the linchpin of much industrial distribution—began experimenting with ITV most prominently in 1952 when Baltimore & Ohio partnered with *Railway Age* Magazine and RCA for a test in their South Chicago Barr yard, one of the nation's busiest railroad yards.[100] The experiment used ITV to assign incoming cars to clear tracks and capture cars' serial numbers, otherwise lengthy manual and potentially error-prone processes.[101] When the demonstration indicated that television could help "handle more trains, at higher speeds, with fewer people"—in short, at greater profit—ITV was increasingly pulled into the massive railroad signaling and communications market—estimated at almost $1 billion a year in 1953.[102] In the air, ITV allowed workers at different airports to share radar information by transmitting video of their traffic control screens, eliminating blind spots and smoothing air travel and shipping processes.[103] At a more modest scale, ITV's broad views of supermarket and department store floors enabled managers to (re)distribute personnel as needed.[104] Throughout these examples, ITV participated in a broad set of twentieth-century experiments, such as just-in-time manufacturing, that sought to increase efficiency by perfecting the flow of material inputs and products.

In turning our attention to the articulation between industrial and televisual flows, ITV prompts revision of the latter term. First, we might consider Williams's discussion of the "mutual transfer" between the discursive strategies of commercials and programming, and how commercial messages saturate and are legitimized by the rest of television's flow. While mapping out flow as a textual and temporal manifestation of programmers' attempts to manage viewers' engagement with television, he also offers a fine description of the urgency of consumption (of both programs and products) embedded within the phenomenon he describes.[105] This extends beyond the economic underpinnings of flow—the exigencies of maximum, sustained viewership—to appear in the "flow of meanings of a specific culture" he identifies in a complicated intertwining of commercials for headache tablets and educational shows, cat food advertisements and news and nature programs, and a loan company commercial playing off the California gold rush and period films.[106] Attending to flow as the meanings that cross television's textual borders reminds us of the place of television within cultural practices of consumption and commodity circuits, and its position as an important part of the production cycle through its marketing function.

We might best understand industrial and broadcast television as different points of transmission and cultural management within the same circuits of production and consumption. The flow of broadcast television—its unending inducement to watch and buy—correlates to the constant flow of materials and products that smoothly ride conveyor systems and freight cars; the temporal rhythm embedded in televisual flow invokes industrial production's continual output.

Second, we can examine the implications of flow's temporality and rhythm for viewer experience and expanded vertical integration. Described by Uricchio as a companion concept for the "viewer-television interface," flow alerts us to axes of power and control, asking us to consider who holds control over television transmission and what technologies participate in those control structures.[107] Within the framework of ITV, these questions translate to a focus on compulsory (rather than compulsive) viewing of television transmissions "scheduled" by employers, factory owners, and shipping agents. Although conclusions regarding the cultural consequences of mandatory television viewing sit at the level of conjecture, importing the theory of flow—and its ability to describe a particular experience of the medium—allows for a partial accounting of workers' experiences within a context in which little historical evidence is forthcoming.[108] Like Williams's notion of flow, ITV content (if not "programming") streams almost continuously. Over the course of an eight-hour shift, a worker might watch and manage a never-ending supply of crushed limestone, the constant fluctuation of furnace flames, or a steady stream of shipping traffic. Even if a viewer cannot turn the TV dial, other dials may well need turning over the course of a viewing session to ensure the proper continuation of the worker's particular outpost in the production-distribution system. Although ITV certainly cannot boast the variability of commercial broadcast television, it nonetheless offers a constant presence (certain technical difficulties excluded) to those it interpellates with its relentless mediation of factory processes. If flow is at least in part about the agency of the viewer in relation to television programming, ITV—through its demand that viewers not only watch, but also act in relation to screen images—may incorporate audiences even more forcefully into the larger cultural and belief systems alluded to by Williams. Audiences do not simply watch ITV flow, they help manufacture it.

While these applications invoke cyborgian visions, these affinities become most apparent in systems that use remote control systems enabling workers to manipulate materials at a remove. These applications—sorting resources into bins, regulating conveyor belt speed—extend the human body doubly.[109] Not only does ITV allow workers to see into spaces the

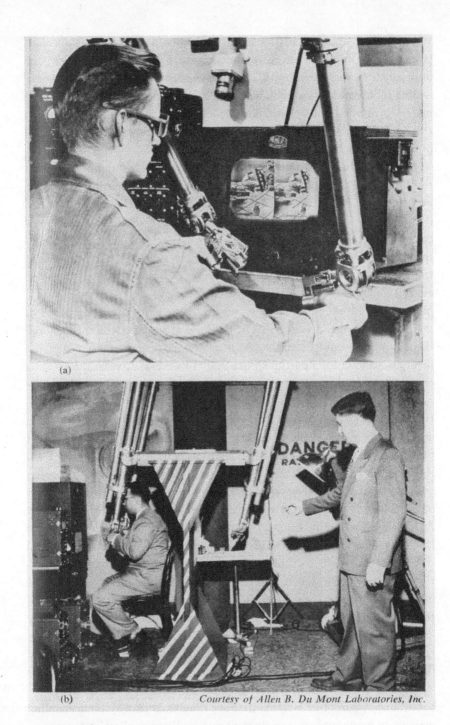

(a)

(b)

Figure 2.4 ITV connected to a remote control system.

Edward M. Noll, *Closed-circuit and Industrial Television* (New York: Macmillian, 1956): 15.

human body cannot withstand, remote control systems enable superhuman action at a distance supported by a visual feedback loop confirming users' spectacular kinetic activity. One highly circulated example (Figure 2.4) of such a system—developed for nuclear research at the Remote Control Engineering Division of the Argonne National Laboratory—depicts an operator intently watching a monitor, both hands grasping controls extending from long overhead arms. A wider shot reveals the body of the technician tucked into a small gap between the screen and the metal frame of the manipulator device, which sits just behind the operator's chair and reaches in front of him like the safety harness of a metal rollercoaster.[110] As explained in the system's description, "the technician places his hands in the device and manipulates it, and every movement of the device is then duplicated at the remote point."[111] In addition to using prosthetic arms and hands, the operator wears three-dimensional glasses that (with a stereoscopic monitor) restore spatial relations flattened by television transmission. Although the man has the power to manipulate nuclear materials at a distance, his own body is subject to tight restraint. If "remote viewing by television does away with both hazard and discomfort," it adds something else in the process—a new relationship between workers, their labor, and television, in which screen technologies augment the limited human body, shaping it to (or making it comfortable within) the rigid mechanical needs of industrial operations.[112] The industrial imagination that attempted to match man to factory envisioned a body stretched so tight over the steam and steel skeletons of manufacture that its fleshy skin, vellum-like, melted into machines.

SMARTER: INFORMATION ARCHITECTURES

Where the preceding projects oversaw product and industrial flows, others targeted information flows. Both attempted to maximize efficiency by incorporating bodies within shifting post-war architectures and increased automation. These latter applications, however, sought to centralize information, homogenize worker access to knowledge, and build networks to rapidly distribute information within the context of ongoing work operations. As a mechanism to coordinate sight, ITV distributed live content to an audience expected to participate directly in time-sensitive processes. A prosthetic pathway to information and expertise, synched sight conditioned its audience to the rhythms of work and transformed humans into nodes within increasingly complex human-machine hybrid information networks—assemblages that anticipated networked computing.

ITV used as an information system could replicate the expertise of a single laborer across several employees and set the pace of work. In one oft-cited example, RCA used ITV's synched sight to meet a fast-approaching deadline for Cinemascope equipment.[113] While a specialist assembled components in close-up view of a camera, 10 monitors transmitted the audiovisual signal to trainees, each working on their own set of components at their own bench. In a "follow-the-leader" process, the trainees duplicated each step carried out by the specialist simultaneously until 10 identical units were completed. Images depicting the process appear in pairs: the male specialist working pliers over an intricate block of equipment in the direct line of sight of an overhead camera, a microphone tucked close by his side, and, in the second image, a bank of television sets with two women performing similar operations. To emphasize the process by which workers do not simply watch, but do, both women's heads are angled down, creating a sight line with their physical manipulation of the components rather than with the television.[114]

Although positioned as a training process, little indicates that the training would ever conclude or that the women—positioned as novices—would ever be able to work free of the temporal regulation of the (male) "leader." Instead, coverage of this example posits a relentless game of Simon Says in which an expert worker automates the bodies of subordinates. Viewer identification becomes central to mechanizing workers. If, as Stephen Groening suggests, "the form of identification suggested by fictional film is required by the training film," ITV intensifies this phenomenon.[115] By demanding that viewers take up the position of the on-screen specialist, seeing and acting along with him in real time (rather than interiorizing a lesson), training processes based in this specialized, homogenized sight embed extreme immediacy within the training experience, reducing the space between instruction, identification, and participation. This immediacy and mechanization, whereby a worker could "learn by doing at the same time he learned by watching," helped position ITV training as "superior" to training film.[116] Furthermore, much like ITV enabled steel workers to replicate their vision across several furnaces to secure workforce efficiencies, interactive television systems enabled experts to replicate their knowledge across multiple production points. While this wouldn't minimize the numbers of bodies needed to work, it would allow employers to swap experts for less expensive novices (a role and function long occupied by women).

Other systems combined synched sight for temporal regulation with experiments in new work architectures developed for growing industries. One example emerges from the beating, highly mediated heart of Western capitalism itself. In 1969, the New York Stock Exchange (NYSE) completed a facility expansion in an effort to increase its average daily volume capacity to 15 million shares.[117] For the exchange, the 1960s and early 1970s were a period of rapid growth and increasing difficulty in managing the paperwork of daily transactions. Looking toward automation as a solution to these issues, the NYSE introduced several new or improved technologies to the floor in the 1960s, including new tickers, electronic pagers, and optical card readers. The NSYE also built the (now closed) "Blue Room," a third trading space neighboring the main floor at 20 Broad Street. From identifying the ideal height of trading posts (the primary "furniture" on the floor that designated where securities would be bought and sold) to testing new electronics and specifying the proper color of each item, the Floor Department overseeing the renovations produced its own paperwork crisis in attempts to achieve maximal efficiency and clarity in the display of visual information.[118] CCTV became an integral part of these efforts. A 7,000 square foot rectangle, the Blue Room featured two horseshoe-shaped trading posts joined together to create a single giant oval. Under the strict policies that regulated floor activities, odd lot brokers worked inside the posts. The height of these posts, however, obscured their line of sight to the electronic ticker posted on the north and south walls of the room. Architects first attempted to raise the height of the electronic tickers by seven feet, allowing the odd lot brokers to see the ticker over the top of the post superstructure.[119] At 19 feet above the trading floor, however, this arrangement distorted ticker visibility for specialists and commission brokers who stood on the outside of the posts and closer to the walls. CCTV provided the solution to this visibility problem when architects returned the ticker to its initial height and installed two CCTV monitors on the inside of the posts for odd-lot brokers.[120]

In an industry serviced in the twenty-first century by a $300 million undersea fiber-optic cable that reduces trading time between New York and London by five milliseconds, even miniscule delays leading to information asymmetries upset the logics by which the exchange works.[121] Experiments with ticker visibility used CCTV to ensure all parties a perfect line of sight to stock prices, and thus instant, simultaneous access to information no matter their position within the architectures of the Blue Room. A similar CCTV system—"Ticker-Tape TV"—distributed a live feed of the ticker to local and branch offices of brokerage firms, promising "the best, most complete, and most automatic communications techniques" vital to "fast decisions."[122] Both systems enabled the growing industry to expand the reach of centralized information. Implicit in the emphasis on synched sight is the belief that traders will understand and act rapidly in accordance with the aims of their employers (and further, that the NYSE is a rational market based on users' access to the same data). ITV allowed traders to be perfectly attuned to the rhythms of market exchange. Vitally, television appealed to existing beliefs about ideal modes of labor by offering a tool that coordinated intensifying systems of automation and employee management. Experiments in business architectures increasingly sought to maximize efficiencies by perfectly matching mediated labor processes to material workspaces.

A third set of applications further confounded the boundaries between human, machine, and architecture. A popular use for early ITV systems was data retrieval and transmission—the "instantaneous 'transportation' of any data seen by the human eye."[123] These applications shared much with ongoing experiments in facsimile: proponents, patrons, interest in streamlining information architectures, early attempts at networking, and FCC classification.[124] However, the temporality of television—liveness and an orientation toward constantly unfolding processes—distinguished it from the fax's emphasis on the distribution of permanent copies.[125] While ITV systems themselves could not permanently *store* data, they were incorporated in various programs that provided the user access to diverse and dispersed information in the manner of an artificial memory. Much like a primitive computer system, ITV enabled users to call up and transmit desired information that had been translated into TV-friendly charts neatly "closeted away" in centralized data pools.[126] Instead of automated systems governing the organization and flow of files, however, people— at the other end of the camera or receiver—often undertook the grunt work of locating and returning needed information via their own camera-monitor setups. Paralleling the facsimile, the data chosen for transmission along ITV's links were often of a visual and static nature: detailed records, signatures, schematics, blueprints, seating charts, and maps.[127] Rehashing earlier claims to speed and perfection, proponents argued, "[t]he eye can take in information at an enormously more rapid rate than the ear can accept it or the voice can communicate it," and suggested that television could—again—prevent "the possibility of error" in communication.[128]

This was particularly attractive in industries in which verbal transmission of visual information was considered unreliable and physical transportation of records too slow.[129] In use as late as 1978, CCTV information systems were also pulled into discourses surrounding the "paperless" office.[130] In the 1960s, companies (and, most famously, the NYSE) increasingly found themselves swamped with paperwork management duties that overwhelmed their capacity to deal with their primary trade. Even computerization presented difficulties, since running queries on bulky machines could produce reams of paper. Using CCTV and centralized information banks (and reducing the overall amount of information shared across the company) enabled businesses to cut material and labor costs associated with too much paper. One company, Toledo-based truck and auto parts manufacturer Dana Corp., credited their CCTV system with the elimination of 500 record-handling jobs across its divisions and 40% of its corporate staff—an expense reduction of about $15 million.[131] As usual, jobs lost were celebrated as efficiency gains—a routine pattern of discounting workers' needs and humanity.

Among the most active early users of ITV information transmissions systems were banks that sought to balance the efficiency of keeping centralized records with making information accessible to workers in dispersed branches.[132] These institutions used ITV to restructure workers' relationship to physical information architectures built into existing bank practices. Before ITV, banks stored depositors' balance and personal signature information at alphabetically organized windows onsite at each branch. ITV, however, enabled banks to build centralized off-site record departments instantly accessible to any teller via intercom.[133] According to manufacturers, this system provided tellers with "a means of 'looking' into the files of the central record room" without leaving their post.[134] Since any available teller could serve any waiting patron "in a matter of seconds—and without leaving their respective windows," fewer employees were needed to staff the floor, backups at certain windows were eliminated, and undersubscribed tellers could be reassigned to other duties.[135] Furthermore, records centers could be relocated to less expensive property, securing literal information economies while safeguarding data off-site.[136] Other early systems centralized retail inventory information for branch salesmen; provided a "complete centralized library" for Navy researchers; supplied delivery schedules, production flow information, and parts requirements to factory workers; and provided airline customers with rapidly changing departure and arrival information.[137] Across these installations, television transmission and retrieval systems promised diverse users—"whether on the same floor, in the same building, in buildings a considerable distance apart, or even in different cities"—instantaneous access to abundant, fluctuating, and distant data.[138] Despite ITV's increasing divergence from the domestic medium, proponents reaffirmed its status as television, declaring, "There is no substitute for the service that television can give."[139]

An installation at the Pennsylvania Railroad demonstrates the appeal of human-machine hybrid networks—which can display public-facing content at the same time they streamline work processes—built into increasingly automated and centralized information architectures. Around 1959, the railroad installed what was then believed to be the largest industrial CCTV system in the world at a cost of over $3.5 million.[140] Comprising over 100 cameras and even more monitors, the system allowed booking agents to instantly examine availabilities and complete ticket-ordering transactions. Incredibly complex, the system connected three different locations: the ticket counter, the telephone sales office, and the coupon file center (where records were kept and tickets reserved). When a customer phoned to purchase tickets, the operator dialed a code representing the date a passenger hoped to book, connecting his or her monitor to one of 40 cameras trained on specially designed availability charts. Once the customer made her selection, the clerk sent a note via Telefax (a fax system using a special pen to send longhand messages) to one of 42 "coupon shaggers" in the coupons file center. The shagger placed the requested ticket under a camera linked to the clerk's monitor. Once the clerk confirmed the ticket selected was correct, it was held at the ticket office until the customer picked it up in person. The in-person process was similar, but the clerk used audio-equipped two-way television to communicate with the coupon center rather than fax. This was for the benefit of the customer, who could witness the technological marvel of the reservation process. The ticket appeared on a public-facing monitor before the client received a copy 10 seconds later via Western Union Intrafax.[141] When public-facing monitors were not in use, they displayed institutional advertising and schedules. According to its designers, ITV allowed for a faster, simpler, cheaper, and more impressive reservation system that reduced their complaints to zero.[142]

A photograph (Figure 2.5) of the railroad's ticketing office alludes to the enormity of this system, depicting dozens of employees sitting at a room-length double-sided bench, each with his or her own television monitor, headset, and dialing system.[143] It is easy to imagine this system as a giant, rudimentary computer in which each camera-availability chart exists as a file within a directory such as "Train availabilities," and the camera-coupon shagger coupling exists as an executable program allowing the user to make changes in a given camera-availability "file." However, this 100-plus node system is, of course, not a computer; it is an intricate, semi-automated system requiring manual inputs at several steps in the chain in order to facilitate the rapid transmission of data across disparate locations. Television thus operates as a mechanism for restructuring information storage and retrieval while it physically and intellectually incorporates people into work processes.

This image—which depicts people literally bound into the machines that regulate their work—may be the most explicit representation of the transformation and extension of the worker's body through television. Although cyborgs by name would not become a part of cybernetic research until the

Figure 2.5 Coupon shaggers in the Pennsylvania Railroad's television ticketing system.
Credit: Bryan Whipple, "Industry's New Tool—T.V.," *The Michigan Technic* (April 1958): 28.

early 1960s, this chapter is replete with uses of ITV that—in cybernetics jargon—"deliberately [incorporate] exogenous components extending the self-regulatory control function of the organism in order to adapt it to new environments."[144] Put plainly, authors Manfred Clynes and Nathan Kline refer to cyborgs as an "approach based on adapting the man to the environment rather than keeping him in a sort of environment to which he was naturally adapted."[145] Sherry Turkle and others have already discussed the capacities of digital screen technologies to function as prostheses.[146] The many examples discussed in this chapter indicate that this phenomenon is nothing new. ITV-as-prosthesis makes the worker's body stronger and bigger in order to fit it to the shifting needs of post-war industry. Or, as in this last example, it incorporates employees into semi-automated information systems. Although we might say the bodies of some are augmented through artificial memory, this comes at a cost of reduced physical mobility and being forced to fit flexible staffing practices that presage on-call staffing. For others, being incorporated into such man-machine systems means taking up rote retrieval activities that would eventually be computerized. These are not the revolutionary, multiple, mutating cyborgs celebrated by

Donna Haraway.[147] Instead, they represent corporate experiments into developing utile relationships between workers and technologies. Indeed, images like the railroad office in Figure 2.5 hew far closer to Karl Marx's description of the "appropriation" of living labor by machines:

> The production process has ceased to be a labor process in the sense of a process dominated by labor as its governing entity. Labor appears, rather, merely as a conscious organ, scattered among the individual living workers at numerous points of the mechanical system; subsumed under the total process of the machinery itself, as itself only a link of the system, whose unity exists not in the living workers, but rather in the living, (active) machinery, which confronts his individual, insignificant doings as a mighty organism.[148]

The "artificial homeostasis" of the ITV cyborg adapts bodies to industrial environments and "the living, (active) machinery" animated by managerial desires.

CONCLUSION

Zworykin and his RCA colleagues waxed poetic about the sight-expanding capabilities of ITV, writing "the desire to extend vision beyond the horizon, to see the unseen, is as old as man's ability to think, to ponder, and to hope."[149] However, ITV built its reputation on the far more mundane goals of reducing costs and increasing productivity in order to secure maximum operating efficiency across a range of industries in the growth of the post-war era. These efficiencies arose from the use of television to properly manage bodies: controlling worker mobility and their use of time, preventing accidents, and building worker capacities so one man could take the place of two.[150] Indeed, the promise to replace expensive human employees was often one of the biggest selling points of ITV equipment, quantified by the numbers of men and "pairs of human eyes" replaced, with one engineer pointing to a future in which cameras could send signals directly to control equipment—removing the need for human workers tout court.[151] The argument that television "reduces accidents . . . reduces operating costs . . . reduces capital investment" also fit into persistent contemporaneous discourses concerning the booming electronics industry's promise to "revolutionize" industrial operations, boost productivity, improve standards of living and even safeguard the nation against the threat of war.[152] Ultimately, in working to establish the value of prosthetic sight, discussions surrounding the development and implementation of ITV reaffirmed the long-standing relationship between industrial efficacy and moving image media promoted by the likes of Frank and Lillian Gilbreth.

As this chapter demonstrates, however, ITV is more than a mechanism of industrial efficiency. ITV provided an opportunity for engineers, public critics, and a wide range of industrial and commercial interests to explore the ideal relationship between the mechanized factory, the mediated office, and the human worker; the size, shape, and location of the ideal workforce; the physical arrangement of the factory and workspace; and even the physical capacities of the ideal employee. In the early 1950s, for example, industrial television was often included in a set of exuberant promises regarding the future shape of television that included the "magic" of color, the "miracle" of three-dimensional programming, and new opportunities for diverse, as well as local programming and station ownership provided by the additional channel capacity of Ultra High Frequency (UHF) television and the 1952 end of the FCC Freeze, which lifted restrictions on new station licenses.[153] However, engineers and reporters took pains to differentiate between the two systems, often relying on gender as a system of difference, hierarchy, and legitimation. Broadcast television was the "more popular sister" and the "glamorous cousin," with industrial television figuring as the "little brother."[154] Femininity became articulated to broadcast television in descriptions of its role as a "show horse": "a highly exotic and temperamental art," "amusing, or boring, or time-wasting, or frankly alarming," ruled by the "dictates of fashion" and focused on "fantasy and deception," with its performance criteria "emotional or subjective."[155] ITV, on the other hand, was the masculine "work horse": "stern," "practical," "useful," "serious," and "entirely functional," with performance criteria that were "intellectual or objective" and content that was "factual and truthful."[156] Engineers invoked domestic, commercial television to disassociate ITV and its users from popular associations of television with mass, feminine, frivolous, and passive audiences. Drawing on gendered value systems allowed engineers to situate their own work as serious and legitimate. Furthermore, reinforcing binaristic gender divisions enabled proponents to sidestep television's threat as a disruptive technology that might undo the masculine logics of the industrial workplace. After all, when ITV makes *any* body stronger, bigger, and smarter, gender no longer operates convincingly as a limit to participation in the workforce.

ITV also provides an example of institutional actors working on the protocols of an emerging medium. As Lisa Gitelman argues, protocols are a "vast clutter of normative rules and default conditions" that "express a huge variety of social, economic, and material relationships."[157] A return to the emergence of ITV in the late 1940s and 1950s provides an alternative understanding of the full institutional ambitions that animated the development of closed-circuit television. It provides an anchor for thinking about workplaces' ongoing attempts to manage employees' physical, economic, and social relationships with media technologies in order to extend workers' capacity to labor. Two decades into the twenty-first century, this work is carried out by scheduling programs, mobile phones, wearable inventory computers, and other tethering devices that attempt to better fit people to contemporary desires for worker elasticity and workforce flexibility.[158] To further condition employees to sedentary desk work, companies offer standing desks, work treadmills, and office Yoga that manipulates workers' sense of time and builds their endurance for constantly increasing demands for this physically and psychologically taxing labor.[159] At stake in these dynamics is nothing less than the question of who gets to help build our bodies and to what ends. The next chapter continues to trace these questions, focusing on early uses of CCTV that centered not on the body, but on the potential productivity of affect and intimacy.

CHAPTER 3

Frankly Boring and Agonizingly Slow: Television Moves to the Office

Immediacy

Sitting on the vault shelves at the Hagley Museum and Library in Wilmington, Delaware, are dozens of U-matic tapes with cabalistic labels, from "35R1 Symbiont changes" to "351 Exec, CKPR/RSTART." The videos themselves are no less arcane, in black and white featuring a single employee in a relentless medium shot that breaks only occasionally for a close-up on a flow chart or title cards—8½" x 11" pieces of paper with invocations like "Base Blank" and "exit" written in a startlingly small, but neat hand. Forgoing any introductory preamble, the presenters begin their talks, staring into the camera, stringing together impenetrable series of acronyms in gibberish incantations:

> So we have to call on the IO complex. And ADH and IO talk back and forth there. ADH sees that it's a printer. Back to IO, back and forth there. There's a lot of interplay here that's too confusing even to put on a flow chart. We do the IO, wait for the interrupt. When all is said and done we're back to the Symbiont.

Fumbling their words and fidgeting with their hands, the narrators forge through their presentations as their clothes rub against their lavalier microphones and their visual aids demand regular readjustment. So proceed these tapes until they wind to their conclusions over the course of some 10–30 minutes.

Television at Work. Kit Hughes, Oxford University Press (2020) © Oxford University Press.
DOI: 10.1093/oso/9780190855789.001.0001

While a few of the videos' confounding qualities originate from their highly specialized goal—to explain computer operating systems to professionals—this does not explain the contrast between their unusually spartan production values and their commitment to a visual form of presentation. Belonging to a larger collection of tapes produced by Sperry Univac in the late 1970s, these are the most rudimentary in their presentation. Certainly, the other tapes have their share of confused movements, boom mics falling into frame, jerky camera work and misaligned close-ups, people inadvertently exiting the frame while others mistakenly enter, and presenters who mumble, chew gum, smoke, pause awkwardly, avoid the camera's gaze, and read slavishly from typed notes. Some of these other tapes, however, also make efforts to exploit the visual form of the video, sprucing up the mise-en-scène with plants, using color, adding animations and other visual interest, employing star power like Kirk Douglas—a onetime spokesperson for Univac—and even drawing on narrative forms and modes of surveillance and co-presence constructed through moments like this one, which begins a video on the distribution industry:

[Open on a factory warehouse. A box with the title of the program, "Introduction to the Distribution Industry," works its way down a conveyor system to the camera until the text is in close-up. We cut to a different space in the factory with a desk and the conveyor line still in partial view. A man in a light blue lab coat enters with a clipboard in hand. He pauses in the center of the frame and addresses the camera in the style oft-parodied by *The Simpsons'* Troy McClure:]

"Oh hi, I'm Albert. Give me a second; you caught me in the middle of something . . . Of course, when you think about it, when you're in a warehouse, you're always in the middle."

Considering that color U-matic would have been available to Sperry Univac in the late 1970s when they made their operating system tapes, the contrast between the two modes of using television is remarkable, leading to a series of questions. Why would Sperry Univac employ impoverished production values when very small adjustments like typed intertitles, formal introductions, set décor, and presentation comportment practices would have resulted in far more aesthetically engaging productions? Or, if they were not interested in visual presentation, why use television at all? The tapes described in the preceding provide no information that could supplement printed materials. Indeed, presenters often read chunks of text at a time and "explained" flow charts simply by reading aloud the names of the steps; it is difficult to see how their "visual" presentation augmented the information in any way. Was Sperry Univac attempting to develop an alternative aesthetic mode based on flaws and heightened immediacy? What did they believe such a strategy accomplished? Given the many such U-matic cassettes in Sperry Univac's collection, the company was clearly committed to the format for training, but why?

This chapter addresses these questions by tracing the early experiments and enthusiasms that marked television's entry into training and employee information contexts. It shifts focus away from television as a means of corporeal extension, turning instead to how closed-circuit television was taken up to coordinate the work of white-collar workers—and to cultivate workers across labor hierarchies—in the 1950s, 1960s, and early-to-mid-1970s. Although the uses that comprise this chapter vary widely—live versus tape, spanning the nation versus displaying the self—they share the desire to exploit and reaffirm television's capacity for immediacy. As John Tomlinson points out, immediacy contains both spatial and temporal components; it invokes direct contact—lacking an intervening agent or substance—and it suggests instantaneous action.[1] Workplace television exploits both: immediacy as co-presence and access to the "real" (the boss, the seat of decision-making and power, company community), and immediacy as speed (for time-sensitive strategic action). Tomlinson further suggests immediacy as the overarching principle organizing the speed of life in the current period of capitalism. We share a concern with how immediacy—as something of a concession offered by capitalism—supports people's acceptance of increasingly poor working conditions (Tomlinson's list includes fast delivery of consumer goods, an easing of physical effort demanded by the machine age, temporal flexibility in working hours, and promises of cultural proximity to distant people and places).[2] However, this chapter retains the specificity of immediacy as it has been articulated to broadcasting and the technological possibility of liveness in particular.

Immediacy also appears in the ad hoc approach to early televisual experimentation outside of the factory. Working quickly to prove the value of television, media workers and entrepreneurs grafted the medium onto existing media systems (theatrical film exhibition) and transformed limitations (the non-portability of early open-reel video) into features (self-observation exercises). The first half of this chapter follows two major uses of television that situated immediacy as key to the medium's management of workers and publics: ad hoc live closed-circuit television meetings and taped self-confrontation training. The second half of the chapter begins to trace how television made the move from an extravagant special-occasion treat to a semi-permanent arm of the corporation following successful experimentation with educational television (ETV) systems and the concerted promotional efforts of institutional media workers. To anchor this discussion, this chapter loosely structures its analysis around a single firm. Although Sperry Univac's extensive tape collection provides some indication of the significant overlap between computers, data processing, and the embrace of videotape to quickly train large workforces in the growing knowledge economy, this chapter centers its focus on another behemoth of communications technology: AT&T.[3]

While AT&T's extensive use of television provides a useful example for exploring the varied applications made of the medium, it should not be taken as representative. However, AT&T distinguishes itself from its counterparts in American business in ways that prove useful for a robust accounting of the practices and promises of "programmatic" television. Like many of television's early industrial adopters, AT&T at mid-century was large, geographically expansive, and resource-rich. A government-supported monopoly (until a court-mandated divestiture took effect on January 1, 1984), AT&T comprised four distinct but interrelated operations: Bell Telephone Labs (research arm), Western Electric (manufacturing), Long Lines (national long-distance telephone service), and Operating Companies (some 20-plus exchanges that provided local service to the contiguous United States).[4] While Bell Labs provided much of the research and development that supported the system, AT&T (for example) compelled its customers to lease Western Electric phones from their local operating company in order to obtain both local and long-distance service. This coordinated, yet nationally dispersed structure likewise meant that AT&T was one of the largest employers in the country, occasionally even taking the top spot.[5] Furthermore, from World War I to the early 1970s, a full half of its employee roll was female, making it one of the largest employers of women.[6] Although these numbers seem to suggest a certain progressive openness to an integrated workforce, Venus Green makes it clear that the Bell System's pursuit of women was part of a bottom-line strategy focused on hiring cheap, tractable workers and placing them within strict, segregated hierarchies of pay, power, and responsibility. In return for its apparent devotion to diversity, AT&T received government training subsidies, good press, and favorable rate increases.[7] To manage this carefully cultivated difference within its massive, geographically dispersed workforce—and to adapt all workers to evolving cost-saving deskilling practices (mechanization, automation, computerization)—AT&T devoted considerable resources to training and employee management (not infrequently, of course, via film and television).[8]

While the company's focus on deskilling and retraining showcases twentieth-century employee management strategies endemic to other large firms that adopted television, AT&T's unique position within the television industry provides an opportunity to examine the medium from the perspective of a firm that was financially invested in its success. Throughout the network era, AT&T's Long Lines division served as the primary national distribution mechanism for commercial television.[9] AT&T thus owned the very infrastructure needed to distribute television signals across the country, whether to home sets, specially equipped movie theaters, convention centers, or its own boardrooms. Not only could AT&T freely use its Long Lines during off hours to spread its own training, meeting, and management programming, the firm stood to profit from the increased use of its network from schools and other institutions. To protect its financial stake in the expansion of non-commercial off-hours television, AT&T traded extensively in the promotion of institutional television. Reading AT&T's public and semi-public pronouncements alongside their own corporate media practices provides a robust sense of the medium's full promise for a range of corporate and institutional users.

AT&T's involvement in television also stretches farther back than most others'. The company's promotional materials often claim a parental role in television's birth via surrogate Herbert E. Ives, a Bell Telephone Laboratories engineer. In the spring of 1927, Ives and AT&T enlisted then-Secretary of Commerce Herbert Hoover in an intercity demonstration of television that stretched from Washington, DC, to New York.[10] The company often took up the mantle of chief inventor, conflating the first long-distance demonstration of television with the first demonstration tout court—likely to the dismay of John Logie Baird and others who had demonstrated some form of mechanical image transmission years prior. In the late 1920s and early 1930s, Bell Labs continued to develop television technology and applications, focusing extensively on two-way television; for two years, the company boasted such a "service" between headquarters at 195 Broadway and Bell Labs' New York address some 2.5 miles away.[11] (A similar technology would return to haunt the AT&T portfolio in the mid-1960s as the PicturePhone.) In the late 1930s—before the war halted "non-essential" research and development—the company turned its attention to the possibility of interconnecting television stations on a network scale, repeating the work it did in radio. The year 1948 saw the first fruits of this labor, when an East Coast network connecting New York, Washington, Boston, and Richmond came online (with a Midwest network not far behind). While AT&T occasionally contracted with theater television producers to transmit special events across its wired infrastructure in the 1940s and early 1950s, the company's internal use of the medium dates to 1953.

When AT&T incorporated closed-circuit television into its shareholder meetings in the early 1950s, it became party to a burgeoning corporate media practice marrying theater and big-screen television. While AT&T first used CCTV for meeting overflow rooms, it quickly moved to more spectacular applications.[12] In 1954, AT&T used CCTV to provide shareholders sitting in assembly rooms at 195 Broadway with a live, behind-the-scenes tour of Long Lines Headquarters (32 Avenue of the Americas). Declared "one of the largest and most complex [CCTV operations] of its kind yet undertaken," the "29 Minutes of Action" presented a "visitor's pass" to the audience before taking a "swing around the building." The presentation also featured a live long-distance telephone call to the San Francisco Weather Bureau, specially produced maps and illustrations, and film strips "to animate the narration." The write-up of the event in the *Long Lines* house organ emphasizes the show's success (measured in "spontaneous applause") and its show-business glamour, fitting similes to both Broadway and commercial television in a two-page spread.[13] Photographs of the event reinforced AT&T's media prowess at both ends of this spectrum. In one image, *Long Lines* showcases the grandeur of a large theater packed with the well-dressed and hierarchically arranged. A blurry but discernable (composite) image of beautiful women graces one of the large projection screens dominating the room and invokes norms of theatrical entertainment (Figure 3.1). A second image displays television in its smaller, more domestic form, albeit arranged as a high-tech command center (Figure 3.2). A shallow depth of field contributes to the sense of overcrowding as men do the important backstage work of adjusting knobs and monitoring screens. Some years later, AT&T extended its programming to internal audiences with "Paging America," a live "closed circuit spectacular" that introduced a new advertising campaign to 13,000 Bell Telephone employees spread across 55 cities.[14] Although more extravagant than most, AT&T's Long Lines presentations represent a key early genre of programmatic CCTV. Live, networked, and geographically expansive, these entertaining programs borrowed from the established modes of sponsored film and radio to manage participants' feelings towards and engagement with the firm (and its many members).

Although a variety of theater television systems existed, all worked by transmitting video and audio signals to specially equipped theaters where they would be projected on large (e.g., 18 x 24 foot) screens. While the technology dated to the 1930s, the immediate post-war era saw significant experimentation in theater CCTV programming and exhibition for sports

One of the scenes as it appeared on the screens at 195 Broadway

Figure 3.1 The crowd at 195 (AT&T headquarters).
Credit: "We Star on TV: Share Owners See How Department Handles Long Distance Service," *Long Lines* (April 1954): 5.

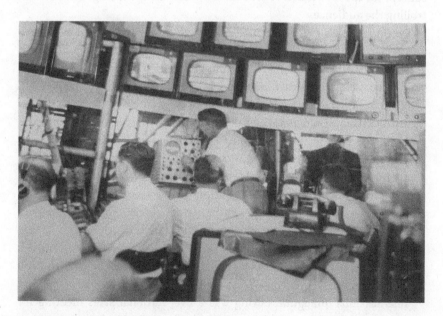

Figure 3.2 "Backstage" with the Long Lines Crew.
Credit: "We Star on TV: Share Owners See How Department Handles Long Distance Service," *Long Lines* (April 1954): 6.

and stage productions.[15] Douglas Gomery suggests this burst of activity represents the apotheosis of the medium, writing, "the attempted innovation of theatre television on a national network level was finished by the end of 1952. And that was about as far as theatre television was to go."[16] This appears to be the case from Gomery's vantage point, which posits theater television as a battleground between two established entities—the "motion picture industry" and "broadcasting interests"—vying for control of the new medium.[17] As he points out, after 1952 (and a failed attempt to win dedicated transmission frequencies from the FCC in 1953 that would have enabled theaters to bypass AT&T's long lines charges) the film industry turned toward widescreen and other strategies for dealing with the small-screen menace. However, setting 1952 as the veritable end of theater television ignores a central use of the medium by firms that don't fit neatly into "the" media industries. Indeed, 1952 is perhaps best understood as a pivot point, when the future of theater television belonged to packaging firms serving industrial clients.[18] Although Hollywood's interest in closed circuits rested on exhibitors' desire to restrict entertainment programming to paying customers, the principles behind theater television distribution challenged what increasingly seemed to be the "natural" correspondence between television and the broadcasting industry, and offered a proof of concept for the restriction of broadcast signals under the exigencies of controlling the audience.

Despite AT&T's infrastructural advantage in the transmission of television signals, they did not orchestrate their CCTV events. They turned to Theatre Network Television (TNT). Founded in 1951 by Nathan L. Halpern, TNT often claimed between 80% and 90% of all CCTV theater business.[19] Depending on whether a storyteller hopes to situate TNT as the progeny of broadcasting or cinema, the salient details of Halpern's biography are either his stint as former assistant to CBS president William Paley or his role as executive for the Motion Picture Theatre Owners of America. The company spent its earliest years focusing primarily on boxing, with limited experimentation in regional distribution of live stage performances, including a Metropolitan Opera performance of *Carmen*. Although business and government meetings represented only a small fraction of early theater television productions, in 1952 this market looked promising enough for TNT to expand, tapping former CBS executive Victor Ratner to head Tele-Sessions, a new division devoted entirely to industrial clients.[20]

Tele-Sessions' inaugural outing was a live, national sales meeting for James Lee & Sons Company—reportedly the first of its kind—telecast from NBC-TV's New York studios to 18 theaters in 17 "key cities" coast to coast from 12:00 to 1:00 EST on December 8, 1952.[21] The program, distributed via

AT&T's coaxial cables, introduced Lee's new line of carpets to a salesman-invited audience of "top retail executives, architects and contractors, home economists for local newspapers, stockholders and community leaders."[22] Kate Smith, a broadcasting personality whose eponymous variety television program had just come under the sponsorship of Lee's, introduced the program, which included speeches from top executives and the presentation of a new line of carpeting and its attendant advertising campaign.[23] To enable "two-way talks between the field and the studio," the CCTV system featured two-way audio that linked each site to NBC studios so audience members could ask questions.[24] Although the presentation's black and white transmission was noted by some as a drawback—especially for interior design products—others suggested that the CCTV meeting was nevertheless superior to its non-televisual counterpart due to the opportunity to "see" and "meet" top executives, whatever grayscale did for their complexions.[25]

While meetings ranged in size and scope, the Lee's event set the mold for theater CCTV programs throughout the 1950s. "Off-hour" exhibition (when theaters would not be sitting movie patrons) allowed employers to tuck their meetings into work hours while providing exhibitors an added source of income that did not compete with their primary business.[26] (Indeed, business meetings were sold to theater owners as "the most promising and profitable purpose to which the costly [theater tv] equipment can be put."[27]) Although sometimes used for local meeting overflow, CCTV was most often pulled into ad hoc regional and national networks.[28] Total screening sites, lists of interconnected cities, and the combined sizes of audiences became de rigueur in press announcements, from the "23,000 doctors in 32 cities" that formed the audience for Smith, Kline, and French's drug marketing to the "1,800 sales and advertising men in 14 cities—ranging from Boston to New Orleans" that formed the target of Esso Standard Oil's sales pitch.[29] Meetings also often featured live celebrity entertainment. While some, like Big Top host Jack Sterling or Kate Smith, were affiliated with a given firm's commercially sponsored entertainment, others employed major stars ranging from Dean Martin and George Burns to President Eisenhower—live from the White House.[30] Whatever the wattage of celebrity star power, one of the main attractions of CCTV business meetings was the appearance of company top brass, which afforded the rank-and-file—or individual shareholder—a rare opportunity to come into (some sort of) contact with organizational leaders. To intensify this sense of immediacy, many meetings—like Lee's—featured two-way audio systems that enabled audiences to ask questions.[31] Because of CCTV's promise to provide an intercession between management and large numbers of geographically spread employees, it appealed to bigger (and more resource rich) companies, including AT&T, IBM, NBC, Westinghouse, and the major automobile manufacturers (General Moters, Ford, Chrysler).[32]

Although business meetings began as a side venture for TNT, by 1955, they were touted as the company's "bread and butter."[33] When the company announced its densest slate yet of theater television productions—10 sessions between the months of December 1955 and April 1956 "representing billings of more than $1,125,000" (over $10 million in 2019 dollars)—at least 8 were for industrial and governmental concerns.[34] In 1957, TNT alone provided CCTV services to 23 firms, with costs per event ranging from $27,000 to almost $9 million, the latter the sum paid by AT&T for its Yellow Book sales event.[35] According to Halpern, his firm represented $23 million of the $28 million in 1957 grosses made by the "Closed-circuit TV communications industry."[36] Although TNT continued to hold large-scale public entertainment spectaculars—like the 1958 Robinson-Basilio middleweight championship fight that busied 25,000 miles of AT&T line spanning 174 locations and 131 cities—their transition at mid-decade to a focus on business was underscored by a major investment in mobile exhibition technologies.[37] Late in 1954, TNT placed an order for over 50 mobile projectors from General Precision laboratories in order to make more meeting-friendly spaces (hotels, auditoriums, theaters, ballrooms) accessible to television signals.[38] The purchase was promoted as a means to expand TNT's own "flexible national operation" to match "the flexible nation-wide coaxial cable network of the [Bell] Telephone Co."[39] Press releases touting the expansion emphasized TNT's increased capacity to "[adapt] its services to the unique needs of each individual client" with ad hoc business communications networks "set up nationally, regionally or locally" across 50 cities coast to coast.[40] By 1958, the company could boast the lion's share of the more than 100 business telecasts that had occurred since Lee's first piloted the practice.[41]

For TNT's industrial clients, CCTV bore a certain bottom-line appeal. By 1960, industry spent an estimated $35 billion annually on meetings and conventions—costs that CCTV promised to defray.[42] For national sales meetings, CCTV minimized the "travel, time and expense" incurred when bringing dispersed participants to a centralized location, and saved valuable "energy spent" by executives who might otherwise travel to several regional meetings.[43] Described by Ratner as the "mass production and mass distribution of meetings," CCTV also meant that it became "economically practical" to expand the ranks of meetings to bring junior executives, local dealers, staff, and even customers into the remit of executives' "authority and competence" (and control) via management communications.[44] The temporal immediacy of CCTV promised money-saving speed, whether for syncing the national rollout of a new product or enabling car dealers to tour a new traveling product exhibition "in a matter of minutes almost without leaving their own showrooms."[45] Sun Oil president Robert G. Dunlop estimated that CCTV reduced the cost of introducing a new gasoline to its dealers by 60%, in part by cutting the previous year's timetable for introducing new products from 40 days of individual dealer meetings to a single hour-long presentation (a promotional figure that conveniently elides the planning time required to produce a national telecast).[46] Halpern himself suggested that CCTV could cost (in 1954) "as little as $2 per important viewer attending a company session," a number that compared favorably to non-televised events.[47] Whether unimportant viewers were discounted remains unclear; this emphasis may be designed to signal the targeting capabilities of CCTV, which, unlike broadcasting, boasted a finite, curated audience. Halpern publicly referred to CCTV as "a kind of narrowcasting—or perhaps it might be called select-casting."[48] Among other banal benefits of CCTV meetings were privacy, high "attendance," and "uniformity of quality" in information distribution.[49]

For the organizational sponsors of meetings, CCTV's splashier main attraction was—echoing the previous chapter—a sort of materials handling. As Ratner puts it, CCTV "is functional because, fundamentally, it saves both time and money in contrast with the cost of moving people and material 'in the flesh.'"[50] While promotional materials discussed the possibility of bringing products to a dispersed workforce, emphasis rested on the ability of CCTV (in contrast to Chapter 2) to move *people*. Ratner himself used this distinction to position television as superior to film, suggesting that while films can present a firm's products, *"television can present the men* who are directly responsible for maintaining leadership in an important field, with an obvious benefit to the 'internal relations' of the company."[51] To be clear, one of the chief values of CCTV was that workers could stay put; Ratner's description of movement and personal presentation rests on ideological constructions of television's capacity for co-presence.

Immediacy and the Corporate Real

Liveness tends to lead discussions of broadcast television's ontology and phenomenology. This may be because the networks worked diligently to establish liveness on a national scale (or at least, its illusion) to justify their control over television in the face of competing interests—the film industry and local stations.[52] However, *immediacy* may be a more useful frame for thinking about the techno-affective affordances and ideological strategies of the medium and its proponents; this is certainly the case for live CCTV meetings. Plainly, immediacy can be understood as television's claim to offer sensibly direct access, in the unfolding present, to someone or something understood to occupy a location distinct from the television set(s); crucially, this access is *shared with other geographically distant viewers*. Immediacy resolves disagreement over whether liveness functions primarily in the temporal or spatial register by consolidating these positions through their shared ideological implications.[53] Supported by a cluster of visual and aural conventions (direct address, interruption, editing), immediacy implicitly promises instant access to some facet of the noncontiguous world "as it really is."[54] Television's "spatial pyrotechnics" likewise offer spectacle that eschews the mise-en-scène of extravagance and calamity to revel in the medium's ability to connect and display the banality of everyday, ongoing modern life (traffic reports, CSPAN, home shopping).[55]

While this temporal and spatial promise to viewers ("*being* there") suggests possible access to "the real" (in real time), it should also be understood as part of a larger program of co-presence that presents viewers to *each other* as part of a meaningfully defined group (nation, family, corporation).[56] Both modes of connectivity appear in twin poles of live programming identified by Mary Ann Doane, catastrophe and information. While the former "produces the illusion that the spectator is in *direct contact* with the [news] anchorperson" addressing them in times of crisis, information "is always *there*, a constant and steady presence, keeping you *in touch*."[57] In the latter scenario, as much as anything else, connection extends sideways—to fellow audience members and participants in the social order. More directly, Jane Feuer argues that careful management of co-presence—in programs like *Good Morning America*—"produces and reproduces [the program's] ideological problematic of family unity and national unity within-diversity"; it is a strategy that can ultimately "create *families* where none exist."[58]

By the 1980s and 1990s, television's ability to transform an audience into a "family" and manage employee-employer relationships would become a hallmark of its promotion (see Chapter 5).[59] As early as the 1950s, however, television's immediacy was already being sold as distinctly personal and communal connectivity. TNT promoted theater CCTV as a way to recapture—and intensify via magnification—"the special qualities of face-to-face communication."[60] CCTV audiences could see "the play of emotion on a speaker's face . . . hear his voice . . . get to 'know' him more intimately than we can through any other distance medium."[61] Descriptions of CCTV often elided mediation to claim that the technology allowed executives to appear "in person" or speak "directly" to their audience.[62] Like commercial television, CCTV promised its viewers unmitigated access to the *corporate* real: the boss, and by extension, the halls of decision-making and power. CCTV likewise provided "the added psychological effect of being part of an audience, of sharing a common experience."[63] It should be unsurprising that clients sought out CCTV when in need of unity and shared purpose (political rallies, corporate milestones, dedications of expanding facilities).[64] While Paddy Scannell contends that liveness is a product of care structures—the unseen labor that makes television a taken-for-granted technology always (invisibly) "at hand" in everyday life—live CCTV productions make this labor visible and spectacular.[65] Care is not an infrastructural undercurrent constituting viewers' relationship to the televisual apparatus; it is a distinct and explicit claim made by companies appropriating the "treat" of splashy, nation-spanning, networked entertainment.[66]

AT&T's use of CCTV at shareholder meetings operated along the same logics of access to the corporate real and personal connection. Ranging from "the rowdy to the dowdy," stockholder meetings grew in size and extravagance as the 1950s wore on.[67] "Well attended, informative, and even newsworthy" annual meetings provided an opportunity for firms to "[nurture] good relations" with shareholders and the public.[68] Firms increasingly courted shareholder participation with beer, hot meals, novel locations (one list counted a circus tent, luxury liner, movie theater, bowling alley, airport, and a snuff mill), and even—in the case of The Chesapeake and Ohio Railroad—free transportation to the meeting.[69] Despite the stiff competition, CCTV and radio were hailed as "probably the most spectacular new development" of such meetings. CCTV's immediacy interested companies that understood relationships as the route to new investment. While bottom line appeals helped sell shares, "something more" was necessary to encourage buy-in; investors needed to "admire and like" corporate management and "feel that they are given fair and friendly consideration."[70] This "feelings job" was the work of the shareholder meeting and, by extension, CCTV. Further, by providing "an opportunity to get a direct personal impression of [top management]," to ask questions and "get on-the-spot answers," CCTV cultivated a sense of transparency and management accessibility—again, access to the corporate real.[71] Celebrating full-throated the promises of immediacy as spatial, temporal, and even cognitive collapse, one onlooker concluded, "So long as telepathy remains outside the realm of the practical, it is hard to conceive of anything more nearly approaching the perfect system of long-distance communication for business."[72]

CONFRONTING THE LIMITATIONS OF THE SELF (AND VIDEOTAPE)

While CCTV meetings built their reputation for effectiveness on co-presence, spectacle, and expansive scale, a second major use of television—self confrontation—instead pursued self-centered intimacy and banality. "Frankly 'boring,'" these videotapes represent the obverse side of immediacy—an aesthetics and approach claiming kin with the Univac videos that began this chapter.[73] The contours of videotape's development in the broadcasting industry are well known. Following similar work on audiotape, Ampex demonstrated their video tape recorder (VTR) to the broadcast networks at several high-profile events and in private meetings in 1956.[74] By April 1957, Ampex units were in operation at all three of the major networks.[75] Tape appealed to the broadcast industry for the same reasons it would be taken up by other large firms. Hailed as a tool of efficiency and economy, tape did away with the common practice of dual performances (one for East-Coast and one, some hours later, for West-Coast audiences). Not only did this avoid duplicating time and resources spent on programs, it provided more flexible working hours to staff who otherwise had to be in-studio for each broadcast.[76] Understood initially as a transmission medium rather than a storage medium, videotape was also cheaper than film, since a single tape could be erased and reused many times. It was faster, since it did not need to be processed and could be shown immediately.[77] This same speed and reusability appealed to New York Telephone, one of Bell's operating companies, when it first began experimenting with video recording in the early 1960s. However, while early VTRs promised economy and efficiency, the machines themselves were expensive, bulky, and wrought with compatibility problems. Tapes could only play back on the machine they were recorded on, circumscribing possibilities of duplication and distribution. Open-reel machines exposed fragile magnetic tape to potentially rough conditions and careless users. Faced with these limitations, industrial media users devised a hyper-local application founded on video's instant replay and reuse capabilities.

Requiring trainees to watch and critique their own taped performances alongside their peers, "self-confrontation" exercises drew from a constellation of group therapy methods gaining popularity in the post-war era. Training groups (or T groups) were pioneered in the late 1940s by psychologist Kurt Lewin with the support of the Office of Naval Research.[78] A therapy methodology, T groups gathered a dozen or so participants to discuss their immediate personal experiences and perspectives as shaped by interaction within the group setting. During the sessions, a trainer probed and contextualized participant encounters using psychological theory. Sometimes referred to as sensitivity training, T groups valued subjective experience and sought to develop bonds of openness and understanding among people with different life experiences (ameliorating, for example, interracial conflict).[79] In the 1960s and 1970s, the methods of T-groups were repackaged as "encounter groups," which often focused more intently on personal growth (via self-disclosure, confrontation, and intense emotional experience) rather than interpersonal dynamics.[80] "Widely implemented" within workplace training regimes by the late 1960s, versions of these group therapy practices provided a minimal theoretical basis that legitimized the incorporation of video as a catalyst for discussion and self-confrontation.[81] Again, industrial trainers followed the example of psychologists; as early as 1966, Frederick H. Stoller created a model for using videotape to provide "focused feedback" on individuals' performance within group therapy.[82] In some ways realizing the long-held ambitions of training film—viewer identification with the on-screen images as a route to perfected performance—videotape's virtue lay in enabling employees to analyze and correct their own personal expression and behavior in minute detail.[83]

Though the broad strokes of video self-confrontation were borrowed from psychology, the aims and ambitions of these methods for employee training were narrower than that of group therapy. In the context of manufacturing, an underwear company filmed women's sewing techniques in pursuit of "increasing quality and efficiency."[84] Much like the Gilbreths' use of film to train workers in the "one best way" of accomplishing a task, employees watched themselves to improve their technique.[85] More commonly, self-confrontation was used to enable white-collar workers to "see themselves as others see them."[86] This form of exteriorization was rarely positioned as a means to achieve meaningful self-actualization within the context of work.[87] The target of video's sharp gaze was often superficial: fiddling, pencil-tapping, overuse of hand gestures, lack of smiling, poor posture, "excessive eye movement"—essentially "any surface type personality mannerisms that may be offensive to a prospect" (or a job interviewer).[88] This emphasis on building the self as a commodity to be consumed superficially by others reached its apex in a "Personal Development" course geared toward aspiring stewardesses enrolled at Cypress College. Over the length of the course, students were taped and evaluated on "poise, grooming, complexion, figure, voice, and attitude."[89] Not only was each student expected to use video to "study her features and bone structure in relation to her make-up, hair styling, and the design of her clothes," taped role-playing scenarios of difficult encounters (a drunk executive, an airsick passenger) allowed her to observe whether she carried out all duties "with a smile."[90]

Even when role-play adds an interactional component to the activity (another example saw receptionists engaging with hostile callers), focus remains on the employee's emotional conduct and performance.[91]

These applications are a far cry from self-actualization and meaningful interaction pursued by psychological applications of video self-analysis.[92] Indeed, they perhaps share more in common with video art of the same period. Persistent concerns with video feedback, mirroring, and engagement with the self-image in artworks by Vito Acconci, Lynda Benglis, Bruce Nauman, and others led Rosalind Krauss to propose, "the medium of video is narcissism"—the "psychological condition of the self split and doubled by the mirror-reflection of synchronous feedback."[93] The subject becomes displaced by itself-cum-object (the mirror reflection), rent from history and offering itself up for visual contemplation. Ways of understanding video as a technology of narcissistic self-display and engagement circulated alongside and shaped industrial take-up of more therapeutic perspectives and practices. Exceptions aside, the target of these applications tends to be the comportment of the (overly idiosyncratic, overly emotional, overly kinetic) self rather than understanding the other; they are an invitation to self-regulate to a degree *far more intense* than anything mandated by an assembly line—often for little more than becoming slightly less annoying or a little more persuasive.[94]

The purported effectiveness of these tapes relied on a different form of immediacy than live programming. Although self-confrontation necessitated a lag between performance and analysis, "instant playback" was nevertheless understood as the route to accessing "the real" (self).[95] While tape could split "the observing-self from the participating-self," if these two temporally distinct "selves" were spread too far apart, it became difficult for a trainee to "bridge back" to their earlier self and identify factors shaping their behavior.[96] Put otherwise, instant playback ensured that students could make profitable use of fresh "feelings."[97] This temporal immediacy, however, also rested on the perfect transparency of videotape and its ability to act as an "infallible mirror" providing an "objective" view of participant behavior.[98] Eschewing the "mediating program contexts of entertainment" (genre, formula, established modes of performance), self-confrontation established its proximity to "pure events"— even lowly training exercises—via aesthetic claims invested in banality as the route to authenticity.[99] Tape captured otherwise ephemeral elements of behavior: words, gestures, the "fleeting nuances of . . . facial and bodily expressions."[100] Because tape could be paused to "pinpoint" mistakes, "*split-second* portions of [a participant's] behavior" or "*exact moments* of loss of control" could be studied in minute detail.[101] Discounting mediation in both the encoding and decoding of a videotaped performance, granularity of movement substituted for clarity in meaning.

Banality was no protection against the "shock and/or amazement" felt when seeing oneself in full detail.[102] Indeed, the emotional intensity of such immediacy was understood as videotape's chief virtue. A "powerful stimulus," television was positioned as an exciting change agent that spurred personal involvement and lively discussion, even among otherwise shy and timid trainees.[103] So impactful was this emotional charge, facilitators routinely discussed the need to carefully manage potentially stressful feedback sessions, for example, by inducing trainees to refer to themselves in the third person and guaranteeing the erasure of tapes.[104] As one trainer put it (invoking, of course, the possibility), "We don't want to destroy anyone with CCTV." However, the negative emotional valence of the process was not a bug, but a feature of the system, one that powered participants' motivation to improve: "the trainee finds himself in a traumatic situation that he usually doesn't forget and thus a need for change is experienced."[105]

Again, immediacy and efficiency made for easy bedfellows. The emotional intensity, clarity, and irrefutability of taped feedback shifted training responsibilities onto participants, who were now charged with identifying, analyzing, and managing the emotions that led to imperfect behavior. Because the trainees could "see for themselves" their mistakes, tape preserved the positive supervisor-supervisee emotional bonds important to successful management while ensuring participants' "acceptance" of the need to change.[106] Video enabled participants to realize faults that "not even their wives or best friends" dared mention.[107] As the stewardess trainer suggests, "If Suzy *sees* that she should lose weight, the instructor need not tell her so. This places the instructor in the positive position of advisor instead of a negative one as critic."[108] Others claimed that the participant's experience provided instruction *superior* to what a trainer could offer: "when an individual sees himself perform a task on television, he clearly observes what he is doing wrong and how to improve. A teacher can offer suggestions for improvement, but there is no substitute for an individual seeing himself immediately after performing a task."[109] In hinting at the possibility of doing away with paid trainers altogether, these discussions of "self-instruction," "auto-observation," and "auto-correction" invoked industry's persistent drive toward efficiency via automation.[110] Not only does video provide a picture-perfect image of what went wrong that (somehow) enables the employee to intuit how to correct her faults, the frisson of visible failure motivates her to become responsible for her own growth.

AT&T was no exception to the increasing interest in video feedback. Illinois Bell, another of AT&T's regional operating companies, launched its own television system under the call sign-moniker "IBTV" in 1966. While early applications of its network included specific skills training (computer use, billing technologies) and informational programs (women's self-defense), the extent of role-play and self-confrontation occurring on their premises was so prevalent it warranted its own dedicated studio. Built in 1970 to free up time in IBTV's two existing studios, the latter studio quickly found itself "in almost constant use."[111] For companies and nonprofits without the massive resources of an AT&T operating company, the relatively low cost of equipment (at its most basic, a VTR and a monitor) and the introduction of "portable" VTRs in 1966 finally made television accessible.[112] Found in spaces ranging from the boardroom to the hospital ward, videotape joined expanding experimentation in personnel training spanning job rotation, programmed instruction, simulation, gaming, and computer-aided instruction.[113] While business only represented 25% of the VTR market in 1970, it was its fastest growing user base.[114] Occasionally decried as "the video fad of psychology," due to its apparently indiscriminant application to "alcoholics, basketball players, counseling, delinquents, diagnosis, engineering, families, nude marathoners, psychiatry, psychodrama, schizophrenics, and T-groups," video self-confrontation nevertheless gained legitimacy by 1970.[115] Though easily forgotten in the shadow of national star-studded television meetings, self-confrontation acted as a Trojan horse, paving the way for expansive cassette-based systems that would dominate in-house corporate communications in the 1980s.

SELLING THE MOVE IN-HOUSE

The work of developing corporate television exceeded technical and textual experiments, requiring persistent attention to the problem of "selling" TV to management. In a speech delivered to fellow corporate television workers, AT&T CCTV staff supervisor Paul Lowry suggested that founding an in-house television system meant first and foremost "developing 'media literacy' among our clients, 'media belief' among management and a 'media plan' for ourselves."[116] Unlike occasional cross-country meetings, in-house systems represented a massive, ongoing investment for firms. Many, however, eventually found it worth the expense. Often comprising both live and taped facilities, in-house systems radically extended the utility of television, merging live events and self-confrontation with increasingly popular taped instruction. Although AT&T was early in its (1963) decision to create in-house television facilities, the company nevertheless relied on over a decade of experimentation with the medium before committing.

One of the most important sites of sustained exploration into the merits of the medium was in the classroom. AT&T was party to the mid-1950s development of Educational Television (ETV), a multifaceted initiative that sought to enrich classroom learning via CCTV. According to the heroic tones of their own promotional pamphlets, in 1956, AT&T "rushed into being" the network that supported the pioneering Hagerstown, Maryland, ETV experiments.[117] The company quickly found itself laying more line as the initial network (interconnecting eight schools with a studio) grew until it reached over 90% of Washington County's 18,000 students.[118] By mid-1961, AT&T operating companies established six additional CCTV networks—including a state-wide system in South Carolina—while some 30 additional systems were in the bidding phase.[119] In addition to providing "transmission services" (often through its local operating companies), AT&T's Bell Labs worked on long-distance cable improvements and ancillary products like amplifiers particularly suited to ETV operation.[120] AT&T's involvement in ETV bolstered its claims that it served the public interest (crucial for a private monopoly ostensibly serving at the pleasure of the government), while fostering a potentially lucrative source of revenue. The firm charged a healthy (albeit discounted) sum to school systems for the leasing of its lines; in the Hagerstown, Maryland, trials, for example, AT&T earned about $1.2 million a year.[121] Indeed, by 1967, Dick James, engineering manager of video at AT&T headquarters, proclaimed ETV a bigger business than even the "enormous" and growing use of private CCTV by corporate interests.[122] While AT&T stood to make a pretty penny on the expansion of ETV, it also provided a wealth of experience that the company could (and did) draw on to develop its own in-house systems.[123]

Some of the most basic arguments corporate video borrowed from ETV concerned television's technical capabilities. Some of these positioned film as Other, emphasizing television's ease of use in comparison—a constellation of affordances that included the ability to watch in a lighted room (enabling note-taking and discouraging sleep) and the ability of *nontechnical people*" (i.e., non-projectionists) to operate equipment.[124] Other highly praised affordances of television, however, (magnification, recording, repeated showings for uniform information distribution) did little to distinguish the medium from its celluloid confrere.[125] (Amnesia, of course, has long been an affliction suffered by new media promoters.) Television was also hailed for its technical flexibility and convergent properties, which combined data retrieval (the slides, charts, and photographs of Chapter 2) with live, taped, and filmed content.[126] Indeed, many in-house television systems gradually became multipurpose. Banks that used CCTV to transmit client signatures eventually developed systems that provided surveillance, distributed instructional video, and allowed for live meetings among managers.[127] Hospitals, military schools, and manufacturing firms did likewise, building multifunctionality into existing or newly planned systems.[128]

Corporate television also borrowed ETV's arguments regarding CCTV systems' ability to save time and money, support growing operations, and make the most of scarce resources. In other words, the same system that helped educators manage rising enrollments, teacher shortages, and increasingly crowded classrooms in the post-war era saved businesses money during their own expansion.[129] For example, although new layers of management supported corporate growth, they exacerbated potential "communications gap[s]" among different segments of the workforce.[130] Beamed directly to workers, television—the medium of immediacy—promised to "shorten . . . lines of communication" and "maintain control" by "eliminating the filtration system" of this growing workforce.[131] Bob Quickstad, who oversaw AT&T AV employee communications, also assured AT&T Vice President Ed Block (via video memo) that television "extend[s] and increase[s] the availability of the best people and resources," saving some four million dollars annually in "time, travel and efficiency."[132] Not only did in-house systems obviate the need to reassemble workers off-site, they introduced new possibilities for embedding training and communications into work architectures.[133] Wheeling a mobile exhibition cart onto a slow sales floor or installing television sets along an assembly line meant "workers had only to turn their heads up" to watch communications tucked into the ebb and flow of the workday.[134] "The classroom had come to the employee at last"; in-house CCTV "made possible almost continuous information and training."[135] Without the "lost" time of movement, every moment could be made profitable.

Television's established identity as a domestic entertainment medium—with a reputation for sales—was also central to its promises of immediacy and impact. According to Halpern, National Dairy Products Company "reasoned that if Tv was effective in selling customers on its product in the home, closed-circuit Tv in the theatre, aimed solely at its dealers and routemen, would be effective in selling them on the company's product" (or even, its advertising campaign for commercial television).[136] Companies likewise blurred the boundaries between corporate and commercial television to showcase their generosity toward employees and to manage morale.[137] That these audiences were conditioned to expect "commercial grade quality" programming was an often-repeated truism.[138] While this demanded greater investment in equipment and production, instructional television could, in turn, borrow the resonance and efficacy of its domestic counterpart. CCTV delivered the authority of *Captain Kangaroo*, the "delights" of *Howdy Doody*, the drama of *Sesame Street*, and the pacing, continuity, and "general informational quality" of *Bonanza*.[139] Here, we might consider the motivations behind the sleight-of-hand that trades adult CCTV audiences for easier-to-influence children. The "powerful spell of the TV image" was further credited with an "almost uncanny ability to hold the attention of young and old alike," a "moving and dramatic" nature, memorability, and credibility.[140]

How then, to explain the spartan production values of the Univac tapes and more mundane CCTV programming? Forgoing showy network aesthetics, these programs instead built similar claims of immediacy on the banal aesthetics of authenticity and access. Informal presentational modes like interviews and panel discussions reportedly lent "honesty and conviction" to management communications.[141] Again conveniently overlooking mediation, users celebrated television's ability to provide lower-level employees "first hand" access to "straight *talk*" and "authentic" information direct from the top brass.[142] AT&T's ETV promotional materials set the stage for these claims, suggesting, "there is something very effective psychologically about television . . . a closeness, an intimacy, a personal something about the television experience."[143] Rehashing the arguments of TNT, corporate CCTV users praised this ability of television to "[bring] about a more personal relationship" between upper management and employees by "conveying . . . the very 'personality' of executives and instructors."[144] San Francisco State College faculty member Stuart Hyde suggested that the "immediate and intimate" nature of two-way CCTV made it the "greatest hope" for community-building in moments of frustration and cynicism; in addition to distributing information, the leader that used the medium could "more importantly . . . send the message that he cares, and that he can be trusted."[145] This capacity for conveying "care" was particularly important to companies that believed that the presence of executives (televisual or otherwise) at major employee events was "vital . . . if only to show the field men that the company is thinking about them."[146] Television—"pleasant," innovative, "liked" by employees, "more interesting . . . than another memo in the 'in box,'"—could, it was hoped, instill a "deep appreciation for a management that used such a dynamic method" to convey important (or "otherwise awkward") information to its employees.[147] Although visually distinct from glamorous special event programming, both modes fit into a growing recognition that "the emotions of the corporation's employees [. . .] have a tremendous but usually ignored effect on job performance."[148]

Like employee knowledge and motivation, feelings—and identification with the boss—became yet another "intangible resource" to be managed toward "the profitable functioning of the corporation and to the well-being of the corporation's personnel, customers and stockholders."[149]

DEVELOPING IN-HOUSE CCTV AT AT&T

Whatever CCTV's promise, concerns regarding its cost, complexity, and efficacy meant that in practice the adoption of in-house television could be described as "agonizingly slow."[150] The precise temporality of CCTV take-up is markedly vague, with one person claiming private television "became a viable market" in 1965, another suggesting 1968 "marked the start of the acceptance" of such systems, and still others hanging the industry's growth around technological advancements—portable VTRs in 1966 or the U-matic in 1971.[151] Even AT&T, with all its advantages, approached in-house television cautiously. While forward-thinking members of AT&T management, training, and public relations were said to "[recognize] the potential" of television "in the late fifties"—the period of high-profile ETV experimentation—the process of internal television development began in earnest in 1963, when AT&T operating company New England Telephone and Telegraph Company established a 17-node CCTV network to connect Traffic Department central offices for training, film distribution, and improving morale.[152] Two years later, the company formed a CCTV Committee composed of representatives from both AT&T and Bell Labs tasked with developing practical, material, and technical information on CCTV systems for "outside customers."

In late 1966, the company turned inward, calling an all-hands meeting at 195 that gathered staff from operating companies, Bell Labs, Long Lines, and AT&T's public relations (PR) department to discuss existing uses of television throughout the firm and devise a plan for future expansion.[153] Southern New England, New England, and New York operating companies all already boasted multi-site networks, with the former two supplementing sites "not yet" interlinked with 8mm film cartridges.[154] These systems served a diverse set of demands, from self-confrontation and video conferencing to operator training, resulting in "an impressive list of programs developed and transmitted" by the operating companies.[155] Long Lines, meanwhile, used their facilities to provide visitors a "tour by C.C.T.V." of their operations in such exotic locales as Nova Scotia, California, and Missouri.[156] Together, these experiments put AT&T in line with other early adopters in the fields of large-scale metal and machine manufacturing and data processing that employed video in the early 1960s.[157] The 195 meeting resulted in a laundry list of potential applications and encouragement to VPs to explore potential television applications.[158] Reproduced in Figure 3.3, it includes 18 broad categories of use—with training "for all departments

SUGGESTED USES FOR CLOSED-CIRCUIT TELEVISION -- INTERNAL USE

- Training programs for all departments and all levels of employees
    - Procedures for handling toll reports (Traffic)
    - Service representatives training on billing, collections, etc.
    - Transmission maintenance (Engineering)
    - Coin telephone training (Marketing)
    - Handling and loading computer tapes (Accounting)
    - Use and care of tools (Plant)
    - Yellow page sales technique
    - Safe operation of heavy construction equipment (Plant)
    - Review of floor care maintenance (Building Service)

- Introduction of new products and service information (Marketing)

- General employee information and announcements

- Policy and organizational announcements (Executive)

- Special events requiring live, on-the-spot recordings (All Depts.)

- Personal evaluation for employee and executives appearing before outside groups and on television (Marketing - Speakers, Trainers)

- Introduction of Departmental practices and interpetations (All Depts.)

- Public Relations Programs and proposed film projects - script readings.

- Trend Reports

- Budget reviews

- Review of Annual Meeting and status reports

- Press releases

- Special Safety messages (Medical Dept., etc.)

- Regional meetings, (All Depts.)

- Tariff changes (Marketing)

- General information of extreme importance to the business (Garlinghouse-Scanlon Report)

- Multi - location meetings

- Presentations of special programs

Figure 3.3 Headquarters planning a (second) media empire.
"Earliest Ref. to TV," c. 1967, 4. John Sheahan Collection.

and all levels of employees" split into a further nine applications—indicating the enthusiasm with which television was articulated to AT&T's labor and communication practices. The vast range of proposed uses runs from discrete, banal tasks linked to a clear audience ("Review of floor care maintenance [Building Service]") to vague, but alluring future possibilities ("trend reports," "presentations of special programs," "multi-location meetings") that suggest a somewhat freewheeling invention of new tele-visual purposes. Combined with "live, on-the-spot" recordings of special events and script readings for proposed film projects that could heighten existing media practice, these hypotheticals indicate how the company hoped to harness the medium's perceived flexibility in almost every aspect of operations.

Ultimately, it was decided that television would become the responsi-bility of Public Relations and Employee Communications. A "stepchild de-partment" often organized on an ad hoc basis, corporate television took up residence in a range of company divisions.[159] The decision at AT&T was based in a desire to make use of existing staff proficient in visual commu-nication, to avoid duplicating production facilities, e.g., of graphics, and to place television in "the department closest to corporate policy making" and "as close to the revenue producing elements of our business as possible" in order to justify continued investment.[160] TV Coordinators were appointed to each operating company to liaise with 195 and act as a clearinghouse for information related to television operations. Outside consultants were hired to provide insight on hardware, studio organization, and operation, and processes of production, distribution, and exhibition.[161] In 1967, an interdepartmental task force "made the medium official" when it put plans in motion to build a permanent studio at AT&T headquarters.[162] Designed "chiefly for experimental work," the studio's primary objective was devel-oping a body of knowledge (regarding new equipment, maintenance, net-working, staffing, distribution, budgeting, and other technical and practical topics) that would be useful to operating companies as they created and expanded their own CCTV facilities.[163] Although initial plans centered on broadcast-quality 2-inch Ampex tape, the studio switched to 1-inch tape to ensure compatibility with operating companies who were already using the less expensive format.[164] Installed in 1968, the studio began full-scale operation in 1969. In the first year of its use, it hosted orientations and trainings for all 23 operating companies and could boast tape distribution to 16 (with 16mm kinescopes sent to the seven laggards still in proposal stages).[165] While the bulk of its early content fell under the rubric of man-agement communications, training applications were its eventual target.[166] Although work at 195 determined that a staff of seven—a director, two cameramen, a technician, an engineering director, a secretary, and a record clerk—was adequate for the medium-sized studios of many of its operating companies, its own staff would grow to 25 by 1977, with extensive use of freelance talent.[167]

The *Business Screen* spread promoting AT&T's New York facilities (Figure 3.4) combines spectacular display of the apparatus with familiar imagery of the mediated workspace. While the boardroom table in plush surrounds recalls RCA's celebration of their business film center published 22 years prior in the same journal (reproduced in Chapter 1, Figure 1.2), differences between the spreads reveals the lengths traveled by television in the intervening years. For AT&T in the late 1960s, it seems, you can never have too many TVs. While film is shunted to the margins (in a single top-right image), the boardroom has more than its fair share of sets and monitors crowding the front of the room: a television sits atop a television, stacked in front of yet another television embedded in the wall. Other photographs round out the display of AT&T's televisual prowess: AV men work against a backdrop of small screens, VTRs, and massive control panels, and a good-sized taping studio displays its extensive equipment. The center's floor plan, which shows that some half of its usable footprint houses video production and its ancillary technologies, further attests to the media commitments of the facility.

Diversity in the local informational and training needs of operating companies resulted in a heterogeneous collection of video subjects and scheduling strategies originating from both local studios and 195. While some programs, like AT&T's daily 30-minute "newscast"—a video house organ that included company news and employee human interest stories— were directed toward a company-wide audience, most programs were more narrowly designed.[168] Audiences might be regional, limited to a single operating company, or even a single building (as in the case of *Info/Net Report*, a daily lunchtime news series aired in the lobby of 195 for headquarters employees).[169] Programming also targeted specific pay grades, as with *Viewpoints*, a hybrid taped/live call-in series developed in 1968 by Illinois Bell; while managers participated in the live program, taped and edited versions were sent to supervisors to share with lower-level employees.[170] Modular programs supported the flexible repackaging of information for different audiences. *RSVP* (Regularly Scheduled Video Programming), for example, consisted of several 3–5-minute "modules" on "job-oriented" topics that could be recombined to form a 20-minute magazine-style program tailored to each of AT&T's varied departments.[171] The style of video programming varied widely, with spectacular special event programming sometimes borrowing above-the-line talent from New York City network

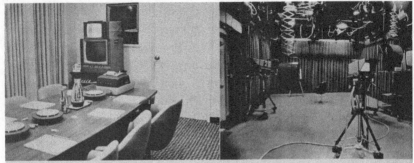

Conference room is shown at left with main studio arrangement illustrated in photo at right.

AT&T's A-V Center: Videotape in Action

Approaching its first full year in operation, AT&T's A-V Center in New York complements VTR activities of ten Bell System companies and serves as a nucleus of information for all 13 other companies.

A NEW Audio-Visual Center, incorporating the latest and most sophisticated industrial videotape production facilities, is now in operation at American Telephone & Telegraph Company headquarters in New York.

An activity of the Film and CCTV Division of the company's Information Department, the A-V Center was first organized on an experimental basis in July, 1968 and began full-scale programming in February of this year. While AT&T has been in the forefront of industrial audio-visual activities for more than 50 years all the mechanics of production have usually been delegated to outside, independent producer contractors working under Film Division supervision. But now, recognizing the increasing importance of videotape in industrial communications and the immediacy with which programs may be planned and produced, the company has set up a small production staff and is currently serving a broad range of headquarters building management.

One reason AT&T has initiated its videotape program is to complement the activities of the ten Bell System companies now with VTR studio facilities, and also to provide a nucleus of information for all 13 other companies, many of whom are contemplating videotape use in the near future.

The way it looks to A.T.&T. audio-visual management at this stage of the game, videotape programming will eventually find its most active use in training, but as of now it is most frequently used in management dissemination and employee information.

Since February, almost all departments of the company have used the center in one way or another. Noted on the activity schedule for one week in August were videotape program origination or playback for Treasury, Maintenance and Engineering, Marketing and Rate Plans, Information, Traffic and Long Lines. All 23 Bell System companies have sent representatives to orientation and training sessions held at the center during recent months.

When AT&T first contemplated a videotape set-up in the summer of 1968 it was recognized that one of the principal problems in any system was compatibility. Videotape recorded on one system can not be played back on another. Because the Ampex one-inch system is in use at other Bell System companies, it seemed logical to continue on with the same system at AT&T's center. Two Ampex VR-7800 VTR's are thus the key to the whole operation. One is used for regular constant taping activity while the other is a back-up. Both are used for editing, which in today's one-inch taping technology is now quick and efficient. Other equipment in use at the center are four GPL cameras, Ampex 400 audio recorders, Gates-Diplomat audio mixers, a TelePrompTer, and a complete Colortran lighting system.

While color taping is not contemplated in the near future, a great deal of the auxiliary equipment in use — lights and assorted electronic hardware — is either immediately ready for color or can be quickly converted.

The Audio-Visual Center is comprised of one main studio 20 by 34 feet, a 19 by 20 foot control room, a small auxiliary studio, conference room, reception area and four offices for staff.

In addition to the fixed studio facilities, a mobile unit consisting of a VTR, small

Figure 3.4A and 3.4B AT&T's 195 Studio and TV facilities, as of 1969.
"AT&T's A-V center: Videotape in Action," *Business Screen* 30, no. 11 (1969): 36–37.

production.[172] Content might be scheduled daily, weekly, monthly, quarterly, or to mimic an event-like conference schedule.[173] However, most (early) programs were one-offs produced as needed. Moving toward more regularly scheduled programming was a key strategy used by CCTV

(b)

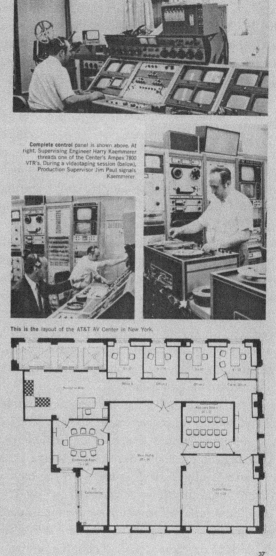

industrial camera, mini-lighting set-up, microphone and monitor can be wheeled to any location in the headquarters or near-by buildings on a cleverly improvised "tea-wagon." This has proved invaluable in taping personnel in their own environment for enhanced naturalness. It also permits instant replay, and approval, by the executives involved, in their own offices.

AT&T's audio-visual staff was fortunate enough to find space for the Center available in a connecting building at the 195 Broadway headquarters. The new Center has 11-foot ceilings and is "reasonably" well-equipped for air-conditioning and good acoustics. Ideally, Film and CCTV Production Supervisor James L. Paul recognizes, a production studio should be built as a box-within-a-box for complete soundproofing, and air conditioning compressors and blowers should be considerably remote from the studio. Neither of these considerations were possible at the new Center, but by good design within existing limitations, and by proper production methods, their lack has not been seriously felt.

Videotape programs produced at AT&T headquarters are now being used in the ten Bell System companies which have videotape facilities operating. They are also used by six other companies which have experimental "starter-sets" and mini-studios. For the seven companies which are not yet equipped with any VTR facilities, programs are converted to kinescopes. All seven of the VTR-less companies are now considering proposals to incorporate videotape into their training and information-dissemination activities.

One important part of the Audio-Visual Center's technical facilities is an audio retrieval system which permits directions from anywhere in the system to request and automatically locate audio information stored on tape at the center.

Willis H. Pratt, Jr., Film and CCTV Director of AT&T, told BUSINESS SCREEN recently that "videotaping and the use of closed-circuit television is one of the most significant breakthroughs in internal communications that we have experienced in many years.

"But, generally," Pratt went on, "business and industry have not moved into the new field of internal communications as quickly as they could have. Whenever any new media comes along there is a long period of development in which standards are not available. We consider it most important that all manufacturers get together and adopt standards. Until then, business will go slowly, always worrying about compatibility.

"Prices of VTR and CCTV equipment are now coming down to attractive levels," Pratt said, "and if the compatibility problem can be solved industry should make great strides in the near future.

"For the audiovisual specialist," Pratt concluded, "videotape holds forth all kinds of challenge for the future. It is one of the most exciting eras we have had." •

Complete control panel is shown above. At right, Supervising Engineer Harry Kaemmerer threads one of the Center's Ampex 7800 VTR's. During a videotaping session (below), Production Supervisor Jim Paul signals Kaemmerer.

This is the layout of the AT&T AV Center in New York.

Figure 3.4A and 3.4B Continued

managers to expand the medium's use in the mid- to late 1970s. By 1976, more than 70 studios spread across AT&T operations boasted a combined annual output of over 3,000 television projects.[174]

Distributing all of these programs—even at AT&T—remained challenging given the increasingly varied technologies available for that purpose. AT&T distributed videotapes by mail and CCTV, and even circulated 16mm and 8mm kinescopes.[175] However, drawing on Long Lines' experience, the company placed particular emphasis on live networking.[176] By 1967, 195's AV center offered two-way transmission to various locations in the building as well as to New York Tel.'s East 56th Street switching center, where they could connect to the national network (and major New York TV and sound studios for additional production facilities).[177] Ed Block, senior vice president of PR from 1974 to 1986, credited the use of its "nationwide video network" to distribute major policy telecasts as the "one unique Bell System capability" that endeared the medium to operating companies. Given its capacity for two-way interaction via telephone and other means, live network programs were frequently used to stand in for in-person meetings, with some programs featuring multiple two-way video feeds to build camaraderie across receiving locations.[178] Indeed, the inaugural (1967) use of the nationwide television network for a "conference" of Bell System management transmitted a presidential message rallying the troops in the face of an unfavorable rate decision announced the day before by the FCC. Although the CCTV arrangements were made in anticipation of a more favorable outcome, President H. I. Romnes's remarks reframed "bad" news as "significant" news, underlining the crucial role of CCTV: "the argument for having this kind of transcontinental get-together is just as good as it ever was. Closed Circuit television provides a means by which we can promptly develop common understanding on important matters and a common response to them."[179]

The seemingly endless pronouncements of television's value—and the $20 million facilities investment made by AT&T corporate between 1968 and 1980 (an amount that does not include the investments made by operating companies)—may seem to suggest that television seamlessly and successfully worked its way into the daily operations of the company.[180] The reality, however, was not so rosy. While the CCTV group was "pumping a lot of information—presumably useful information—out to the [operating] companies" by the late 1970s, their efforts were marred by a lack of coordination, duplication of effort, redundancy in content, and even a lack of oversight to ensure that programming aligned with policy.[181] Interviews with managers about their perspective on the utility of CCTV revealed ambivalent feelings toward the medium. While a number found television useful, many believed it was overused, leading to decreased effectiveness and too-heavy time demands on the part of viewers.[182] One respondent admitted he never watched CCTV at all.[183] AT&T was not unique in its mismatch between televisual ambitions and reality. For many mediated companies, daily and weekly newscasts remained a common way "to make as much use as possible of expensive videotape equipment and staffs" despite high failure rates and evidence of their unpopularity.[184]

AT&T's emphasis on television also contradicted its own workplace initiatives. Their "motivation to work" program addressed the increasing dissatisfaction experienced by "the people in 'dum-dum' jobs" who, it was feared, would "become increasingly hard to manage."[185] By undoing elements of Taylorism—extreme division of labor, deskilling, circumscribed work processes—and giving workers more responsibility and more holistic duties, the "work itself" was positioned as the key to employee satisfaction. Robert N. Ford, who developed this theory at AT&T, placed his project in direct opposition to media efforts. In the 1969 Presidential Address at the American Association for Public Opinion Research, he argued that "only a profound optimist" could believe in the motivational efficacy of workplace initiatives like CCTV, movies, and house organs.[186] Ironically, the same speech used a televisual metaphor of "program involvement" and preventing "channel turnover" to describe the quality of engagement his project attempted to cultivate: "Am I involved at all in my thinking and feeling with these cowboys and Indians—or whatever—or am I completely passive? . . . the challenge is to add elements to jobs so that employees can get involved, can make up their own 'program' or soap opera for the day."[187]

In brief, although AT&T's television operations received a high level of support across its first two decades, its persistence in the company was never entirely assured. In the face of negative feedback, AT&T created a System Support Group and assigned new leadership to more carefully orchestrate use of the medium company-wide.[188] In establishing television's enduring presence as a critical part of firm operations, AT&T's audiovisual men (and some women) shared the burden of corporate video producers across the country. To support these efforts, workers within corporate television founded the National Industrial Television Association (NITA) in 1970, which merged with a similar West-Coast organization (ITS) to become the International Television Association (ITVA) in 1978.[189] A wealth of publications likewise supported the spread of corporate television. Manuals and trade journals (*Educational and Industrial Television, Training, Video Systems, Video User, Videography*, and eventually *BusinessTV*) provided wide-ranging and explicit guidance on how to found, operate, and sustain support for television.[190] Specialized publishers, particularly Knowledge Industry Publications, Inc. (KIPI), founded by Elliot Minsker, offered self-study programs in video production. KIPI also published one of the well-used

Brush Reports, five book-length volumes of market research compiled by Douglas and Judith Brush designed to help companies adapt television to their operations.[191] Obtaining the support of upper management was often the primary preoccupation of these publications, with "selling" the overwhelming logic that undergirded this process.[192] This work never quite ended for television departments, which needed to "constantly justify [their] existence in terms of the space, capital investment, and the monetary resources [they] require."[193]

At AT&T this justification came in several forms, the most ambitions of which—the "systems approach"—sought to build a media empire into the company's literal foundations.[194] As explained by Lowry, television "must be developed as a complete system; hardware and software, people and programming, design and distribution . . . a complex unit of interconnecting and interdependent parts which requires a single planner and operator with end to end responsibility."[195] Based in metaphors of the nervous system and custodianship, the systems approach sought to consolidate control (as close to the upper echelons of management as possible) and to encourage the growth of increasingly sprawling television operations via logics of extensibility.[196] It reinforced television's status as a tool of logistical control and employee cultivation that expanded alongside the business. As new markets opened up, employee ranks swelled (or shifted, necessitating retraining), and new client bases emerged, television was incorporated in burgeoning visions of corporate communication in an "always and everywhere accessible" model (see Chapter 4) wherein any space—and any audience—could be reached by organizational directives and corporate messaging: "Today, a videotape produced at AT&T can find its way into any number of locations, before all kinds of audiences, edited into any number of other programs."[197] Put otherwise (by Quickstad), rather than operate in the traditional mode of "top-down, one-way" corporate communications, television "was, and is filling some new and immediate employee communications needs which help extend the vision, perception and knowledge of ^employees at all levels ~~of employees~~ . . . and it's doing it from top down, horizontally, bottom up . . . one way and two way."[198]

In a speech to ITVA members on the "philosophy" of AT&T television operations, Lowry reinforces this expansive purview for his department:

> CCTV is the application of television's widest technological capabilities (now or in the future) to my company's broadest communications needs for the purpose of helping the company reach its corporate goals through more efficient communications. This defines Corporate Television as a problem solver, a tool of the business like a computer, telephone or the copy machine.[199]

Demurring, he notes, "[s]uch a broad definition with its implied organizational size might bring a few charges of 'empire building.'" (Of course, his goal.) However, he argues, in order to manage AT&T's telecommunications empire, television needed to operate on the same vast scale and under centralized control. Mobilizing the mission of AT&T, Lowry further legitimated this approach:

> Luckily, such a broad concept of media responsibility is not new to our business. We have long believed in "end to end responsibility" regarding the nationwide telephone network to avoid duplication, insure compatibility and maintain a co-ordinated growth for the best communications service to all. That same principle was applied to this television communications system within the company.[200]

While front-end technological compatibility is taken up elsewhere as a banal means to reduce "costly re-engineering and re-arrangement," here Lowry bends the AT&T motto of "universal service" to the media department's imperial ambitions.[201]

Practically, the systems approach took a number of forms. "Phase one" (the first decade) of AT&T corporate's television strategy built operating companies' production capacities while serving their training and information needs "in every way" possible. By producing content that appealed to operating companies, PR and Employee Communications sought literal buy-in in the form of playback equipment purchases. In turn, operating companies and specialized user departments helped establish the value of TV communications, laying the "groundwork for a broader system yet to come."[202] "Phase two" engaged "a more 'mass media'" approach to content that "formalized" television "into a regularly scheduled, recognized and dependable flow and source of information." Modular programs like *RSVP* provided "greater interchangeability and uniformity in the production, processing and packaging of information" (as with any studio system), and helped generate the large "feed" of programming necessary to warrant an expansive distribution system.[203]

To further secure a future for the medium, television's operatives embedded these distribution systems within work architectures. While companies certainly accommodated cinematic technologies in a range of spaces, television was hardwired into buildings' electronic systems as they were constructed and renovated. Distinguishing television from film, Lowry promoted this approach as the "natural outcome" of television's radical flexibility (a signal that could be "transmitted, recorded, duplicated, translated, retrieved, stored, processed, manipulated" anytime and anywhere) and user-friendliness (programming available at the turn of a dial and a flick of the switch).[204] Locally, AT&T experimented with projects like "conversation areas" that imagined a sort of water cooler effect wherein employees came together not for office gossip and relaxation, but to tune in to the company message:

> These are areas within departmental space made up of four to five chairs, a coffee table, a television set wired to the cable system, a telephone, a rack for company publications and, perhaps, a coffee maker. The cable system will carry several channels of tape, live and/or text information ranging from company stock quotes to live management programs with call-in questions from the phone.[205]

In addition to stitching television into the everyday spaces and practices of individual departments, AT&T pursued the promise of early live CCTV experiments by connecting far-flung operations. The "450 Room," for example, a management-training facility in their Basking Ridge, New Jersey, headquarters, connected via CCTV to their 195 Broadway building in New York City. More formalized than a gathering space, the connected classrooms enabled AT&T to more directly control the flow of information (and spread the knowledge of "distinguished" speakers) between two key facilities and groups of employees.[206] In the late 1970s, television was increasingly incorporated into AT&T buildings—in boardrooms, auditoriums, meeting and conference rooms, classrooms, offices, and even dormitories—and combined with other communication technologies, such as teleconferencing and noise control systems for open spaces.[207]

While interlacing television and infrastructure enabled media workers to position themselves as experts in yet another field of corporate operations, it also opened up space for a new kind of media worker, the communication facilities or A/V consultant. Both titles were used by Hubert Wilke, who founded his own consulting firm in 1965 and eventually worked with dozens of Fortune 500 companies throughout the 1970s and 1980s, including AT&T.[208] Wilke's company, aptly called "Hubert Wilke, Inc.," advised firms on how to best incorporate audiovisuals into their spatial and technological infrastructures. Under the company's purview were spatial plans (room size and height, power and environmental controls, speaker and screen locations), the "visual and aural environment" (seating patterns, screen dimensions, light levels), equipment (slides, filmstrips, film, television, recording and speaker systems, remote control, projection), audio control (speech intelligibility, noise control, voice transmission, audio reproduction), paging and music distribution, television and film studios, electronic distribution, surveillance and electronic security, data transmission and translation for multi-language discussion, and in-house production facilities.[209] For AT&T, Wilke completed dozens of projects, helping to wire boardrooms, classrooms, labs, and even their elaborate shareholders' meetings.[210]

While the extent to which television and its ancillary technologies spurred a reconfiguration of work architectures deserves a longer discussion, television's system possibilities evidently opened up new specialization opportunities for media laborers in the corporate sector. These professionals, in turn, further promoted the establishment of television in the hopes of expanding their own fields of paid employment. In addressing these workers' pursuit of their material interests, we might again consider how the AV sector intensified industries' mediation. Inventing new applications, relentlessly incorporating television into every arm of the corporation, even championing its extension beyond the workday, AV proponents may well have had a measurable role in the transition to "perpetual training" and the dissolution of boundaries demarcating enclosed spheres of institutional authority.[211] Although Gilles Deleuze associates these shifts with computers, the following chapter's discussion of cassettes suggests that television supported corporations' attempts to make temporal and physical limits of work meaningless in the pursuit of appropriating more labor from employees. It is hard to imagine, however, that this goal was top of mind for many AV workers. Rather, this process is perhaps better understood as symptomatic of a workplace system defined by competition and a need to constantly prove one's own value and entrepreneurialism. It is easy to forget that AV workers were often subject to the same post-Fordist employment conditions as those they targeted with television at work.

CONCLUSION

Univac's tapes represent the most aggressively boring video programming I encountered over the course of this project (including an hour-plus equipment check discussed in Chapter 5). While their content continues to be curious, the preceding discussion provides some explanation of their presumed value. Although aesthetically at odds with glittering CCTV extravaganzas that connected workers live across the country, both keyed into ideas about the value of immediacy and its companions, co-presence and speed. These strategies foreshadow the hard turn to "soft" management in the 1980s that focused intently on community feeling, identification, and personal engagement. Further, both fit into an approach to televisual experimentation that scaffolded a new sector of media production onto the existing entertainment industry and made virtues out of technical limitations.

Offering a unique perspective on the early development of corporate television, AT&T possessed characteristics common to early adopters as well as an unusual financial stake in the medium's institutional success. Following AT&T's initial attempts to make television useful beyond the factory hints at two interrelated processes directed largely toward white-collar workers. First, in the 1950s and 1960s, employers were beginning to close the loop between laborer and (media) consumer by reconciling these two positions in a more intimately manageable subject. Increasingly, corporate leadership would attempt to fold pleasure and leisure into the workplace to make employees more tractable and to blur the lines between work and nonwork and thus extend claims over workers' time, attention, and even affection beyond the factory gates (so to speak). Second, the move from ad hoc theater television to in-house television systems built into quotidian workspaces represents an intensification in the proximity and ubiquity of mediated corporate communications, furnishing the technological infrastructure for the former strategy. Corporate networking of the 1960s only intimated what the realization of these desires might look like. "Flexibility" was still measured against commercial broadcasting technology; AT&T boasted of the dynamism of the services they offered to business clients, claiming that though their corporate networks were "small compared to CBS, NBC or ABC . . . there are hundreds of them—hundreds of additional networks stitched into our system, each one subject to change" (swapping, for example, an Atlanta meeting room with a Denver ballroom at a moment's notice).[212] Despite the apparent radical modularity of such systems, they would be no match for what was to come next.

CHAPTER 4

The Other Format Wars: Cartridges, Cassettes, and Making Home Work

Time-Shifting

A 1970 ad (Figure 4.1) for CBS's EVR (Electronic Video Recording) displays three men tucked around a desk just large enough to hold a 16-inch CRT and a bulky cartridge player. A techno-labor triptych, the men on the left and the right face the center, aligning the viewer's attention with the middle figure. We are left gazing at the image on the TV screen: yet another man sitting at a yet another desk, with a figure hovering over him gesturing toward an open briefcase. A dark rectangular box, the briefcase echoes the nominal proportions and position of the TV set in the foreground. A composition worthy of the High Renaissance, the briefcase operates as a second "screen" that anchors the pyramidal looking relations of the two men—and provides the conclusion for a series of sight lines beginning with the foreground figure on the left. If the parallel between television and the more traditional sales tool of the briefcase is unclear, the tag line is less subtle: "Your salesmen might bring in extra business if they spent more time watching TV." The joke, of course, depends on the juxtaposition of businessmen amid the trappings of work with a medium linked to popular entertainment. Rather than back down from television's leisure status, the first line of copy suggests this reputation can be made useful: after all, "[p]eople like to watch television." Another firm, Pepsi, was more explicit in its hopes to channel the appealing qualities of television into corporate skilling: "TV places the learner in a situation that is

Television at Work. Kit Hughes, Oxford University Press (2020) © Oxford University Press.
DOI: 10.1093/oso/9780190855789.001.0001

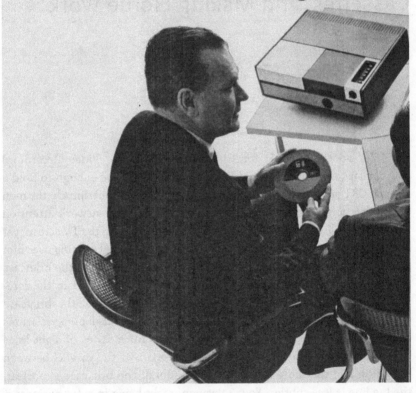

Your salesmen might bring in extra business if they spent more time watching TV.

Figures 4.1A and 4.1B All work and no play? For these three, EVR suggests there's little difference.
Credit: *Business Screen* 31, no. 6 (1970): 16–17.

informal, emotionally comfortable, and familiar—particularly in view of the fact that a trainee has probably spent more hours of his life before a TV set than in a classroom."[1] Television becomes a means to transform the process of training from a discouraging experience into an "almost . . . fun" activity "sensitiv[e] to the feelings of the learner."[2] Yet another industry

Figures 4.1A and 4.1B Continued

professional claimed gleefully, "TV is watching with cookies in bed"—intimate, comfortable, and ever-so-slightly transgressive.[3]

As is clear from the previous chapter, companies had long been interested in mobilizing the resonance of the small screen. However, if CCTV and videotape offered the affective impact (not to mention speed and savings) of television, videocassettes promised all of this at "revolutionary" intensity.[4] For the first time, employers could do more than invoke feelings of home and leisure—they could transform domestic space into a site of exhibition for corporate communications. A far cry from the sort of "time-shifting" hailed as an increase in consumer choice, home viewing materially extended the workday while discursively positioning this labor as near-leisure (fun! comfortable! cookies!) and blurring meaningful distinctions between work and nonwork.

Referred to as "the single development which has most improved the institutional utility of television" the audiovisual cassettes of the 1960s and 1970s proved again that flexible, expansive distribution was as important—if not more—than strong production.[5] In an era of growing workforces and geographic expansion, industry insiders situated cassettes as a means to "reach further into the organization" and "get our information out to more people, more cheaply and with equipment easier to operate than ever before."[6] However, while the utility of portable, easily duplicated media was clear to many, the material form this would take was a matter of intense debate. Almost 15 years before Betamax opened the field of home video in 1975, experiments with moving-image cassettes provided a flashpoint for discussions about the use of small-screen media within industrial and educational contexts.

By looking to technologies that predated consumer video, this chapter intervenes in our understanding of "the" format wars. As it is commonly told, the story begins in 1975 when Sony brought its ½-inch videocassette player—the Betamax—to market with an advertising campaign that promised consumers freedom from the broadcast schedule and antagonized content producers with the threat of decreased control.[7] The rising action occurs in 1977 with JVC's introduction of its competing ½-inch format, the VHS. Besides the loading mechanism, the primary difference between the two machines, which used remarkably similar technologies for scanning, recording, and signal adjustment, was the length of their tapes.[8] Following VHS's entry into the market was a series of volleying price cuts and attempts to extend recording time on both machines. Although Betamax holds pride of place as the format that introduced and made meaningful the practice of time-shifting as an audience behavior, the VHS dominated after a single year of global distribution.[9]

Infamous in media and business history, the battles between Betamax and VHS have been used to demonstrate numerous arguments about media standardization, consumer behavior, and the impact of corporate alliances.[10] The primacy of the home market in these discussions, however, has limited most histories to the aforementioned formats (while contemporaneous analyses of video art and activism often center on Sony's Portapak).[11] When devices such as CBS's Electronic Video Recording (EVR) or Avco's Cartrivision appear in video histories, they often function as an amuse-bouche to the VHS-Betamax main course, a short but entertaining story of failed technologies that draws out the flavors of the central event: successful penetration of videocassettes in the home. Even Frederick Wasser's wide-ranging *Veni, Vidi, Video* describes its six video formats (and their failures) only insofar as they can be understood as home entertainment technologies.[12] Unfortunately, sidestepping the relationship between institutional users and manufacturers shortchanges analysis. In Wasser's case, for example, alternative systems of content production within the business communication sector complicate his claims regarding the crucial role that software played in determining the success of video formats. Even if we take home use as the ultimate goal of manufacturers—though industry and education continued to use VHS throughout the format's lifetime—limiting our analysis to commercial entertainment ignores the extent to which institutional users operated as key intermediaries during experimentation phases of the medium when its features and cultural meanings were under development.

Tracing the earlier standardization battles of the 1960s and early 1970s thus offers insight into how decisions made within one media sector (corporate communications) can impact decisions made in another (home entertainment) as technologies moved between them. Referring to standards as "politics by other means," Janet Abbate argues that standards shape technologies' adoption and use with far-reaching consequences that unevenly affect stakeholders.[13] Attuned to vacillations between hope and anxiety on the collective corporate emotional register, an analysis of the major discussions surrounding the development of cassette technology indicates what technological capabilities industry sought, how they understood their users, and how different actors—manufacturers, professional organizations, corporate users, software suppliers—attempted to make affordances and choices between competing systems meaningful. In tracking these relationships "beneath, beyond, and behind the boxes our media come in," this chapter builds on what Jonathan Sterne terms "format theory" and my own discussions of "threshold formats" as "formats that never reached saturation or even standardization but which occupy pivotal positions within (material and discursive) experiments into how 'old' technologies can be refigured to offer new possibilities and opportunities."[14]

This expansive approach provides insight into otherwise well-known histories, not least of which is Sony's famed marketing campaign for Betamax that sought to make cassettes' time-shifting affordances legible to early adopters with the invitation to "Watch Whatever. Whenever." Advertisements that exhorted viewers to "Make Your Own TV Schedule" and "Add Hours to Your Day" emphasized users' ability to reprogram the flow of network television, exerting greater control over content and the use of their own time.[15] Both popularly and academically, these discourses expanded into paeans to video's ability to "free" audiences from the "tyranny" of network scheduling practices.[16] Some even parroted the language of Sony's ads, positioning the VCR as the "very first video communication medium that allows us to 'take control' of when, where, how, and what to watch on television."[17] More measured analyses pointed out that the "control" promised to viewers was fairly limited. Time-shifting—the key promise of these ads—doesn't result in more diverse programming or greater quantities of amateur production; instead it reinforces the consumer model of television by celebrating expanded choice.[18] What continues to evade critiques of time-shifting-as-empowerment, however, is an acknowledgment of its role in assisting workers (especially the upscale early adopter professional class targeted by these ads) to accommodate employers' increasing demands on their leisure time.

While many of Sony's Betamax ads trumpet the generic value of watching programs scheduled against each other or airing past one's bedtime, some comment explicitly on viewers' temporal demands. One invokes the following scenario: you've watched the first six episodes of a seven-episode series—"Wall Street: A Novel for Television"—only to be called away for a "business dinner" during the climactic last episode ("Alas!"). But fortunately ("lucky thing"), "while you're out going about your business, Betamax is home going about its business of videotaping that TV show, so that you can play it back when you get home."[19] The masculinity of this "you" is signaled by the (presumably fabricated) title of the series and its associations with both economic rationality and literary traditions—as well as an aside that assures the reader that the machine is just as ready to record Game Seven of the World Series. The Betamax thus allows a man working a traditional first-shift job to expand his temporal commmitment to his employer without suffering an unbearable degradation of his leisure time. In other words, television helps lessen the blow of work's encroachment.

Other ads are more subtle in their suggestion that the video's value is its accommodation of work. Alluding to the increasing number of women abandoning daytime television to enter the 9–5 workforce, another ad entreats, "Imagine. Watching the Late Show in the morning. Or a soap opera in the evening. Or Whatever Whenever. What power!"[20] Among other things, this formulation suggests that viewers can become empowered to push against industrial assumptions about gender and viewership by taking up individualized tactics to embed women's stories within the masculinized prestige of prime time. It is important to remember, however, that the temporality of (gendered) labor and that of televisual leisure have always been deeply intertwined. As Nick Browne noted over 20 years ago, "the position of programs in the television schedule reflects and is determined by the work-structured order of the real social world."[21] During much of the network era, this meant women's programming during the day and men's and general-interest programming in evening prime time, with the attendant assumptions about who should be at home and when. The television schedule, in short, helped naturalize "the logic and rhythm of the social order."[22] However, the mass Fordist organization of activity based on a 40-hour work week and a gendered division of labor presumed by this particular televisual mode underwent significant destabilization in the 1970s as more women entered the workforce, unionism faltered, and the seeds of precarity took root.[23] As these shifts became legible, television *once again* supported and accomodated new labor-leisure relations—via videocassettes and time-shifting. Crucially, when the "empowerment" to personalize the temporality of one's own TV viewing experience is read in the context of existing industrial strategies to use television to maximize workers' capacity to labor, the "flexibility" of time-shifting (here, articulated to its ability to accommodate work) seems more aligned with a post-Fordist organization of labor and life than it does with viewer power and choice.

Further, this temporal play can be read in line with a transition toward "immaterial labor"—labor organized to produce immaterial goods including "communication, affective relationships, and knowledges" (e.g., in now-dominant service and information industries).[24] Because this work relies on "the everyday human capacity to communicate, consume, empathize, cognize, and emote," it is characterized by a "boundary-breaching intangibility" that threatens to completely undo any distinction between work and nonwork time.[25] As explained by Paolo Virno,

> What is learned, carried out and consumed in the time outside of labour is then
> utilised in the production of commodities, becomes a part of the use value of
> labour power and is computed as profitable resource. Even the greater "power to
> enjoy" is always on the verge of being turned into labouring task.[26]

Language, learning, memory, reasoning, reflection, relationships—all become corporate resources to be managed. Cassettes doubly reinforced this deconstruction of spatio-temporal boundaries, first by expanding employees' contact with work duties beyond the workday and workplace, and second by engaging workers' "everyday human capacities"—*especially* the so-called "power to enjoy."[27] While pleasure (or otherwise "rewarding" work) and temporal flexibility (especially in the form of autonomy) were pursued *by workers* in the 1970s, these features—as operationalized by employers—ultimately served to increase and intensify labor time.[28]

Tracing videocassettes' continuity with technological precursors, this chapter argues that Sony's promotion of temporal flexibility and empowerment was the culmination of years of experimentation and application wherein the key terms for cartridges and cassettes were not simply "Whatever. Whenever," but "Whenever. Whomever. Wherever." Rather than promise freedom from the broadcast schedule, this triadic promise of perfect flexibility—and power—responded to industrial concerns with employee management in an era when the temporal demands on worker time—due to speed-up, downsizing, and part-time labor—were becoming more complex (whenever), when workforces were becoming more diverse (whomever), and when—through mergers, acquisitions, and globalization—companies were growing more expansive (wherever). Tracing the pursuit of whenever-whomever-wherever as a *management strategy* through a series of three case studies—8mm cartridge projectors (1961–1970s), CBS's EVR (1960–1971), and Sony's U-matic (1961–1980s)—this chapter reveals the limits of technological histories bounded by a single medium and the dangers in substituting single-sector analyses—in video's case, of the home market—for the history of a medium tout court.

LOOPS, SATELLITES, AND SINGLE CONCEPTS: 8MM CARTRIDGES BUILDING THE WHENEVER-WHOMEVER-WHEREVER TRIAD

According to James Lardner, the degree to which educational and industrial users took up the U-matic came as surprise to Sony, which subsequently responded to institutional interests by developing accessories and modifications that addressed their specific needs (e.g., for editing).[29] While advertising suggests that Sony was well aware of the importance of the institutional market, their surprise regarding the level of support for the new technology may have been in part because the company invested little time and resources into market research.[30] Had Sony attended to these spaces—particularly within American markets—they would have noticed the steady, though unwieldy, development of a set of instructional technologies, exhibition practices, and theories of audiovisual learning and skilling that increasingly drew on cartridges. At the center of these experiments was the endless-loop cartridge, which preceded the introduction of the U-matic by almost 10 years.

In 1961, Technicolor introduced the first loop film projector. Neatly encased in a rectangular silver box without visible supply or takeup reels, the seven-pound Technicolor 800 Instant Movie Projector looks like a cross between a slide projector and filmstrip projector. The "800" draws its film from Magi-Cartridges, small plastic cases that house up to four and a half minutes of 8mm film. As in later loop film cartridges, the film is spliced together in a single, continuous loop so that as soon as the film completes its run it is ready to show again—no need for threading or rewinding.[31] Similar in application were a number of reel-rewind systems that stored their film in cassettes. While not as neatly self-contained as loop films, reel-rewind cassettes allowed for rewinding to review specific moments in a film.[32] Although the "800" was silent due to technical limitations, research and development led to sound-capable machines six years later in the form of the "1000" Super-8 film projector. Fairchild, Technicolor's primary competitor in the early years of endless-loop projection, offered a sound rear-projection unit—the Cinephonic—the same year. By 1970, cartridges could hold up to 30 minutes of sound film.[33] While cartridges were marketed to educators and amateurs, business heavily dominated early cartridge purchases.[34] By the time the U-matic was making inroads in the industrial and educational sectors, at least six different companies were in competition for the top spot in the endless-loop market, while six others invested in reel-rewind systems.[35]

Whenever

Evidence suggests that little demand existed for short, cartridge-based films prior to Technicolor's introduction of the "800." It was up to the firm's promotional materials to make the technology's utility legible for institutional users. Foreshadowing Sony's campaign for the Betamax, one of the 800's key selling points was its "whenever" temporal flexibility, which Technicolor linked to good pedagogical practice.

> "Only" 4½ minutes? Technicolor answers it's better that way because it eliminates running 15 minutes or more of film to find the short section you really want to use. This feature may commend itself to classroom use also for its greater flexibility in illustrating a specific part of a lesson. The film's immediate readiness for a second run may well encourage repetition for emphasis. The 4½

minute film run may well prove a better teaching device for many purposes than a longer picture rushed through to fit a time schedule.[36]

This promotional discourse eventually materialized in the "single concept" film.[37] In contrast to conventional 16mm films that covered multiple facets of a broad topic (the solar system), films created for endless-loop projectors contained a single lesson (Saturn), and could be arranged in series (each planet, the sun, the moon). Single concept films' short duration and quick set-up allegedly made them easy to integrate into larger lesson plans designed and orchestrated by the teacher according to their professional expertise.

Proponents of the single concept film for business likewise emphasized its temporal flexibility, hailing its abbreviated length as audiovisual best practice. "Cap" Palmer, founder of corporate film studio Parthenon Pictures, argued that teaching works best in short bursts that give students time to "assimilate," and attributed the length of most training films (20 or 30 minutes) to the "cost and clutter" of 16mm projection:

> To show a 16mm movie, the sales manager has had to locate a projector, find someone who knows how to thread and operate it, reserve a room he can darken, and make miscellaneous other preparations. Having gone to all this trouble, he can't show just two or three minutes of film to one waitress or mechanic or office worker, he has to make the effort worthwhile.[38]

Cartridges allow instead for the easy integration of screening (of precise blocks of essential "gut content") into the rhythms of the workday.[39] In these visions of cartridge films, there is no need to put an entire office or shop floor off their work; instead, any individual needing training on a specific task can screen for themselves a "pamphlet-sized lesson"—as many times as needed.[40]

In addition to teaching workers, single concept became a tool in the mission of "consumer education," where the temporal flexibility of cartridge exhibition was translated into efficiently managing "customers' time."[41] Put another way, shorter films maximized the salesman's opportunity for valuable interaction with their target. Technicolor suggested that the endless-loop function was designed in part to accommodate salesmen who couldn't "afford" the time to rewind a film upon its conclusion when they needed to make a final point to drive their pitch home.[42] The repetitive capabilities of endless-loop cartridges were likewise articulated to the imagined rhythms of sales. One Massachusetts-based company, Cabot Corporation, attributed increased sales of Cab-o-Sil, a fumed silica product, to a selling speed-up enabled by Technicolor "1000" projectors. Cabot suggested the complexity of a new product like Cab-o-Sil required extensive "consumer education," but found its initial methods (a four-hour seminar and a 25-minute 16mm film) inefficient due to "elaborate planning" before each presentation.[43] The company claimed that cartridge projectors enabled them to shrink this preparation period from days and weeks to no time at all. According to Cabot, the resultant "instant meetings" not only allowed them greater control over the pacing of sales by allowing them to set up customer calls wherever and whenever, it reinforced their image as an "aggressive, modern, and well organized" company—no doubt the same impression Cabot hoped to leave with the readers of *Business Screen*, where its effusive praise for cartridges appeared. Whereas educational single concepts positioned the loop as a means to re-watch material for self-directed mastery of content, the repetition built into corporate single concept loops served a desire to repeat the sales performance for as many different viewers as possible, incrementally building an audience that matched the ambitions of expanding industries.[44]

Whomever

A corollary to the temporal precision of single concept films was their ability to target audiences. Although cartridge films could be shown to medium-sized groups in classrooms and boardrooms, they were promoted heavily as a medium of individualized use. Films shown to an entire class could be later reviewed independently, "free[ing] the teacher" from the "burden" of "repetitive demonstration" (and allowing the instructor to accomplish other work), while films "repeat, and repeat again" for the neediest students.[45] Films teaching manual skills (e.g., violin technique) were likewise designed for individualized instruction so that users could follow along with the film as they practiced the demonstrated task.[46] In both instances, cassettes' ease-of-use ("no reels, no sprockets, no threading, no rewinding, no oiling, no cleaning") was central to claims of their adaptability to varied audiences.[47]

Another pedagogical approach using endless-loop films, the "satellite film idea," attested to the perceived value of this flexibility and precision. Developed by Curtis Avery and the E. C. Brown Trust Foundation, the satellite film concept used a mix of 16mm and 8mm films for a modular and extensible approach to teaching. Each set of films included an 8–10 minute "base" film with "built-in launching pads"—points in the base film that could be expanded through the use of 8mm single concept films (the satellites that orbited the base film).[48] A sort of analog hyperlinking, this approach again suggests the role that television played as a ground for experimenting with what we consider computer functionality. By stripping down the base film to general information and allowing users to customize their teaching with orbiting films (including those they made themselves), the system accommodated multiple target audiences, including teachers, students, and parents who wanted to review or preview information with their children at home.[49]

The satellite film's investment in tailored content may have been in part due to the nature of the E. C. Brown Trust Foundation, a nonprofit that sponsored sex education initiatives. Its pilot satellite project comprised a set of films explaining human reproduction. Given the different rates at which children develop, the Trust imagined that satellite films could be used by parents when they felt their children needed them, essentially customizing the audiovisual curriculum to the biological and social needs of each child.[50] While it is unclear to what extent the "satellite film idea" influenced educational cinema practice, this example showcases how proponents imagined cassettes' pinpoint accuracy.

Industry joined educators in the practical development of single concept films as a means to reach targeted, site-specific audiences—including schoolchildren. "Schooled in Safety," a drivers' education program sponsored by American Oil Company, used eight cartridge films to reach "young motorists and potential future customers" in the only location American Oil could reliably reach them, high school.[51] Looking toward internal users, Chrysler sent its dealers cartridge sets for customer screenings of product information and for internal training in sales and service.[52] Rear-projection devices were also popular for point-of-purchase displays at trade shows and in stores.[53] The portability of machines supported promises of targeted use; as one advertisement for the Fairchild Cinephonic Sound Movie Projector boasts, "You simply pick it up and go . . . to the right prospects in the right place."[54]

A substantial site of theorization about projectors' utility, ads also visually underscored this promotion of small, spatially situated audiences. The previously mentioned Cinephonic ad uses a mosaic framework to stitch together a series of individualized viewers across a range of business locales. These tableaus are linked by upward-moving arrows—originating from the salesman's projector-cum-briefcase—that denote the machine's mobility as it "GOES ANYWHERE, SELLS ANYTHING" (Figure 4.2). While the ad's copy further suggests that the Cinephonic can address audiences of up to one hundred members, the accompanying images focus instead on small groups and individuals, emphasizing unique viewers and distinct work

THIS IS A BEST SELLER...

IT GOES ANYWHERE, SELLS ANYTHING on 8mm Sound Motion Pictures

Whether you sell in a show room or board room, you'll find the Cinephonic Repeating Sound Movie Projector to be the best sales assistant your men ever had.

The Cinephonic can show and tell your story at a moment's notice . . . at any point of sale. It weighs just 15 pounds, probably less than your briefcase. You simply pick it up and go . . . to the right prospects in the right place. Show your story to one viewer, a dozen or a hundred at a time.

Cinephonic is complete in its own case, even to its screen. It works at the turn of a knob, shows brilliant movies; plays crisp, vibrant voice and music. Your film, in an automatic cartridge replays thousands of times. You can count your cost in pennies per showing.

Are you preparing a new film, or do you already have a winner? In either case — see and hear the Cinephonic now. See how your story can reach more of the right people in the right place. It can help you to sell more of what you're selling.

For a demonstration in your office, write or call:

FAIRCHILD CAMERA AND INSTRUMENT CORPORATION

580 MIDLAND AVENUE, YONKERS, N.Y. INDUSTRIAL PRODUCTS DIVISION

Figure 4.2 1962 Advertisement for the Fairchild Cinephonic 8mm projector. Only one image features more than a single audience member.
Credit: Business Screen 23, no. 5 (1962): 3.

spaces, a signal of its flexibility to meet diverse needs. Fairchild renewed this strategy in a 1968 ad for the Mark IV and V (Figure 4.3) that features nine vignettes illustrating the projector's deployment on desks and shop floors, as well as in trade show displays, military briefing rooms, and medical facilities.[55] The later ad not only showcases a more expansive set of

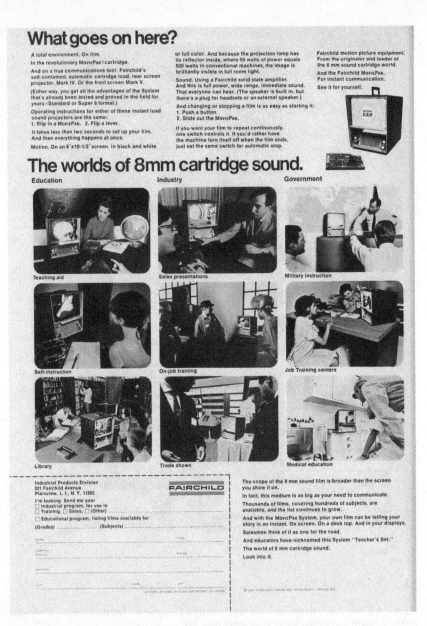

Figure 4.3 Promises of usability for varied audiences (and diverse spaces) remained central to the promotion of later models, evidenced in Fairchild's 1968 ad for their Mark IV and Mark V projectors.
Credit: Business Screen 29, no. 1 (1968): 36.

users and applications, it offers a vision of the projector's colonization of "worlds" not determined by the route of a single salesman, but by the wholesale permanent adoption of the technology by a range of institutions. It is a more ambitious articulation between audience, space, application, and machine flexibility, underlined by an emphasis on diverse screen content that is almost wholly absent from the preceding ad.[56] Combined, both of these ads—and many others—draw on and reinforce pedagogical theories of situated learning and long-standing beliefs about the impact of place and proximity on the effectiveness of sales. Their emphasis on "wherever" is central to their claims of reaching "whomever" most effectively.[57]

Wherever

The flexibility, precision, and targeted audiences described in the preceding became coupled to industrial capital's needs for constantly growing markets and geographic expansion. One of cartridges' primary values thus lay in their ability to render the world—customers, clients, coworkers, and employees—perfectly and permanently accessible to business communications. As noted earlier, projectors' portability was a point of pride in advertisements, which tended to list not the size of the cartridge, but the weight of the machine and whether it could fit nicely in a briefcase.[58] This portability was further reinforced by promotions that contrasted projectors' size with that of filmed subjects (e.g., demonstrations of bulky and expensive-to-ship agricultural equipment).[59] The durability of projectors and cassettes—their ability to "withstand rough riding in the trunk of a salesman's car" and "cop[e] with today's increasingly rugged shipping conditions"—was commonly invoked as a testament to their ease of movement.[60] Notably, in this particular land-and-sea pairing, cartridges span two distinct scales: the local weaving and wending of the traveling salesman and the globe-crossing leaps of a shipping vessel. More mundane were the regular litanies of exhibition locations that assured readers that cartridges could reach "exactly the right spots, from cafeteria to locker room to foreman's cubicle to prospect's desk to machine-side."[61] Foreshadowing video, promoters even suggested the home could be turned into an exhibition space via "Home Study" courses for training after the workday.[62]

This enthusiasm over the colonizing capacities of cartridges built on existing discourses regarding portable film technologies' service to capital and hegemonic geo-political interests.[63] In particular, cartridge machines were represented as devices of international trade. While Europe and the foreign office were common targets of ads' imagined globetrotting, manufacturer MPO likewise touted its device's cooling system for allowing exhibition "in the tropics."[64] Editorials and advertisements discussed the prevalence of silent loop films and extolled the ease of overdubbing, linking the physical portability of the projector to the linguistic flexibility of its content.[65] Optisonics' Mastermatic endless-loop 35mm filmstrip projector—a sibling of 8mm cartridge machines—even separated its image and sound tracks into two separate cartridges that users could switch out "in a wink."[66] Billed as a "multilinguist," the Mastermatic's duel cartridge system addressed both global and highly local audiences (via their own "buzzwords"), offering companies a modular system for fully extensible corporate communication.

In an editorial for *Business Screen*, Ott Coelin touched even more explicitly on the possible role of cartridge machines in global trade.[67] Locating a great need for skilled workers "in under-developed lands of Africa, the Near and Far East," he imagined a second Marshall Plan comprised of "simpler, less costly, and highly effective" cartridge projectors and single concept films to teach foreign office, service, and sales workers. For Coelin, underpinning this international aid is a "wisely-selfish purpose"—the "trade [that] follows basic training." Noting that overseas sales make up "over a generous quarter" of US business, Coelin situated cartridges as a stimulant to this international economy. Though his prognostications were far more ambitious than any activity to come out of the industrial audiovisual sector in the late 1960s and 1970s, they touched on a current of interest in cartridges as a key player in an ongoing and uneven process of international economic development that would eventually be recognized in the popular imagination as globalization.

A seemingly unlikely place to begin the story of the "other" video format wars, 8mm and Super 8 cartridges set the conditions by which video would be taken up by the industrial audiovisual sector. Cartridges promised users the ability to transmit exactly their desired message to a targeted audience whenever they wanted—wherever and whomever that audience might be. Offering new means of distribution and exhibition, the industrial sector promoted cartridges as uniquely portable and effective tools of corporate expansion and efficiency. Salesmen became hyper-mobile distributors of the mediated company message as they drove along their territory, a Technicolor Instant Projector in the trunk. Using new modes of individualized exhibition (or, more accurately, erasing the extensive use of filmstrips that proceeded and accompanied them), films took over desktops, shop floors, and merchandise aisles. Considered in conjunction with discussions of their ability to facilitate communication at a distance—whether with foreign clients or locals speaking their own language—cartridges' power lay in the efficiency promises of greater logistical control using fewer resources.[68]

According to their marketing departments and even some of their users, cartridges also allowed for a level of interactivity with the screen that had never before been possible; various models allowed users to pause, rewind, and even screen in slow motion. Unlike traditional 16mm film projection, the audience had some power to direct the process of projection. This interactivity translated to the industrial setting both in the form of more efficient, individualized instruction and easier, more effective selling to prospects who become perforce involved— and, as the selling logic goes, more invested—in the salesman's pitch. New modes of textuality, e.g., the single concept film, exploited the early limitations of the cartridge, newly valuable spaces of exhibition, and shifting theories of learning and reception. Although cartridges never quite caught on as some predicted (or hoped), they nevertheless offered a productive site for discussions of mediated skilling and selling. Despite the obvious self-interest that motivated Jeorg Agin, the director of Sales Development for Eastman Kodak, to argue that the "Super 8 sound movie is more than a different way of doing the same old thing. It is the beginning of a new concept in communications," when we consider cartridges as the forerunner of videotape cassettes, he may not have been off the mark.[69]

What might be missed in these enthusiastic endorsements of cartridges is the extent to which manufacturers developed a dizzying array of new technologies—cartridges among them—spurred on by an infusion of government money into education via the National Defense Education Act of 1958.[70] Provoked by Cold War fears regarding the national security consequences of the Soviets' scientific supremacy—ostensibly demonstrated by the launch of Sputnik 1 in 1957—the legislation earmarked funds for audiovisual education.[71] The cartridge-load filmstrip, a close companion to Super 8 cartridges, testifies to the somewhat chaotic activity that resulted from manufacturers' attempts to profit from increased investment in education: 38 different machines, with nine different mechanisms for synching sound and image, and four different cartridge formats—only one of which was compatible with more than one machine—graced the market in 1970 alone.[72] Non-standardization for 8mm cartridges likewise remained a significant problem.[73] Given the threat of increased competition and the possible loss of a leadership position if and when their standard won out, manufacturers of Super 8 cartridges saw little benefit in overhauling their products to offer interchangeability. As a result, despite all of the predictions of 8mm cartridges' ability to perfect corporate communications, the tone of those outside of manufacturer circles was often tentative and skeptical. A wide variety of formats would persist into the 1970s, providing an elaborate equipment landscape for video players' debut.

From the perspective of the present, the EVR appears as an interstitial technology occupying a unique position between Super 8 cartridges and videocassettes. Technologically, the device married film with the electronic medium of television. Although EVR cartridges required a custom playback machine, just as any film cartridge might, the deck transformed every television—home or office—into a potential exhibition site. This articulation of cartridge capabilities to the most domestic and user-friendly of technologies intensified its whenever-whomever-wherever claims. Designed by President of CBS Laboratories Peter Goldmark in 1960 as "a visual counterpart of sound reproduction from a long-playing record," the EVR (Electronic Video Recording) used a cartridge to play sound and image embedded on a thin strip of film on "any home television set."[74] Or, it was supposed to. After 11 years of lurching development, two CBS funding rejections, the dissolution of four potential funding and manufacturing partnerships, a cartridge duplication plant beset with mechanical and staffing difficulties, two years of release date push-backs, and only 11 months on the market, CBS abandoned the EVR and its stake in the rapidly intensifying race to invent a small format video player in 1971.[75] Promised longer than it was produced, the EVR nevertheless contributed to ongoing discussions regarding the ideal shape of mediated labor and leisure.

Just as 8mm and Super 8 cartridges emphasized their ease-of-use for diverse audiences, CBS sold the "convenience" of the EVR as a guarantee of the machine's suitability for whomever, wherever. Convenience, in this context, stood for a constellation of attributes: EVR's speedy installation ("use a dime as your screwdriver"), easy operation for non-expert audiovisual users (though its hyped pushbutton control and automatic threading were not as novel as CBS wanted its consumers to believe), portability (just connect "to any conventional television receiver, regardless of its location"), and the planned availability of software ("wherever people shop . . . in public and private libraries, in theatre lobbies, record shops, through cartridge clubs and probably super markets").[76] Although CBS's desire to eventually break into the home market—literally everyone, everywhere—helped shape its user-friendliness, these same attributes were attractive to a corporate communications sector increasingly transferring employee-training responsibilities to workers—whether they learned "on site" or through home study.[77] Likewise, industrial visions of a highly networked workforce in constant communication demanded all parties' full participation in audiovisual media practice. As the 1971 president of the Industrial Audio Visual

Association suggested in a discussion of video cartridges, "Television equipment cannot be the sole preserve of AV specialists at Headquarters if it is to reach its optimum potential as a communications tool as commonplace as the telephone."[78]

The EVR's "wherever" promises borrowed Super 8 cartridges' emphasis on low cost, ease of use, and flexibility. However, CBS publicly compared their invention not to Super 8, the closest technological relative, but to more expensive 16mm and video formats.[79] In so doing, they positioned their device as an "economical" solution to the problem of mass duplication and distribution of corporate audiovisuals across a geographically dispersed workforce.[80] According to an EVR ad, these low costs enabled one early adopter—Equitable Insurance—to equip its 8,000 salesmen "located anywhere in the United States" with the projector.[81] Arthur Brockway's attempts to position the EVR as the standard bearer of the cassette market likewise promoted international hardware and software agreements with the EVR Partnership as a boon to global corporate communications.[82]

Like discussions that attended Super 8 cartridges, the ability of the technology to penetrate diverse spaces fed into larger concerns regarding the value of specialized audiences. Examples hewed close to those proposed for Super 8 (e.g., point-of-purchase "electronic merchandising"), but also included a wider range of home users bound by profession, from surgeons to paper merchants.[83] Optimistic predictions speculated that the EVR might expand media use "into areas untouched by conventional film projection as we know it today."[84] In these neglected and heretofore impenetrable spaces, so the argument went, makers of sponsored media would find new audiences, such as adults working in isolated industrial parks, who would serve as a ready (and captive) audience during breaks and lunch hours.[85] Further, "conceptual packages" built from audience research attempted to generate content a given user would choose to watch "for his own benefit."[86] So great is the potential targeting capacity of the EVR, audiences might voluntarily screen materials for themselves.

The EVR's spatial flexibility was likewise articulated to overcoming an increasingly saturated media environment. Citing the work of Alvin Toffler and management guru Peter Drucker—authors central to concerns over the rapid acceleration of demands on individuals' capacities to acquire information—Thomas Hatcher, president of the audiovisual trade group National Industrial Television Association (NITA), declared to his fellow members, "No longer can we afford to deal with these situations in the traditional manner of moving people to the information . . . we must find an effective way of moving visual information, supported with audio, to the individual, where he wants it, when he needs it."[87] While exhibiting a

Fordist impulse to move the work to the men, rather than move the men to the work, this is no centralized assembly line. Instead, the promise of increasing workers' contact with industrial information arises from the flexibility of media to radically adapt to diverse temporal and spatial conditions. This understanding of EVR becomes explicit in a review of the machine that could have been lifted almost wholesale from a Fairchild or Technicolor press release:

> With EVR, the teacher might integrate educational films more effectively into the smooth flow of his classwork. He could preview and choose. He could stop the program for comment for general discussion. He could schedule lessons at his own discretion, and show his films either to individual students or to large groups simply by linking a single EVR player into as many television sets as he needs.[88]

Much like a Super 8 cartridge, the EVR promised the precise manipulation of audiovisual content, the folding in of media with the rhythms of the (teacher's) workday, and the ability to scale the program to meet the needs of different sized audiences. Ultimately, however, the EVR could make good on one promise 8mm cartridges could not: incorporating the home as a central node in these institutional information networks.

The Home as Privileged Subject of Whenever-Whomever-Wherever

While the EVR's globally expansive capabilities were important to its promotion, the most socially and politically productive work it accomplished was intimately local. Due to its ancillary status relative to television—already a home and workplace technology—the EVR operated as a flashpoint for negotiations between home entertainment and industrial markets. In this context, whenever-whomever-wherever became redefined beyond generalized flexibility. Whenever targeted off-the-clock leisure time; wherever exploited domestic associations with comfort and pleasure; and whomever is not "anyone," but everyone—the mass broadcast audience. By rendering the home accessible to corporate communication projects, the EVR expanded workers' capacity to labor, promising industry a greater ability to colonize previously restricted time, space, and affective relations of their employees.

A scion of the television industry, the EVR saw the home as its rightful place. CBS's decision to market the machine initially to industrial and educational users was pragmatic. Targeting industry first—those with the deepest pockets as well as economic and image-conscious incentives for early adoption of new technologies—enabled manufacturers to turn to the more lucrative home market with an improved and often cheaper device.[89] Furthermore, positioning the device as a tool for the expanding knowledge industry may have enabled CBS president Frank Stanton to persuade network leadership that it would not present a serious threat to the company's broadcast interests.[90] However, rather than reinforce a vision of these markets as distinct, CBS and Goldmark united institutional users and commercial entertainment audiences via the EVR's capacity to provide a single home-work knowledge/information/entertainment interface.

This cultivation of both markets in tandem manifests in manufacturing licensing agreements and discussions regarding EVR software. Despite CBS's ownership of—and brand association with—the device, they never produced the playback equipment. Instead, the broadcast behemoth licensed the design to manufacturers on a royalty basis. CBS's decision to work with Motorola underlines the importance they placed on the industrial market. According to Stanton, CBS chose the equipment manufacturer in part for their leadership in four important product categories: solid state color television, hotel-motel television, hospital communication systems, and educational television.[91] While CBS did not choose a strictly industrial/educational equipment manufacturer (e.g., Fairchild), neither did they choose a company invested only in consumer entertainment products. Furthermore, Motorola's experience in the hospital, hotel, and educational fields became important to the development of EVR software. After initial announcements that Modern Talking Picture Service would transfer corporate-sponsored films and educational titles to the EVR format, Motorola reported that they planned to offer "marketing related groupings of programs" to hospitals, hotels, and public safety outfits.[92] During 1969–1971, Motorola developed software packages for a broadening horizon of institutional users, including universities, retailers, and the American Bankers Association.[93] Motorola's emphasis on these "specialized" (i.e., non-domestic) markets became a hallmark of the device's promotion to the industrial sector.[94] Perhaps unremarkably, the first company to adopt the EVR as a training tool was Motorola itself, which announced software packages covering management, sales, training, and motivation for its distributors in 1970.[95]

Given the key role played by Motorola and early industrial adopters—in the identification of specialized markets, the development of software packages, and the promotion of the machine as an industrial/educational tool—it is easy to overlook the home as CBS's ultimate goal. However, the home market was integral not only to how CBS imagined the significance of their device, but also to how the *industrial* market recognized the potential of the EVR. The perceived value of this home-work interface to institutional interests becomes clear in discussions of EVR software. In a *Business Screen* promotion of the EVR's early success, Brockway celebrated a deal of "strategic importance" reached with 20th Century Fox Films CEO Darryl F. Zanuck to release 1,500 Hollywood features on the new system.[96] While Brockway was no doubt interested in what this would mean for the primacy of the EVR in the emerging home video player market, the CBS executive explained the meaning of the deal to readers of *Business Screen* in terms of what it meant for the EVR's position in standardization battles. Tucking the "Zanuck endorse-ment" into a longer discussion of the "corporate and educational com-munity investment" in the EVR, Brockway implicated the home market in the success of the industrial market, concluding, "for education and business uses in the field of pre-recorded video, EVR will remain the dominant if not only system of choice."[97]

For employers, the ability of domestic video players to move audiovisual training and employee communication into the home, where users could learn at their own pace—and on their own unpaid time—was one of its chief values.[98] For industrial software producers, the opening of the home market to institutional and instructional media was likewise appealing. NITA president Hatcher—a prominent EVR user in his capacity as manager of learning systems at Equitable Life Insurance—clarified the significance of the EVR's dual-market approach in an address given to those filmmakers directly, explaining:

> remember that the users of these company systems are also consumers and, since the consumer market will mostly likely be developed through the insti-tutional market, it may be wise for you to develop a shrewd marketing strategy that will allow you to identify these users and gain access to them. What better way to obtain consumer market demographics on a test basis, so you can have relevant and saleable programming available when the consumer market finally does break open.[99]

Industrial users were often critical of their perceived role as the "guinea pigs" for manufacturers' R&D, which supported the latter party's entry into home markets.[100] However, Hatcher recalibrates distinctions between nominally distinct markets by pointing to possibilities inherent in a larger, mass market for "knowledge industry" goods tied to the *audiences* who span both contexts. Outsized predictions—centering on content like "teaching a five-year-old to read, learning a foreign language and improving a golf swing"—suggested that if the EVR caught on, industrial film producers would experience "demands for product far exceeding anything the industry has ever known"—and the "entertainment giants of Hollywood" would be put on notice that *they* have to "compet[e] for time on the same screen."[101]

At first blush, the likelihood of corporate media producers creating content for the consumer market might seem strange given traditional constructions of the home as a site of leisure (for men). However, EVR software blurred boundaries between work, learning, and entertainment, targeting upscale professionals as they moved in and out of institutional settings. To attract these typical early adopters, CBS selected software that gave home video "the sheen of high culture," particularly in contrast to a broadcast system increasingly characterized as a lowbrow "wasteland."[102] Promotional materials and cultural critics highlighted the possibility of watching ballet, opera, and off-Broadway productions, positioning video as an "instrument for the edification of sophisticated connoisseurs and the self-improvement of status-conscious members of the professional-managerial class."[103] Even in the context of this home "entertainment," loosely didactic EVR software rehearsed discourses of independent learning common to Super 8 cartridges. Further, the "professional-managerial class" that provided the desired demographic of home video adopters was further identified by *Variety* as composed of "doctors, lawyers, teachers, and business leaders."[104] In short, the intended "home users" of the EVR were not just well-off elites; they were a *professional* audience, one composed of workers in key markets for institutional media production.

More strictly "institutional" software likewise established the EVR as a skilling, corporate communications, and entertainment machine as suited to the organization as it was to the home. This is evidenced in one of Motorola's signature software initiatives, "Prescription TV," a "Hospital TV Network," that included 126 cartridges containing "sports, entertainment, enrichment, motivation, training, and education."[105] The first project produced especially for the "network" was an entertainment series created by *Laugh In*'s Rowan and Martin, starring Jack Benny, George Burns, and other comedians in features such as "Exercise . . . It Couldn't Hurt."[106] Later programs included "three of the most exciting motor sports films ever produced," football and fight films, and more staid patient informational programming like "Your Hospital Bill."[107] Motorola marketed its entertainment offerings as a means to prevent male patients from becoming "restless" (and overusing the call button) in the afternoon when soaps and game shows dominated the broadcast schedule.[108] Other

"Prescription TV" programs sought similarly narrowed audiences, albeit for training and education. Specialty shows like "Safety on the Job" and "Patient Feeding" targeted healthcare workers, as did series for surgeons and anesthesiologists.[109] Using hospitals as their entry point, Motorola positioned the EVR as a labor/leisure agnostic before the very audiences who might make up future home consumers.[110]

This strategy continued in another major programming effort targeted at public safety organizations. Initially, programs were geared primarily toward police training (with programs such as "Shoot/Don't Shoot" and series including "Cops and Other Humans"). However, the EVR's capacity for entertainment programming and exhibition— "Imagine how a crowd of young people would respond to this renewed showing of attention and care when a policeman with a Motorola Teleplayer shows a great shorts film at a local store-front community service center"—bolstered the promise of its institutional utility, transforming the EVR from a training mechanism to a public relations tool—for both the police and Motorola.[111] As in the ad that opened this chapter, the value of the EVR comes from its ability to consolidate organizational communications and entertainment, as well as its extension of institutional claims to private subjects' time, attention, and affective orientation to television.

A short-lived device with little in common with the tape-based video systems that dominated in the following decades, the EVR might seem like little more than a technological curiosity. It was one of some dozen machines promised to achieve nearly the same basic thing: affordable and highly portable moving images hooked up to any standard television receiver. For his part, Wasser positions the EVR as the pioneering home video player that first pressed broadcasters, manufacturers, software producers, and critics to consider developing video for the home consumer market.[112] However, we can also read the EVR as a manifestation of negotiations over the relationship between the industrial and home entertainment markets, the blurring of leisure and labor in software development for professionals, and the expansion of industry's claims to workers' time and attention. While other devices were locked into similar debates, the EVR offers a compelling pivot point from Super 8 cartridges to the success of the U-matic given its technological and discursive proximity to film cartridge systems, its position as one of the first devices to catalyze conversations about the value of electronic televisual communication, and its status as a technology that was long promised, and only briefly delivered. This last quality in particular, which meant the EVR was nothing more material than a site of speculation for almost three years, allowed room to develop the needs and desires of the industrial communication sector without worrying about the limits of a functioning device.

SONY'S U-MATIC: "A REVOLUTIONARY NEW MEANS OF COMMUNICATION"

Throughout the 1960s and 1970s, industry chroniclers reported a score of interests that had, at some point, announced plans to enter the video player market.[113] While some used discs, several, like EVR, used the popularity of LP records as a framework for understanding how users might eventually collect and reuse audiovisual software. Still others were inspired by a different audio technology: the compact cassette tape introduced by Phillips in 1962.[114] The majority of proposed systems followed this model, using videotape wound in small plastic cassettes.[115] Of these, the U-matic was the first on the market—a position that helped lead to its success as a veritable institutional standard. Although Sony developed the U-matic in 1969, the machine would not be available to consumers for two more years. Unlike many of its more delicate competitors, the delay was not caused by manufacturing issues. Rather, in the interest of presenting its format as *the* standard in videocassettes, Sony shared the technical specifications for its ¾-inch cassette with Matsushita and its independent subsidiary Japan Victor Company (JVC) in 1970 to build intra-industry support around their format and to offset consumer hesitation to purchase equipment amidst an unsettled market. U-matics went on the market in 1971.[116]

Targeted to an institutional audience comprising business, military, medicine, education, and government interests, the first U-matics were adopted by large firms ranging from Lord & Taylor department stores to Pepsi soft drinks (two companies that featured prominently in advertising).[117] 40,000 machines were sold to institutional users in 1972, with half of that number reaching businesses and educators in the United States and Canada.[118] Claiming a backlog of 70,000 unit orders by 1973, Sony announced plans to double production every year until it reached one million player recorders manufactured by 1975.[119] After a couple of boom years, U-matic was declared the "*de facto* standard among private television users" in 1974.[120] By 1977, the statistically "typical" user of U-matics produced over 20 programs a year for about 10,000 employees distributed across 18 locations for multiple rounds (4–10) of viewing.[121] Use ranged wildly. "The largest video network on the globe" (in 1975) belonged to Ford, which stocked 5,400 U-matics in its dealer showrooms for customer information, sales and service personnel training, and executive news briefs.[122]

Almost a decade after its initial demonstration, a small, but supposedly representative study of corporate television users in the United States revealed that *every* participant used ¾-inch cassettes as some part of their audiovisual program.[123]

Whenever

Although the U-matic's whenever-whomever-wherever claims were overwhelmingly redundant with earlier cartridges, the ¾-inch videocassette—more than any of its twentieth-century counterparts—represented a concrete realization of corporate desires for post-Fordist flexibility in the mediation of work. An efficiency machine, Sony's cassette married the abbreviated temporalities of Super 8 cartridges with the expediency and economy of videotape, a medium marked by fast processing (including erasure and reuse). Even when Motorola promoted the EVR's "rapid distribution of information," boasting, "we can have a videotape made in less than a day," the slippage between tape and film in their comments belies the temporal difference between the two media.[124] While Motorola could create a film quickly, processing time delayed cartridges' distribution to "a little over two weeks."[125] With U-matic, producers could mail finished cassettes within 24 hours of their completion.[126] No one promoted the speed of the U-matic quite like Sony, whose advertisements suggested that their machine's speed saved lives. Although based on a fictional scenario in which a doctor discovers a new treatment for cancer—and records, duplicates, and distributes his success immediately rather than wait for "some future medical convention"—the ad nevertheless estimates a precise jump in survival rates from 30% to 50%.[127] Nonsense science aside, the U-matic "dramatically expedit[ed]" the production and distribution of business audiovisuals, aiding in the reconfiguration of knowledge economies and infrastructures.[128]

The U-matic's temporal efficiency went beyond simply reducing the length of time needed to complete generalized tasks. Paralleling the productivity logics of the detailed division of labor, discourses surrounding the U-matic emphasized the particular qualities of temporal economies based on *whose* time was used and saved. U-matic became a means to save the costly time of experts, borrow the unpaid time of prospects, and adapt to the temporal orientation of contemporary audiences. In an era of rising training costs and "excessive demands" made on the time of internal specialists, U-matic was hailed as an ideal mechanism for cost-effective distribution of expertise.[129] One video proponent even suggested that a professional trainer's annual salary could be pocketed once unsupervised trainees learned to screen material for themselves.[130] Videotapes enabled companies to off-load temporal burdens on customers as well, making "selling time" "more effective."[131] Salesmen claimed that prospects were more likely to spend additional, uninterrupted time with them—"customer exposure time"—when they gave media presentations.[132] Tucking video into longer presentations also enabled salesmen to appeal to the allegedly short attention spans "of most people."[133] This second grouping of the U-matic's "whenever" affordances—inducing customers to relinquish their personal time and replacing the paid time of experts—ultimately made time expenditures more "efficient" by quantifying, differentiating, and redistributing time use based on how directly the company shouldered the "cost" of time spent.

Whomever

Perhaps because U-matic was the first widely adopted video format to materially substantiate many of the claims and promises of videocassettes, its "whomever" affordances were often articulated to specific ongoing shifts in workplace and labor relations, rather than to vague fantasies of reaching everyone, everywhere. Introduced on the cusp of the Equal Employment Opportunity Commission's (EEOC) most active period of workplace reform, the machine offered itself up as a means to quickly and efficiently train minoritized people and women as companies scrambled to reverse discriminatory hiring practices under the threat of federal reprimand. Precipitated by Civil Rights activism in the early 1960s as well as piecemeal stabs at improving the employment landscape for non-white workers at the federal level (by presidential executive order and voluntary "plans for progress" established with large governmental contractors), the Civil Rights Act of 1964 finally banned workplace discrimination in its Title VII, tasking the EEOC with ameliorating historically racist and sexist hiring and promotion practices.[134] However, because the EEOC was given no authority to enforce its findings in workplace discrimination cases, the commission's impact was slow to materialize. Further, due to gradual phase-in and generous loopholes, Title VII only applied to 40% of the workforce as of 1968.[135] Even still, the commission's limited funding and small staff were little match for the 8,856 complaints it received in its first year (a number that would rise to over 71,000 by 1975).[136] How to address complaints was a matter of intense debate, since the letter of the law prohibited considering race in employment decisions—a colorblind approach that would do little to improve existing practices when skills tests, educational requirements, and other practices strategically limited candidate pools.[137] In 1969, President Richard Nixon put disagreement to (temporary) rest when he shepherded what became known as the "Philadelphia Plan" through Congress, a law mandating measurable "target ranges" for government contractors hiring minority workers.[138] That same year, the first substantial appellate decisions took place under the purview of Title VII.[139]

If the late 1960s began to chip away at minority employment discrimination, the same could not be said for sex discrimination. Despite the addition of "sex" to the Civil Rights Act before it passed in 1964, the EEOC explicitly deprioritized sex discrimination in its early years.[140] Further, Order No. 4 (February 1970), which expanded the Philadelphia Plan's quotas and timetables to all businesses, did not include women as a "protected class" until it was revised in December 1971.[141] The reticence of government actors to pursue sex discrimination provoked considerable action from individual women, activist groups, and women's workplace caucuses. Taking the law at its word, tens of thousands of women submitted complaints to the EEOC in its first three years.[142] Due to frustration caused by tepid EEOC response, the National Organization of Women (NOW) was formed in 1966—in part by two EEOC staffers who helped the activist organization shape its strategy for working with and against the government body.[143] The turn of the decade also witnessed the development of women's caucuses—groups of working women organizing within their own workplaces to detail discrimination and push their employers for equitable treatment—that would lay the groundwork for successful class action lawsuits in the early 1970s.[144] By the time Revised Order 4 took effect, feminist activists were well-positioned to take advantage of its expanded protections.

Although Nixon distanced himself from the Philadelphia Plan in his re-election campaign, the EEOC entered its most active phase of enforcement in 1972. Benefiting from added resources and more expansive legal frameworks for fighting workplace discrimination, the EEOC filed 90 antidiscrimination suits in 1973 alone.[145] Drawing up consent decrees with major American employers including AT&T, US Steel, Bethlehem Steel, and major trucking companies, the government secured significant victories via settlements that often required companies to open up positions previously restricted to white men (particularly at higher levels of organizations) and invest in training women and minorities.[146] Although the terms under which the EEOC would finally enforce Title VII were narrower than many wanted—for example, focusing more on white women's attempts to enter the upper echelons of corporate structures than establishing more inclusive work cultures to improve the working conditions of working-class and minority women—the mid-1970s nevertheless transformed the American workplace. By 1980, for example, 25% of minority workers were employed in positions that had been closed to them in 1965.[147] The days of peak EEOC enforcement came to a brutal close under Ronald Reagan, who appointed Clarence Thomas as chair of the EEOC.[148] Cases brought and considered under the EEOC dropped precipitously in the early 1980s, and cases were closed whether they were fully investigated or not.[149] The Justice Department under Reagan likewise considered equal opportunity cases as if the existing guidelines and case law "did not exist."[150] However, despite the department's "energetic conduct opposing affirmative action," previously agreed-upon hiring timetables and goals remained intact through the early 1980s, allowing for some continuation of equal employment efforts.[151]

The fight for employment opportunity coincided with several other workplace shifts of the 1970s. Unions—primarily the province of white males and the strongest voice for collective bargaining over workplace relations—came under harsh attack as business leaders lobbied against union protections and increasingly moved their operations to low-regulation "right to work" and non-union states.[152] This signaled a move away from an employer-employee relationship (for many) negotiated through working-class solidarity to one based more squarely on the pursuit of individual opportunity and protections—a process compounded by the tenor of increasingly narrow affirmative action struggles.[153]

As the American workforce expanded and transformed, so too did the corporate training industry. By the early 1980s, this sector comprised over 325 firms specializing in published training materials, live seminars, and custom training programs. The market for published (film and video) materials alone grew over 300% between 1976 and 1983.[154] Within the industrial film sector, the share of films geared toward training more than doubled between 1969 and 1972, reaching 38% in the latter year.[155] Many of America's largest firms (GE, IBM, AT&T, Sears, JC Penney) also developed their own internal video systems.[156] Although these expenditures represented only a quarter of the of the estimated $3.9 billion 1983 training industry, these numbers would continue to climb as companies attempted to meet equal employment mandates and cut travel costs by using tapes at home rather than pay for off-site seminars.[157] As noted, training programs were a common remedy utilized in the government's equal employment efforts—either in the form of federal grants or in settlement agreements that required employers to devote funds to developing qualified candidate pools of minority and women workers.[158] Major employers including

General Motors, Sears, and American Airlines—all of which were found responsible for employment discrimination by the 1980s—invested heavily in technologically sophisticated training centers and headquarters.[159] Simultaneously, the growth of new employment sectors, especially in information technologies and data processing, introduced jobs that required specialized on-the-job training in continuously evolving skills.[160] (Indeed, one of the U-matic's chief uses was data-processing training; see the UNIVAC tapes of Chapter 3). Training via tape was also positioned as a solution to fields with "naturally high turnover," such as the ballooning service industry.[161] Although the dawn of the 1980s witnessed a shift in emphasis away from concrete skills training toward employee news and morale-building, by 1985, somewhere between $3.5 billion and $4.7 billion were spent on corporate video.[162]

The U-matic's ability to speak directly to the broadening identities of the American workforce was positioned as one of its key advantages. Market researchers and private television champions Douglas and Judith Brush wrote extensively on video's utility as a means to accommodate differences in identity, education, and employment status exacerbated by the geographical spread of institutions and waves of conglomeration uniting diverse industries under a single organization. Describing this scenario to a fictional professional manager, they note:

[In the past,] your work force was probably a fairly uniform group, usually white and male—and, often, poor. Even if they didn't speak the same language, either yours or each other's, they generally lived the same way and shared the same value systems. . . . They all perceived things pretty much the same way.

That was before unions, before government regulations, before consumerism, before EEO and OSHA. It was before TV, space flights, conglomerates, before multinationals, and before Vietnam and Watergate. This was before the events and changes in society that have divided and sub-divided us into myriad little groups, combining and recombining our affiliations and identities, making communications an increasingly complex task.

Today's professional manager, however, will never know more than a small fraction of his organization's employees, and most will never know him. Himself an employee, he is a cog in an organization that may extend several layers above him, many layers below him and to hundreds of locations throughout the country and around the world.

His work force is far from uniform. It now includes women, Blacks, Hispanic Americans, blue-collar workers, technicians, Ph.D.'s, unskilled laborers, clerks, engineers, computer operators, union members, accountants, and professional managers like himself. His language problem is not between nationalities but more often between professions, specialties, age groups, and lifestyles. Furthermore, neither he nor his diverse fellow employees has a single clear-cut identity. They are multi-dimensional people—more than just an audience for job-related communications. . . . They come from different environments, have varying educations and different points of view on many matters. Whatever activity they are pursuing at a given moment, all their other roles and activities influence their perceptions and actions.[163]

The U-matic became a centerpiece of expansive training efforts to corral these differences, establishing homogenous knowledge across heterogeneous workforces via individualized and highly local use.[164] Alluded to earlier, the commercial media industry's contemporaneous turn toward niche audiences (some containing the very same groups targeted by EEO training initiatives) was explicitly invoked elsewhere as a model for corporate communications.[165] Unsurprisingly, for example, television was positioned as particularly suited to younger workers—the "Sesame Street" and "MTV" generations "weaned on media, and as comfortable turning dials as turning pages."[166] Just as cable was beginning to accommodate viewers sidelined by the network era's focus on white middle-class men and families, targeted tape distribution provided a means to deliver "special interest" programming tailored by content and style to niche employee groups.[167]

Video's "whomever" flexibility was also eventually incorporated into downsizing strategies of the 1980s, supporting increased profits by accommodating a "greater emphasis on individual worker productivity."[168] U-matic could "take limited resources (the new lean management staff) and spread them consistently to a large number of people," or cross-train employees "so that fewer people with more skills can do a greater variety of tasks."[169] Video could also aid continuous retraining of workers to meet the shifting demands of post-Fordist production processes like flexible specialization.[170] Television's status as an increasingly mundane household appliance supported corporate fantasies of hyper-efficient, self-guided instruction that could "be used with confidence by almost totally inexperienced personnel."[171] Media managers hopefully suggested that tapes' "'any time, any place' aspect" could even "stimulate voluntary viewing" and facilitate an introspective orientation to self-training wherein individuals willingly diagnosed and overcame their perceived shortcomings through self-screening.[172] As one put it, "It is the ability to control it yourself, that stop and start. That little push of the finger makes all the difference in the world."[173] Delegating training responsibilities to individual U-matic users, this strategy promised audiences ease, convenience, and marginal autonomy in exchange for increased work expectations. Ultimately, workers became the ideal candidates for determining just how to fit mediated communications most efficiently into the wherever and whenever of their labor—whether on the clock or off, at work or at home.

Wherever

Much like the EVR, the U-matic's most radical potential lay in its ability to add the home to its stock of "wherever" distribution sites. Laundry lists of the U-matic's ideal use locations were as expansive as those that came before, including insurance offices, elementary schools, social clubs, tanker fleets, retail stores, assembly lines, bank branches, prison training rooms, and "where Captain Kirk was always talking about going."[174] Put more succinctly: "Video is everywhere."[175] While in the late 1970s portable cassette and monitor systems enabled workers to haul presentation equipment to a variety of locations, by the 1980s, the penetration of consumer units within outside organizations and the home dramatically expanded the possible distribution outlets for video communications, making video as portable as a cassette tape.[176] Industrial participants made sense of this expansiveness—and, eventually, corporate ambitions to colonize the home—through the language of networking.

A messy term, "network" invokes mass media infrastructure, centralized commercial entertainment, and decentralized computer systems.[177] While vague and indiscriminate invocations of networking were common to industrial video discussions, the Brushes defined video networks as five to seven-plus locations served by videocassettes.[178] In a 1974 survey of some 200 firms, 78 reported such networks, with 36% claiming 20 locations (the largest network, IBM, boasted over 900).[179] Just six years later, 83% of respondents claimed networks with a median of 34 locations.[180] Networking language promised radically expanded media distribution and increased efficiency—again based in part on what moves (the tape, information) and what stays put (the player, the viewer).[181] As the Brushes described it, "[t]elevision, like the computer, is going to where the user is instead of the other way around."[182] Looking ahead, video consultants considered the possibility of moving beyond computing as mere model and integrating video access into Local Area Networks: "the mind runs wild. . . . Important company messages seen by *everyone* throughout the plant at *the same time* with no one *having to leave their work stations* . . . dial-up access to libraries of training tapes . . . videoconferencing . . . the potentials are endless."[183] Although this convergence—an intensification of whomever-whenever-wherever—would be first attempted via the satellite systems of the next chapter, networking logics also had more immediate effects.

Growing "networks" supported the proliferation of increasingly complex and geographically dispersed institutions. In particular, cassettes addressed the needs of loosely bound organizational forms by promising a "uniform, cost-effective" method of communication and, more importantly, control within complicated hierarchies and diverse employee bodies.[184] For franchises, banks with branches, and retail stores moving into suburban shopping centers, the U-matic promised to help manage dispersed organizational structures via more consistent (and "personal") communication using fewer resources; this is certainly what endeared the machine to The Manufacturers Life Insurance Company, which contracted independent agencies "in wildly scattered locations": eight countries spanning two continents home to 1,800 field agents.[185] Early users also promoted "connecting up the organization"—producing video reports in the field to inform management—for easier and more efficient surveillance of distributed workers.[186] Networking, in short, enabled video managers to promote their medium as a mechanism to oversee increasingly labyrinthine organizational charts and support geographical expansion and territorial convergence in multi-divisional companies (conveniently ignoring, of course, international differences in color television broadcast standards).[187]

A continuation of the discursive work of the EVR, networking also invoked broadcast television. Cassette distribution provided a mechanism to reach a mass (and later, narrowcast) audience over a national (and later, international) expanse, *with the home as potential access point*.[188] As consumer models of videocassette players found their way into homes in the late 1970s, industry observers broached the possibility of using cassettes to extend the bounds and claims of institutional communication networks by creating "home-office, home-plant and home-school interfaces permitting the (viewer) to take some of his audiovisual work home with him."[189] Expanded home networks built from consumer technologies (both cassettes and computers) were promoted as a means to develop "*new uses and applications* that would be impractical, too costly or simply impossible for the larger, centralized systems to execute."[190] While some positioned the home as a convenient space to reach dispersed field agents, more obviously, sending tapes into the home provided companies the opportunity to extend workers' time devoted to laboring and preparing to labor by moving training outside of the regular workday.[191]

Industry's positioning of labor-based communication and skilling as workers' responsibility to take up during unpaid time and within the domestic sphere represents a form of what Nonay Y. Glazer refers to as "work transfer."[192] Glazer's research on the nursing and retail industries describes how (mostly) women have been asked to take on work previously assigned to a paid employee as part of their domestic and gendered responsibilities—and how changing business architectures (e.g., the use of open-stock floor plans) materially support these shifts.[193] While the gendered dimensions of self-skilling within industry may be somewhat more complex than in Glazer's study, the turn to corporate communications in the home likewise troubles boundaries between labor and leisure, as well as between the workplace and the domestic private sphere.[194] As with the forms of work transfer discussed by Glazer, the demand that workers watch at home and on their own time corresponds to corporate interests in profitable efficiencies; it also serves as a reminder that under capitalism, the valuing of subjects' time is uneven and hierarchically arranged to serve powerful (often institutional) interests.[195] Businesses hoped that by moving into the home and beyond the traditional workday they could secure unpaid labor while continuing to demand high levels of productivity during the increasingly packed workdays that resulted from the lean workforces of the 1980s.[196] Building on earlier practices of distributing management communications in employee lunchrooms and lounges for workers to consume "on their own time," these attempts to exploit agnostic labor-leisure technologies to increase workers' capacity to labor would only expand with the mass adoption of home computing and internet-connected mobile devices. As Sarah Sharma reminds us, these demands were not and are not experienced equally—"bodies are differently valued temporally and made productive for capital."[197] Videotape cassettes provided a locus for these jumbled demands.

Even when viewers were not *at home*, invocation of the domestic viewing experience attempted to harness television's ability to facilitate distinctly *personal* communication between distant parties.[198] While one human resources researcher believed that TV placed the instructor and the student "in direct contact with little distance between them," another company using videotape claimed it was actually *less impersonal* than *in-person visits*.[199] Industry surveys likewise placed video's "personal" quality as one of its strongest advantages—right after instant replay and cost.[200] Many of these more "personal" uses revolve around communication not as training or merchandising, but as building relationships among people and with the firm: an interview with a successful female employee to recruit other women, a president's "motivational welcome" during employee orientation, taped shareholders' meetings to make top brass accessible, or leadership carefully explaining problems affecting the company so "as many employees as possible get the word straight from top management."[201] A hosiery merchandiser for a department store, for example, reported that she sent tapes to branches when she could not attend important meetings in person, claiming that use of audiovisuals makes sure people at the branches "don't feel neglected."[202] Others emphasized the perceived authenticity of television, going so far as to say that the medium's affective resonance was more important than any content:

> due to its acceptance as a believable news medium in the home, video is also
> a believable medium in the corporate environment. Its use is perceived by
> employees and managers alike as a sign of an open climate of communications.
> The act of communicating is frequently more important than the message itself
> and video's innate impact intensifies this effect.[203]

Recalling the EVR advertisement discussed earlier, television offered employers a unique opportunity to deliver the company message to workers in comfort borrowed from their domestic watching habits, entreating workers to understand mediated corporate communications as benevolent, a fun and comforting technology inviting them to participate more fully in the aims of the corporation.

The home as viewing site also provided access to workers' families as expanded audiences for strategic communications campaigns.[204] United Airlines, for example, responded to its 1985 pilots' strike by sending 5,000 cassettes directly to pilots' homes. The tapes attempted to defend the company's position, likely hoping that the domestic context and an audience of dependent loved ones would shape pilots' reception of their anti-strike message.[205] Other uses—sending general update tapes home with executives—were broader in their intended effects ("his family gains a better understanding of his firm and his duties").[206] At-home viewing also hoped take advantage of an environment supposedly more conducive to the reception of corporate messages—where workers were more comfortable and could "concentrate more on the message."[207]

In short, these authors hoped to exploit television's status as an intimate, domestic medium already tied up in many workers' social relationships for affective management, and "to provide cohesion" among increasingly diverse employees and management.[208] Furthermore, for the U-matic and the consumer formats that followed on its heels, the home is one "wherever" that promised a particularly powerful realization of the always-accessible workforce.

Sony likewise stood to benefit from this industrial expansion into the home. When demonstrated for reporters in 1970, the U-matic was presented as a home entertainment technology with the caveat that it would be rolled out first to industry.[209] However, after two years, the consumer market faded from certainty as institutional orders outpaced Sony's production capabilities.[210] Ultimately, Sony's campaign for the U-matic—"Sony. The Proven One!"—staked a leadership claim within standardization battles while solidifying the U-matic as an institutional technology by reproducing the same litany of users in almost every ad: business, industry, education, medicine, government.[211] The home market became confined to occasional asides in marketing materials, as in an ad that wistfully suggests, "Perhaps, some day, there'll be a U-matic in every living room."[212] While this vision appealed to Sony and industrial employers alike, the Betamax ended the U-matic's run at developing home-work interfaces. A miniaturized, ½-inch tape version of the U-matic, Betamax transformed the U-matic into the "commercial model" against which Sony contrasted its new "home model."[213] While this split between U-matic and Betamax muddied when smaller or more diversified companies adopted the cheaper Betamax system, U-matic remained widely used in business well into the 1980s.[214]

CONCLUSION

Although the U-matic was the only format to come close to SMPTE's specifications for standardization, conversations that attended the unwieldy "format wars" precipitating Betamax and VHS illustrated reccurring institutional and business desires. Ideal communication machines were not only themselves cheap, fast, and efficient—they made the company cheaper, faster, and more efficient to run. In part, they accomplished this task by finding new utility in linking work and home. As an incubator for consumer electronics, the workplace became a place where R&D expenditures could be recouped on higher-priced machines, where kinks could be worked out, and where companies could build interest in new technological affordances (e.g., home recording) from the same individuals poised to become the upscale early-adopters of their home consumer models. Cassettes likewise reconfigured domestic exhibition practices and applications to serve employers' interests. Certainly, a big part of the history of "home" video is audiences pushing back against the broadcast schedule, confronting the power of copyright holders, sharing bootlegs, consuming and circulating pornography, participating in guerrilla tape networks, making home movies, and making art. However, if we focus only on how videocassettes empowered audiences, we miss how their flexibility, economy, and ease-of-use also served the needs of capitalism during a key period of national and global industrial expansion. When we think about the institutional and home markets in tandem, "Whatever. Whenever. [Whomever. Wherever.]" is not simply a marketing claim appealing to consumer desire for flexibility in their leisure-time entertainment options, but a continuation of longstanding corporate attempts to make temporal and spatial flexibility profitable. It is also an assurance to employers that they can manage a heterogeneous workforce increasingly defined by difference—in skill, position, education, gender, race, culture, and geography. This is the ultimate corporate fantasy that videocassettes purport to fulfill: at any time, anyone anywhere (or, everyone everywhere) can be incorporated into ever-expanding corporate networks of communication and control.

CHAPTER 5

The People's Network: Soft Management with Satellite Business Television

Narrowcasting

"Office geography matters."[1] So says a 2017 *New York Times* article celebrating the "newest" trend in the reorganization of workspaces. Accompanied by a picture of a Microsoft employee contorted to fit in a soundproof glass and plastic "isolation room" the size of a telephone booth, the article describes a modular approach to workspace design that combines open floor plans with "huddle rooms" and smaller, private spaces for temporary hunkering down. Drawing on long-standing tradition, these experiments pursue increased productivity via an intensification of the speed and proximity of work. Spaces are designed to spur unavoidable run-ins with colleagues—that is, "casual collisions" and "creative clusters" that replace time-wasting email chains—while maintaining opportunities for employees to (take turns to) work in intense concentration.[2] Space is time, is productivity; "It's like increasing the clock speed of a computer. If you rev things up, you should be able to do more."[3] Tucked into discussions of increased "worker well-being" framed as interpersonal connection and choice are statistics on cost-benefits. Moving to flexibly shared workspaces enables employers to decrease overhead spending; whereas the average space occupied per employee was 225 square feet as recent as 2010, with new models of organization, as little as 60 square feet can suffice. Informed by studies in workplace analytics that track workers' physical movements, time spent in meetings, and

Television at Work. Kit Hughes, Oxford University Press (2020) © Oxford University Press.
DOI: 10.1093/oso/9780190855789.001.0001

communication practices, these material environments hope to engender a maximally productive working body at the lowest cost possible.

Although the "geography" of white-collar work addressed in this chapter expands far beyond the cubicle and open floor plan, it draws on similar imaginaries of efficiency and productivity that envision space as a mechanism to manipulate time and interpersonal relationships. Like re-spatializations of the office, satellite business television (BTV) understood the collapse of space as a means to bring workers into productive proximities with the site of work and the moment of labor. While BTV furthered earlier technologies' interest in access, speed, spread, and precision, it sought additional sociocultural productivities. Coming a little over a decade after videotape became a practical reality, BTV intensified breakdowns between labor and leisure. While tapes could bridge the spaces of work and home, satellite programming represented a more perfect union with domestic television content strategies, including cable's approach to niche narrowcasting. While this chapter describes the rise of BTV networks as yet another mechanism for increasing the scale of corporate empire, my focus rests on how companies took up satellite television networks to appeal more intimately to their employees, emphasizing affective and community bonds important to strengthening human infrastructure as a means to paper over worsening working conditions. Through two case studies, I describe how companies used, commented on, and attempted to formally augment satellites' claims to liveness and global (but perfectly targeted) connectivity. I argue that they did this in order to position themselves before their employees as global powerhouses, generous purveyors of information, and concerned employers interested in developing community and shared understanding across corporate hierarchies. At their most ambitious, BTV systems formed part of (neoliberal) capitalist attempts to replace the nation as anchor of worker identity.

These goals were important to companies in the mid-1980s and 1990s—the prime of BTV's short life—when working conditions for most Americans were worsening due to corporate attempts to engineer an economic and ideological climate suited to profit maximization. Diverse strategies, many outlined in the Powell Memorandum, sought to maintain the power of the capitalist class in the face of increasing criticism (and gains) from a wide swath of American citizens. Business was also reacting to a regulatory environment increasingly misaligned with their interests: new pan-industrial regulatory bodies like the Environmental Protection Agency, a Republican presidential administration (Nixon) that supported this regulation contra expectations, and rising inflation (as Mark Blyth points out, "*a class-specific tax*" that hurts capitalists and helps debtors).[4] Written as a confidential letter from Lewis F. Powell, Jr., to the US Chamber of Commerce in 1971, the letter offered a blueprint for re-securing free enterprise hegemony. Business needed to establish its intellectual legitimacy by reshaping university faculties and business school curriculum, gain public support via television panel programs and the popular press, and control the courts by developing a bench of conservative lawyers and intervening in court cases.[5] With particular relevance here, the memo suggested redeploying house organs targeting workers to support free enterprise. Although David Harvey notes that it is difficult to gauge the impact of the Memo, he nevertheless offers an evocative statistic: the Chamber of Commerce swelled from 60,000 member firms in 1972 to about 250,000 firms by the early 1980s.[6] We might also consider the laundry list of organizations founded or re-energized in the 1970s to support the consolidation of corporate power in the ways outlined by the memo: the Business Roundtable (1972), the Heritage Foundation (1973), the American Legislative Exchange Council (1973), Cato Institute (1974), the American Council for Capital Formation (1975), the American Enterprise Institute, the Olin Foundation, the Center for the Study of American Business, the Hoover Institute, the National Bureau of Economic Research, and others.[7]

These Right-leaning organizations' promotion of individualism, personal responsibility, and market solutions were aided by national and global crises that shook faith in prevailing economic policy. In the face of rising oil prices abroad, an energy crisis at home, and rates of inflation and unemployment hitting 30-year highs, Keynesian economics' focus on government intervention and full employment was recast as flawed and unpredictive.[8] An alternative economic orthodoxy, ensconced in the University of Chicago and championed most famously by Milton Freidman, used these crises as an opportunity to redirect focus to monetarist questions of controlling inflation.[9] Buoyed by Freidman's controversial win of the so-called Nobel Prize in economics in 1976, the neoliberal approach—"faith in the wisdom and efficiency of markets, disdain for big government taxation, spending, and regulation, reverence for a globalized world of flexible labor pools, free trade and free-floating capital"—became official government policy in 1979, when Carter's chairman of the US Federal Reserve Bank ignored unemployment concerns to move toward inflation-directed policy.[10] The result was a severe economic recession and double-digit unemployment through the early 1980s.

The abandonment of the goal of full employment in favor of controlling deficits and inflation—by a Democrat president—would have lasting repercussions for US workers. Carter effectively cratered the state's ability to offer meaningful social programs due to his (and subsequent Democrat) administrations' affirmation of the need to tightly control deficits. When Reagan continued Carter's fiscal policy, he shifted presidential rhetoric, swapping out the onerous (obligation and collective sacrifice) for the optimistic (boundless "privatized and personalized" freedom); the state became little more than the enemy of individual liberty.[11] To cover for this repudiation of national society, conservative writers of the early 1990s recommended a turn the local in the form of civic organizations like charter schools, crime watches, and soup kitchens. As observed by Daniel T. Rodgers, "The social contract shrank imaginatively into smaller, more partial contracts: visions of smaller communities of virtue and engagement—if not communities composed simply of one rights-holding self."[12] In this context of weakening social ties and niche affiliations, Reagan destroyed one of the most important anchors of nationwide worker solidarity when he transformed the National Labor Relations Board into a steward of business interests.[13] Combined, these practices created a vacuum of affiliation and care that soft management practices would attempt to exploit.

Globalization compounded the precarious position of American labor. As countries recovered from infrastructural losses of World War II, American industry lost market share to foreign firms. This resulted in increased price competition, exacerbated in the United States by the deregulation of major domestic industries (e.g., the airlines, also the site of Reagan's most dramatic strike-breaking). While provoking cuts to the company balance sheet, globalization also offered firms lucrative opportunities to expand and outsource. Companies went global to avoid protectionist regulation, source cheap labor, weather regional currency fluctuations, speed their reaction times to changing economic conditions, and make up fixed costs no longer covered by the domestic market.[14] Domestically, the rise of institutional investors (e.g., mutual funds)—combined with executive pay newly tied to stock performance—put additional pressure on CEOs to chase short-term stock gains and "shareholder value."[15]

The profit maximization strategies deployed by American business leaders were euphemistically described as "re-engineering." Taking many forms, among the most visible was downsizing—the permanent elimination of staff positions. While once a survival strategy, in the 1980s and 1990s, downsizing was used to increase profits by lowering overhead; it was also a means used by CEOs to make their companies appealing targets for lucrative mergers.[16] Between 1993 and 1995 alone, over nine million people lost their jobs to re-engineering.[17] Deskilling also reshaped labor. Aided by advances in office automation, companies simplified complex jobs into simple discrete tasks. These "rationalized pieces" of work were then offloaded onto low-skill, low-wage American workers (especially women and people of color), cheap outsourced labor, and computers.[18] By 1992, over half of American companies outsourced some part of their business.[19] Duties that were not easily rationalized were recombined, still allowing for the elimination of jobs (and, at times, the elimination of entire management layers). This model was doubly economical for American companies that relocated their low-level domestic workers to cheaper buildings and zip codes. A companion practice, moving to part-time, on-call, and contract work, enabled companies to "treat labor as a variable rather than a fixed cost," reducing their overhead and their accountability to government-mandated employee protections (e.g., retirement minimums) in one fell swoop.[20]

Fewer of the jobs that remained post-re-engineering were what Arne L. Kalleberg calls "good jobs"—those that pay well (with opportunities for future raises), provide sufficient fringe benefits, allow for autonomy in the execution of duties, and give some control over scheduling, employment terms, and termination.[21] Gone was the psychological contract between employer and employee that exchanged job security for hard work and loyalty. Instead, "open employment relations" became the new norm, with workers taking on most of the risk of at-will employment.[22] Furthermore, the decline of trade unionism—due in part to hostile regulation and the massive growth of historically non-union white-collar and service professions—left many with no recourse to push against the precarious position they found themselves in. Even within the field of management, theorists worried over the impact of these changes on worker loyalty, morale, and performance. Citing increasing worker feelings of betrayal, alienation, isolation, fear, self-interest, distrust, anomie, and cynicism, Terrance E. Deal and Allan A. Kennedy blamed the previously described management practices for "destroy[ing] the social fabric of life at work for employees."[23] As these processes continued to intensify into the 1990s and later, job satisfaction trended downward while fears over instability increased.

Complicating the felt impact of these shifts were major changes in workforce demographics. Due to a range of factors—including civil rights employment legislation, women's higher educational achievement, the stagnation of men's wages, and the rise of employment sectors friendly to women—the share of women in the workforce increased dramatically over the last four decades of the twentieth century. Immigrants, older workers, and people of color also found themselves represented more robustly in the American workforce (see Chapter 4). The rise in dual-earner households led some workers to exchange better working conditions and pay for flexibility (e.g., to manage child-care responsibilities).[24] Many employees thus faced the challenges of navigating organizations that were in the throes of often legally mandated cultural shifts wherein companies were tasked with accommodating difference (or, at the very least, refraining from overt discrimination). Tensions around difference were heightened in international companies that sought to leverage local knowledge to support global operations.[25]

MANAGEMENT'S CULTURAL TURN

Faced with an increasingly diverse workforce and fallout over the "degradation of [office] work," business leaders took to pen and paper.[26] The 1980s ushered in the era of the management bestseller—"business bibles" like *Out of the Crisis* and *The New Corporate Cultures: Revitalizing the Workplace after Downsizing, Mergers, and Reengineering*—that promised the secrets of corporate success, often via adjustments in management style rather than material changes in working conditions or pay. Classified by their authors and the Library of Congress as business theory, we might likewise think of them as "a sort of indigenous *cultural* theory"—to borrow a phrase from John Thornton Caldwell.[27] In other words, the now-canonized books that accompanied management transitions of the 1980s and 1990s represent a publicly available, widely disseminated locus of corporate sense-making about labor cultures. These are works of theory that take seriously the proposition that a given firm's employee base forms a distinct cultural community, and that correctly managing worker identity, values, and emotion is *central* to heightened productivity and corporate success. While think tanks, university economics and law departments, and businesses of the 1970s and beyond worked hard to foster a libertarian individualism that could protect their interests against class-based solidarity, companies *also* attempted to redirect workers' affective bonds away from the nation and toward the firm.[28] Ultimately, this "cultural turn" in management theory helps explain the pride of place (and millions of dollars) given BTV in the 1980s and 1990s.

The US American firm's turn to cultural management was often modeled on one of the country's biggest rivals—Japan. *The Art of Japanese Management*, published in 1981, created a vogue for mimicking the Asiatic powerhouse. In a formulation common to the business books of its time, *Art* offered a model of seven "S's." Three "hard-ball" (i.e., Western) targets of managerial efficiency—strategy, structure, and systems—were set against four "soft-ball" (i.e., Japanese) foci—skills, style, staff, and the cumbersome "superordinate goals."[29] While the definitions of these categories can be found in the original, relevant here is the distinction drawn between bureaucratic management focused on impersonal efficiency and an employee-centered program that envisioned workers as human capital to be developed to their full potential. In this latter mode, it becomes *management's* duty to attend to each employee as a "whole human being" with "economic, social, psychological, and spiritual needs."[30] Published in the same year, William Ouchi's *Theory Z* likewise looks to Japan to promote the "subtle and subjective" (human relationships, trust, personality, intimacy) as new bases of strategy and decision-making.[31] A hybrid work, *Theory Z* invokes a once forgotten mid-century entry in American business theory that received renewed attention in the 1980s. In *The Human Side of Enterprise*, Douglas McGregor's "Theory X" and "Theory Y" describe opposing understandings of employee behavior.[32] Theory X assumes that workers are lazy, indifferent, and resistant to change, and thus in need of explicit direction and surveillance. Theory Y draws on Maslow's hierarchy of needs to explain how organizational conditions transform workers into the type posited by Theory X because they are not given the opportunity to address *through their work* higher-level needs such as belonging, status, and self-fulfillment. Filtered through books like *Theory Z*, Theory Y's insistence on decentralized decision-making, participatory management, and "empowerment" became de rigueur in the management literature of the 1980s and 1990s at the same time that Japanese techniques like quality circles—voluntary groups of mostly lower-line workers that suggested improvements on company operations—reached fad status in the States.

Business cultural theory argued that identity and "core values" were management's most effective tools, especially as expansion made direct oversight of employees increasingly difficult. *Built to Last*—a much-heralded study of "visionary companies," several of which used BTV—argued that the "fundamental element" of a visionary company "is a *core* ideology—core values and sense of purpose beyond just making money—that guides and inspires people throughout the organization."[33] By ensuring commitment to the firm's core values through extensive indoctrination, "cult-like" work cultures, and targeted hiring practices focused on "fit," visionary companies could "empower" workers to take up decision-making roles, comfortable in the belief that choices made independently would nevertheless conform to company desires. This was particularly important in the context of globalization.[34] Where spatial and temporal barriers disconnected workers from headquarters and cultural differences threatened worker harmony and shared purpose, strong company values (and the mechanisms for making them "stick") promised control.

These "softer" management methods were a corporate attempt to reconfigure workers' allegiances as part of a larger global political strategy that envisioned identification with the firm as key to profitability, expansion, and ideological support for the purposes of capital. Kenichi Ohmae's *The Borderless World* explicitly championed this redirection when it suggested that firms must "create a system of values shared by company managers around the globe *to replace the glue a nation-based orientation once provided.*"[35] Within these logics, attending to the "whole" worker required companies to usurp the support and sense-making functions previously executed by governmental, familial, and religious institutions.[36] Indeed, the favored 1980s and 1990s models for corporate organization and action were the family, clan, cult, and religion.[37] Crucially, these social formations were not *metaphors* to guide the company, but outright goals for reconstituted social relations. These models demanded commitment, trust, and sacrifice for the greater good; engaged in individuals' identity work; and purported to provide meaning to the lives of individuals. Work became the privileged site of self-actualization.[38] Following Arjun Appadurai and Zygmunt Bauman, who mark an ongoing disarticulation among identities, loyalties, and the state as a feature of globalization and liquid modernity, this chapter proposes BTV as one way in which corporations actively supported and attempted to benefit from this disarticulation.[39]

In the epigraph to their chapter on "Cult-like Cultures," management theorists James C. Collins and Jerry I. Porras choose a telling opening gambit to illustrate successful cultural leadership:

> "Now, I want you to raise your right hand—and remember what we say at Wal-Mart, that a promise we make is a promise we keep—and I want you to repeat after me: From this day forward, I solemnly promise and declare that every time a customer comes within ten feet of me, I will smile, look him in the eye, and greet him. So help me Sam."
>
> —Sam Walton, *to over one hundred thousand Wal-Mart Associates via TV Satellite Link-up, mid-1980s*[40]

For Collins and Porras—as for the field more generally—communication was the linchpin of soft management.[41] Frequent and direct communiques from leadership could supposedly defuse rumors, assuage worker anxiety, enforce preferred interpretations of corporate actions, and maintain esprit de corps in periods of transition.[42] In this epigraph, Walton takes all of two sentences to position himself as God and country, establishing the company as an "imagined community" bounded by rituals and shared values.[43] While a fine illustration of Collins's and Porras's cultish advice, the medium of Walton's address goes unremarked upon. Satellites as such were rarely invoked directly by management theorists. However, many of the marquee firms they praised (Hewlett Packard, IBM) were heavy users of BTV. Further, management gurus the likes of Peter Druker, Tom Peters, and Rosabeth Moss Kanter used BTV to deliver seminars and talks on management theory.[44] Excavating satellites from the margins of management books, this chapter demonstrates how they helped structure Ohmae's "borderless world," a global capitalist efficiency project realized through self-management pressures, communication technologies, and post-national identity projects:

> a network of offices and entrepreneurial individuals, connected to each other by crisscrossing lines of communication rather than lines of authority. . . . What holds this network together is our shared sense of identity, which is supported in turn by our commitment to a shared set of values.[45]

If identity and values provide the affective infrastructure for these communication networks, BTV represents one of its most extensive material manifestations.

In reconfiguring the reach of the corporation beyond national boundaries, satellite BTV operated as a major "scale-making project."[46] Helping corporations imagine the world as a near-endless store of cheap labor and soon-to-be discovered markets made proximate via spatial annihilation, satellites contributed to a new school of cartography invested in deterritorialization. Defined by weakening national borders and the disembedding of local experience, deterritorialization transforms cultural-spatial relationships in ways scholars are still coming to terms with.[47] Appadurai argues that bound nation-states were superseded by disjunctive systems of circulation and power ("scapes") that distribute people, technology, capital, media, and ideologies as needed for the global cultural economy.[48] Michael Hardt and Antonio Negri pose the rise of Empire—a "new global form of sovereignty" that recreates the world as a single boundless, universal space enveloped in its eternal reign—in part, to fully realize the potentialities of capital as a dominant vector of power and control.[49] Writing in 2013—well after satellites promised corporate conquest of outer space—Zygmunt Bauman argued that power has become "truly *extraterritorial*, no longer bound, not even slowed down, by the resistance of space."[50] These formulations share with corporate users of BTV an embrace of a world marked by dramatically shifting social-spatial relations that reconfigured and, at times, intensified existing power structures (whether a phenomenon to be dreaded or fervently wished-for). Supported by the distributive capacities of global media technologies, the process of deterritorialization via BTV drew likewise on existing imperial and colonial strategies that used spectacle—of infrastructural power, unequal looking relations—to lay discursive claims on territories and people as a strategy of scale-making.[51]

Envisioning a world where it could be claimed that "nationality scarcely matters," BTV also extended the work of the global commercial media industries.[52] The technological capabilities of satellites to stretch beyond national borders coincided with a shift to post-national modes of imagining (and desiring) audiences. In the United States, the multichannel transition— marked by Amanda Lotz as beginning in the mid-1980s—witnessed the proliferation of cable, VHS, and satellite programming and a consequent fragmentation of the national audience across these varied outlets. This fragmentation was likewise supported by advertisers and media producers who increasingly recognized the value in carving out niche audiences to match the rise of post-Fordist modes of production and product differentiation within the consumer goods industries. The televisual form that arose from these shifts, *narrowcasting*, turned to what Michael Curtin refers to as "edge," a distinction strategy based in narrative, aesthetic, or representational appeals to niche audiences united on one or more vectors of identity and taste.[53] This shift to narrowcasting was further exacerbated by an acceleration in media companies' global ambitions. Television workers charged with buying and selling programs in the global marketplace used professional understandings of demographics, psychographics, and meaningful audience differences to help create "post-national imagined communities" connected along alternate lines of affinity and cultural proximity.[54]

While others have explored the implications of a commercial media landscape attuned to these geo-linguistic and geo-cultural identities, BTV—as an example of narrowcasting—represents an opportunity to examine how some of the country's most powerful companies *directly* engaged in edge and distinction, ideological and symbolic management, and post-national identity work in the 1980s and 1990s.[55] This is the other side of the story of the multichannel era: the creative deployment of *employees* as niche audience. Put another way, at the same time that post-national consumer identities became lucrative as a means of gathering and selling audiences on the diverse products of flexible specialization, proper cultural management of worker identity in-house (but not at home) supported profit-maximization strategies based in cuts to employees' material welfare.

FOUNDATIONS

Most academic analyses of satellites focus on commercial entertainment industries and audiences within national and globalized media landscapes. Scholars have traced (or registered their own) hopes and concerns regarding satellites' capabilities to distribute cultural resources across national borders, to "undermine twentieth-century sovereignties and their attendant social relationships and cultural and ethnic identities," to establish difference and distance, to fragment audiences, and to shape international relations.[56] Others have taken up questions of policy and law to mark how satellite technology has been constrained along established lines of power, to map the consequences of utopian rhetoric in the development of satellite and cable policy in the United States, and to predict future policy needs with the coming of technological competitors, such as fiber optics.[57] Still others have mapped related issues of competition, technological development, and ownership in the multichannel era and earlier.[58] Within cultural studies, researchers have asked after the relationship between satellites and viewer "mobility," as well as the place of the satellite dish as an object embedded in British taste hierarchies.[59] The most in-depth cultural treatment of the satellite comes from Lisa Parks, whose book *Cultures in Orbit* argues that accounting for satellites demands that we reconfigure and expand our understandings of the televisual itself.[60] Parks's book lays the groundwork for my analysis of business satellite television.

Most visible as a distribution mechanism for audiovisual programming to national publics and paid subscribers, the active field of satellite applications is much wider. Data applications include the distribution of market information to stockbrokers, client transaction information (car rentals, credit card verifications), and client records.[61] Never quite shedding the connection to their militaristic roots, satellites continue to be used for reconnaissance and information gathering, as well as many other "remote viewing" operations (many with commercial applications) in meteorology, hydrology and oceanography, agriculture, geography, and geology.[62] satellites also distribute voice signals, aid navigation through global positioning systems, send distress signals, and offer early warning systems in the case of catastrophe. And, as explored in this chapter, satellites formed the backbone of private television networks interconnecting business offices, distributing content to manage the identities, aspirations, and affiliations of white-collar workers. However, before even the largest companies adopted BTV in the mid- to late 1980s, experiments across educational, governmental, and international organizations established satellites' border-spanning ability to distribute resources and develop the faculties of its audiences.

The US response to the launch of Sputnik in October 1957 cemented satellites' links to global power and prestige. Although analyses of public opinion cast doubt on most Americans' concerns over the threat of Soviet scientific and technological supremacy, Sputnik unsettled Washington.[63] The Soviets' successful launch of Sputnik II (containing the doomed space dog Laika) and the United States' failure to reach orbit by the end of 1957 further stoked the concern of US government officials regarding the nation's status as "the laughing-stock of the whole Free World."[64] Establishing spatial supremacy as a Cold War battleground, the United States poured resources into the founding of NASA, the creation of political positions and a new State Department, and major science and education initiatives.[65] Eventually, the United States successfully launched Explorer 1, in February 1958. In the ensuing decade, satellites became inextricably linked to national, global, and interplanetary power.

Governmental projects established the globe as the natural scale of satellite communications. The International Geophysical Year (1957–1958) brought together 67 countries in a collaborative effort to collect data relating to several interrelated scientific fields. UNESCO and others quickly recognized satellites as an international phenomenon due to their vast infrastructures and questions of policy that arose given satellites' capabilities for (potentially unwanted) border-crossing distribution.[66] As one author warned—foreshadowing the intentions of 1980s business bibles—satellites "might penetrate or undermine twentieth-century sovereignties and their attendant social relationships and cultural and ethnic identities."[67] The United States Information Agency (USIA) followed this thread when promoting Worldnet's ability to "mak[e] the global village a reality."[68] Launched in 1983, the live satellite television service operated in the tradition of Voice of America, seeking "foreign publics" in Africa, Europe, and the Middle East with content that promoted "greater global understanding" of "the real America."[69] Cheerleading their Cold War propaganda project, USIA insisted, "satellites recognize no national borders. . . . Satellites have indeed made the world a smaller place."[70] Arthur C. Clarke, the science fiction author credited with predicting geosynchronous orbit, suggested even more vividly the end of geography (in part, quoting himself), "'What we are building now is the nervous system of mankind. . . . The communications network, of which the satellites will be nodal points, will enable the consciousness of our grandchildren to flicker like lightning back and forth across the face of this planet' . . . the conquest of space will be complete."[71]

In education, satellites transformed global populations into audiences for knowledge projects. Early targets were isolated or otherwise "communications poor" communities (Alaska, Appalachia, the Rocky Mountains, and Hawaii in the United States; rural villages and poor classrooms in India and

Brazil).[72] Designed for varied publics (schoolchildren, workers, families, medical and educational professionals), satellites distributed programs on science, health, agriculture, public affairs, literacy and foreign languages, religious and cultural programming, professional training, homemaking, and entertainment. Despite being billed as educational, many early experiments also focused on unemployment and worker shortages, e.g., "education for work."[73] Satellites' reach became *the key in making specialized resources from many places available wherever they are needed.*[74] They provided the individual educator with superhuman powers to work at a global scale, functioning as "an Aladdin's lamp through which he can command resources from over the entire globe. At long last, the teacher will be able to say: 'The world is my classroom.'"[75] The Orientalist overtones of this formulation lay bare the extent to which, even in the context of educational initiatives, satellites' colonizing capabilities nipped at the heels of giddy proclamations of their power.

Although satellite technologies required considerable up-front investment, efficiencies in resource distribution, notably qualified labor, promised eventual savings.[76] While often cloaked in the high-minded rhetoric of serving citizenries, an educational economist translated these discussions into the language of the market:

> Education is a "labor-intensive" industry, using large amounts of high-level, high-cost manpower. In competing with less labor-intensive industries whose efficiency and labor productivity are steadily rising, education will continue to lose the race, badly, until it does more to improve its own efficiency and the productivity of the human talents it employs.[77]

Glossing over systemic problems regarding states' willingness to devote adequate funding to the development of their citizenry, it is this particular emphasis on workforce efficiencies—surrounded by a foggy accounting for the factors that *create* these conditions—that returns in corporate promotions of the medium.

For Business

NASA indicated as early as 1959 that it hoped to lay the groundwork for a commercial system.[78] In 1962, Congress enacted the Communications Satellite Act, creating COMSAT (Communications Satellite Corporation), a partnership between common carriers (AT&T, ITT, RCA, Western Union), public stockholders, and the government, charged with overseeing the establishment of this commercial system.[79] Comsat General (a COMSAT subsidiary), IBM, and Aetna Life and Casualty partnered in 1975 to develop and operate the first satellite system targeted toward business users. Under the aegis of Satellite Business Systems, the group launched its first satellite in 1980 with the hopes of appealing to users with voice and data transmission as well as videoconferencing. Several of BTV's first users were in the resource-rich, temporally stingy finance industry. Aetna Life and Casualty began working with NASA to develop satellite systems for point-to-multipoint narrowcasting and point-to-point videoconferencing on a test basis in 1978.[80] They were quickly joined by Merrill Lynch, MONY Financial Services, Chase Manhattan Bank, and Empire of America Federal Savings Bank.[81] Other early adopters included automotive and tech companies like Chysler, Ford, General Motors, Hewlett-Packard, and Texas Instruments. Despite this early entry of Fortune 100 companies, as late as 1985, the vice president of corporate development for COMSAT bemoaned, "the only people making any money on teleconferencing are the people writing about it."[82] Eventually, however, the increased availability of Ku-band satellites—which transmitted to smaller, cheaper VSATs (very small aperture terminals, or two-way dish antennas)—made BTV accessible to more users.[83] Ad hoc special events—often a test run for companies considering in-house systems—topped 600 in 1986. By 1988, over 50 companies boasted permanent systems (some 75% of which were installed in the previous two years), accounting for more than 10,000 satellite dishes strewn across the country—and, increasingly, internationally.[84] Programming—mostly live and in-house—served varied purposes similar to CCTV and cassettes before them (product introductions, employee newsletters, up-to-date market and regulatory information, interactive communication across employee hierarchies). Satellites were also pulled into a booming business theater industry—live, often multimedia stage productions for employees, some of which licensed acclaimed business bibles to serve familiar aims of group identification, motivation, recognition, and taking the "edge" off unsavory news.[85] However, increased training needs were cited as the primary factor shaping satellite video adoption and use in the late 1980s and early 1990s—estimated to represent as much as 75% to 90% of all BTV use.[86]

The other major driver of BTV was an interest within companies using satellite data systems to increase their functionality and "operational value."[87] Data-driven systems—for credit card verification, inventory control, price verification, and stock quotes—represented the largest segment of the business satellite industry by 1991.[88] They were especially prevalent in retail chains, many of which sought additional network capabilities including in-store music and ad distribution; BTV for training and corporate communications; and even screening the short-lived Turner Broadcasting Systems Checkout Channel for customers.[89] Corporate orthodoxies of efficiency maximization—"economizing" by doubling up services—sometimes overshadowed existing needs. As the director of systems at Copps grocery stores noted, "We've got the video feeds in and we've got TVs in each store. Now it's just the matter of us sitting down and working out the program."[90] Under these conditions, private satellite use grew to over 150 private company systems in 1992.[91] The private satellite market was estimated at $1.4 billion in 1994 and (overly optimistically) was expected to hit $2.7 billion in 2001.[92] The US market dominated globally, though the early 1990s saw significant adoption rates in Europe and Canada.[93]

A number of different BTV models waxed and waned in popularity. In the early 1980s, hotels and packagers served corporate clients on an ad hoc basis. Holiday Inn, Hilton, Hyatt, Sheraton, Intercontinental, and Marriott all offered BTV and videoconferencing facilities in attempts to appeal to business users, who might use their facilities for events similar to the CCTV productions of Chapter 3.[94] Blue chip companies—early users of hotel facilities—began moving in-house in 1982–1983.[95] Hotel and packaging services recalibrated to appeal to smaller companies and to offer additional screening locations for large special event broadcasts like Coca-Cola's 100th "birthday" celebration, which crossed six continents and connected 15,000 Atlanta headquarters employees with celebrations in London, Tokyo, Nairobi, Rio de Janeiro, and Sydney.[96] While companies' private BTV networks often targeted their own members (using scramblers to encode signals), some, like Kodak and John Hancock Mutual Life, used satellites to engage customers and other publics with educational and informational programs at universities and other locations.[97] Companies might also lease satellite time to other companies, sell ad space in their internal programming, share programming across networks for cross-industry communications, or use their networks to deliver promotional materials and packaged stories ("video news releases" or VNRs) to the press and other "influencers."[98]

Not all BTV called a single corporation home. Special interest networks—both subscription-based and pay-per-view—sought wider (but still narrowcast) audiences. Supported by rising VSAT adoption at American workplaces, these inter-firm, intra-professional networks carved out their audiences like any cable channel of the multichannel transition. The American Hospital Association and the Institute of Electrical & Electronics Engineers were the first organizations to boast their own narrowcast networks (1982). The next few years saw the founding of additional offerings both commercial and nonprofit, including the American Law Network (ALN), the Satellite Education Network (insurance industry), and the Food Business Network.[99] By the end of 1986, 11 networks offered special-interest programming; by late 1987, this number would reach 27 (and then fall to 15 the year after—this number was volatile, with networks shuttering, reopening, and even moving to cable).[100] In 1988, six channels offered regularly scheduled programming on a subscription basis (from a semester to two years), while nine operated on a pay-per-view basis, offering viewers anywhere from two to 68 programs per year.[101] Channels like the Financial Satellite Network (FSN) spanned national borders to narrowly target audiences united by a job title—securities traders willing to pay $1,300/month for "motivational seminars," sales training, and market trend information.[102] Pay-per-view channels—often sponsored by professional organizations—offered somewhat broader programming (best practices, new regulations, news) targeting an entire industry.[103] Unlike single-company BTV systems, which established the internal audience as an emotionally bonded unit, special interest networks created knowledge communities built on broad-based professional or guild identities. Both, however, were indebted to a logic of narrowcasting and edge that envisioned labor as a key vector of connection and distinction.[104]

SELLING THE SYSTEM

As re-engineering reduced management layers and spread responsibility for corporate decision-making, worker oversight became increasingly difficult. Satellites' space-binding capabilities realized long-standing fantasies of a mediated "command center" that could contain unwieldy corporate operations amidst shifting global market conditions.[105] In newspapers and trade journals—including *BusinessTV*, the self-proclaimed "TV Guide" for BTV—satellites promised "ubiquitous" communications "available literally everywhere," from "Quiet Creek and Cricket Chirp America" to far-flung international metropolises.[106] BTV testimonials gushed over the value of this ubiquity—to "leverage the skills of fewer and fewer experts over broader and broader audiences" or to overcome language barriers in global manufacturing operations with visual instruction.[107] One of the oft-repeated success stories of satellites' spatial conquests told the tale of increased profits via localization. JC Penney—department store and early investor in satellite systems—installed a hybrid voice/data/video network to demonstrate new products to its stores nationwide.[108] Prior to the system, stores were divided into four regions, with every store in a given region selling the same products in the same quantities. BTV, however, enabled local buyers to shape their stock according to their patrons' tastes and pocketbooks; reportedly the company saved over $7 million in travel expenses, product samples, and product markdowns in the first year.[109] While these capabilities were particularly important to geographically dispersed companies—multinationals, franchises, those with mobile vehicle fleets—they also appealed to companies cutting travel due to global threats like the Gulf War.[110] The celebration of satellites' global reach was matched only by fervor over their "targeting precision," which promised "complete control" over audience composition.[111] IBM, for example, was hailed for its three distinct "networks," each of which distributed narrow content to carefully curated internal and external audiences.[112] Direct, simultaneous communication *across* employee hierarchies also promised tighter coordination for companies with increasingly murky lines of command and communication.[113]

Creative accounting positioned BTV as economical—compared to the travel expenses and productivity losses of in-person communications.[114] Satellite technology appealed to corporate accountants due to its distance insensitivity; VSAT purchases aside, it cost the same to transmit programming next door as it did to a remote island 500 miles away (provided both were within the same satellite's footprint).[115] Furthermore, on a one-off basis, the cost of an average 30- or 60-minute live BTV program compared favorably to formal video production and tape duplication and distribution.[116] The economic value of BTV was also reckoned in the same currency of immediacy articulated to CCTV meetings. Among other things, the constant hum of corporate communications connecting workers and the firm was credited with speeding product introductions, responding immediately to changing market conditions, raising capital faster, updating workers' specialized knowledge, and making the most efficient use of workers' time on the clock.[117] Because many live satellite programs incorporated question-and-answer sessions (via telephone), misunderstandings and unexpected questions could be resolved immediately; one Kodak representative boasted taking "as many as 100 questions" in a single 2-hour show.[118] Satellites also became a primary medium of crisis communications. Johnson & Johnson's response to the 1982 Tylenol scare—when bottles of their pain reliever were spiked with fatal doses of cyanide—became a textbook case for how satellites could be used to quickly distribute VNRs to the press as an emergency unfolded.[119] In the language of business, satellites' high-speed, globetrotting, scale-making capabilities were routinely marketed as the "competitive edge" that increased productivity and gave their users an advantage.[120]

The most suggestive appeals to satellites' value, however, reformulated this "edge" along the lines imagined by Curtin and management theorists: as a mechanism to draw boundaries around homogenous audience groups linked by identity, values and shared purpose. Narrowcast "events" that provided employees the opportunity to "interact as a corporation" were promoted as the path to unity and, more ambitiously, "a sense of oneness" between field workers and the firm.[121] The feelings of belonging "create[d] and cement[ed]" by BTV translated to "winning understanding for (and contribution to) management decisions, identification with the company, and establishing a cohesive attitude with respect to economic and social issues."[122] BTV was also praised for lending credibility to management communications, acting as a visual "polygraph" that testified to executives' honesty and ability to deliver the trust-building "straight talk" so important within management circles.[123] Described as the corporate sector's "fireside chats," BTV communiqués represented "the personal side of office automation . . . the power of presence."[124] The glamour and glitz of satellites likewise attempted to build morale and "inspire" greater productivity via entertainment that reaffirmed corporate culture.[125] Workers were engaged directly via employee recognition segments and opportunities to "star" in satellite programs to generate excitement and reinforce an understanding of BTV as a service by and for employees.[126] These widely shared aspirations for BTV—to reinforce a sense of corporate community and reposition the firm as central to workers' self-actualization and self-governance—stretch to their full conclusion in Domino's Pizza's suggestive sobriquet for their BTV system: "the people's network."[127]

BTV was particularly praised for handling moments when the category of "the people" was under transformation due to re-engineering and demographic shifts (see Chapter 4).[128] Studies of workplace change suggested that managers could "smooth" these processes by providing workers with timely information to shore up sense-making (the guiding corporate "vision") of the new situation, by lending emotional support for the "survivors" of downsizing, and by distributing explicit educational material on topics like stress management.[129] "Candid, companywide" BTV Q&A sessions, which allowed workers to voice their concerns and ask questions of management, ostensibly gave workers a sense of personal involvement in changes and allowed executives to position themselves as empathetic leaders.[130] As an anonymous executive put it: "You get to be seen as a person who understands what's happening, who is cognizant of feelings, who doesn't have all the answers but is willing to listen and learn, and who has a vision so that others will say, 'I'll work for that guy for a few months and see how it goes.'"[131] Federal Express's acquisition of rival Flying Tiger

Line became a favored case study in timely "straight talk": "Less than two hours after the Dow Jones wire service announced the merger, FedEx Chairman Fred Smith and Chief Operating Officer Jim Barksdale gave an unscripted, unrehearsed address over the company's satellite television network—FXTV—to 35,000 employees in 800 locations."[132] Using terms like "merger" instead of "acquisition," speakers attempted to maintain worker loyalty by suggesting that FedEx "really did want" the former Flying Tigers on their "team."[133] Daily television broadcasts following the merger targeted employee trust and feelings of involvement: "questions and answers traveled back and forth, up and down the organization."[134] Successful change communications were to operate as "a steady hum, 'white noise'" that constantly reassures workers that management *cares* and knows what it's doing.[135] Ultimately, while the speed and reach of satellites were indeed central to global logistics applications, their perceived strategic value lay in the ability to bend massive infrastructures toward the softer management goals of the 1980s and 1990s.

Narrowcasting's Expanded Cultural Project

As noted, this corporate emphasis on identity management coincided with a larger shift toward narrowcasting within the media, advertising, and consumer goods industries. In the face of post-Fordist production methods that increased consumer choice, new outlets for differentiated media content (e.g., cable), rising income inequality that punctured advertiser interest in broad middle-class consumers, and increasingly sophisticated and granular means of dividing and aggregating consumer groups, media firms became interested in creating what Joseph Turow calls "image tribes"—"gated communities" of narrow, homogeneous groups linked by demographics and lifestyle.[136] While target marketing held roots in earlier practices (e.g., day-part programming for women listeners), commercial satellites—due to the reach and precision championed earlier—intensified media firms' ability to gather physically scattered individuals aligned with increasingly narrow categories (e.g., young, urban, professional white women interested in theater and high fashion) into groups large enough to sell to advertisers. Media firms pitched the value of these smaller groups by claiming a "special relationship" with audiences that translated into heightened consumer loyalty, and by asserting "efficient separation" of advertisers' target audiences from undesirable viewers, leading to zero waste circulation.[137] To make viewers feel like "part of a family," media firms purchased and produced content that appealed intimately to their chosen demographics on the basis of identity, shared concerns, and personal beliefs (strategically alienating everyone else).[138] Special interest programming was also seen as a solution to threatening *employment* shifts—the rise of "career" working women, dual-earner households, and intensifying work demands on employees' leisure hours—that meant "desirable" viewers spent less time watching television.[139]

In transforming the shape and nature of the commodity audience, narrowcasting sought to "maximize the system's potential for selling," whatever the social and political fallout.[140] Highly critical of narrowcasting, Turow argues that audience fragmentation damages peoples' ability to recognize themselves as citizens, members of a *diverse* national community who bear the shared responsibility of self-governance. When relationship marketers "surroun[d] individuals with mirrors of themselves, their values, and their activities," they in effect "emphasiz[e] to their targets a world that [begins] and [ends] with their personal needs."[141] Confrontation with discomfort and (political, ideological, cultural, economic) difference becomes increasingly rare as a function of the sorting strategies of narrowcasting. Others argue that narrowcasting functions as a release valve for hegemonic representational practices within mainstream broadcasting. By offloading programs that feature minority concerns onto cable (where they can be easily ignored by non-minority viewers), the televisual system as a whole can claim to serve diverse constituencies while reinforcing a center-marginal model. Further, the financial goals and constraints of cultural narrowcasting result in channels like BET (Black Entertainment Television) that *still* serve only the economically desirable members of its target group while—in BET's case—erasing meaningful differences within blackness.[142] Last, while narrowcasting may link audiences via race or gender, for example, its ultimate goal is not cultural connection, but viewer perception of "belonging *within particular consumer categories*."[143] The hoped-for primacy of this mode of self-recognition is troublesome, especially when considered within a larger cultural context that encourages people and groups to imagine their (and others') public standing as indexed to their legibility as markets.[144]

The purveyors of BTV pitched themselves on the very same bases of loyalty, family-feeling, and identity formation that appealed to advertisers. However, whereas commercial narrowcasting trains viewers to engage in identity formation at the *point of purchase*, BTV asks its viewers to undertake the same process at the *point of profit*. Both are alluring moments of incorporation into capitalist ideological systems. Building on a long tradition of industrial media that attempts to engender workers' support for deregulation, right-to-work legislation, and other "business-friendly" policies, narrowcasting—and management's cultural turn—attempted to create work cultures that envisioned employee identity as synonymous with firm identity. While this possibility might seem laughable in the context of widescale "re-engineering," it is worth remembering that, as per US custom, professional identity is often positioned as a key vector of a subject's individuality *but not a base from which to build class solidarity.* Similar to the commercial system, where viewers are asked to see group membership merely as a sign of shared (but) individual consumer habits, BTV encourages viewers to see themselves not as Labor, but as individuals with shared goals and (potentially) shared fortunes.

In short, narrowcasting, as a force that directs our attentions and affinities along some lines and not others—operates in *both* labor and leisure contexts to support an orientation to identity formation as a pleasurable and reassuring process of distinction, individuality, choice, and power.[145] In both commercial narrowcasting and BTV, the emphasis on personal and group identity formation along economic lines is made to overshadow any potentially uncomfortable recognition of exploitative production systems (both those that people experience as workers and those that result in otherwise desirable consumer goods). These dynamics become readily apparent in the programs themselves.

THE EMPLOYEE NEWSLETTER

A video newsmagazine, *JCI Report* is a paradigm of one of the most common genres of business satellite programming. Johnson Controls (JCI), its producer, was founded in 1885 in the environmental controls business (founder Warren S. Johnson invented the electric room thermostat). The company underwent significant expansion in the second half of the twentieth century, entering several additional industries, most notably batteries, plastic containers, and car seats and interiors. JCI referred to 1990s globalization as the "tidal wave trend" it anticipated and responded to nimbly by pursuing international markets, beginning with a European manufacturing facility built in 1964.[146] Outsourcing in the automotive and building industries provided "new opportunities" for JCI to enter growing markets in Asia, South Africa, and South America, while the dissolution of the Soviet Union left new countries open to privatization and commerce.[147] JCI also saw the geographical reach of its ventures grow with the transformation of integrated facilities management into a larger portion of their overall business in the mid-1990s, leading them to oversee facilities for international and multinational corporations like IBM, Mobil Oil, British

Petroleum, American Express, and Xerox.[148] JCI's global transformation and its adoption of satellite technology are coterminous, forming part of the same project. *JCI Report* featured in an extensive slate of BTV programming that packaged the company's economic performance for workers, encouraging employee buy-in throughout the 1990s.

Johnson Controls Conference Network (JCCN) eventually reached over 170 branches across the United States and Canada. Its earliest ambitions, however, were more modest. In an interview, Dave Sobczak, who built JCI's satellite program and oversaw much of the company's video production beginning in 1974, recounted JCCN's origins. He described a pre-satellite era marked by difficult, slow communication between headquarters and the field dominated by "snail mail" and computing resources stretched uselessly thin. In the late 1980s, JCI contracted with Private Satellite Network and Scientific Atlanta for data distribution to over 100 North American branches. Realizing the system "was a perfect fit" for BTV (doubling services to "economize"), Sobczak proposed developing several strategic Ku Band satellite downlinks for video. In 1988, JCI ran a year-long pilot program, distributing training materials to 11 sites. When BTV reduced training costs to a third of the cost of videotape, Sobczak's supervisor expanded the scope of the project, and receiving dishes were installed at every branch office within their satellite's footprint. BTV became JCI's primary means of video distribution, overtaking (though not entirely replacing) tape cassettes. The inaugural edition of *JCI Report*—which explicitly discusses the value of the young BTV system—reveals how company leadership used satellite narrowcasting to fold soft management strategies into attempts to build its reputation as a global power.

Employee newsletters were a well-established communication genre long before *JCI Report*. Dating to at least 1807 with National Cash Register's house organ, the format bears a consistent set of conventions:

There are the usual personal items—births and, unfortunately, deaths. There are stories about company social events and sports groups and how the company band brings joy to its community engagements. There are reports about company performance—new offices opening up, promotions, awards won at trade fairs. There are employee profiles, mixing, as profiles are wont to do, little insights into a worker's off-the-job activities with motivational messages about how the worker got to where he is today through hard work and loyalty to the firm. There are safety messages. There are details about how external conditions will likely affect corporate performance. There are explanations of company policies, such as a ban on smoking in the workplace. There's even a story about a recent strike—a story which dares to say that if management had handled things better, the strike might not have happened.[149]

By way of punch line, the author—writing in 1990—reveals that the issue described in the preceding was published in the 1880s. If the genre's form had changed little over the course of a hundred-plus years, neither had its aim. Writing in 1920—boom times for the development of house organs—another author outlined the goals of the employee magazine: cooperation, unity, morale, education, and building acquaintances across institutional membership.[150] Combined, these functions promised to incorporate workers more effectively (and affectively) into the workplace by "sell[ing] the employees to each other. The departments to each other. The plants to each other. The management to employees."[151] Almost 70 years later, in the era of *JCI Report*, house organs were still understood as a significant managerial tool—one that could "upgrade the company's image, motivate the employees, encourage camaraderie, improve safety awareness, and provide employees with constant reminders of the management's desire to break down communication barriers between different levels of the work force."[152] The newsletter remained part of a sales and influence job, promoted as "the ideal vehicle for selling your company's philosophy and promoting strategic objectives among your employees."[153]

JCI Report recombined the newsletter with broadcast and cable news aesthetics, borrowing the authority and trustworthiness of a form that was quickly proving itself central to geopolitical maneuvering amid CNN's spectacular coverage of the First Gulf War.[154] Beginning November 19, 1991, *JCI Report* ran on a fairly regular monthly basis through the end of 1997. Clocking in between 18 and 30 minutes, each episode was hosted by Jamie Marvin-Casey, a former news anchor for a local Wisconsin news station. A seamless imitation of a television news broadcast, the show comprised feature stories, in-depth and remote reporting packages, headline announcements, interviews, commercial-like act breaks, interviews, and puff pieces. The Premier Edition of *JCI Report* quickly establishes the program's credentials through savvy replication of news aesthetics. The *JCI Report* logo—which prominently features a large satellite dish—swoops in against a 3-D graphic of the world (Figure 5.1A). Through the narrow interstices of the logo, we can see what appears to be a live feed of a news studio. As the graphic falls away, viewers are left with a wide shot of the newsroom that includes production crew. Silhouetted by stage lights, a man miming the role of "director" cues the anchor. This shadow theater is accompanied by lively orchestral fanfare—trumpets, strings, and the percussive staccato chimes of a xylophone—and a booming voice announcing,

"From the studios . . . of the Johnson Controls Conference Network, this is . . . *JCI Report*. With your host, Jamie Marvin-Casey." The camera zooms, centering Marvin-Casey. Sitting at the anchor desk in a bold red power suit (Figure 5.1B), she welcomes audiences to the program with a cadence

Figures 5.1 A and 5.1B
The mock newsroom—embellished with glowing television monitors—peeks through the interstices of the *JCI Report* logo (a) just before Marvin-Casey welcomes her audience (b). *Screen capture.*

and tone of voice indistinguishable from broadcast news. Throughout the remainder of the program, graphic intertitles, chyrons, and a faux in-set graphic "screen" accompany Marvin-Casey's reading of the news and further mark the program within the genre of serious broadcast journalism. Cloaked in the costume of news, JCI borrows the authoritative "vantage point" from which television declares it knows the world and its inner workings.[155]

Every episode of *JCI Report* contained dozens of stories (the 30-minute premier episode boasts 26). While features, video packages, and in-studio interviews might run as long as 7 minutes, news items ranging from 10 to 90 seconds comprised the majority of each episode. Segments might describe changes in compensation packages, cover new products, provide financial reports and business overviews, celebrate new initiatives and major contract wins, challenge workers to meet goals, post opportunities for training, introduce new executives and branch managers, invite participation in sweepstakes and competitions, announce celebrated retirements, and feature frontline workers in human interest pieces (e.g., "New Year's Resolutions"). "Fun" quizzes and advertisements for training sessions masquerading as commercials divide larger program segments. Marvin-Casey's cadence and aural transitions smoothed the flow of disparate stories, as did sequencing that exploited tangential thematic relations between consecutive items.[156] If the conveyor line ITV of Chapter 2 offers a new way of conceptualizing Raymond William's notion of "flow," BTV invokes its roots in commercial entertainment television. As *JCI Reports* jumps between worker recognition, business plans, humanizing profiles of management, and celebrations of company power, the "mutual transfer" of meanings across segments "sells" the traditional product of the employee newsletter: the company. The wide-ranging flow of *JCI Report* represents the constituencies of JCI—increasingly varied in the period of expansion and diversification—as part of a cohesive and intelligible whole.

In purporting to unfold in real time, the program's jumbled amalgamation of segments staked claims to the company's ability to oversee global markets and pivot quickly in response to breaking news from around the world. Previews of coming stories—both at the top of the episode and throughout—emphasize the forward momentum of the show and the tight control the anchor, and, by proxy, JCI, held over the unfolding of events. This same control appears in Marvin-Casey's temporally marked speech, e.g., "Jim will join us again in a few minutes to announce the first ever best branch of the year award, but first, let's take a look at some of the stories making headlines at Johnson Controls," or "We'll be back in a moment [. . .] but first a bit of trivia." A 90-second "headline" segment, which highlights branch activities spanning North America, likewise reinforced JCI's managerial knowledge of its dispersed operations and its ability to understand and organize an otherwise dizzying array of different projects, geographical locations, and customers.

Likewise borrowed from television news, liveness—or, more accurately, the *insinuation* of liveness—positioned *JCI Report* as a glossy, consumer grade, shared experience, with all the implications explored in Chapter 3. *JCI Reports* was almost exclusively edited on film.[157] However, producers went to great lengths to cheat the look of liveness, commonly featuring remote reporting and what appeared to be double satellite feeds (an in-studio anchor conversing with an on-site reporter). This charade appears in routine form in a segment on a new pricing program for the South West Region. Marvin-Casey mentions the pricing program before cutting to a reporter on the scene "joining them today" to talk more. During their conversation, *JCI Report* moves into a split screen featuring both reporters against a flattened globe graphic with the date (December 29, 1992) crawling along the bottom of the screen. As Marvin-Casey asks questions, the other reporter pauses thoughtfully—earpiece visibly displayed—before responding in detail. Marvin-Casey concludes the piece, remarking to her interviewee, "I appreciate your time today." Surprised by the fidelity of the program's "liveness," I turned to Sobczak (also a veteran of the broadcast industry) to ensure that *JCI Report* was indeed taped. Laughing, he explained, "It was all faked."[158] For him and his team, it was important that the program look like "any regular television news show."[159] A question of professionalism, perhaps, Sobczak's quest for verisimilitude also underscores why the news format is useful for a particular kind of corporate storytelling.

Satellite news undergirded the program's claims of offering hard-hitting, important information ("straight talk") and global vision. When first introducing the purpose of *JCI Report*, Marvin-Casey describes its content as "in-depth interviews, financial reports" and "news and information" covered in a "consistent and straightforward manner." As evidence, the first episode features a lengthy and seemingly candid discussion of company finances—including a $26 million shortfall of planned earnings—straight from the comptroller. Repackaging corporate communications as "news," JCI positions programming as both objective and relevant to a workplace community that extends beyond the bounds of individual branches. The pitch-perfect simulation of news aesthetics also supports JCI's attempts to situate itself as a global power that is nevertheless intimately invested in the narrow concerns of its workforce. This self-positioning centers on *JCI Report*'s ability to establish its "global presence"—a claim to modernization defined by "the capacity to be technologically and culturally integrated within a new system of global satellite exchange" serving Western interests.[160] Described by Parks in relation to early satellite spectaculars like *Our World* (a 1967 program on world population that combined mostly live feeds from 24 countries in a 2-hour show), by 1991, the once flashy signifiers of global presence's orchestration—live international remotes, displays of the television apparatus—had been domesticated by the news. For companies whose profits lay far afield of media production, however, the aesthetics of satellite-enabled global presence remained a powerful means of demonstrating institutional agency on the world stage. The vast communication infrastructure and corporate empire exhibited in *JCI Reports* showcases the firm's status as a corporate neocolonial power well equipped to manipulate temporal and geographical relations to serve the interests of its employees. Just as the *CBS Evening News* might bind the country for 30 minutes of shared consideration of timely national and international issues, so too could JCI instantly survey and connect its employees and operations, wherever they might be.[161] Furthermore, in an era of rampant mergers and conglomeration, flawless satellite news aesthetics testified to companies' ability to absorb yet another industry—and not just any industry, but communications, the storied linchpin of corporate success.

Rather more quotidian content reinforced BTV as community-based narrowcasting. Segments signaled their highly targeted audiences through narrow, mundane appeal (the energy efficiency retrofit business, frontline sales promotions) and segments featuring audience members (branch activities, the winners of an employee competition). Insider language bordered on nonsense for "cultural interlopers," as in the case of JCI Comptroller Rich Kolashefski's "tips" for meeting FY92 fiscal goals: "drive to a 60-40 mix, seek out a 75% markup on new PSAs, look for a 50% portfolio markup, ask at least a minimum 8% escalation on PSA renewals [and] go for a 90% markup on unscheduled."[162] To create a sense of intimacy and family feeling, executives were addressed by their first names and lower-level employees were frequently asked for program content suggestions. Promoting the quasi-collaborative nature of *JCI Reports*—as well as its value—Wilson described the program as featuring "stories *from* branches *to* branches that convey success that others may be able to use."[163]

To reinforce feelings of unity and shared purpose, *JCI Report*'s exhibition simulated synchronous connection. Despite being taped, *JCI Report* was "broadcast" only once on its release day, intended to be seen by all branch office employees at the same time.[164] Addressing the audience of the inaugural episode, JCI Vice President Jim Wilson explains, "The intent here is that all of our people—in the field, in our branches, our frontline service providers—have an opportunity to view this information with the branch management teams and have some healthy discussion." *JCI Report* ostensibly offered a springboard for interaction across employee hierarchies. Even when the vagaries of work schedules and too-small conference rooms made this mode of viewing difficult, Wilson encouraged employees to maintain the social experience of communal viewing through activities like (self-funded) pizza (or—in the spirit of localized culture—blintz) parties. Following management literature that suggested fun, social workplaces could extract higher commitment and productivity from workers, this scenario reinforces understandings of the employee audience as a close community—with a stake in *JCI Report* and the company it represented.[165]

The opportunities for "visible management" provided by *JCI Report* also enabled executives to reinforce their vision for the company and its core values. This practice appeared explicitly in moments of direct address from JCI's top brass—as when Wilson exhorted viewers to "get back on track and meet our commitment in our '92 plan"—and in stories that reinforced the cultural and economic ambitions of JCI. The feature story of *JCI Report*'s inaugural edition touted JCI's attendance at a government-sponsored energy conservation forum and their parallel involvement in sponsoring energy-efficiency legislation. While the report relayed the economic value of JCI's participation in the form of "3 to 5 billion dollars in opportunities," it also excerpted a speech from former Energy Secretary James Schleshinger who described energy efficiency as a public good. Invoking the Gulf War, Schleshinger suggests, "It's a hell of lot easier and a hell of a lot more fun to kick ass in the Middle East than it is to actually make sacrifices in order to reduce the importation of oil." Implicitly, the latter operation—the purview of the assembled audience and, in turn, *JCI Report* viewers—is equally as important as global foreign policy *and* more difficult. In its pursuit of energy efficiency contracts, JCI bills itself as a company that cares about—and is deeply involved in—sustaining the well-being of the country through core values of hard work and sacrifice.

Workers were further encouraged to focus on their productivity in motivational speeches that borrowed the Japanese focus on "empowerment" via self-management and increased responsibility. Before outlining increased profitability expectations for the upcoming year, Controls Group Vice President Joe Lewis took pains to describe the important role played by the Systems and Services Division (SSD, *JCI Reports'* target audience) within the larger company.

> As I've said before, the Systems and Services Division is the *heart and the soul* of the controls group. . . . It's where we've got the greatest market share and it's

a growing business. . . . Of course the flip side of that is that we do expect the strongest financial performance from the Systems and Services Division. So you can see, *with that kind of importance* to the Controls Group, what happens in the Systems and Services Division really affects the Controls Group as a whole. When the Systems and Services Division is doing well, the Group does well, when Systems and Services is off-plan, why, the Controls Group is off plan.

Continuing, Lewis describes next steps, placing the onus of "managing the margins" on lower-level employees: "If we don't have a good tough-minded manager *right at the branch level*—the branch manager and the sales people—to keep those margins up we won't get the job done." Local branches must accept responsibility to support the financial health of the entire company. When asked if the "high expectations" laid out in his plan are realistic, he responds affirmatively, situating higher productivity expectations as naturally suited to the quality of employees (and the company's products and know-how):

> You know, the Systems and Services Division has got really good people in it. I think that our sales force is second to none in the industry. We know and we really believe that our construction expertise and prowess is better than anybody else that's in the marketplace and we got good technical people that have been trained. We've got a good product to install. . . . We got the best people and I think they can live up to our expectations. I'm counting on it.

The next segment, which profiles the winner of JCI's "Best Service Branch of the Year" award, reinforces corporate's emphasis on branch performance, self-management, and initiative. Further, the strategies that won Halifax the award—"maintain and continue to build a positive team, promote the philosophy of empowerment, and make the necessary investment"—are the very same productivity-enhancing goals pursued by *JCI Reports* itself.[166] Ultimately, JCI deployed satellites as a cutting-edge sales weapon to be wielded against outsiders, as a mechanism for collaboration and community formation for insiders, and as a means to build a desirable and highly consumable identity as a powerful, appealing employer and business partner. It is a textbook case of media experiments in an age of uncertainty and soft management.

While the company's evolving data and information needs enabled the founding of the system, they also contributed to its collapse. With rising speeds, the internet became a preferable mechanism of data transfer, not least because of the rising cost of satellite time. When Sobczak began programming broadcasts in 1991, the cost to run an hour of programming on an occasional use satellite was roughly $350. In 1997, this reached $2,500 due to decreasing availability of satellite time because of older satellites' obsolescence and several failed launch attempts. While Sobczak and his team adapted by using more pre-recorded material to "tighten" time usage, costs remained high. Furthermore, due to shifts in JCI labor coordination—frontline technicians and key branch office employees worked increasingly on location, calling in rather than physically checking in to the branch office—fewer workers actually watched "live" broadcasts. Sobczak wryly noted, "by mid '95, the satellite network became the most expensive videotape distribution media there was because they would put a tape in and hit record."[167] JCI's satellite network ceased operation after 1997. JCI continues to produce and distribute significant levels of media for their employees, but their primary distribution mechanism is the internet.[168]

EDGE AESTHETICS:
ENTERTAINMENT, SINCERITY, INTERACTIVITY

While the newsletter was one of the most popular genres of BTV, satellite television programming was highly diverse, as might be expected in such a decentralized media system. To provide a more granular look at aesthetic and technological strategies that crossed program boundaries, my next case study turns to Steelcase. A significant producer of BTV, the company's focus strikes at the very heart of workplace reorganization. Founded in Grand Rapids, Michigan, in 1912, Steelcase manufactures industrial furniture, interiors, and office technologies. Their products and marketing have long provided the material and discursive base for restructuring the white-collar office in ways similar to the example that opened this chapter.[169] Like many satellite users, Steelcase is an international firm. The company began investing in overseas operations in the mid-1970s through partnerships with companies in Japan and France that appealed to the Asian, European, and North African markets. The company entered the Middle East shortly thereafter with the establishment of dealer distributors in six countries in 1977.[170] By 1991, Steelcase's manufacturing operations alone spanned 11 countries; their products, meanwhile, could be purchased in 68.[171] While records indicate that Steelcase began internal media production in the mid-1970s, few details remain regarding the founding of their satellite systems, referred to simply as BTV (identified in the following as SBTV for clarity.) However, several extant SBTV recordings document and self-reflexively comment on Steelcase's understanding of satellite television as

Figure 5.2 The opening, fast-paced graphic of "BTV" describing why workers might find themselves exclaiming, "I want my BTV." *Screen capture.*

a workplace communication tool. Taking each in turn, I explore how they manifest, alternatingly, corporate interest in the managerial value of edgy entertainment, sincerity, and interactivity.

Edgy Entertainment

Building on decades of corporate and educational theorizing that suggested people learn better visually, promoters of BTV claimed that workers could process and remember audiovisual information better than print. Following the previous chapter, as the "TV generation" matured, television was positioned as a medium that could borrow use and behavior patterns from employees' "social life."[172] "Entertaining" BTV and "riskier [television] formats" could (ostensibly) hold viewers' attention, demonstrate care, evoke utile emotions, and better engage viewers' identification with narrowcast programming.[173] It became BTV producers' charge to create programming "equal to what people are seeing on TV at home."[174] For Steelcase, this ambition is clearest in "I want" (STCS-V60, n.d.), a promotional reel pitching the content and value of SBTV to Steelcase dealers (Figure 5.2).

The six short minutes of "I want" capture the "fast-paced and exciting" look of commercial television, running rapidly through seven different satellite programs and their accompanying promises of "tools for your edge," "action steps," "competitive review," and "success chat."[175] The televisuality of this sizzle reel—expressed here as an "acute hyperactivity and an obsession with effects"—draws on satellites' futuristic associations to posit Steelcase as hip, high-tech, and innovative.[176] The reel begins with the slogan "*I Want my BTV*" backed by flashes of bright colors and rock music as rapid-fire text cycles through the promises of SBTV: "corporate information faster," "digital communication," "interactive experience," "sales opportunities," and "training." A clear allusion to MTV's "I want my MTV" campaign, which used massively popular rock stars like Mick Jagger, David Bowie, and Pat Benatar—and, of course, space imagery—to promote the new cable channel, the intro draws on the slogan's cultural connotations to construct SBTV as a provider of highly desirable, unique content narrowly suited to its intended audience.[177] This explicit invocation of cable television was matched with a collage structure and pastiche aesthetics that juxtaposed a mock workout program, talk shows, training films, satellite news coverage, and a television commercial in extreme postmodern style.

The aesthetic pressure on "I want" was high. It was not enough to entertain and engage viewers; "BTV" sought to demonstrate the communication acumen of its producers while establishing SBTV's utility and power. This overlap is clear in a segment showcasing a television advertising campaign. The scene opens on a gothic skyscraper towering over a post-apocalyptic landscape. A grey pallor saturates the scene as a zombie-like crowd of besuited workers shuffles toward the castle. The commercial cuts to a medium close-up of a man lifting a computer monitor over his head (Figure 5.3A) as the booming voice of an announcer chides, "It is foolish to think that technology alone can solve our business problems. People, and how well they work together will. We can show you a way. Steelcase furniture and office environments: a smarter way to work." After a cut back to the mob, the camera moves into an extreme close-up of an eye. Without conclusion or resolution, "I want" cuts, jarringly, to a clownish set reminiscent of a children's program. A man in a teal shirt and vividly patterned tie stands amid blockish, brightly colored geometric forms (Figure 5.3B). With all of the excitement of an infomercial pitchman, he gestures wildly and exclaims, "I told you it had wow power! Can you believe it! And that's just the beginning. That's television!" The contrast between the commercial—developed for broadcast distribution—and the SBTV program exaggerates the commercial's high production values. Leaving aside the irony of the

Figures 5.3A and 5.3B "BTV" emphasizes wide-ranging aesthetic acumen through contrasts such as these. A dreary techno dystopia captured in varied camera angles and shot distances (a) finds its foil in the cartoonish mise-en-scène of the studio set (b). *Screen capture.*

commercial's dismissal of technology in a BTV promo, the segment testifies to Steelcase's ability to manipulate visual styles for persuasive communication, as well as the power of television itself.

Ultimately, "I want" invokes the visual speed endemic to entertainment programming—particularly fast-paced editing—as evidence of the *technical capacity* of satellite communications to provide viewers a "competitive edge" based in near-instant information. This spectacular sleight-of-hand is reinforced by Steelcase dealer testimonials that emphasized speed of information distribution:

> One of the biggest things [BTV] does is that it enables us to get real time information to our sales people that they can then deploy against the marketplace . . . anytime we can get information from Steelcase through the dealer to the customer in a more timely manner that's a valuable tool.
>
> —Ed Bonner, *Office Environments*

> We think [BTV's] state of the art, we think it gets the message out there quick. We think it's going to grow to interactivity. And we think it gives us an edge on the competition. It's a communication edge and I would encourage you to use BTV. I wouldn't be without our BTV.
>
> —Mark Mayhew, *Chairman, Dealer Council*

This BTV is doubly "edgy." It provides viewers a speed advantage against their competitors and it takes up the narrowcast work of distinction and community formation.

Edgy Sincerity

Deploying a starkly different aesthetic mode, a second Steelcase video pursues this latter function to even greater effect. Nearly four times longer than "I want," "Larry Leete's BTV Message to the Sales Organization" (STCS-V59, 1994, henceforth "Message") unfolds almost entirely as a single medium close-up (Figure 5.4). The program cuts away from its speaker— Steelcase President Larry Leete—three times: once for an 8-minute video clip of COO Jim Hacket addressing a dealers' meeting and twice to insert the same chart regarding recent company performance. The remainder of the broadcast consists of Leete directly addressing the camera. Wearing a grey suit and tie, he sits before a soft cloud-like background and appears to read from a teleprompter. While one might attribute this simplistic staging to the live nature of the presentation, this explanation is unsatisfying;

Figure 5.4 Larry Leete and the aesthetics of sincerity. *Screen capture.*

many other live Steelcase programs use far more involved mise-en-scène, cinematography, and graphics.

Instead, the video is an example of corporate understandings of the aesthetics of sincerity and connection as a direct response to management theory that emphasizes visible management during difficult change. For Steelcase, the early to mid-1990s was a "time of change and challenge," due in large part to re-engineering.[178] In his address, Leete runs through a litany of obstacles faced by the company, including "implementing a new organizational structure, moving into and learning new frontline roles and responsibilities, refocusing our dealers on their lead sales role, and making the personal transition to a new compensation program," as well as the president's resignation, delivery problems, and a new early retirement program that shrunk their workforce. In order to tackle these difficulties, Leete suggests that increased communication—in part, via SBTV—will provide a critical tool:

> the real purpose of this broadcast [. . .] is to begin the process of improving our communications with you. As you know, this broadcast is only for Steelcase sales people. This is the first time this year that we've used BTV exclusively within our sales organization, but it won't be the last. We recognize the need to do a better

job of communicating with you. We know that we haven't done it well enough in this time of transition and turbulence. We intend to improve our performance in the communication arena and we're taking a first step right now.

Following the managerial playbook, Leete's message appears "empathetic and concerned about people" and offers viewers evidence of corporate interest for the particular plight of the Steelcase dealer.[179] A "straight talk" *mea culpa*, "Message" further suggests that the home office is actively working to correct these problems—and has invested time and money in the necessary solutions.

> Better communication wouldn't eliminate the problems you faced this year, but it would go a long way towards helping you develop a *better understanding of the corporate situation*, which would allow you to develop a *better personal perspective* on the customer and dealer situations you've been managing on our behalf. It would also give you *added confidence* to know that the people in Grand Rapids are aware of the difficulties you face and are acting to correct these difficulties [emphasis added].

The goal of increased communication in this instance is not information to mobilize in the context of sales, but closer communion with the head office (and its guiding vision), and increased awareness of one's own role within the company. Despite Leete's acceptance of fault, the emphasis on worker perceptions and understandings also neatly absolves Steelcase of total blame, since it is a change to workers' capabilities that provides a partial answer to the crisis.

"Message" suggests that BTV's connectivity can likewise strengthen the Steelcase community by opening communication channels between dealers and executives. Though Leete acknowledges that SBTV might not function well for "true conversation," he nevertheless includes it in his discussion of two-way communication "targeted at the items and concerns that you care most about." Likewise, Leete suggests that SBTV grants "access to all areas of the company and to the decision makers that most affect the work you do." As an illustration, the program cuts to the clip of Hacket talking to dealers in which the COO declares, "we hear you." Leete further promotes this "access," noting, "You'll be hearing a lot from Jim Hackett in the coming weeks and months. In fact, he'll be appearing on our next BTV broadcast to the sales force." Alongside these explicit affirmations of BTV's capacity for connection and dialogue, the broadcast's earnest, no-frills visual style undergirds its promise of "down-and-dirty, roll-up-your-sleeves, no bull information."[180]

Drawing on the meanings accruing around satellite technologies and liveness, the simple style of the broadcast pursues a doubled sense of immediacy in continuation of practices described in Chapter 3. First, its lack of detailed staging establishes its urgency—and corporate's desire to act quickly and decisively in a moment of crisis. Second, by eschewing the traditional markers of media presentation, *especially* when other SBTV presentations closely mimic commercial entertainment, "Message" suggests to viewers that they are being granted unfiltered, *nearly unmediated* access to "the big guys."[181] The medium close-up focuses viewer attention on Leete's facial expressions and emotional performance as he details company failures and foibles in the collaborative, highly personal language of soft management:

> I want to *personally* thank you for the sacrifice and effort you've put forth this year. And *I will hope you will join me* in looking forward to the days ahead which I believe are bright . . . *you've made it possible for us all* to look forward to the team satisfaction and personal fulfillment that will come from leading *our* dealers and *our* company into the future. Thank you [emphasis added].

It is a virtuosic performance of "corporate personhood," wherein an executive stands in for the company to foster easy identification and emotional connection that ward against Labor's attempts to instigate change.[182] The duration of the shot likewise attempts to build intimacy and trust with a leader who appears to provide unembellished insight into higher-level happenings. We might think of this as the aesthetics of access, to borrow a phrase. However, unlike the aesthetics described by Lucas Hilderbrand—the material evidence of viewers' shared and repeat engagement with videocassettes that builds palimpsest-like on magnetic tape—the access aesthetics of "Message" are illusory.[183] In a bid to exaggerate co-presence and connection with leadership, "Message" attempts to *efface* the material evidence of mediation in an attempt to represent the "breaking down of barriers" between leadership and lower line employees.

Edgy Interactivity

Proximity and connectivity discourses reached their apex in the call-in show. These types of BTV programs often began with a formal presentation followed by a period of "open lines." Ostensibly, any of the hundreds or thousands of viewers "tuned in" to the program could call or fax their questions to be answered live and on-air, though questions were often screened. While popular for training, these programs' much-hyped "interactivity" was also folded into larger attempts at community-building and emotional management. "No-holds-barred" question-and-answer sessions with the boss became a popular strategy for projecting concern and managing anxiety and rumors in periods of change.[184]

"Interactive" satellites' associations with high-tech proximity and care were likewise useful to Steelcase's cultivation of its reputation for industry-wide leadership. In 1995, Steelcase partnered with the International Development Research Council (IDRC) to produce "BTV Enhancing Productivity" (STCS-V67, 89 minutes, henceforth "Productivity") for an audience of blue-chip companies including Microsoft, AT&T, Cisco Systems, and Federal Express, likely on a pay-per-view basis or as free institutional advertising. The program centered on IDRC's research describing how altering the spatialization of office work could lead to higher levels of productivity and employee retention. Over the course of the first half hour, the program's three panelists discuss different facets of workspace reorganization, including telecommuting, hoteling, and new mobile technologies that enable work outside of the office.[185] The remaining hour of the seminar comprises an extended Q&A session. Steelcase and IDRC's use of satellite television—yet another vanguard technology restructuring the spatialization of work—reinforces their corporate identities as cutting-edge global entities that anticipate major industrial shifts for the benefit of clients. This is particularly important for Steelcase, whose product line is implicitly promoted by IDRC's research. The lengthy Q&A session—which draws more from distance education traditions than it does from "straight talk" management communications—helps establish the seminar's credentials as an "educational effort" rather than a sales pitch.

A range of visual and discursive strategies further position "Productivity" (Figure 5.5) as a collaborative learning environment that balances personal attention with expansive scale. The moderator begins by emphasizing the broadcast's reach—to 1,500 people in "22 sites internationally." (Later, this group would be described less ambitiously as a North American audience.) Describing the Q&A's limited interactivity as dialogic connection, the host declares, "It *is* a discussion." The screen confirms, routinely displaying telephone and fax numbers entreating the audience to participate in cross-country conversation. Periodic invitations to call and fax in—alongside compliments reinforcing proper behavior ("OK, we've got some more questions and it's great. You're doing

Figure 5.5 Like *JCI Report*, "Productivity" emphasized the apparatus and the news format's claims to global reach and access. *Screen capture.*

what you're supposed to and what we hoped you would, which is calling in.")—both interpellate viewers to participate in the "discussion" and repeatedly demonstrate the accessibility of the expert panel. Localization strategies that emphasize satellites' precise reach further complement satellites global bona fides. When viewers call in, they are asked to identify themselves and their location. For the duration of their question, an on-screen map pinpoints their location, emphasizing satellite television's power to connect the dispersed international audience with the home office in Grand Rapids, Michigan. However, unlike *JCIReports'* "live" news remotes, live Q&A maps operate less as testament to the satellite's conquest of global markets and more as a demonstration of intimacy and proximity. Using callers' names and speaking as if addressing them individually, panelists pursued recognition strategies credited with creating "personal television."[186] The host's conclusion—a request for feedback made to coincide with the distribution of a survey at each downlink site (more managed interactivity)—further established the corporate satellite broadcast as a mechanism of collaborative communication. Again, BTV claims to cater to its audiences by folding them more deeply into circuits of corporate communications and decision-making.

Satellite users' attempts to manage immediacy and connectivity became most pronounced in moments of failure. One of the most spectacular failures in "Productivity" occurs when the one-way nature of the phone systems (and the panelist's attempts to dissemble its limitations) becomes evident. This exchange occurs between two panelists (Tina Facos-Casolo, Program Manager for IBM Real Estate Services, and Bill Agnello, Vice President of Real Estate and the Workplace for Sun Services), the host (Franklin Beker, director of the International Workplace Studies Program), and a caller from Chicago:

> CHICAGO: Hello, this is a call from Chicago. How do you address the security issues involved with location independence?
> [Silence then short exasperated laugh from Facos-Casolo.]
> FACOS-CASOLO: [With her mic slowly being turned up.] Uh Ok, Uh, excuse me. What do you mean by security implications, what are you trying to secure?
> [Becker and Agnello respond, somewhat overlapping, with physical gestures toward Facos-Casolo.]
> BECKER: I don't think we can do this; you can't do this.
> AGNELLO: Yeah, they can't respond.
> FACOS-CASOLO: Oh, I'm sorry. [Softly laughing.] Oh right, thank you.
> [Agnello takes over, speaks about encryption.]

Though the Steelcase system allowed for back-and-forth telephone discussion, it appears the programmers of "Productivity" chose not to take advantage of it. A small moment, this failure hints at the extent to which discourses of satellites' interactivity and global connection were often more fantasy than fact.[187] Notably, BTV's "immediate connectivity" falls short of the interactivity offered by the technologies that many describe as videoconferencing (multipoint-to-multipoint live video).[188] Although "videoconferencing" was often used to describe BTV, the inverse rarely, if ever, occurred; the misnomer never went in the direction of insinuating *less* interactivity.[189] Whatever the intentionality of this slippage, it furthered the illusion of closer affective proximity, access, and dialogic participation in management decisions that were elsewhere supported by aesthetic and practical strategies (faked dual satellite pickups, two-way audio, program hosts directing on-site activities).

If, as noted in Chapter 3, liveness "is the worked at, achieved and accomplished effect of the human application and use of technologies whose ontological characteristic is immediate connectivity," then BTV indeed worked hard to establish liveness and its consequent connotations of community and co-presence.[190] This effort is the centerpiece of SBTV's "Broadcast Coordinators Equipment Test" (STCS-V397, 1991, 84 minutes; henceforth "Test"). A live trouble-shooting program, "Test" asked receiving branches to call in so that on-site technicians could better calibrate their systems in light of recent technical difficulties. The network coordinator describes the aim of the program, cataloging the system's difficulties:

> The purpose of today's broadcast is to eliminate any technical problems that you have been having out there, especially with the Darome [call-in] system. What we're going to do is eliminate all of those embarrassing moments—we've all been through 'em—uh, you know when the whine is there and the squeal is there and the uh people sounding like they're in caves and there's those dreaded moments of silence that we've all been through.

Indeed, call-in programs like "Productivity" exhibit many of these characteristics—whining, echoes, popping "p's," calls cut off, phone-handling noise—that testify to the technology's limited capacity to provide a sense of perfect immediacy. While programs like "Test" offer the company an opportunity to demonstrate sincere interest in developing a sense of reciprocity between field workers and the home office, it also makes clear that the coordination of co-presence requires extensive discussion of microphone use, coaching people "too afraid to talk," labeling confusing switches and knobs, complicated protocols for calling in, attending to the time constraints of receiving stations, and developing architectural solutions to accommodate broadcast audiences.[191] In short, although producers agreed that Q&As "should be seamless and transparent," this was not always the case in practice.[192]

Just as various parties papered over the discrepancy between the promise and reality of immediate connectivity, satellites' global reach was also crafted with care. Despite ads dripping with space-age imagery and exotic locales—as well as promises of the ability to "train the world" and broadcast "Live . . . from anywhere to anywhere"—the "globe" delivered by BTV was piecemeal.[193] A number of practical and economic barriers precluded anything approaching complete global reach, including zoning ordinances restricting antenna placement, interference in urban areas (especially in the C band), time zone discrepancies, incompatible scrambling systems and television standards, program translation costs, fixed earth stations that could only receive signals from a particular satellite, and slower adoption of downlinks in Europe (not to mention corporate disinterest in global audiences considered irrelevant to profit-seeking ventures).[194]

Technological and economic problems were exacerbated by cultural differences that made securing user engagement difficult. At Ford, for example, attempts to use BTV (there named Ford Communications Network, or FCN) to foster a transnational corporate identity spanning employees in France, the United Kingdom, Spain, Germany, and Belgium floundered amid the specificities of non-US work cultures. While German safety regulations prohibit showing television at the site of labor, German unions successfully protested FCN's encroachment on nonwork hours in break areas, reducing worker exposure to FCN virtually to nil.[195] According to a former producer for FCN, viewers across the continent found ethnocentric paeans to Ford's global power "distasteful," while more regionally specific news ranged from boring to a source of tension (as when Ford described corporate plans to move production jobs from one of its locations to another).[196] Beyond Ford, some workers felt BTV bore the sheen of "Big Brother" and increasingly dehumanizing communication technologies, while others simply had difficulty operating the equipment.[197] Even executives reportedly feared being portrayed as "telenerds" with their every personality tic on display.[198] What is significant about satellites' temporal, global, and cultural ambitions, however, is not their unblemished success; it is their lasting resonance for corporate management projects supporting worsening working conditions for most employees.

CONCLUSION

Eventually, BTV units were hit by the same belt-tightening that ruled other corporate divisions.[199] Additionally, BTV, like videoconferencing, began an irreversible transition to the desktop in the late 1990s.[200] If it is useful to invoke Kenneth Lipartito's argument that even failures are "socially resonant, and they shape our options for the future," it is not because BTV was a failure.[201] Indeed, though relatively short lived, BTV was championed by some of the most powerful companies in the world, pulled millions of dollars into its orbit, and, at times, even spanned continents. BTV and its many representatives likewise did "narrative work," spinning the strands of several stories that continue to be told in the service of creating "a new technological world."[202] Like concurrently developing technologies— videoconferencing, two-way institutional cable, and supersonic flight— BTV helped naturalize the global scale of private business, suggested that companies could (and should) remake geographies in order to achieve advantage in capitalist systems of exchange, and deepened understandings of information access as the key to success in the "knowledge economy."[203] It also supported an increasingly salient vision of multipurpose information networks to manage labor and logistics, and celebrated the replacement of physical contact with virtual interaction as a measure of increased liberty and flexibility.

BTV also added new chapters to our stories of technology, labor, and life. Working on the affective level, BTV legitimated corporate management that targeted worker identity and relationships in a bid to usurp other modes of affiliation—while simultaneously dissuading broader-based class solidarity. Corporate narrowcasting reinforced viewers' existence within hyper-individualized media systems that constantly and continuously asked them to recognize themselves as inside/outside increasingly niche interest groups. Working on (and against) Labor, BTV sold mechanisms for maximizing white-collar worker productivity as signs of empowerment and care; much like the gleaming "huddle rooms" of Microsoft, BTV bore the sheen of economic investment in employee well-being while working conditions and remunerations declined. Further, BTV's visible management broadcasts suggested that proximity to the boss's image equals access to useful knowledge and power; that participation in a question-and-answer session could be tantamount to self-governance and even control. Last, satellite television confirms one of the guiding narratives of this book: that for the business communications sector—ever infatuated with Marshall McLuhan—the medium was, indeed, the message.

Conclusion

Acknowledgments

Throughout this book, I have argued that television operated for American business and industry as an instrument of orientation. It allowed businesses to locate themselves and their workers within complex cultural circuits, workplace hierarchies, institutional communication practices, and the physical space of the plant, region, nation, and globe. As an efficiency machine, television enabled expanding industries—from American post-war manufacturers to globalized conglomerates—to work on their employees' physical and mental capacities as well as their relationships with the company. I have shown how both logistical and cultural management were long-standing industrial desires articulated to communication technologies that, though associated today with desktop computing, discovered much of their form and function in television. In addressing television beyond commercial and public broadcast systems, I have described private networks whose contours are determined first and foremost by the map-making of company operations rather than the geo-politics of the nation. Tracking the many ways in which commercial and industrial media sectors mutually inform one another has likewise led me to reconsider some of the conceptual foundations of television as we thought we knew it (flow, immediacy, time-shifting, narrowcasting).

Leaving that work to lengthy chapters, I reserve my conclusion not to address "ends" but to ponder the conditions of possibility that enable beginnings. I offer, in other words, my acknowledgments: my "statement of indebtedness" to the many people and institutions that shared their

Television at Work. Kit Hughes, Oxford University Press (2020) © Oxford University Press.
DOI: 10.1093/oso/9780190855789.001.0001

resources with me; my "recognition of an obligation" to the audiovisual professionals who pursued television at work not as a tool of control, but as a mechanism of a more humane workplace; and my "acceptance"—or better, recognition—"of the authority" of the archive/s that provided me a place from which I could credibly speak.[1]

Though sometimes positioned as an authentic gateway to the past, "the archive" undergirds the sense-making of the present. For Jacques Derrida, who returns to the historical meaning of *Arkhé* as commencement and commandment (origin and authority), the archive strategically and continuously transforms and reproduces the past, even determining what is archivable in the first place.[2] For Michel Foucault, the archive operates as the system that governs the formation and intelligibility of utterances; it enables us to make sense of our world and our relations with one another.[3] For both, the archive is a mechanism of power and policing that controls what can be said (and remembered) and how meaning is created and understood. While acknowledging the legitimating function of "the archive" as a site of empowered discourse, in the following I focus instead on *archives*: brick-and-mortar institutions driven by varied missions and funding arrangements, professional cultures, technical expertise and best practices, localized theory, archiving and preservation technologies and infrastructure, as well as law and policy. These *particular institutions* remain under-acknowledged (and under-theorized)—not least because historians have long colluded with archival power by effacing the labor of archivists; recognizing the active role of archives workers indeed diminishes some of the historian's own authority as a mediator of the past.[4] However, accounting for archivists' professional practices enables greater awareness of the relations of power that create sources, select certain records and not others for preservation, and mediate between the researcher and access. As a theorist of "the" archive suggests, "archivization produces as much as it records the event."[5]

The neglect of television's "work life"—although due largely to the concerns of television studies as it developed since the 1970s—should be understood in part in relation to the difficulty of preserving and securing access to historical corporate (audiovisual) records.[6] While this book draws from some public-facing archives that actively solicit researcher attention (the Wisconsin Historical Society, the New York Public Library, the Prelinger Collection, the Hagley Museum & Library, the University of Rochester Rare Books and Special Collections), others I visited were closed to the public or required special permission for researcher visits. Although I contacted some 30 companies that I knew to have (had) major television operations, I was granted (sometimes very partial) access to only five institutions: Johnson Controls, Motorola, New York Stock Exchange, Steelcase, and AT&T. Here, however, I was fortunate. Having worked at an archives myself, I was able to draw on the advice and expertise of my colleagues—Mary Huelsbeck, Maxine Fleckner Ducey, Vance Kepley, Laurel Gildersleeve, Heather Heckman, Emil Hoetler, Allison Neely, and Rick Pifer—who helped me navigate corporate archives and their contact lists. I am indebted to these institutions and their archivists, including Bruce Bruemmer, Drew Davis, Lee Grady, Sheldon Hochheiser, Charles Kempker, Janet Linde, Carol Lockman, Kevin Martin, Kathy Reagan, Sue Topp, Melinda Wallington, Melissa Wasson, and Ken Wirth, who so generously attended to me and my project, which would not—could not—exist without them.

While the work of these archivists—and the support of others who could not grant me access to their collections, but sent along helpful files and leads—testifies to a robust, collaborative archives community invested in research, there remains reason for concern over the long-term preservation and access to corporate audiovisual records. For one, the archives field is not immune to the precarious working conditions that have come to define labor in the twenty-first century.[7] Many archivists find themselves in a field increasingly defined by significant underemployment, an over-reliance on unpaid internships and temporary contract work, outsourcing, and downsizing.[8] At least twice over the course of this project, archivists cited their precarious employment status (temporary contract workers) as part of their rationale for denying access to corporate records, pointing to a potentially troubling vector of precarious access to American business records. When companies organize their archives according to the hyper-flexible conditions most favorable to their profit-seeking operations, they reinforce their own authority over certain discursive formations by limiting access to historical records (and access to the authority they grant the speaker). It becomes difficult (but not impossible) to speak in certain ways from the corporate archive.

Compounding these problems is television's precarious materiality. One of video's key selling points was easy erasure and reuse, leading to routine destruction of taped content.[9] Further, for all of the temporal control video promised the institutions that used it, the medium has a remarkably short lifespan (an estimated 30 years). Far more delicate than film, video is highly susceptible to chemical deterioration and magnetic field distortion. Difficulties increase for companies that—as guinea pigs of the electronics industry—were at the forefront of new media adoption. As a consequence of the mass proliferation of cassette, cartridge, and disk formats before interchangeability and (temporary) standardization, it is not unusual for archives to hold unplayable formats.[10] Even supporting three or four widely used formats becomes prohibitively expensive as the equipment and exper- tise to repair legacy machines becomes more difficult to acquire over time.[11] Indeed, while one very generous archivist purchased a VHS player expressly so I could watch tapes in their collection, EVR cartridges are unplayable— even at the Motorola archives where an EVR player sits in storage.

Precarity also attends corporate audiovisual collections in the process of appraisal. Audiovisual materials might be discarded entirely (the most common fate in the archives I contacted) or they might languish, unproc- essed until a corporate heritage project calls them forth from well-stowed boxes. Over the course of my research, I found that even when audiovisual records persist, the paper records created alongside them have often been discarded due to assessments at some time or another that they lack "per- manent" value. Fortunately again, however, appraisal practices are not con- fined solely to the formal structures of corporate archives. This book has benefited immensely from the work of amateur archivists (but professional TV men). John Sheahan, a producer and director for AT&T and Johnson & Johnson, consulted his personal papers, using his judgment to select materials he believed (rightly) would be of interest to my research. My un- derstanding of the rise of television in AT&T would not have been possible without his forward-thinking appraisal and retention decisions. In a pro- ject that we might more traditionally classify as amateur archives work, Richard (Dick) Van Deusen appraised, weeded, and digitally published "The Wilke Papers," a series of reports, newsletters, photographs, and essays created in the course of business at Hubert Wilke, Inc., a pioneering au- diovisual consulting firm. Designed as an archival project, the liner notes accompanying the CD-Rom he gave me argues for the importance of these records—and hints at the sincere investment in knowledge communities indicative of the audiovisual sector members I've come into contact with:

> When Hubert Wilke first showed me some of the original documents,
> I recognized an archive that deserved to be preserved and made widely available.
> It is a textbook on AV systems technology based on principles that are arguably
> as relevant today as they were when first formulated. The resource is Hubert's,
> and my, contribution. It is free to share.

Although appraisal may be a precarious process, the diversity and scope of the audiovisual sector blunts the force of corporate control over business history records.

Archival power thus recognized, I turn to other debts and obligations, namely those owed to the audiovisual professionals who helped me map an unwieldy terrain. We must remember that those who worked most intimately with workplace television—many of whom are still alive, and some of whom are still working—had goals and ambitions that overlapped only partially with the heightened efficiency and control aims of the companies that employed them. For them, then, the meaning of "television at work" resonates somewhat differently from the ways I discuss it in the preceding pages. I believe it is in these differences that we might locate the conditions of possibility for a more humane workplace.

I had the great fortune to meet a number of corporate communications professionals who were intimately involved in the development of television at work over the course of this project. Judith Brush, corporate communications consultant, author, cofounder of *The Brush Report*, and adjunct faculty at Marist College, submitted to two separate interviews and three hours of conversation regarding her engagement with the field and her experience creating one of the most important bodies of data on corporate video use. The late Thomas Hope, founder of institutional audiovisual market research firm Hope Reports (and winner of a Congressional Gold Medal for photography work during World War II), spoke at length about how his research fit into a larger interest in global education and worker training. Bill Smith, founder of the processing, duplication, and distribution company Allied Film, identified serving educational messengers with "quality information" as the linchpin of his business. Television producers and directors for major media users—including John Sheahan (AT&T, Johnson & Johnson), Steve James (GTE Biznet), and Dave Sobczak (Johnson Controls)—were not only key to my understanding of the field, they are delightful and engaging people whose passion for their work is palpable. Mentioned earlier, television director, researcher, and author Dick Van Deusen (Prudential) patiently explained why he cofounded the National Industrial Television Association, the East Coast organization that merged with its West Coast counterpart (Industrial Television Society) to become the most important trade organization for video professionals in the country: the Industrial Television Association (ITVA). Ron Brown, one-time president of ITVA, likewise helped me understand the significance and mission of the organization for its members. Combined, these folks' wide-ranging backgrounds in theater, journalism, educational media, military audiovisual service (both World War II and Vietnam), public relations, advertising, and commercial broadcasting testify to the diverse intellectual energy of the field.

Across our conversations, many emphasized their role as communications professionals (rather than technicians) sincerely invested in the project of improving the workplace. Sometimes explicitly positioning their work against "promotional" content, interviewees were often most interested in larger questions of corporate culture and the impact of messaging on employees and the community (as well as its ability to prevent exhaustion for trainers and other workers). Steve James, for example, emphasized video's ability to show respect and deference to an audience (due to its expense and time-intensiveness), and create bonds among workers:

> You're doing something that ultimately is engaging people on an emotional level. . . . If you can get them to laugh or you can get them to cry or you can get them to relate on a human level to what's going on with this character in front of them, well that's huge. And that's what video is for. It's for engaging people on an emotional level. If you're not doing that you might as well do a white piece of paper.

Judith Brush likewise emphasized the way video could lessen feelings of disenfranchisement and lack of connection as firms grew. Used well, she claimed, video "made people feel they were part of something" and provided important information and training support. In a corporate context where middle management would sometimes restrict access to information as a power strategy, Brush also saw video as "inclusive" and inherently democratic; "everyone gets the same message . . . it's an equalizer."

This optimism and passion shouldn't be confused for naïveté. While those I talked with emphasized the power of corporate communications as a tool—fostering improved skills and a stronger community for workers, as well as economic success and innovations for firms—some candidly acknowledged it could also be a weapon wielded against the best interests of employees. One producer (who asked to remain anonymous) shared with me the story of his first day on a job. He was asked to supervise the edit of a video for Wall Street analysts that starred an executive celebrating cost reductions and a recent mass layoff.

> He was *crowing* about how wonderful it was that he cut all these jobs. Then he goes into the studio and goes on the live satellite TV and he's going to the employees, "we know how difficult it is and we feel for every single one of you that's lost a job but we have to do this to stay competitive." And I'm sitting there watching this guy, just astounded. I go, OK I'm not in Kansas anymore. This is the world I'm in now. That I think was the most difficult thing about the job. . . .
> On the other hand, there are people who really want to train people and want them to be trained well. They want to do their jobs well because they know it impacts the success of their company and so they put everything they've got

into it and those are the clients that you love to work with. Because you want the same thing they do.

Others acknowledged that corporate work was a space of negotiation and potential frustration. As James noted, even if you're "being called on to spin something in a certain way . . . you have your personal integrity, you're not going to participate in a complete subterfuge or falsehood. . . . We did the best we could to make it as honest as we could." As freelancers gained experience, they could be more selective about their clients. Indeed, Brush indicated that a potential client's "philosophy" needed to match theirs before they agreed to take a job (and today she finds herself working "passion projects" primarily with community and nonprofit organizations). Even with well-matched clients, however, the Brushes found that some companies refused to take the necessary steps and investment to follow their research findings, leading to disappointment.

While excellent work has sought to understand the production cultures of the entertainment industries, much work remains to be done, especially in other media sectors. In my limited pursuit of the audiovisual field, I have found a community of workers engaging in incredibly wide-ranging knowledge projects on behalf some of the most powerful institutions of the twentieth century. As indicated throughout this book, the prolific annual output of in-house studios spanned training, communicating across employee hierarchies, and making company activity legible to shareholders, product users, and the public.[12] Both producers and consultants informed me they were drawn to the field in part because of the routine ability to experiment and learn new subjects as they worked with different internal and external clients across these expansive areas. Sheahan, for example, recounted a program that he made in concert with Western Electric's corporate psychiatrist designed to stem an uptick in alcoholism, suicide, and other mental health problems resulting from the relocation of the company's human resources headquarters from New York City to Greensboro, North Carolina; he relished the opportunity to visit a private psychiatric clinic in New Jersey "to learn and observe." Other projects people mentioned by name ranged from explaining the legal process of discovery and how to sell a particular water treatment system to exploring the implications of the Madrid Fault for oil production. Exactly how audiovisual men and women (though mostly men) translated the research and interests of other workers (from trainers and psychiatrists to a firm's legal council) is a crucial area of future research. Further, production workers also saw these projects as opportunities for visual and aesthetic innovation, from the adoption of computer graphics to figuring out how to perfectly cheat the look of dual satellite feeds when funds and technical constraints prevented it. How trade knowledge circulated among media professionals and interpenetrated the translation efforts between experts and their clients remains an important question.

Routinely, corporate audiovisual workers made the argument that we need to understand their field as partially integrated with the commercial entertainment industry. Many clarified that they often worked with professional talent—both above and below the line—who raised the production values of their projects. (Professional local news anchor Jamie Marvin-Casey's star turn on *JCI Reports* is just one such example.) Many also described live television—via systems sometimes developed in collaboration with broadcast television workers—as an exciting challenge on par with entertainment work. At the same time that workers situated their work parallel to the entertainment industry, however, they also claimed special technical expertise that occasionally surpassed their commercial brethren. The men I talked with were often responsible for managing operations that spanned media—including still photography and new computer learning systems—and impossibly fast turnover in video formats. Some were charged with building studios from the ground up that might link multiple buildings or comprise a million dollars worth of facilities and equipment. Underscoring the importance of television workers' specialized technical expertise, Sheahan tells of his experience designing the media facilities for the new Johnson & Johnson World Headquarters, commissioned to architect I. M. Pei. According to Sheahan, the initial plans included poor lighting and design decisions that would hamper media production. As he puts it, "architects back in those days didn't think about those things. I will tell you right now, I. M. Pei didn't think about it in our building." In other words, it was up to Sheahan and his staff to teach the superstar firm a lesson or two in television facilities design.

One of the founding stories of the business television field—which demonstrates the relationship between commercial and corporate television—also belongs to Sheahan, who played a pivotal role in Johnson & Johnson's media response to the Tylenol crisis. Soon after it became clear that someone was spiking bottles of the painkiller with cyanide, the president and CEO of Johnson & Johnson called Sheahan into their offices, asking for a live press conference later that day. Despite the fact that Johnson & Johnson did not have an onsite satellite dish, forward-thinking planning by Sheahan (the pre-installation of television cables in the facility he designed) and his intimate knowledge of the long lines system (due to his stint at AT&T), the company had their press conference hours later, sending the video to every affiliate in the top 20 American markets. Shortly thereafter, Sheahan got another call, this time from Tom Brokaw, asking to interview CEO Jim Burke live on the 6:30 news. Scrambling once again to reconnect their studios to the broadcast networks, he succeeded. He recalls talking to an old friend at New Jersey Bell—the man who helped him set up the feed—"He couldn't believe it. Actually he told me later the people at NBC—his brother—couldn't believe we could do that." While trade literature often invokes this story to demonstrate the speed and efficacy of satellite communications (as noted in Chapter 5), here it reads as a testament to the ingenuity and technical knowledge of television workers.

Ron Brown explained the need for these kinds of stories for the field's professionals: "somehow industrial television is always looked down at as some sort of child or something and if you wanted something really good produced [e.g., a commercial], you went to an agency outside." This led to frustration "because people who worked in industrial television were just as good as the people who worked outside, but the perception was not there." How workers fought for recognition of their creative and technical capabilities within larger work worlds is a classic question of production cultures analysis. One small vector of this phenomenon I noticed in my interviews was an emphasis on the corporate communications worker as a sophisticated global agent. Hope told me stories of being wined and dined in Japan by Sony during their development of the videocassette. Others shared tales of traveling to Mexico and Canada and the challenge of getting gear through customs, sleeping in airports, shooting in South Africa in verité style without a script (but with carefully planned reserves of batteries and stock), working across incompatible national video standards and formats, navigating global cities with the help of local talent and international crews, and wiring the conference rooms of the world for videoconferencing. The usual trade stories of daring and ingenuity, perhaps, but it would be a shame if we—like those Brown discusses—allowed production cultures hierarchies to get in the way of seriously considering this work in the context of globalized media(ted) industries.

Audiovisual professionals also developed an extensive body of ideas regarding the utility of media, working both with and against popular management theories. The meticulous data collection of Judith and Douglas Brush and Thomas Hope are among the most prominent examples, though smaller-scale efforts were undertaken by a range of actors. While some used their experience to build and share industrial media theories (television's immediacy, mystique, cultural centrality, credibility, and domestic familiarity as keys to its efficacy), many also consulted and even developed media research to guide best practices. Van Deusen, for example, undertook a two-year study for Prudential to compare the impact of their videotaped roleplay training to the use of textbooks, video programming, and a control group. Further, though some embraced popular management and media theories—particularly those of Marshall McLuhan, Peter Drucker, and Rosabeth Moss Kanter—others asserted their professionalism in contrast to the revolving door of management trends. As Steve James put it,

> Management theories come and go. One year it's outsourcing and another year it's Cowboy Ethics. Then one year it's Genghis Khan. Then . . . Six Sigma. *Oh my god, Six Sigma!* OK, fine, that's what we're doing this year and it will run its course . . . I think it's more about integrity. . . . My theory has been you look for the people with integrity, you look for people that want quality work that want to pay for it, and you give them the absolute best you can give them.

The measures of "quality work" developed by James and others, in turn, shaped television at work and the professional field that undergirded it.

One of the most important sites for this theorizing was ITVA, which also provided a model of workplace community for many. Repeatedly, interviewees described the trade organization as an invaluable site of intellectual and personal connection. Though eventually reaching upwards of 12,000 members across North America and Europe in the 1980s, ITVA was remembered (by Brush and others) as "really, really a close-knit group." Sheahan concurs, "we all knew each other, all of us who worked in this little field. It was kind of a clique." ITVA provided television workers the opportunity to share knowledge and strengthen bonds. "We got together twice a year and we talked about emerging technologies, we talked about programming, we talked about budgeting, we talked about some of the challenges that we had—staffing, budgets, not enough money."[13] Outside of their biannual meetings, workers engaged in writing toward the field (Van Deusen described a popular white paper he wrote—and sold—on the "continuous problem" of "selling management on the value of what we're doing"), as well as seminars and trainings for future video workers (the Brushes brought media producers to their Marist College classes to share their work with students, sometimes before they even premiered it for their commissioning client). Throughout, these endeavors were described in the terms of sharing, connection, and care.

This emphasis may be the result of the personal stake some held in the industry. Several mentioned one of the appeals of the job was its ability to accommodate workers' family lives, unlike the broken shifts of commercial broadcasting. For others, BTV was itself a family affair (replete, too, with many "dear friends"): three of the eight I spoke with were married to someone they worked with, Tom Hope eventually passed his business down to his son, Vincent, and Judith Brush tells me her young son became such a fixture at ITVA events, he earned the sobriquet "baby video." Indeed, this sense of connection and concern was cited by Brush as one of the reasons she and her husband pivoted away from the field in 1993, as video departments themselves became victims of re-engineering and they saw their friends and students fired. While the Brushes helped their associates write résumés and land new positions, as she puts it, "that kind of soured us a little bit on some of the corporate work, because we saw so many people get hurt." This compassion and care that unites a field but spans disparate workplaces returns us to the possibilities of work as a site of solidarity and mutual recognition, and proposes an understanding of labor that must yield to workers' lives beyond the factory gate. Although deeply implicated within the post-Fordist project of labor efficiencies, many of those within the field of corporate television staked out and cherished a vision of their own workplaces as sites of creative autonomy, personal fulfillment, and community engagement. In acknowledging my great debt to those I spoke with—individuals who gave me hours of their time, shared important documents from their personal collections, provided contacts to further my project, contentiously pored over timelines and confirmed details, trusted me to tell some small part of their story—I want to emphasize *this* vision as one of the enduring products of their labor.

As my conclusion—and this book—comes to a close, I am left thinking of the scholarly community that shaped the conditions of possibility for my own work. I am immensely indebted to Michele Hilmes, who advised the dissertation research that found its way into these pages. Jonathan Gray has offered truly extraordinary support and guidance in every way imaginable. Eric Hoyt's many invitations to collaboration and methodological exploration have invaluably deepened my approach to my own work. Caroline Frick guided me to questions regarding marginal majority media, institutions' role in supporting certain media histories, and our responsibility in challenging those histories. Derek Johnson and Jeremy Morris both generously helped me refine my ideas and arguments here and elsewhere. I am especially grateful to Myles McNutt, Sarah Murray, and Alyx Vesey, who ensured I passed my Wisconsin Thursdays in good company and challenging conversation. Others whom I'd be remiss in not acknowledging for their influence and insight are Mary Beltrán, Andrew Bottomley, Michelle Caswell, Brandon Colvin, Christopher Cwynar, Liz Ellcessor, Brian Fauteux, Daniel Herbert, Kyra Hunting, Josh Jackson, Amanda Keeler, Alex Kupfer, Danny Kimball, Caroline Leader, Elana Levine, Derek Long, Lori Kido Lopez, Wan-Jun Lu, Cynthia Meyers, Amanda McQueen, Michael Z.

Newman, Jenny Oyallon-Koloski, Nora Patterson, Allison Perlman, Josh Shepperd, Jen Smith, Nora Stone, Tony Tran, Shawn VanCour, Jennifer Wang, and the larger, confoundingly generous Wisconsin intellectual community. I often feel I spent more than a year in Oxford, Ohio, where Ron Becker, Mack Hagood, Jen Malkowski, and Rosemary Pennington helped me develop my approach to my subject in a particularly formative phase. I am especially grateful to Katie Day Good for her thoughtful feedback on a draft of a book proposal. Now, as a teacher and researcher myself, I often think back to the exhilarating and formative experiences I had as an undergraduate at Bucknell University; it is perhaps impossible to express how grateful I am to Eric Faden, Jean Peterson, Roger Rothman, and especially Michael Drexler, who challenged me to the limits of my capabilities. I am likewise grateful to those I first met as a fledgling UT graduate student, including Janet Staiger, Mary Celeste Kearney, Michael Kackman, Charles Ramírez Berg, Lalitha Gopalan, Peter Alilunas, Bo Baker, Alex Cho, Candice Haddad, Tiff Henning, and Leigh Goldstein, who helped me begin to figure out what it means to be an academic. I have been delighted to find the intellectual community at CSU supportive and encouraging, and I already owe much to the kind mentorship of Kari Vasby Anderson, Hye Seung Chung, Greg Dickinson, Scott Diffrient, Elizabeth Williams, and especially Eric Aoki. Carl Burgchardt, Martín Carcasson, Tom Dunn, Meara Faw, Katie Gibson, Julia Khrebtan-Hörhager, Ziyu Long, and Elizabeth Parks make department meetings—and the routine, but crucial work of shared governance—a pleasure. Gloria Blumanhourst, Dawn McConkey, Nancy Schindele, and Eliza Wagner-Kinyon have been far more patient with me than my overdue travel documentation deserves. It's not easy to make a new institution and a new city home; Peter Erickson, Katie Knobloch, Nick Marx, John Pippen, Allison Prasch, and Abby Shupe have made it easier. Institutionally, my research benefited tremendously from research support from the Department of Communication Studies at Colorado State University, a UW Chancellor's Fellowship in the spring of 2015, and an exploratory research grant from the Hagley Museum and Library in the summer of 2014. At Oxford University Press, this project improved due to the care and enthusiasm of Hallie Stebbins, Hannah Doyle, and Meredith Keffer, and I am particularly grateful for the insightful suggestions of the manuscript's anonymous reviewers.

Leaving aside my work life, as impossible as that may be in practice, I am indebted to many others as well. My educational ambition comes from my mom (Janet Hughes), herself a third-generation alumna of Juniata College, my Nana (Laura Jane Bartschat), a beloved middle school teacher, and my Aunt Kay (Hughes), who's held just about every educator job there is. My father, Greg Hughes, encouraged me to be creative and confident in these and countless other ambitions. Harry Hughes, my grandfather and family chronicler, and Helen Hollingshead, my great-grandmother and author of the popular local newspaper column "Do you Remember?," taught me that a wide range of stories constitute history and memory, and it's up to us to recognize and preserve them. My grandmother, Louise Hughes, has always been one of my kindest champions. My Papa, Fred Bartschat, loved me, even when I broke his very nice pen. Bob and Sue Elkins have been incomparably patient with me any time I've had to tuck work into otherwise lovely family visits. Steph Anzman-Frasca has been so important to my intellectual and personal development, I'm not sure who I'd be without her. Zildjian, my childhood cat, was my near-constant companion for over 17 years, moving with me to five states, two grad school stints, and my first tenure-track job. While a mediocre editor, she contributed to the project in countless other ways. And then there's Evan Elkins, to whom I owe so much that to detail it would require another conclusion and perhaps another book.

While these acknowledgments reflect on the factors that enabled this particular bit of academic labor, they also document my interest in work as a precondition for broader class-based and social solidarity. Throughout, this book focuses on the special productivity of the conjuncture between business and television to better understand how media shape our everyday relations with one another; our labor, learning, and leisure activities; and the institutions in which we participate. While the story I tell is not optimistic, it is not the only story possible to tell about the state of labor in late capitalism. For one, this conclusion invokes my friends, my family, my cherished interlocutors, and my coworkers (many one-and-the-same) who support my work, and who make my everyday experience of life—labor and leisure—meaningful. For another, as I finished a draft of this manuscript, a historic wave of teacher strikes, including the state-wide wildcat West Virginia strike, reopened what many understood to be a concluded chapter regarding the strength of union power in the United States. While these are disparate stories, both describe the importance of work as a site of self-actualization, social connection, and community. It is in following these other narratives—and in the mutual recognition of those with whom we "walk around on the same bit of carpet for eight hours a day"—that we might find the conditions of possibility for a more humane world.

NOTES

INTRODUCTION

1. This discussion of the centrality of work to identity is centered in a Western context.
2. Lisa Parks, *Cultures in Orbit: Satellites and the Televisual* (Durham, NC: Duke University Press, 2005), 2. While my use of "interface" alludes to computing (and I argue throughout that some television uses anticipated or duplicated computer applications), I am more interested in less specialized definitions of the term, i.e., as "a means or place of interaction between two systems, organizations, etc.; a meeting-point or common ground between two parties, systems, or disciplines; also, interaction, liaison, dialogue" that point to the relationship between American labor and capital. "interface, n." OED Online. December 2018. Oxford University Press. http://www.oed.com.ezproxy2.library.colostate.edu/view/Entry/97747?rskey=tZo7lN&result=1 (accessed December 17, 2018).
3. Anna McCarthy, *Ambient Television: Visual Culture and Public Space* (Durham, NC: Duke University Press, 2001), 11, 14–15, emphasis in original.
4. John Durham Peters, "Calendar, Clock, Tower," in *Deus in Machina: Religion, Technology, and the Things in Between*, ed. Jeremy Stolow (New York: Fordham University Press, 2013), 41–42.
5. Raymond Williams, *Keywords: A Vocabulary of Culture and Society*, rev. edn. (New York: Oxford University Press, 1985), 176–179.
6. See Hannah Arendt on the "fertility of human labor power." Arendt, *The Human Condition*, 2nd edn. (Chicago: University of Chicago Press, 1998), 118.
7. Keith Grint, *The Sociology of Work* (Cambridge: Polity Press, 2005), 42.
8. Ibid., 7.
9. Karl Marx, "Alienated Labor," in *Karl Marx: Selected Writings*, 2nd edn., ed. David McLellan (Oxford: Oxford University Press, 2000), 90–91; Harry Braverman, *Labor and Monopoly Capitalism: The Degradation of Work in the Twentieth Century* (New York: Monthly Review Press, 1974); Michael Burawoy, *Manufacturing Consent: Changes in the Labor Process under Monopoly Capitalism* (Chicago: University of Chicago Press, 1979), 82; Gillian Creese, *Contracting Masculinity: Gender, Class and Race in a White-Collar Union, 1944–1994* (Toronto: University of Toronto Press, 1999); Rosabeth Moss Kanter, *Men and Women of the Corporation* (New York: Basic Books, 1993).
10. See, for just one example, Arne L. Kalleberg, *Good Jobs Bad Jobs: The Rise of Polarized and Precarious Employment Systems in the United States, 1970s–2000s* (New York: Russell Sage Foundation, 2011).

11. E. P. Thompson, "Time, Work-Discipline, and Industrial Capitalism," *Past & Present* 38 (1967): 59–97.
12. Braverman, 278.
13. Nona Y. Glazer, *Women's Paid and Unpaid Labor: The Work Transfer in Health Care and Retailing* (Philadelphia: Temple University Press, 1993).
14. Rosalind Gill and Andy Pratt, "In the Social Factory? Immaterial Labour, Precariousness and Cultural Work," *Theory, Culture & Society* 25, no. 7–8 (2008): 17. Before calling for greater "work-life balance," we would be wise to consider Sarah Sharma's argument that "work-life balance is an idea bout the time of work and the time of life that sees no alternative temporal order beyond the corporate control of bodies . . . it is a way of giving meaning to time precisely to manage time." Instead, we should be looking for ways of reconfiguring our temporalities that are not indebted to capitalist systems. *In the Meantime: Temporality and Cultural Politics* (Durham: Duke University Press, 2014), 106.
15. The rise of the digital economy has also led to further elucidation of Autonomist Marxist thought. See, for example, Tiziana Terranova, "Free Labor: Producing Culture for the Digital Economy," *Social Text* 63, vol. 18, no. 2 (2002): 33–58.
16. See, for example, Phoebe Moore and Andrew Robinson, "The Quantified Self: What Counts in the Neoliberal Workplace," *New Media and Society* 18, no. 11 (2016): 2774–2792; and Sharma, 16–18.
17. On bio-capitalism, which appropriates workers' "vital faculties" for the material benefit of capital, see Cristina Morini and Andrea Fumagalli, "Life Put to Work: Toward a Life Theory of Value," *Ephemera* 10, no. 3–4 (2010): 240–241.
18. Andrew Ross, *No-Collar: The Humane Workplace and Its Hidden Costs* (New York: Basic Books, 2003): 19.
19. John Tomlinson, *The Culture of Speed: The Coming of Immediacy* (London: Sage, 2007), 88.
20. David Morley, *The Nationwide Audience: Structure and Decoding* (London: BFI, 1980), 18.
21. Ibid., 15. Emphasis mine.
22. See, for example, Creese, 25–29, 65–78, on how this is managed, especially with regard to the strategic reframing of women's work to legitimate different pay.
23. This is one of the primary concerns of Kanter's landmark work, originally published in 1977. See also Grint, 319.
24. David Harvey, *The Condition of Postmodernity* (Cambridge, MA: Blackwell, 1990), 124.
25. Dallas Smythe, "On the Audience Commodity and Its Work," in *Media and Cultural Studies: KeyWorks*, eds. Meenakshi Gigi Durham and Douglas M. Kellner (Oxford: Blackwell, 2006), 233.
26. Ibid., 239; Sut Jhally and Bill Livant, "Watching as Working: The Valorization of Audience Consciousness," in *The Spectacle of Accumulation: Essays in Culture, Media and Politics*, ed. Sut Jhally (New York: Peter Lang, 2006), 32.
27. Brett Caraway, "Audience Labor in the New Media Environment: A Marxian Revisiting of the Audience Commodity," *Media, Culture & Society* 33, no. 5 (2011): 700–701.
28. Jérôme Bourdon and Cécile Méadel describe a similar dynamic, though they focus on France, where this work is unpaid. "Inside Television Audience

Measurement: Deconstructing the Ratings Machine," *Media, Culture & Society* 35, no. 5 (2011): 42.

29. Deborah Tudor, "Who Counts? Who Is Being Counted? How Audience Measurement Embeds Neoliberalism into Urban Space," *Media, Culture & Society* 31, no. 5 (2009): 838.

30. Philip Napoli, "Revisiting 'Mass Communication' and the 'Work' of the Audience in the New Media Environment," *Media, Culture & Society* 32, no. 3 (2010): 511.

31. Terranova, 33–58; Mark Andrejevic, "Watching Television without Pity: The Productivity of Online Fans," *Television & New Media* 9, no. 1 (2008): 30; Derek Johnson, "Inviting Audiences In: The Spatial Reorganization of Production and Consumption in 'TVIII,'" *New Review of Film and Television Studies* 5, no. 1 (2007): 74; Alison Hearn, "Structuring Feeling, Web 2.0, Online Ranking and Rating, and the Digital 'Reputation' Economy," *Ephemera* 10, no. 3–4 (2010): 421–438; John Banks and Sal Humphreys, "The Labour of User Co-Creators: Emergent Social Network Markets?" *Convergence* 14, no. 4 (2008): 409; Vincent Manzerolle, "Mobilizing the Audience Commodity: Digital Labour in a Wireless World," *Ephemera* 10, no. 3–4 (2013): 455–469; Mark Andrejevic, "Estranged Free Labor," in *Digital Labor: The Internet as Playground and Factory*, ed. Trebor Scholz (New York: Routledge, 2013), 149–164.

32. Christian Fuchs, *Digital Labour and Karl Marx* (New York: Routledge, 2014), 268–270; Julian Kücklich, "Precarious Playbour: Modders and the Digital Games Industry," *Fibreculture Journal* 5 (2005): np.

33. Yochai Benkler, *The Wealth of Networks: How Social Production Transforms Markets and Freedom* (New Haven, CT: Yale University Press, 2006), 96.

34. Johnson, 74, 78; Terranova, 35; Banks and Humphreys, 409, 411–412; Andrejevic, 2008, 34–35; Axel Bruns, *Blogs, Wikipedia, Second Life, and Beyond: From Production to Produsage* (New York: Peter Lang, 2008), 29; Napoli, 512; Ethan Tussey, *The Procrastination Economy: The Big Business of Downtime* (New York: New York University Press, 2017), 6.

35. Ian Bogost, "Hyperemployment, or the Exhausting Work of the Technology User," *Atlantic* November 8, 2013. https://www.theatlantic.com/technology/archive/2013/11/hyperemployment-or-the-exhausting-work-of-the-technology-user/281149/ Accessed December 13, 2018.

36. ERC, *ERC 2012 Social Media in the Workplace Study* (Mayfield, OH: ERC, 2012).

37. Shannon Baker, "How Do You Best Engage Employees about Corporate/Internal CSR Efforts? *PRWeek* (September 2011): 51–21; Andrejevic, 2013, 160.

38. Fuchs, 133. This became starkly evident in the 2018 data-harvesting scandal whereby Cambridge Analytica used Facebook in attempts to influence American politics.

39. Melissa Gregg, *Work's Intimacy* (Cambridge: Polity, 2011), 88–89.

40. Vicki Mayer, *Below the Line: Producers and Production Studies in the New Television Economy* (Durham, NC: Duke University Press, 2011), 124, 133. We might also think about the long-standing social division of labor, which impacts access to certain jobs. See, for example, Elana Levine, "Toward a Paradigm for Media Production Research: Behind the scenes at *General Hospital*," *Critical Studies in Media Communication* 18, no. 1 (2001): 66–82.

41. David Hesmondhalgh, *The Cultural Industries*, 2nd edn. (Thousand Oaks, CA: Sage, 2007), 69.

42. Ibid., 186.

43. John Thornton Caldwell, *Production Cultures: Industrial Reflexivity and Critical Practice in Film and Television* (Durham, NC: Duke University Press, 2008); Derek Johnson, *Media Franchising: Creative License and Collaboration in the Culture Industries* (New York: New York University Press, 2013).

44. Haidee Wasson and Charles R. Acland, "Utility and Cinema," in *Useful Cinema* (Durham, NC: Duke University Press, 2011), 3. In addition to sources mentioned across these footnotes, see Devin Orgeron, Marsha Orgeron, and Dan Streible, eds., *Learning with the Lights Off: Educational Film in the United States* (Oxford: Oxford University Press, 2012) and Geoff Alexander, *Academic Films for the Classroom: A History* (Jefferson, NC: McFarland, 2010).

45. I use "marginal majority" to emphasize the extent to which "useful" and other non-commercial media genres are both central to everyday life and actively obscured by much media studies work. Raymond Williams, "Culture Is Ordinary," in *Raymond Williams on Culture & Society*, ed. Jim McGuigan (Los Angeles: Sage, 2013), 3.

46. Arlie R. Belliveau, *Micromotion Study: The Role of Visual Culture in Developing a Psychology of Management*. Master's thesis, York University, 2011: 2; Rudmer Canjels, "Films from Beyond the Well: A Historical Overview of Shell Films." In *Films That Work: Industrial Film and the Productivity of Media*, eds. Vinzenz Hediger and Patrick Vonderau (Amsterdam: Amsterdam University Press, 2009), 241; Mats Björkin, "Technologies of Organizational Learning: Uses of Industrial Films in Sweden during the 1950s," in *Films That Work*, 303.

47. Heide Solbrig, *Film and Function: A History of Industrial Motivation Film*. Doctoral dissertation, University of California at San Diego, 2004; Anna McCarthy, *The Citizen Machine: Governing by Television in 1950s America* (New York: The New Press, 2010); Ramón Reichert, "Behaviorism, Animation, and Effective Cinema: The McGraw-Hill *Industrial Management* Film Series and the Visual Culture of Management," in *Films That Work*, 298. Khary Oronde Polk, "'Easy to Get': Race, Regulation, and the Black Venereal Body," in *Subaltern Soldiers: Race, Sexuality, and American Militarism in the Early to Mid-Twentieth Century*. Doctoral dissertation, New York University, 2011; and Devin Orgeron, "Spreading the Word: Race, Religion, and the Rhetoric of Contagion in Edgar G. Ulmer's TB Films," in *Learning with the Lights Off*, 295–315.

48. Miriam Posner, *Depth Perception: Narrative and the Body in American Medical Filmmaking*, Doctoral dissertation, Yale University, 2011; Belliveau, *Micromotion Study*, 2012; Haidee Wasson, *Museum Movies: The Museum of Modern Art and the Birth of Art Cinema* (Berkeley: University of California Press, 2005); Jennifer Horne, "A History Long Overdue: The Public Library and Motion Pictures," in *Useful Cinema*, 213–257. On other disciplinary studies into similar questions of media and professional expertise, see Christopher Sellers and Joseph Melling, "Towards a Transnational Industrial-Hazard History: Charting the Circulation of Workplace Dangers, Debates and Expertise," *The British Journal for the History of Science* 45, no. 3 (2012): 401–424; Charles L. Briggs, "Communicability, Racial Discourse, and Disease," *Annual Review of Anthropology* 34 (2005): 269–291; Linda F. Hogle, "Introduction: Jurisdictions of Authority in Science and Medicine," *Medical Anthropology: Cross-Cultural Studies in Health and Illness* 21, no. 3–4 (2002): 231–246; Yves Dezalay and Bryant G. Garth, eds., *Lawyers and the Rule of Law in an Era of Globalization* (New York: Routledge, 2011); Janice Radway, "Research Universities, Periodical Publication, and the Circulation of

Professional Expertise: On the Significance of Middlebrow Authority," *Critical Inquiry* 31, no. 1 (2004): 203–228.

49. McCarthy, *Ambient Television*; Amanda R. Keeler, *Sugar Coat the Educational Pill: The Educational Aspirations of Emergent Film, Radio, and Television*. Doctoral dissertation, Indiana University, 2011; Stephen Groening, *Cinema Beyond Territory: Inflight Entertainment in Global Context* (London: British Film Institute, 2014).

50. Stephen Groening, " 'We Can See Ourselves as Others See Us': Women Workers and Western Union's Training Films in the 1920s," in *Useful Cinema*, 67, 69.

51. Solbrig, *Film and Function*, 93–99; McCarthy, *Citizen Machine*, 83–116.

52. McCarthy, *Citizen Machine*, 31–80; William L. Bird, Jr.,*"Better Living": Advertising, Media, and the New Vocabulary of Business Leadership, 1935–1955* (Evanston, IL: Northwestern University Press, 1999), 3–7. Rick Prelinger likewise points to Jamison Handy, the figurehead of one of the most prolific institutional media production houses of the twentieth century, as a key agent of the growing commercialization of public discourse. Rick Prelinger, "Eccentricity, Education, and the Evolution of Corporate Speech: Jam Handy and His Organization," in *Films That Work*, 215.

53. Vinzenz Hediger and Patrick Vonderau, "Record, Rhetoric, Rationalization: Industrial Organization and Film," in *Films That Work*, 40.

54. On the issues of Hollywood and the home, see Michael Z. Newman, *Video Revolutions: On the History of a Medium* (New York: Columbia University Press, 2014); Daniel Herbert, *Videoland: Movie Culture at the American Video Store* (Berkeley: University of California Press, 2014); Frederick Wasser, *Veni, Vidi, Video: The Hollywood Empire and the VCR* (Austin: University of Texas Press, 2002); Ann Gray, *Video Playtime: The Gendering of a Leisure Technology* (New York: Routledge, 1992); and Eugene Marlow and Eugene Secunda, *Shifting Time and Space: The Story of Videotape* (Santa Barbara: Praeger, 1991). On the format wars, see Joshua M. Greenberg, *From Betamax to Blockbuster: Video Stores and the Invention of Movies on Video* (Cambridge, MA: MIT Press, 2008) and James Lardner, *Fast Forward: Hollywood, the Japanese and the Onslaught of the VCR* (New York: Norton, 1987). On the rest, see Lucas Hilderbrand, *Inherent Vice: Bootleg Histories of Video and Copyright* (Durham, NC: Duke University Press, 2009); Dennis Redmond, *The World Is Watching: Video as Multinational Aesthetics, 1968–1995* (Carbondale: Southern Illinois University Press, 2003); and Gladys D. Ganley and Oswald H. Ganley, *Global Political Fallout: The VCR's First Decade* (Cambridge, MA: Program on Information Resources Policy, Harvard University, 1987). Others look at video as a distinctive art form or cultural practice. Sean Cubitt, *Videography: Video Media as Art and Culture* (Hampshire: Palgrave MacMillian, 1993) Gray, Video Playtime; Michael Renov and Erika Suderburg, eds., *Resolutions: Contemporary Video Practices* (Minneapolis: Minnesota Press, 1996). The only monograph-length humanities-based study of corporate video is Eugene Marlow's dissertation, *The Reported Use of Videotape in American Corporations 1956–1980*. Based in the work of Marshall McLuhan, Harold Innis, and Neil Postman, Marlow provides a broad introduction into the use of video in corporate settings focused on its impact and temporal and spatial communications and relations. Eugene Marlow, *The Reported Use of Videotape in American Corporations 1956–1980: A Media Ecology Approach*. Doctoral dissertation, New York University, 1988.

55. Joy V. Fuqua, *Prescription TV: Therapeutic Discourse in the Hospital and at Home*. (Durham, NC: Duke University Press, 2012). See notes 3 and 47 for McCarthy citations.

56. JoAnne Yates, *Control through Communication: The Rise of System in American Management* (Baltimore, MD: Johns Hopkins University Press, 1993); Paul A. Argenti, *Strategic Corporate Communications: A Global Approach for Doing Business in the New India* (New York: McGraw-Hill, 2008); Paul M. Leonardi "When Does Technology Use Enable Network Change in Organizations? A Comparative Study of Feature Use and Shared Affordances," *MIS Quarterly* 37, no. 3 (2013): 749–775.

57. Of course, television had not yet been invented (even if film had already found its way to the workplace in spectacular ways, cf. Frank and Lillian Gilbreth). Obviously, I don't fault the lack of attention to electronic media, but point to the limitations of the communication media she does study.

58. JoAnne Yates, *Structuring the Information Age: Life Insurance and Technology in the Twentieth Century* (Baltimore, MD: Johns Hopkins University Press, 2005). Notably, her case study, the life insurance industry, was a major user of both film and video technologies.

59. Edgar H. Schein, *Organizational Culture and Leadership: A Dynamic View*, 3rd edn. (San Fransico: Jossey-Bass (2004), 17; Scott D. N. Cook and Dvora Yanow, "Culture and Organizational Learning," *Journal of Management Inquiry* 2, no. 4 (1993): 375; Harrison M. Trace and Janice M. Beyer, "Changing Organizational Cultures," in *Classics of Organization Theory*, 6th edn., eds. Jay M. Shafritz, J. Steven Ott, and Yong Suk Jang (Belmont, CA: Thompson Wadsworth, 2005), 383–392.

60. Cook and Yanow, 372; Joanne Martin, *Organizational Culture: Mapping the Terrain* (Thousand Oaks: Sage, 2002), 77–80.

61. Pushkala Prasad, "The Protestant Ethic and the Myths of Frontier: Cultural Imprints, Organizational Structuring, and Workplace Diversity," in *Managing the Organizational Melting Pot: Dilemmas of Workplace Diversity*, eds. Pushkala Prasad, Albert J. Mills, Michael Elmes, Anshuman Prasad (Thousand Oaks, CA: Sage, 1997), 132; Albert J. Mills, "Dueling Discourses: Desexualization versus Eroticism in the Corporate Framing of Female Sexuality in the British Airlines Industry, 1945–1960," in *Managing the Organizational Melting Pot*, 171–198; Blake E. Ashforth and Fred Mael, "Social Identity Theory and the Organization," *The Academy of Management Review* 14, no. 1 (1989): 20–39. See also Chapter 5 in this book.

62. Raymond Williams, "Dominant, Residual, and Emergent," In *Marxism and Literature* (Oxford: Oxford University Press, 1977), 146.

63. William Boddy, *New Media and Popular Imagination: Launching Radio, Television, and Digital Media in the United States* (Oxford: Oxford University Press, 2004), 166; Jay David Bolter and Richard Grusin, *Remediation: Understanding New Media* (Cambridge, MA: MIT Press, 2000).

64. Geoffrey Pingree and Lisa Gitelman, "What's New about New Media?" in *New Media, 1740–1915*, eds. Lisa Gitelman and Geoffrey Pingree (Cambridge, MA: MIT Press, 2003), xv; Carolyn Marvin, *When Old Technologies Were New: Thinking about Electric Communication in the Late Nineteenth Century* (New York: Oxford University Press, 1988), 5; Hilderbrand, 35.

65. Jonathan Sterne, *The Audible Past: Cultural Origins of Sound Reproduction*, (Durham, NC: Duke University Press, 2003), 3; Boddy, 16; Lisa Gitelman, *Always*

Already New: Media, History, and the Data of Culture (Cambridge, MA: MIT Press, 2006), 6; Bolter and Grusin, 60; Hilderbrand, 11.

66. Susan J. Douglas, *Inventing American Broadcasting, 1899–1922* (Baltimore, MD: Johns Hopkins University Press, 1987), 322. Janet Abbate, *Inventing the Internet* (Cambridge, MA: MIT Press, 1999), 179; Gitelman, 6; Sterne, 8.

67. Abbate, 179; Gitelman, 7–8; Jonathan Sterne, *MP3: The Meaning of a Format* (Durham, NC: Duke University Press, 2012), 7. Bruno Latour (as Jim Johnson), "Mixing Humans and Nonhumans Together: The Sociology of a Door Closer," *Social Problems* 35, no. 3 (1988): 299, 301, 307. Particularly in the context of industrial television (Chapter 2), my analysis of struggles over the potential affordances of television likewise follows Bruno Latour's interest in questions of delegation (the human tasks given to objects) and prescription (the demands objects then make on human users).

68. Although Michele Hilmes uses this passage to refer to radio, it applies equally well to television in this context. *Radio Voices: American Broadcasting, 1922–1952* (Minneapolis: University of Minnesota Press, 1997), xiii.

69. Jonathan Sterne, *The Audible Past* (Durham, NC: Duke University Press, 2003), 7–8, 182; Gitelman, 7.

70. Michel Foucault, "Nietzsche, Genealogy, History," *The Foucault Reader*, ed. Paul Robinow (New York: Pantheon Books, 1984), 81.

71. Here we might also consider Foucault's claim that the conditions that regulate the appearance of new objects in effect produce them by making them *legible*: "They do not define its internal constitutions, but what enables it to appear, to juxtapose itself with other objects, situate itself in relation to them, to define its difference, its irreducibility, and even perhaps its heterogeneity, in short, to be placed in a field of exteriority." Michel Foucault, *Archeology of Knowledge* (New York: Pantheon Books, 1972), 45. I argue that standards battles can be seen best through this lens, wherein formats become legible through certain shared characteristics, and the characteristics that do not matter in this way are forgotten; I address this point in depth in "Record/Film/Book/Interactive TV: EVR as a Threshold Format," *Television and New Media* 17, no. 1 (2016): 44–61. As an added methodological point, as Sterne notes, new technologies tend to be accompanied by copious informational and illustrative material as their promoters attempt to make them meaningful to potential users; this provides a logical source of evidence revealing the carving out of possibilities (7).

72. Ann Laura Stoler, *Along the Archival Grain: Epistemic Anxieties and Colonial Common Sense* (Princeton, NJ: Princeton University Press, 2009), 34, 106, 138–139.

73. Sterne, *Audible Past*, 341.

74. Indeed, the production of archives is one of the four key moments identified by Michel-Rolph Trouillot in which silences—understood as the products of power—impact the production of official histories. Michel-Rolph Trouillot, *Silencing the Past: Power and the Production of History* (Boston: Beacon Press, 1997), 26, 28, 48.

75. Antoinette Burton, *Archive Stories: Facts, Fictions, and the Writing of History* (Durham, NC: Duke University Press, 2005), 9. While Burton is most directly referring to political, cultural, social, and economic factors (e.g., private companies' need within capitalist systems to manage a growing workforce or meet regulatory requirements regarding document retention), it is

particularly important within media histories to also consider how discourses of preservation themselves weigh on historiographical possibilities. Caroline Frick, *Saving Cinema: The Politics of Preservation* (Oxford: Oxford University Press, 2011).

76. On the overwhelming dominance of a few marquee trade magazines in media historiography, see Eric Hoyt, "Lenses for Lantern: Data Mining, Visualization, and Excavating Film History's Missing Sources," *Film History* 26, no. 2 (2014): 146–168.

77. Trouillot, 22, 49. In using snowballing beginning with prominent industry leaders, e.g., those who had led one of the major professional organizations, my sample was restricted largely to men who worked at the largest firms, primarily as producers.

78. Jennifer Karns Alexander, *The Mantra of Efficiency: From Waterwheel to Social Control* (Baltimore, MD: Johns Hopkins University Press, 2010).

CHAPTER 1

1. Dallas W. Smythe, "On the Audience Commodity and Its Work," in *Media and Cultural Studies: KeyWorks*, eds. Meenakshi Gigi Durham and Douglas M. Kellner (Oxford: Blackwell, 2006), 230–256.

2. For more on the utility and limitations of this framework for understanding audience activity as work, see Kit Hughes, "Work/Place' Media: Locating Laboring Audiences," *Media, Culture & Society* 36, no. 5 (2014): 644–660.

3. See, for example, Michael Curtin, "On Edge: Culture Industries in the Neo-Network Era," in *Making and Selling Culture*, ed. Richard Ohmann with Gage Averill, Michael Curtin, David Shumway, and Elizabeth G. Traube (Hanover, NH: Wesleyan University Press, 1996), 181–202.

4. To be clear, many firms that used television were not vertically integrated, making expanded vertical integration something of a misnomer. I use this term here for its analytical utility in drawing attention to companies' attempted "production" of their own workers.

5. While the vertically integrated studio system considered labor in the form of its parallel star system, stars (and directors) were also products marketed to audiences. Furthermore, although earlier organizations may have emphasized promoting from within, these practices did not represent a wholesale understanding of employee development—at all ranks—as crucial to mass production processes. Burton W. Folsom, *The Myth of the Robber Barons: A New Look at the Rise of Big Business in America* (Herndon, VA: Young America's Foundation, 2010), 65.

6. Harry Braverman, *Labor and Monopoly Capital: The Degradation of Work in the Twentieth Century* (New York: Monthly Review Press, 1974); Wiebe E. Bijker, Thomas P. Hughes, and Trevor Pinch, eds., *The Social Construction of Technological Systems: New Directions in the Sociology and History of Technology* (Cambridge, MA: MIT Press, 1987). See also David F. Noble, *America by Design: Science, Technology, and the Rise of Corporate Capitalism* (New York: Alfred A. Knopf, 1977) and Alfred D. Chandler, Jr., *The Visible Hand: The Managerial Revolution in American Business* (Cambridge, MA: Harvard University Press, 1977).

7. Kent T. Healy, "Transportation," in *The Growth of the American Economy*, ed. Harold F. Williamson (New York: Prentice Hall, 1944), 366–387; Gerald Berk, *Alternative Tracks: The Constitution of American Industrial Order, 1865–1917* (Baltimore, MD: Johns Hopkins University Press, 1994); William G. Roy,

Socializing Capital: The Rise of the Large Industrial Corporation in America (Princeton, NJ: Princeton University Press, 1997).

8. See, for example, Thomas C. Cochran, "The Business Revolution," *The American Historical Review* 79, no. 5 (1974), 1449–1466, esp. 1452–1460. On the impact of communication technologies' material form on the expansion of societies and their economic and political systems, see Harold Innis, *Empire and Communications* (Oxford: Oxford University Press, 1950).

9. Although widely retold, this story is rarely sourced. This account draws from "Alfred Vail," *The National Cyclopædia of American Biography, Volume IV* (New York: James T. White, 1897), 450.

10. John Tomlinson, *The Culture of Speed: The Coming of Immediacy* (London: Sage Publications, 2007), 26.

11. Richard B. Du Boff. "Business Demand and the Development of the Telegraph in the United States, 1844–1860," *The Business History Review* 54, no. 4 (1980): 467, 474–475.

12. Ibid., 465.

13. After Great Britain nationalized its inland telegraph companies in 1866, Canada and the United States became the only two countries with privately operated and owned telegraph lines. Richard B. Du Boff, "The Telegraph in Nineteenth Century America: Technology and Monopoly," *Comparative Studies in Society and History* 26, no. 4 (1984): 571–586, 572.

14. JoAnne Yates, "The Telegraph's Effect on Nineteenth Century Markets and Firms," *Business and Economic History* 15, no. 2 (1986): 152. Message rates decreased rapidly in following years, but remained high enough to discourage heavy "social" use of telegraph lines.

15. Ibid.

16. Du Boff, "American Technology," 580–581.

17. Christopher H. Sterling, Phyllis W. Bernt, and Martin B. H. Weiss, *Shaping American Telecommunications: A History of Technology, Policy, and Economics* (Mahwah, NJ: Lawrence Erlbaum Associates, 2006), 52.

18. George David Smith, *The Anatomy of a Business Strategy: Bell, Western Electric, and the Origins of the American Telephone Industry* (Baltimore, MD: Johns Hopkins University Press, 1985), 78–79.

19. US Congress, Senate, *Investigations of Western Union and Postal Telegraph-Cable Companies*, 60th Cong., 2d sess., S. Doc. 725 (Washington, DC, 1909), 21–22.

20. James Carey, *Communication as Culture: Essays on Media and Society*, rev. edn. (New York: Routledge, 2009), 157.

21. Ibid., 164. The company that became Western Union explicitly targeted railroads as their primary customers, contracting for exclusive rights to build wires along train tracks. Sterling, Bernt, and Weiss, *Shaping American Telecommunications*, 42.

22. Alexander James Field, "The Magnetic Telegraph, Price and Quantity Data, and the New Management of Capital," *The Journal of Economic History*, 52, no. 2 (1992): 401–413, 412.

23. The American rail system was comprised primarily of single tracks (as opposed to double tracks, which allowed trains to pass the same tracked area in opposite directions or move in the same direction at different speeds without the possibility of collision). The telegraph—and its continuous, rapid communication capabilities—was thus critical to rail's operation in the United States. See Field, 406–409; Du Boff, "American Technology," 575; Leonard S.

Reich, *The Making of American Industrial Research: Science and business at GE and Bell, 1876–1926* (Cambridge: Cambridge University Press, 1985), 32.

24. Du Boff, "Business Demand," 478; Carey, 158–159.
25. Yates, 149; Du Boff, "American Technology," 573.
26. Field, "The Magnetic Telegraph," 405. More specifically, we could trace the increased need in communication to what Yates calls "asset specificity" and "complexity of product description" (156–157). On how the *type* of information passed along the wires, e.g., price and quantity data, affected which industries benefited most from the telegraph, see Field, 403–405.
27. Yates, 155, 161.
28. Reich, 341.
29. The codes had an additional benefit of shortening messages for cheaper communications. Du Pont, for example, substituted "habitadme" for the lengthier (and more troubling) "how many were killed?"
30. Reich, 579. Other industries that benefited from the "timeliness" of the telegraph included journalism, gambling, and, as I discuss later, finance. On the agreement between Western Union and the Associated Press whereby the telegraphy company refused service to the AP's competitors in return for favorable news coverage, see Reich, 581–582. Jonathan Sterne, *The Audible Past: Cultural Origins of Sound Reproduction* (Durham, NC: Duke University Press, 2003), 140.
31. David Hochfelder, *The Telegraph in America, 1832–1920* (Baltimore, MD: Johns Hopkins University Press, 2012), 109.
32. Sidney H. Aronson, "Bell's Electrical Toy: What's the Use? The Sociology of Early Telephone Usage," in *The Social Impact of the Telephone*, ed. Ithiel de Sola Pool (Cambridge, MA: MIT Press, 1977), 26; Hochfelder, 109.
33. Du Boff, 581–583.
34. Hochfelder, 102–103, 115.
35. Ibid., 121, 116.
36. Ibid., 102.
37. Carey, 157.
38. Ibid., 13, 27.
39. Ibid., 131.
40. Yates, 161.
41. Glenn Porter, *The Rise of Big Business, 1860–1910* (Arlington Heights, IL: Harlan Davidson, 1973), 43.
42. Aronson, 23; Smith, 8.
43. Kenneth Lipartito, *The Bell System and Regional Business: The Telephone in the South, 1877–1920* (Baltimore, MD: Johns Hopkins University Press, 1989), 8.
44. George B. Prescott, *Bell's Electric Speaking Telephone: Its Invention, Construction, Application, Modification, and History* (New York: Arno Press, 1984), 46. It would not be until the close of the nineteenth century, however, that telephone use surged in rural areas and homes of the non-elite. See Smith, 125.
45. Alexander Graham Bell, Letter "To the capitalists of the Electric Telephone Company," Kensington, March 25, 1878. Reprinted in Ithiel de Sola Pool, Craig Decker, Stephen Dizard, Kay Israel, Pamela Rubin, Barry Weinstein, "Foresight and Hindsight: The Case of the Telephone," in de Sola Pool, 156.
46. Smith, 25. Robert M. Pike, "Kingston Adopts the Telephone: The Social Diffusion and Use of the Telephone in Urban Central Canada, 1876 to 1914," *Urban History Review* 18, no. 1 (1989): 33.

47. Prescott, 46–47. On the emphasis telephone companies placed on "serious" masculine uses of the technology (as opposed to women's "idle talk"), see Sterne, *The Audible Past*, 192–194, 199.
48. Aronson, 26.
49. Garnet, 22.
50. Pike, 42.
51. Reich, 136.
52. Smith, 22; Aronson, 27.
53. Garnet, 22–23. As with the telegraph, the telephone used different rates for home and business use. Smith, 25, 43; Robert MacDougall, "The Wire Devils: Pulp Thrillers, the Telephone, and Action at a Distance in the Wiring of a Nation," *American Quarterly* 58, no. 3 (2006): 732. Sterne, 197.
54. Bell letter, in de Sola Pool, 157.
55. Bell's nationally placed advertisements (which began around 1910) primarily targeted businessmen by emphasizing time thrift, connecting on vacation, and the impressive nature of the new technology for clients. When advertisements incorporated the home in their sales pitch, the telephone was promoted as a management device, convenient for the woman of the house to handle logistical tasks like ordering goods. Claude S. Fischer, "'Touch Someone': The Telephone Industry Discovers Sociability," *Technology and Culture* 29, no. 1 (1988): 39.
56. Pike, 41; Lipartito, 19.
57. Lipartito, 42, 103–106; Emily Bills, "Connecting Lines: LA's Telephone History and the Binding of the Region," *Southern California Quarterly* 91, no. 1 (2009): 28.
58. Aronson, 28.
59. This was the case in both the United States and the United Kingdom. Quote from Leslie Hannah, "Managerial Innovation and the Rise of the Large-Scaled Company in Interwar Britain," *The Economic History Review* 27, no. 2 (1974): 252–270. For a primer on shifts in managerial practice that coincided with the adoption of these technologies, see Chandler, *The Visible Hand*, 1973.
60. Hannah, 257.
61. This same practice resulted in the centralization of headquarters in cities that could act as hubs for managerial work across industries. Jean Gottmann, "Megalopolis and Antipolis: The Telephone and the Structure of the City," in de Sola Pool, 310; Bills, 37–38.
62. Aronson, 29; Lipartito, 8, 19.
63. Lipartito, 102–106; Bills, 28, 37–38, 56–57.
64. Bills, 41, 57.
65. Aronson, 29–30.
66. Asa Briggs, "The Pleasure Telephone: A Chapter in the Prehistory of the Media," in de Sola Pool, 43–45.
67. Fischer, 41–43.
68. Martin Mayer, "The Telephone and the Uses of Time," in de Sola Pool, 244.
69. Alan H. Wurtzel and Colin Turner, "Latent Functions of the Telephone: What Missing the Extension Means," in de Sola Pool, 246–261, 257.
70. As early as 1909, for example, a Maine inventor used radio as a "wireless telephone" to communicate between Portland and nearby islands (Reich, 156). Eventually, wireless telephony drastically intensified the telephone's promises of "universal service." However, while AT&T eventually incorporated microwave transmission into its systems, their pursuit of such applications served primarily to develop patents that protected their long line service. Reich, 170, 175.

71. Paladugu V. Rao, "Telephone and Instructional Communications" in de Sola Pool, 473, 484.
72. R. L. West, "Supervisory Control Systems With Leased Telephone Circuits," *Journal: American Water Works Association* 53, no. 8 (1961): 979–983.
73. Andre Millard, *Edison and the Business of Invention* (Baltimore, MD: Johns Hopkins University Press, 1990), 59.
74. Ibid., 65.
75. Patrick Feaster, "The Artifice of Nineteenth-Century Phonographic Business Dictation," *The Velvet Light Trap* 72 (2013): 6.
76. "Edison Photographs a Sound," *Macon (GA) Telegraph*, December 25, 1885, 5. Graham's Dictaphone, on the other hand, first targeted government workers in the nation's capitol. Woodbridge, *Dictaphone*, 12–13.
77. Millard 75, 77–78.
78. Ibid., 77, 79.
79. In 1888, Edison sold his interest in the machine to Jesse Lippincott, a businessman who had already purchased the American Gramophone Company in the hopes of creating his own electronic communications monopoly. Lippincott also saw business as the primary target for the machines. See Millard, 79.
80. Ibid., 254.
81. Editing dictations mid-composition also ranged from difficult to impossible, making them impractical as a replacement for a critically thinking stenographer (Feaster, 10–11). For a discussion of the difficulties faced by the machine's earliest users (and the reluctance of employees to use them), see Millard, 79–81, 264. On the quality of their sound reproduction, see Emily Thompson, "Machines, Music, and the Quest for Fidelity: Marketing the Edison Phonograph in America, 1877–1925" *The Musical Quarterly* 79, no. 1 (1995): 134–138.
82. Millard, 265.
83. Ibid., 262.
84. As one Edison ad puts it, "It is easy to replace a typewriter operator, but a competent stenographer is hard to find." "Ten Reasons Why Edison's Phonograph Is Superior to Any Stenographer," *Phonogram* 3, nos. 3–4 (1893): 410.
85. Millard, 267.
86. Sterne, 212.
87. Millard, 85; Feaster, 8.
88. Millard, 86.
89. Jeremiah Courtney and Arthur Blooston, "Mobile Radio Communications: The 'Work-Horse' Radio Services," *Law and Contemporary Problems* 22, no. 4 (1957): 633.
90. Ibid., from title.
91. Susan Douglas, *Inventing American Broadcasting, 1899–1922* (Baltimore, MD: Johns Hopkins University Press, 1987), 66–68.
92. Ibid., 82
93. Ibid., 95–97.
94. "Marconi's Great Triumph," *San Francisco Call 86*, no. 128 (October 6, 1899): 6.
95. Ibid., 1–2, 6.
96. Michele Hilmes, *Radio Voices: American Broadcasting 1922–1952* (Minneapolis: University of Minnesota Press, 1997), 44–50; Douglas, 207, Susan Smulyan, "Twisting the Dial," in *Selling Radio: The Commercialization of American Broadcasting, 1920–1934* (Washington, DC: Smithsonian Books, 1994), 93–124;

Robert McChesney, *Telecommunications, Mass Media, and Democracy: The Battle for the Control of U.S. Broadcasting, 1928–1935* (New York: Oxford University Press, 1993).

97. For an overview, see Elizabeth Fones-Wolf, "Creating a Favorable Business Climate: Corporations and Radio Broadcasting, 1934 to 1954," *The Business History Review* 73, no. 2 (1999), 226–246.

98. C. B. Jolliffe, "Radio and Safety," *The Annals of the American Academy of Political and Social Science* 142 (1929): 68–69.

99. Joseph A. Poli, "The Development and Present Trend of Police Radio Communications," *Journal of Criminal Law and Criminology* 33, no. 2 (1942): 194.

100. G. A. Playfair, "Radio Communication in Forest Protection and Administration, British Columbia Forest Service," *Empire Forestry Review* 32, no. 4 (1953): 342; W. Victor Weir and W.W. Hurlbut, "Emergency Radio Communication," *Journal: American Water Works Association* 33, no. 7 (1941): 1166.

101. Karl G. Larew, "From Pigeons to Crystals: The Development of Radio Communication in U.S. Army Tanks in World War II," *The Historian* 67, no. 4 (2005): 664–677; Weir and Hurlbut, 1166.

102. Lee B. Hertzberg, "Radio Communications for Water Utilities," *Journal: American Water Works Association* 51, no. 5 (1959): 604.

103. Hertzberg, 599.

104. Harry E. Jordan, "Application of the Public Water Supply Industry for Radio Channel Allocations," *Journal: American Water Works Association* 36, no. 12 (1944): 1285–1293.

105. "The Detroit Police Department Radio System," *The American Journal of Police Science* 1, no. 5 (1930): 457.

106. Hertzberg, 600.

107. Jordan, 1286.

108. Courtney and Blooston, 627. Emphasis mine.

109. Ibid., 627.

110. In pre-war Los Angeles, for example, when extreme weather or "social disturbances" (e.g., telephone operator strikes) incapacitated the physical telecommunications infrastructure, radio restored communication between the city's power and water facilities (Hertzberg, 601; Weir and Hurlbut, 1174). The Delaware, Lackawanna & Western Railroad, which experimented with wireless to enhance the allure of buying tickets, found it came in handy during a 1914 blizzard that knocked out the telegraph system. Tommy Meehan, "Fighting a Blizzard with the Wireless," *Railroad History* no. 199 (2008): 45.

111. Playfair, 347.

112. Larew, 676.

113. Tyler Watts and Jared Barton, "'I Can't Drive 55': The Economics of the CB Radio Phenomenon," *The Independent Review* 15, no. 3 (2011): 383–397.

114. Considine, 460. See also M. W. Baty, "Remote Control of Small Water Systems with Voice Frequency Carrier Equipment," *Journal: American Water Works Association* 48, no. 8 (1956): 1051.

115. Samuel C. McLendon and Michael Zihal, "Telemetering and Remote Control by the Long Island Water Corporation," *Journal: American Water Works Association* 49, no. 11 (1957): 1371–1377.

116. "The Detroit Police Department Radio System," 456, 459. See also Jordan, 1286.

117. "The Detroit Police Department Radio System," 459.

118. Hertzberg, 599.
119. Courtney and Blooston, 628, 633; Hertzberg, 599.
120. Douglas M. Considine, "Modern Instruments and Controls," *The Scientific Monthly* 54, no. 5 (1942): 455.
121. Ibid., 460. Emphasis mine.
122. Poli, 195; Hertzberg, 599.
123. Hugh R. Slotten, "Radio's Hidden Voice: Noncommercial Broadcasting, Extension Education, and State Universities during the 1920s," *Technology and Culture* 49, no. 1 (2008): 8.
124. Liberal arts lectures and music programs provided cultural enrichment. Ibid., 4–5.
125. Amanda Keeler, "Defining a Medium: The Educational Aspirations for Early Broadcasting," *Journal of Radio & Audio Media* 23, no. 2, 2016; William Bianchi, "The Wisconsin School of the Air: Success Story with Implications," *Educational Technology & Society* 5, no. 1 (2002): 142.
126. Katie Day Good, "Radio's Forgotten Visuals," *Journal of Radio & Audio Media* 23, no. 2 (2016): 367–368.
127. Jerri Ann Husch, *Music of the Workplace: A Study of Muzak Culture.* Doctoral dissertation, University of Massachussettes, 1984, 52–54.
128. Marek Korczynski and Keith Jones, "Instrumental Music? The Social Origins of Broadcast Music in British Factories," *Popular Music* 25, no. 2 (2006): 148–149, 155.
129. Simon C. Jones and Thomas G. Schumacher, "Muzak: On Functional Music and Power" *Critical Studies in Mass Communication* 9 (1992): 159; Korczynski and Jones, 162, footnote 6.
130. Term borrowed from Jones and Schumacher who use it to refer to "prerecorded and programmed sound systems used in commercial and industrial contexts . . . music used principally to support and encourage some other primary activity, whether the production and consumption of goods and services or the reproduction of social and symbolic order in public spaces" (166).
131. William Benton (of major advertising firm and radio program producer Benton & Bowles) became the sole owner of the company in 1941. Benton would promote another "functional" use of sound technologies when he championed Voice of America as Assistant Secretary of State for Public Affairs. Husch, 58, 61.
132. Ibid., 62.
133. Husch, 62–64. Jones and Schumacher report its instillation in "most major American firms," though their classification schema is unclear (159).
134. Husch, 67–71, 74, 128.
135. Jones and Schumacher, 159.
136. Ibid., 158.
137. Korczynski and Jones, 146, 147.
138. Joseph Lanza, *Elevator Music: A Surreal History of Muzak, Easy-Listening, and Other Moodsong* (Ann Arbor: University of Michigan Press, 2004), 27.
139. For a close reading of these themes, see Husch, 93–149. Quotation from Jones and Schumacher, 161.
140. Jones and Schumacher, 162.
141. Joy V. Fuqua, *Prescription TV: Therapeutic Discourse in the Hospital and at Home* (Durham, NC: Duke University Press, 2012), 2.
142. Alexander Russo, "An American Right to an 'Unannoyed Journey'? Transit Radio as a Contested Site of Public Space and Private Attention, 1949–1952,"

Historical Journal of Film, Radio and Television 29, no. 1 (2009): 1–25; Ronda L. Sewald, "Forced Listening: The Contested Use of Loudspeakers for Commercial and Political Messages in the Public Soundscape," *American Quarterly* 63, no. 3 (2011): 761–780; On "care," see Jones and Schumacher, 162.

143. Jones and Schumacher, 163.

144. On the temporality of mediated spaces and labor, see Anna McCarthy on waiting room television in *Ambient Television: Visual Culture and Public Space* (Durham, NC: Duke University Press, 2001), 195–224. We might also consider Russo's discussion of Transit Radio, which used content looped to the temporalities of consumer travel rather than driver shift work (6).

145. Good, 367–368.

146. Jonathan Coopersmith, *Faxed: The Rise and Fall of the Fax Machine* (Baltimore, MD: Johns Hopkins University Press, 2015), 17.

147. Much of the early experimentation was undertaken by radio giant RCA, which imagined a fax network on par with radio; newspapers and radio stations would lease machines to their subscribers who would receive (over the course of some 15–20 minutes) a 4–6 page newspaper. Although abandoned due to costs and technical difficulties, a second (faster) generation of newspaper facsimile was taken up in 1944 by papers including the *New York Times* that broadcast to banks, hotels, restaurants, and other businesses. Coopersmith, 58, 62, 84.

148. Ibid., 44.

149. Television's developers also saw fax as a possible adjunct to broadcasting that could transmit schedules and synopses to subscribers. Ibid., 45, 194.

150. Ibid., 161. See also pages 40, 49, 92, 124.

151. Ibid., 162. The speed of the fax may have been particularly appealing in the United States, where major cities could be quite distant from each other. See also pages 39, 66, 125, 137, 156, 169.

152. Terry Ramsaye, *A Million and One Nights* (New York: Simon and Schuester, 1926), 345.

153. Uncertain is how the film would have been projected, since it was still two years before the Lumière brothers exhibited their Cinematograph.

154. "Camera! Action! Sales!" *Business Week* (May 27, 1939): 38.

155. Patricia Murray, "When Advertisers Tried Films in the Gay '90s" *Printers' Ink* 205 (November 19 1943): 25–26. This account—told by the canonical advertising trade paper—likewise serves its industry, arguing advertising films were "*too* popular" for their own good. Disrupting traffic and overloading city streets, they were quickly banned, "a tragic story" that nonetheless testifies to the skill of advertisers and the enthusiasm of consumers for commercial messages.

156. Peep shows, however, make for a more evocative origin, binding industrial film ever more tightly to the entertainment industry. Charles Musser, *The Emergence of Cinema* (Berkeley: University of California Press, 1994), 169–170. William Boddy, "Advertising Form, Technological Change and Screen Practices in the USA," in *Films That Sell*, eds. Bo Florin, Nico de Klerk, and Patrick Vonderau (London: British Film Institute, 2016), 166.

157. Though the stories' inaccuracies can be clarified. It is most likely that *Dewar's— It's Scotch!* was produced in 1897, the same year as a handful of other early advertising films. See Rick Prelinger, *The Field Guide to Sponsored Films* (San Francisco: National Film Preservation Foundation, 2006), 111.

158. Terry Ramsaye, "The Romantic History of the Motion Picture" *Photoplay* 22, no. 2 (1922): 60. The tale of Porter's pioneering textual work—the first narrative film—comes vividly some chapters later. Ramsaye, *Nights*, 345.

159. Though often the province of the nation, in this instance, cinema heritage served an industry hoping to build its own empire. Caroline Frick, *Saving Cinema: The Politics of Preservation* (New York: Oxford University Press, 2011), 12–14.

160. Citation from the first of three times *Business Screen* recounts the origin story. "First Advertising Film?" *Business Screen* 1, no. 4 (1938): 17. Though the first *Business Screen* version of the story follows closely *A Million and One Nights*, several discrepancies exist: different dates (1987 or "somewhere between 1986 and 1900"), the name of the distiller (Haig & Haig or Dewar's), and—most curiously—a direct quote allegedly from *Nights* published in *Business Screen* that does not appear either in Ramsaye's *Photoplay* series or his book. This suggests that *Business Screen* was more invested in the politics of citation and affiliation than it was in dutifully following its sources. Later *Business Screen* retellings drop this facet of the story, focusing primarily on the legitimating power of long-ago dates (even if an improbable 1893) and figures like Porter and Edison. "Early History of Sales Film Dates Implement Company Sales Pix to 1911," *Business Screen*. 15, no. 4 (1954): 10; "Audiences, U.S.A." *Business Screen* 14, no. 2 (1953): 34.

161. "Camera! Action! Sales!" 38.

162. *The Harvester World* 2, no. 14 (1911): 2, 6, 17. IHC materials almost always list the date of *Back to the Old Farm* as 1911, though no evidence of the film's distribution exists prior to 1912.

163. Gregory A. Waller, "International Harvester, *Business Screen* and the History of Advertising Film," in *Films That Sell*, 41–42, 44–46.

164. "Those Wonderful First 30 Years . . . ," *Business Screen* 34, no. 4 (1973): 19.

165. "The Birth of the Sales Film," *Business Screen* 1, no. 4. (1938): 17; "Early History of Sales Film Dates Implement Company Sales Pix to 1911," *Business Screen* 15, no. 4 (1954): 10.

166. Prelinger, 111.

167. "International Harvester: A Pioneer of 1911 Shows the Way in 1938," *Business Screen* 1, no. 1 (1938): 14–16.

168. Waller, "International," 47–48; *The Harvester World* 1, no. 12 (1910): 5.

169. "A Warning," *The Harvester World* 3, no. 3 (1912): 17.

170. For a thorough accounting of Ford's considerable motion picture activity in the 1910s and 1920s, see Lee Grieveson, "The Work of Film in the Age of Fordist Mechanization," *Cinema Journal* 51, no. 3 (2012): 25–51. On other companies early to the film game, see "Those Wonderful First 30 years," *Business Screen* 33 (1973): 19.

171. Yet another source claims Vitograph's "Adventures of Billiken," created by J. Alexander Leggett for Monash Sales Company, as the first industrial (c. 1909). See "The Pioneer Industrial Film Man," *Educational Film Magazine* 1, no. 1 (1919): 30.

172. Heide Solbrig, *Film and Function: A History of Industrial Motivation Film*. Doctoral dissertation, University of California, San Diego, 2004, 116.

173. Lee Grieveson, *Cinema and the Wealth of Nations: Media, Capital, and the Liberal World System* (Oakland: University of California Press, 2018), 2.

174. As Scott Curtis notes, the Gilbreths' films were (at least) equally invested in promoting the Gilbreths themselves to potential clients—a reminder that media workers' self-interest has often shaped how film has been popularly configured as a potential tool for industrial purposes. Scott Curtis, "Images of Efficiency: The Films of Frank B. Gilbreth," in *Films That Work*, eds. Vinzenz Hediger and Patrick Vonderau (Amsterdam: Amsterdam University Press, 2009), 85–99.

175. Stephen Groening, "'We Can See Ourselves as Others See Us': Women Workers and Western Union's Training Films in the 1920s," in *Useful Cinema*, 34–58.

176. W. H. Offenhauser, Jr., and F. H. Hargrove, "Some Industrial Applications of Current Sound Motion Picture Equipment," *SMPTE Journal* 34, no. 2 (1940): 164.

177. See, for example, John S. Bird, "Vocational Training Offers Field for Moving Picture," *Reel and Slide* 2, no. 2 (1919): 21. Many of the perceived virtues of film as a training medium parallel the attributes identified by educators as central to its pedagogical value. Devin Orgeron, Marsha Orgeron, and Dan Streible, "A History of Learning with the Lights Off," in *Learning with the Lights Off: Educational Film in the United States*, eds. Orgeron, Orgeron, and Streible (Oxford: Oxford University Press, 2012), 21–25, 31.

178. Association of National Advertisers (A.N.A.) Films Steering Committee, *The Dollars and Sense of Business Films* (New York: A.N.A., 1954), 39.

179. This common refrain enabled advocates of business film to compare it favorably to print by establishing film as a medium with no "waste circulation." In other words, circulation numbers equated readership/viewership numbers, since anyone confronting a film in the proper situation devoted "undivided attention to absorbing the sponsor's message." A few decades later, with the advent of rear-projection machines and CRT television exhibition, lighted room screenings would be promoted as an advantage over film. "Camera! Action! Sales!" 38; A. L. Parker, "Progress in Film Advertising," *Associated Advertising* 13, no. 4 (1922): 17; A.N.A., 7.

180. Solbrig, *Film and Function*, 2004.

181. H. Walker and Paul Sklar, *Business Finds Its Voice: Management's Effort to Sell the Business Idea to the Public* (New York: Harper & Brothers, 1938), 1, 8.

182. Anna McCarthy, *The Citizen Machine: Governing by Television in 1950s America* (New York: The New Press, 2010), 31–80; William L. Bird, Jr., *"Better Living": Advertising, Media, and the New Vocabulary of Business Leadership, 1935–1955* (Evanston, IL: Northwestern University Press, 1999), 3–7.

183. Industrial film developed differently across international contexts. These examples merely point to the scope of film use. Rudmer Canjels, "Films from beyond the Well: A Historical Overview of Shell Films," 247; Martin Loiperdinger, "Early Industrial Moving Pictures in Germany," 69, 72; and Nicolas Hatzfeld, Gwenaële Rot, and Alain P. Michel, "Filming Work on Behalf of the Automobile Firm: The Case of Renault (1950–2002)," 192, 204, all in *Films That Work*.

184. Dolph Eastman, "How Shall We Break the Deadlock," *Educational Film Magazine* 6, no. 4 (1921): 3–4. A similar logic operated within the educational sector. See Victoria Cain, "'An Indirect Influence upon Industry': Rockefeller Philanthropies and the Development of Educational Film in the United States, 1935–1953," in *Learning with the Lights Off*, 236–236.

185. C. H. Moore, "Importance of the Film in Industrial Education," *Educational Film Magazine*, 1, no. 2 (1919): 30.

186. Parker, 17.

187. *The Harvester World*, an internal magazine, provides a good, though imperfect, record of the distribution practices of IHC dealers. Wisconsin Historical Society, McCormick-International Harvester Collection. This protocol lasted until IHC shifted to distributing training films for the war effort.

188. Walker and Sklar, 37. The Bureau of Commercial Economics circulated film prints donated by business, manufacturing, newsreel outfits, churches, civic groups, government, and trade associations. According to its founder, the audience for *BCE* films reached 34 million people in 1920. Sean Savage, *The Eye Beholds: Silent Era Industrial Films and the Bureau of Commercial Economics*. Master's thesis, New York University, 2006. See also Orgeron, Orgeron, and Streible, 54; "Announcement," *Educational Film Magazine* 5, no. 6 (1921): np; see also page 11 of the same issue. For Levey's distinguished moniker, see C. H. Moore, "Importance of the Film in Industrial Education," 30.

189. Solbrig, 125–126.

190. Grieveson, *Wealth*, 103.

191. Walker and Sklar, 35.

192. Parker, 17.

193. "Camera! Action! Sales!," 38; Walker and Sklar, 32, 35.

194. Under different names, e.g., *Business and Home TV Screen, Computer Pictures*, the journal ran until 1995. However, its primary relevance to the industrial film sector can be dated up through the 1970s and its first name change (1978), which coincided with a decrease in publication rate. Ott H. Coelin, the journal's founder and long-time editor, also served as vice president for the educational magazine *See and Hear*, a keen reminder of the overlaps between nontheatrical sectors. Indeed, one of the earliest sources of trade information geared to industrial interests was *Educational Film Magazine* (*EFM*), which began publishing soon after World War I's conclusion lifted restrictions on paper and pulp use. Each issue contained a range of special-interest sections, including "Industrial." Dolph Eastman, "Our First Anniversary—and Our Future," *Educational Film Magazine* 3, no. 5 (1920): 5; "Industrial Section," *Educational Film Magazine* 1, no. 1 (1919): 29. For more on the appeal of (often free to rent) sponsored films as classroom films, see Orgeron, Orgeron, and Streible, 45. For his part, Coelin also founded the American Archives of the Factual Film at Iowa State University in 1974, a large collection of nontheatrical business and educational 16mm films later absorbed by the Library of Congress.

195. Eric Hoyt, "Lenses for Lantern: Data Mining, Visualization, and Excavating Film History's Neglected Sources," *Film History* 26, no. 2 (2014): 155–156.

196. Technicolor," *Business Screen* 1, no. 1 (1938): 20–21; "Food," *Business Screen* 2, no. 3 (1940): 11–16; "Markets," *Business Screen* 2, no. 4 (1940): 11; "The ABC's of Business Film making" *Business Screen* 1, no. 4 (1938): 13, 28; "Pioneer," *Business Screen* 1, no. 5 (1939): 17, 42.

197. See, for example, "1955 Audio-Visual Projection, Tape Recording and Related Equipment including Projection Screens and Film Handling Accessories," *Business Screen* 15, no. 8 (1955): 1A–22A.

198. Benedict Anderson, *Imagined Communities: Reflections on the Origin and Spread of Nationalism*, rev. edn. (London: Verso, 2006), 5–7.

199. Sub-Committee on Sponsor-Producer Responsibilities of the Films Committee of the Association of National Advertisers, "A Check-List for Producer and Sponsor Responsibility in the Production of Motion Pictures," *Business Screen*

12, no. 2 (1951): 25, 26. Pushing newcomers away from the fatted calf of government contracts, this report explicitly declares, *"It is most certainly evident from this Review that there is no need to set up new production resources"* (emphasis original, 27).

200. World War II is credited with establishing a reliable nontheatrical audience, scraping away suspicions linked to film's low-culture status, solidifying networks of 16mm film use, and providing "ideological commitment" to film for education and training. Kirsten Ostherr, "Health Films, Cold War, and the Production of Patriotic Audiences: *The Body Fights Bacteria* (1948)," in *Useful Cinema*, 104; Orgeron, Orgeron, and Streible, 41, 107; Gregory A. Waller, "Projecting the Promise of 16mm, 1935–45," in *Useful Cinema*, 135–137; Quote from Solbrig, 137.

201. Kathryn Cramer Brownell, "'It Is Entertaintment, and It Will Sell Bonds!': 16mm Film and the World War II War Bond Campaign," *The Moving Image* 10, no. 2 (2010): 60–82; Waller, 135–137.

202. Kevin Hamilton and Ned O'Gorman, *Lookout America!: The Secret Hollywood Studio at the Heart of the Cold War* (Hanover, New Hampshire: Dartmouth College Press, 2019), 17.

203. Ott Coelin, Editorial, *Business Screen* 4, no. 6 (1942): 6; "News of the Associations," *Business Screen* 5, no. 4 (1943): 36.

204. The National Association of Visual Education Dealers (est. 1939, first major meeting 1946) also included industrial members in their conferences and print damage insurance programs. Orgeron, Orgeron, and Streible, 3–66; "The Fifth Midwest Forum," *Business Screen* 3, no. 2 (1943): 41. "NAVED Insures Films," *Business Screen* 4, no. 8 (1944): 26.

205. "Industrial Audio-Visual Association Holds Annual Meeting," *Business Screen* 9, no. 2 (1948): 19.

206. "Industrial Audio-Visual Association Elects Board," *Business Screen* 11, no. 2 (1950): 28. John Thornton Caldwell, *Production Culture: Industrial Reflexivity and Critical Practice in Film and Television* (Durham, NC: Duke University Press, 2008), 88–90.

207. "14 Festival Awards to Sponsored Pictures," *Business Screen* 8, no. 8 (1947): 25; Irene A. Wright, "Government's Interest in Film Festivals," *Business Screen* 11, no. 8 (1950): 8, 10; "Cleveland's Festival Surprise Hit," *Business Screen* 5, no. 9 (1948): 8, 48.

208. "Ferguson Library Extends Civic Film Interest in Stanford, Conn.," *Business Screen* 11, no. 5 (1950): 10; "Toledo Chamber of Commerce to Sponsor Business Film Festival," *Business Screen* 13, no. 7 (1952): 4; "Boston Holds First Annual Film Festival," *Business Screen* 12, no. 4 (1951): 24.

209. I am indebted to Brian Real for pointing out the connection between CINE and USIA in his 2019 Society for Cinema and Media Studies Presentation, "Networks of Screen Diplomacy: The USIA as a Patron of Nontheatrical Art," March 14. Seattle, Washington. For more on the USIA's motion picture activities in this period, see Brian Real, "The Hidden History of the American Film Institute: The Cold War, Arts Policy, and American Film Preservation," *The Moving Image* 18, no. 1 (2018): 25–47.

210. Wright, 10.

211. Orgeron, Orgeron, and Streible, 48; for more on the exhibition of sponsored films on television, see Kit Hughes, "Disposable: Useful Cinema on Early Television," *Critical Studies in Television* 12, no. 2 (2017): 102–120.

212. Thomas W. Hope, *Hope Reports: AV-USA* (Rochester, NY: Hope Reports, 1969), 2. Rhees Rare Books, Hope Reports Collection, University of Rochester (henceforth HRC).
213. Ibid., 14, 28.
214. Ibid., 37.
215. Ibid., 37, 39.
216. "Camera Eye," *Business Screen* 1, no. 6 (1939): 10; "Technical Production, Projection, Equipment, Development," *Business Screen* 1, no. 6 (1939): 27. Another major problem that diffused the threat of television was qualified staffing shortages. In "Chicagoans Take to Television: A Progress Report on Telecasting in the Midwest," authors discuss the limited base of skilled technicians for local stations and the attendant value of cooperation through training initiatives for *everyone* in the audiovisual industry—since stronger television operations meant more opportunities for business film producers to exhibit their product. *Business Screen* 8, no. 8 (1947): 18–21, 32.
217. "Business Theaters: RCA's Plant Center," *Business Screen* 8, no. 7 (1947): 28–29.
218. "Large Screen Theatre Television," *Business Screen* 8, no. 7 (1947): 41.

CHAPTER 2

1. Richard Koszarski and Doron Galili, "Television in the Cinema before 1939: An International Annotated Database, with an Introduction by Richard Koszarski," *e-media studies* 5, no. 1 (2016): http://journals.dartmouth.edu/cgi-bin/WebObjects/Journals.woa/1/xmlpage/4/article/471. This first film cited is *La photographie électrique à distance*, directed by George Méliès, which portrays television as a leisure technology in the vein of photographic portraiture.
2. Chaplin would likely have been familiar with experimentations on videophones in the late 1920s and 1930s, which may have inspired the two-way communication screen device.
3. R. C. G. Williams, "Industrial and Professional Applications of Television Technique," *Proceedings of the IEE* 99, no. 20 (1952): 651; David Sarnoff, "Electronics and the Engineer," *Proceedings of the IRE* 41, no. 7 (1953): 837; V. K. Zworykin, "The Evolution of Television," *Electrical* Engineering 72, no. 3 (1953): 209; V. K. Zworykin, "Industrial Television and the Vidicon," *Electrical Engineering* 69, no. 7 (1950): 624–627; Anthony R. Michaelis, "Some Uses of Television in Science and Industry," *The Quarterly of Film Radio and Television* 7, no. 2 (Winter 1952): 170; G. H. Wilson, "Television in Industry," Paper presented at AIEE Fall General Meeting (February 1953): 125; H. F. Schneider, "How Can Industry Use Television?" Paper presented at the 3rd annual Conference of the Professional Group on Industrial Electronics (September 5, 1955): 23.
4. Raymond Williams, *Television: Technology and Cultural Form*, ed. Ederyn Williams (London: Routledge, 1997 reprint), 86.
5. Ibid., 85.
6. William Uricchio, "Television's Next Generation: Technology/Interface Culture/Flow," in *Television after TV: Essays on a Medium in Transition*, eds. Lynn Spigel and Jan Olsson (Durham, NC: Duke University Press, 2005), 232–261.
7. On work systems and the conditioning of capitalism, see Rosabeth Moss Kanter, *Men and Women of the Corporation* (New York: Basic Books, 1993), 10; Vicki Mayer, *Below the Line: Producers and Production Studies in the New*

Television Economy (Durham, NC: Duke University Press, 2011); and David Harvey, *The Condition of Postmodernity: An Enquiry into the Origins of Cultural Change* (Hoboken, NJ: Wiley-Blackwell, 1991). On labor and technology, see, for example, Harry Braverman, *Labor and Monopoly Capital: The Degradation of Work in the Twentieth Century* (New York: Monthly Review Press, 1974) and E. P. Thompson, *The Making of the English Working Class* (New York: Vintage, 1966).

8. Inga Kroener, *CCTV: A Technology under the Radar?* (Farnham, UK: Ashgate, 2014); Clive Norris and Gary Armstrong, *The Maximum Surveillance Society: The Rise of CCTV and Social Control* (Oxford: Berg, 1999); Kelly A. Gates, *Our Biometric Future: Facial Recognition Technology and the Culture of Surveillance* (New York: New York University Press, 2011).

9. "Industrial Television Solves a Mystery by Watching Thieves at Work," *The Michigan Technic* 72, no. 2 (1953): 44; "TV Catches a Thief," *New York Times* (September 6, 1953): E7; Bryan Whipple, "Industry's New Tool—T.V.," *The Michigan Technic* (April 1958): 28; P. B. Reed, "Industrial Television Demonstrated," *Radio Age* 9, no. 3 (1950): 14; *SMPTE Journal* 54 (April 1950): 512–513.

10. While educators were sometimes classified as ITV users, they were also set apart through the terminology of E-ITV or ETV. A wealth of trade materials document educational CCTV programs. See, for example, *Educational Television*, which became *Educational and Industrial Television* in 1972.

11. "Review," *Journal of the Institution of Electrical Engineers* 4, no. 45 (1958): 512–516.

12. James D. McLean, "Industrial Television Systems," *Televiser* 1, no. 1 (1944): 53–54.

13. Reviews of Edward M. Noll's and V.K. Zworykin's books, for example, point out that their focus is narrow, excluding major manufacturers or focusing heavily on a single lab. The author of these reviews published his own book on CCTV in 1957. "Books," *Proceedings of the IRE* 44, no. 9 (1956): 1203; "Books," *Proceedings of the IRE* 46, no. 10 (1958) 1769–1772.

14. Robert J. Connors, "The Rise of Technical Writing Instruction in America," *Teaching Technical Communication: Critical Issues for the Classroom*, ed. James M. Dubinsky (Boston: Bedford/St. Martin's, 2004), 84, 89.

15. Patrick Moore, "Myths about Instrumental Discourse: A Response to Robert R. Johnson," in *Teaching Technical Communication*, 54.

16. Anna McCarthy, *Ambient Television: Visual Culture and Public Space* (Durham, NC: Duke University Press, 2001), 63–88.

17. A broader cultural understanding of CCTV as the manifestation of the desire to create rigidly defined but potentially expansive networks can look to theater television. Using intra-city and even national closed-circuits, theater television distributed live and filmed programming via radio relay, coaxial cable, and/or telephone lines to a limited set of participating movie theaters (and therefore a highly restricted television audience). Predating ITV, theater television likewise built its reputation in part on live remote viewing. In the keynote delivered to the 1944 National Electronics Conference, for example, Ralph R. Beal alluded to the shared qualities of both systems when he discussed theater TV's capability to deliver the "thrills and drama of actual events as they occur at a distance in real life" *alongside* the promise of ITV's "use of radio sight as the 'eyes' of factories, the means of co-ordinating and controlling giant manufacturing enterprises, and the means also of looking into places that otherwise might be inaccessible or

dangerous." Ralph R. Beal, quoted in "Chicago Conference Presages Expanding Electronic Applications," *Electrical Engineering* (November 1944): 419. See Chapter 3 for more.

18. Morris A. Mayers and Rodney D. Chipp, *Closed Circuit TV System Planning* (New York: John F. Rider, 1957), v. Hints of earlier uses exist, such as Diamond Power's claim to have used a CCTV system to monitor water gauges as early as 1945, though little information substantiates these instances.

19. R. C. G. Williams, 651; "TBA Conference Highlights," *The Film Daily* (December 12, 1944): 8; David Sarnoff, "Reconversion Is Dominant Factor," *The Radio Annual* (1946): 59; A. P. Peck, "Previews of the Industrial Horizon," *Scientific American* (June 1947): 244.

20. Michaelis, 173.

21. Whipple, 28–30. All figures in this chapter adjusted for inflation and represented in 2019 dollars via CPI Inflation Calculator.

22. "Industry's Electronic Eye," *Steel* (July 21, 1958). Accessed at the Hagley Museum and Library, Wilmington, DE.

23. Richard W. Cook "Transistorizing the Industrial Image Orthicon Camera," *IRE Transactions on Industrial Electronics* 8, no. 2 (1961): 1.

24. W. R. G. Baker, quoted in "Glowing Prospects on His Screen," *New York Times* (December 18, 1955): F1; E. S. Hall, "The New Look in Industrial Electronics," *Proceedings of the IEE* 108, no. 37 (1961): 23–14.

25. For more on the specifics of transmission, see Mayers and Chipp, 108–113. Both AT&T and the Bell System devised special rates for closed-circuit television transmission by 1957.

26. Creighton Peet, "TV's Little Brother," *Popular Mechanic* (November 1950): 82; Schneider, 23.

27. E. R. Thomas and W. L. Norvell, "Television for Monitoring Stack Emission," *Electrical Engineering* 72, no. 3 (1953): 224–227; L. W., "Industrial TV Plays Big Role in Many Fields," *Chicago Daily Tribune* (May 10, 1952): C1; Michaelis, 173; Wilson, 135.

28. J. Higsom, "Electricity in the Expansion of the Iron and Steel Industry," *Proceedings of the IEE* 103, no. 7 (1956): 35.

29. Schneider, 23.

30. "Industrial TV Showing Set," *Los Angeles Times* (October 9, 1954): P14; L. W., C1; Alfred R. Zipser, Jr., "C.B.S. Unit Lifts Military Orders from 0 to $5 Million in 5 Months," *New York Times* (February 13, 1955): 11; Sarnoff, "Reconversion," 59; Peet, 84; Julian K. Sprague, "Industrial Electronics," *Financial Analysts Journal* 11, no. 3 (1955): 83–85.

31. Zipser, 11.

32. Peet, 81–85, 260.

33. Joseph M. Guilfoyle, "Industrial Television," *Wall Street Journal* (August 29, 1955): 14; Zipser, 11; Michaelis, 173; Baker, quoted in "Glowing," F1; Whipple, 30.

34. Michaelis, 170–177; Sarnoff, "Electronics and the Engineer," 837.

35. Peet, 81–85; "IRE Convention: DuMont Color System," *Broadcasting—Telecasting* (March 13, 1950): 28; "Proceedings of the Meeting of the Associates of Stanford Research Institute," Volumes 5–10 (1951): 34; Michaelis, 170–177.

36. Harold R. Walker, "A Low Cost Industrial Television System," *IRE Transactions on Industrial Electronics* 9, no. 2 (1962): 97–101; Arthur D. Caster, "Television for Sewer Inspection," *Sewage and Industrial Wastes* 31, no. 7 (July 1959): 860;

"DuMont Labs Announces Line of Industrial TV Equipment," *Broadcasting—Telecasting* (May 27, 1957): 88; "Electric Product Sales Post Record," *New York Herald Tribune* (January 7, 1957): B14.

37. Radio Corporation of America, "Industrial Television Meeting May 24, 1951," 1. Accession 2069, RCA (Camden, NJ Technical Reports) Box 165, Folder Z 164-Z-170. Hagley Museum and Library, Wilmington, DE.

38. Edward M. Noll, *Closed-Circuit and Industrial Television* (New York: The Macmillan Company, 1956), 10; Allen B. Dumont, "The 'Telectronic Age,'" *Variety* (January 6, 1954): 102; Wilson, 130; Schneider, 23.

39. See, for example, Morris and Chipp, *Closed Circuit TV System Planning* (New York: J. F. Rider, 1957); Henry Arthur McGhee, *Industrial Television: Design and Application of Television Equipment in Industry, Education, and Science* (London: George Newnes, 1957); V. K. Zworykin, E. G. Ramberg, and L. E. Flory, *Television in Science and Industry* (New York, John Wiley & Sons, 1958). Respectively, the corporations represented by these authors are DuMont, Pye Limited, and RCA.

40. Zworykin et al., 11, 272.

41. Quotation from Zworykin et al., 22 and Schneider, 23–31. Variations on this "too" formulation appear as early as 1952 in "Industrial Television Expands," *Radio Age* 3, no. 11 (1952): 21, and became a point of reflective comment by 1957 (Mayers and Chipp, 62). "Industrial Television Solves a Mystery," 44; L. W., C1.

42. David E. Nye, *America's Assembly Line* (Cambridge, MA: MIT Press 2013), 8, 10.

43. On the conceptual history of efficiency, see Jennifer Karns Alexander, *The Mantra of Efficiency: From Waterwheel to Social Control* (Baltimore, MD: Johns Hopkins University Press, 2008).

44. Leon A. Wortman, *Closed-Circuit Television Handbook* (Indianapolis: Howard W. Sams, 1969), 155.

45. Whipple, 29; R. C. G. Williams, 652, 657.

46. Mayers and Chipp, 62.

47. "Steel Mills Make Use of Television," *New York Times* (February 21, 1954): F2; Mayers and Chipp, 63; P. Barratt and I. M. Waters, "The Application of Closed-circuit Television in the Nuclear Industry," *Journal of British IRE* (March 1940): 229; Wilson, 127; Schneider 24; J. E. H. Brace, "Industrial Television: A Survey of History, Requirements and Applications," *Journal of British IRE* (June 1960): 443.

48. Brace, 443; Wortman, 160.

49. Barratt and Waters, 225–241; Whipple, 29; R. C. G. Williams, 657; Noel Ashbridge, "Television Development," *Address Delivered at the Television Convention* (April 28, 1952): 11; Zworykin, "The Evolution of Television," 40. It was also suggested that improving safety measures with television would lift morale. Scheider, 25.

50. "Electronics for Greater Safety," *Radio Age* (January 1957): 20.

51. Wortman, 177.

52. Noll, 13.

53. "Eye-Witness Reports from a Fiery Furnace," in *Broadcasting* (October 2, 1950): 95, *Popular Science Monthly* (October 1950): 243, and *New York Times* (September 10, 1950): 180. Emphasis in original.

54. Caster, 196–197; Peet, 84. The language of "inaccessibility" and even "extreme inaccessibility" recurred throughout these formulations. Barratt and Waters, 231; Dumont, 102; Schneider, 23; Whipple 28–30; R. C. G. Williams, 652.

55. This quote is attributed to a "steelworker in Virginia," though similar formulations circulated elsewhere, as in a sewage industry trade paper that credited television with solving the "centuries old problem of 'seeing where you can't look.'" "Electronics for Greater Safety," 20; Caster, 855.

56. Noll, 12; Schneider, 23.

57. Noll, 11; Zworykin et al., 28.

58. Noll, 12.

59. Zworykin et al., 27; Ashbridge, 11.

60. Zworykin et al. 202; Caster, 196–197.

61. Zworykin et al., 26.

62. Whipple, 29; "Three Dimensions Achieved in Video," *New York Times* (April 16, 1950): 82; Zworykin, "The Evolution of Television," 40; Schneider, 24.

63. Zworykin et al., 24.

64. Ibid.

65. Ashbridge, 11; F. Roberts and J. Z. Young, "The Flying-Spot Microscope," *Proceedings of the IEE* 99, no. 20 (1952): 755; Wortman, 172. See also Zworkin et al. 24; Mayers and Chipp, 63, 78.

66. Noll, 17, 21; Mayers and Chipp, 78.

67. Mayers and Chipp, 63.

68. Leonard C. Showalter, *Closed-Circuit TV for Engineers and Technicians*. (Indianapolis: Howard W. Sams, Bobbs-Merril, 1969), 9, emphasis mine.

69. Zworykin et al., 38.

70. Ibid.

71. Noll, 13.

72. David Morley, *Home Territories: Media, Mobility and Identity* (New York: Routledge, 2000); Lisa Parks, *Cultures in Orbit: Satellites and the Televisual* (Durham, NC: Duke University Press, 2005); Harold A. Innis, *Empire and Communications* (Lanham, MD: Rowman & Littlefield, 2007); James W. Carey, "McLuhan and Mumford: The Roots of Modern Media Analysis," *Journal of Communication* 31, no. 3 (September 1981): 162–178.

73. Zworykin et al.; Sight at a distance was also brought into the field of education, with a common refrain suggesting that television operated as a transporter—bringing viewers to scenes and scenes to viewers. Reed, 14.

74. Whipple, 29.

75. "Seventy Makers of Automation Equipment to Open 4-Day Exposition Here Tomorrow," *New York Times* (November 28, 1954): F7.

76. Sprague, 83; "25,000 to Inspect Handling Devices," *New York Times* (May 19, 1953): 41; "Electronics for Greater Safety," 20.

77. L. Landon Goodman, "Materials Handling and Automation," *IEE Journal* (December 1959): 689. "Equipment Makers See Record Output," *New York Times* (May 14, 1951): 44; "New Uses for TV Found in Industry," *New York Times* (October 8, 1950): F8.

78. "25,000 to Inspect," 41.

79. Goodman, 689.

80. "Show of Robot Load Toters," *New York Herald Tribune* (May 15, 1955): A12; "25,000 to Inspect," 41; "Seventy Makers," F7; Sprague, 83; W. R. G. Baker "Electronics—Promise and Reality," *Transactions of the IRE Professional Group on Vehicular Communications* 3, no. 1 (1953): 40.

81. "25,000 to Inspect," 41; Baker, "Promise," 41; Schneider, 24.

82. Zworykin et al., 164.

83. "Steel Mills Make Use," F2.

84. Lisa Parks's definition of satellite footprints offers a useful corollary insofar as both offer the promise of homogenized coverage and perfect sight (49–52). See also Chapter 5.

85. Johanna Drucker, *Graphesis: Visual Forms of Knowledge Production* (Cambridge, MA: Harvard University Press, 2014), 81.

86. Noll, 4, 6; Wortman 163; Zworykin et al., 166, 167; Mayers and Chipp, 71, 72.

87. Wortman, 165; "Industrial Television Transmitted via Telephone," *Electrical Engineering* 75, no. 2 (1956): 212; Thomas and Norvell, 224; Guilfoyle, 14.

88. Zworykin et al., 166; Noll, 4, 6; Wortman 160, 163.

89. Mayers and Chipp, 82, 79; Zworykin et al., 38, 192.

90. Mayers and Chipp, 79, 82.

91. Zworykin et al., 26, 191; Mayers and Chipp, 79; Noll, 10.

92. Noll, 4, 10.

93. Noll, 4. Observers were quick to run back-of-the-envelope calculations to demonstrate the potential labor costs saved. McGhee, 117; Mayers and Chipp, 69–70.

94. Mayers and Chipp, 63; Noll, 12l; "Industrial Video Holds Great Future Promise," *The Science News-Letter* 62, no. 17 (October 25, 1952): 269; Wilson, 125, 127; Noll, 32; R. C. G. Williams, 656; Brace, 443.

95. Noll, 4; Mayers and Chipp, 69–72; Zworykin et al., 164; Peet, 84; Schneider, 24.

96. Wortman, 164.

97. Noll, 4; Zworykin et al., 166.

98. Zworykin et al, 161.

99. Mayers and Chipp, 69–72; 84–87, Noll, 6–7; Zworykin et al. 177; "Electronics for Greater Safety," 20–21; "TV Slated to Keep Eye on New Midtown Shuttle," *New York Times* (January 14, 1955): 12.

100. "Kaiser Aluminum Adding to Trentwood Mill," *Wall Street Journal* (September 12, 1952): 17; Felix C. Smith, "An Investment Trust Views the Rails," *The Analysts Journal* 14, no. 1 (1958): 45–47; Schneider, 29.

101. Zworykin et al., 175–176; Whipple, 29–30; "'Midget' Televising Helps Run Railroad," *New York Times* (September 17, 1952): 49; Schneider, 29.

102. Mayer and Chipp, 87; Fred B. Stauffer, "IT&T Steps up Activity in Rail Field," *New York Herald Tribune* (November 22, 1953): A7; Smith, 45–47; "Comment Heard on Wall Street," *New York Herald Tribune* (July 21, 1956): A3; "Roadhouse TV Scans 2 Miles of Track," (advertisement) *New York Herald Tribune* (December 11, 1957): B7; Guilfoyle, 14.

103. Noll, 10.

104. Wortman, 148.

105. Raymond Williams, 79.

106. Ibid., 111.

107. Uricchio, 256.

108. In a suggestive analysis of 21st century CCTV workers, Kevin Walby shows how mall surveillance professionals internalize and reproduce their employers's racist, classist, and capitalist ideologies (a cultivation function) through their work of coordinating coworkers and shoppers on the sales floor. Kevin Walby, "How Closed-Circuit Television Surveillance Organizes the Social: An Institutional Ethnography," *The Canadian Journal of Sociology* 30, no. 2 (2005): 209.

109. Mayers and Chipp, 69–71; Zworykin et al. 191.

110. Noll, 15.

111. Ibid., 14.

112. Zworykin et al., 13.

113. Mayers and Chipp, 74; Zworykin et al. 247; Noll, 24.

114. The largest reproduction of this image, found in all three books in the preceding citation, is in Mayers and Chipp, 77.

115. Stephen Groening, "'We Can See Ourselves as Others See Us': Women Workers and Western Union's Training Films in the 1920s," in *Useful Cinema*, eds. Haidee Wasson and Charles R. Acland (Durham, NC: Duke University Press, 2011), 40.

116. Mayers and Chipp, 74, 77.

117. Floor Department memorandum dated December 22, 1966, quoted in Tyrell G. Rogers, "Status Report—20 Broad Street Project," October 12, 1967, page 3. Senior Vice-President, Market Surveillance Jeremiah J. O'Donahue Papers. Box 100, Folder "Trading Floor, Raulitier, 1965–1971," New York Stock Exchange Archives (henceforth NYSE).

118. See Meeting Minutes in O'Donahue Papers, Box 100, Folder "Trading Floor Expansion (20 Broad Street) 1966–1968," NYSE.

119. "Meeting held Tuesday, November 14, 1967 at 10:00 AM in Room 1901," 3. O'Donahue Papers, Box 100, Folder "Trading Floor Expansion (20 Broad Street) 1966–1968," NYSE.

120. Ibid, 1.

121. Christopher Williams, "The $300m Cable That Will Save Traders Milliseconds," *The Telegraph* (September 11, 2011). http://www.telegraph.co.uk/technology/news/8753784/The-300m-cable-that-will-save-traders-milliseconds.html (accessed August 3, 2014); "Hibernia Express, a Game Changer for the Financial Industry, Links Global Markets with the Lowest Latency Transatlantic Connection Available," *Business Wire* (September 26, 2005): np. http://www.businesswire.com/news/home/20150916005805/en/Hibernia-Express-Game-Changer-Financial-Industry-Links (accessed January 9, 2016).

122. Wortman, 155–156.

123. Ibid., 139.

124. Jonathan Coopersmith, *Faxed: The Rise and Fall of the Fax Machine* (Baltimore, MD: Johns Hopkins University Press, 2015), 44.

125. F. K. Becker, J. R. Hefele, and W. T. Wintringham, "An Experimental Visual Communication System," *The Bell System Technical Journal* 38, no. 1 (1959): 141–142.

126. "Cutting Administrative Expenses with Closed-Circuit TV," *Management Review* (April 1971): 49.

127. Zworykin et al., 36. Static image transmission realized additional economies by using slower scanning rates accommodated by telephone wires, eliminating the need for expensive coaxial cables associated with television transmission.

128. Zworykin et al, 36; Schneider, 27.

129. Wortman, 139; Zworykin et al., 36.

130. "Keeping Informed: Updates on Management," *Management Review* (May 1, 1978): 5.

131. "Cutting Administrative Expenses with Closed-Circuit TV," *Management Review*, Condensed from *Business Week* January 30, 1971, (April 1971), 50–51.

132. Schneider, 27. "CCTV Verifier Links Remote Bank Locations," *Banking* 65, no. 9 (March 1973): 48.

133. Noll, 24; Mayers and Chipp, 87; William M. Freeman, "Closed-Circuit TV Aiding Industry to Check Processes, Spur Output: Closed Circuit TV Boon," *New York Times* (March 29, 1953): F1, 5; "Philadelphia Bank Trying New System," F4.

134. Schneider, 27.

135. Noll, 24; Mayers and Chipp, 90. The language of "in a matter of seconds" appears again in Freeman, 5.

136. Zworykin et al., 251; Noll, 25–26; Schneider, 27.

137. Noll, 26–27; Guilfoyle, 14; Schneider, 28; Michaelis, 175; W. L., C1; Wortman, 166; Mayers and Chipp, 84; Zworykin et al., 181.

138. Noll, 26; Zworykin et al, 261.

139. Noll, 27.

140. Mayers and Chipp, 87; Zworykin et al. 179–180.

141. J. W. Alinsky, "Dial-Selected Industrial Television for Ticket Reservation Facilities," *Transactions of the American Institute of Electrical Engineers, Part 1: Communication and Electronics* 79, no. 2 (May 1960): 175.

142. Alinsky, 174; Mayers and Chipp, 87, 174.

143. Whipple, 29.

144. This definition is borrowed from the first article to mention the term. Manfred Clynes and Nathan S. Kline, "Cyborgs and Space," *Astronautics* (September 1960): 26–27, 74–75.

145. Nathan Kline, quoted in Ronald Kline, "Where Are the Cyborgs in Cybernetics?" *Social Studies of Science* 39, no. 3 (2009): 339.

146. Sherry Turkle, *Life on the Screen: Identity in the Age of the Internet* (New York: Simon & Schuster, 1995).

147. Donna Haraway, "A Cyborg Manifesto: Science, Technology, and Socialist-Feminism in the Late Twentieth Century," in *Simians, Cyborgs and Women: The Reinvention of Nature* (New York; Routledge, 1991), 149–181.

148. Karl Marx, *Grundrisse: Foundations of the Critique of Political Economy*, trans. Martin Nicolaus (London: Penguin, 1973), 693.

149. Zworykin et al., 1.

150. Sarnoff, "Radio Review . . . and a 1948 Preview," *Radio Age* 7, no. 2 (1948): 5; Wortman, 139, 160, 162; Whipple, 30; Schneider, 25; Henry M. Lewis, Jr., "TV in Work Clothes," *The Rotarian* (August 1955): 34; Ashbridge, 11; Peet, 81–81; Reed, 14; Wilson, 127; Michaelis, 174.

151. PYE Advertisement, "Do You Employ People to Watch Clocks," *The New Scientist* (January 7, 1963); Alexander R. Hammer, "Industry Posting More Electronic Guards," *New York Times* (October 4, 1959): F1; "Closed Circuit TV Protects Defense Plant," *New York Times* (August 28, 1956): 33; Schneider, 31.

152. R. C. G. Williams, 167; Baker, "Promise," 42; Hall, 24; "Electronics for Greater Safety," 20–21; Smith, 46; Wilson, 125; Ernest B. Gorin, "Long Term Industry Outlook," *The Analysts Journal* 12, no. 3 (June 1956): 80; "Big Rise Forecast for Electronics," *New York Times* (December 19, 1955): 4.

153. David Sarnoff, "TV Comes of Age, Stands Ready for the Future," *The Billboard* (December 1, 1951): 13; Lewis, 32–34, 54–55; "R.C.A. Net for 1953 to Show Gain," *New York Herald Tribune* (December 15, 1953): 43; Dumont, 102.

154. Peet, 81; Guilfoyle, 14; Schneider, 23.

155. Wilson, 125; R. C. G. Williams, 651; Brace, 441, 444.

156. Ibid.; Dumont, 102; Michaelis, 172.

157. Lisa Gitelman, *Always Already New: Media, History, and the Data of Culture* (Cambridge, MA: MIT Press, 2006), 1.

158. ITV, in other words, can be understood as the prehistory of wearable computers and augmentation devices proposed for workplaces, the military, and other institutional settings. See Ana Viseu, "Simulation and Augmentation: Issues of Wearable Computers," *Ethics and Information Technology* 5 (2003): 17–26.

159. Sarah Sharma, *In the Meantime: Temporality and Cultural Politics* (Durham: Duke University Press, 2014), 84.

CHAPTER 3

1. John Tomlinson, *The Culture of Speed: The Coming of Immediacy* (Los Angeles: Sage Publications, 2007): 74.

2. Ibid., 86–89, 124–145.

3. Peter Caranicas suggests large firms' adoption of video often "followed the installation of major data processing divisions," in part due to the ability of video to "endlessly repeat complex material" and reduce the tedium of intricate and boring tasks. "The Rise of Private Television," in *The Handbook of Private Television: A Complete Guide for Video Facilities and Networks within Corporations, Nonprofit Institutions, and Government Agencies*, ed. Nathan J. Sambul (New York: McGraw Hill, 1982), 1-4. (The page numbers in this volume are hyphenated, with the first number indicating the chapter.)

4. In 1974, the year the US government brought the antitrust suit against AT&T that would result in divestiture, 17 of these operating companies (e.g., The Mountain States Telephone and Telegraph Company) were wholly owned by AT&T. The company had majority or minority stakes in 6 others. Local exchanges were the primary casualties of the break-up of "Ma Bell" when they were recombined into seven independently owned and operated Regional Bell Operating Companies (RBOC). AT&T, *Annual Report*, 1974, 19.

5. Marjorie A. Stockford, *The Bellwomen: The Story of the Landmark AT&T Sex Discrimination Case* (Newark, NJ: Rutgers University Press, 2004), 14.

6. Venus Green, *Race on the Line: Gender, Labor, & Technology in the Bell System, 1880–1980* (Durham, NC: Duke University Press, 2001), 2.

7. Ibid., 226–228. Eventually AT&T would be sued for sex discrimination in a landmark case brought by the Equal Employment Opportunity Commission. Stockford, 7–20.

8. See Heide Solbrig, "The Personnel Is Political: Voice and Citizenship in Affirmative Action Videos in the Bell System, 1970–1984," in *Films That Work: Industrial Film and the Productivity of Media*, eds. Vinzenz Hediger and Patrick Vonderau (Amsterdam: Amsterdam University Press, 2009), 259–282.

9. On AT&T's immediate post-war maneuvers to supplement its telephone infrastructure with coaxial cable and microwave relays that would strengthen its voice-distribution capacities while placing the firm in a monopolistic position relative to television signal distribution, see Jonathan Sterne, "Television under Construction: American Television and the Problem of Distribution, 1926–62," *Media, Culture & Society* 21, no. 4 (1999): 512–515.

10. "Two-Way Television: A Development of Bell Telephone Laboratories." Folder "Television (3 of 5)," 458 04 04 01. AT&T Corporate Archives. Warren, NJ (henceforth AA).

11. It's unclear when this service existed. Its chief function appears to have been publicity rather than intercommunication. Mark Schubin, "Video Research," *Videography* (May 1979): 61–66, "Television (3 of 5)." AA.

12. "News of the Advertising and Marketing Fields," *New York Times* (July 16, 1953): 35.

13. "We Star on TV: Share Owners See How Department Handles Long Distance Service," *Long Lines* (April, 1954): 5–6. AA.

14. "AT&T New Advertising Drive to Open on Closed-Circuit TV," *Broadcasting/ Telecasting* (March 18, 1957): 60.

15. Proponents cooed over its ability to offer content—for example, live theater acts, A-list performers, and major sporting events like the World Series—too expensive for commercial sponsorship alone since ticket sales could help cover costs and generate profits. John Evans McCoy and Harry P. Warner, "Theater Television Today," *Journal of the Society of Motion Picture Engineers* 53 (1949): 346–348; Austrian, 379. On theater television as a "closed-circuit" that extended a business model focused on per-person ticketing, see Barton Kreuzer, "Progress Report—Theater Television," *Journal of the Society of Motion Picture Engineers* 53, no. 2 (1949): 134; "Progress Committee Report," *Journal of the Society of Motion Picture and Television Engineers* 56 (May 1951): 581; and Austrian, 385.

16. Douglas Gomery, "Theater Television: The Missing Link of Technological Change in the US Motion Picture Industry," *Velvet Light Trap* 21 (1985): 59.

17. Timothy R. White, "Hollywood's Attempt at Appropriating Television: The Case of Paramount Pictures," in *Hollywood in the Age of Television*, ed. Tino Balio (Crows Nest, Wales: Unwin Hyman, 1990), 149–155. According to RKO Executive Vice President Ralph Austrian, Hollywood also feared drops in theater attendance due to changing labor patterns, namely the end of wartime shift work, which replenished the film audience three times a day. Ralph B. Austrian, "Some Economic Aspects of Theater Television," *Journal of the Society of Motion Picture Engineers* 44, no. 5 (1945): 13.

18. Gomery's brief aside about the "enterprising entrepreneurs [who] even tried industrial clients" (59) downplays the extent to which informational and institutional applications of theater television may have shaped the medium's imaginary even before 1952. In public statements circulating while the FCC was deliberating on whether to provide special frequencies to theater television, Halpern pointed to his experience with industry and government productions to paint the medium (in the FCC's preferred lingo) as a "a new and different service . . . a valuable national resource." Nathaniel Halpern, "Progress," *International Projectionist* (September 1952): 17. The years 1952 and 1953 alone saw the announcement (if not the realization) of three new theater TV companies devoted to business and government applications. "Business Telecasts Aim of New Firm," *Motion Picture Daily* 72, no. 104 (1952): 1. Yet another firm, Closed-Circuit Television Co., would be announced in early 1953. "Ex-Gov't Video Director Enters Theatre TV Field," *Motion Picture Daily* 73, no. 10 (1953): 1.

19. "Lindsley to Head TNT Unit Sales," *Motion Picture Daily* 76, no. 79 (1956): 11; "Closed Circuit TV Firms Expect Record Business Volume in '57," *Broadcasting/ Telecasting* (January 28, 1957): 93; "Closed-Circuit Spectaculars?" *Television Digest with Electronics Reports* 14, no. 2 (1958): 9.

20. Halpern, "Progress," 140; "Personal Notes" section in *Television Digest* 8, no. 29 (1952): 6.

21. There is, however, some evidence that GM used a limited form of the technology as early as 1946. Thomas Kenny, "TV's Little Brother Grows Up," *Duns Review and Modern Industry* (July 1956): 48; "To Theatre Telecast Nat' Sales Conference Dec. 8," *Motion Picture Daily* 72, no. 79 (1952): 1; "Lee's Toppers Enthusiastic over Telecast," *Motion Picture Daily* 72, no. 110 (1952): 1; "Theatre TV: Lee's to Air Sales Meeting," *Broadcasting/Telecasting* (November 1, 1952): 92. While this may have been the first "sales meeting," the Federal Civil Defense Agency used theater television as early as 1951 to train civilian defense workers. "Defense Training: FCDA to Try Movie TV," *Broadcasting/Telecasting* (September 10, 1951): 34; "Civil Defense: Plans More Theatre TV," *Broadcasting/Telecasting* (November 5, 1951): 80.
22. "To Theatre Telecast," 1; "Lee's Toppers," 5.
23. "Theatre TV Has Busy Week in Showings," *Broadcasting/Telecasting* (December 15, 1952): 104. See also Victor M. Ratner, "Television for Business Meetings," *Harvard Business Review* (June 3, 1953): 67–69.
24. It's unlikely that receiving sites were wired for two-way audio (many simply used phones to call in questions). However, one article intimates that the meeting was equipped for two-way image transmission, using split screens to show "conversations" between executives at the centralized studio and the distant audience. "To Include Remote Pick-up on Lees TV," *Motion Picture Daily* 72, no. 106 (1952): 4.
25. "Lee's Toppers," 5.
26. One exception is a meeting for Dodge employees that was held after the workday so workers could put in a full day without "losing" time to presentations and entertainment. "TNT Books Dodge Sales Show for Theatre TV," *Motion Picture Daily* 74, no. 13 (1954): 1, 7.
27. "Calls Off-Hours Theatre TV Most Promising Now," *Motion Picture Daily* 72, no. 56 (1952): 1. Likewise, for projectionists, televised business meetings were positioned as job opportunities. "In the Spotlight," *International Projectionist* (November 1954): 20.
28. On overflow, see "Now All Can See," *Broadcasting/Telecasting* (November 23, 1953): 46; "Sidelights of the Day in the Financial and Business Fields," *New York Times* (April 19, 1955): 43; Alfred R. Zipster, "Cordiner, Carey Quietly Discuss Job Security at G.E.'s Meeting," *New York Times,* (April 23, 1959): 41.
29. GE's 1958 "Live Better Electrically" Tele-Session, which transmitted to 79 cities, was touted as the largest CCTV meeting of its time. "More Firms Switching to Closed-Circuit TV Meetings," *Sponsor* 16 (November 1953): 60; "Closed-Circuit TV Contract," *International Projectionist* (June 1955): 19; Edward F. Addiss, Jr., "Operations Planning Closed-Circuit TV," *International Projectionist* (February 1958): 10.
30. MH, "Theatre TV Gets Lively Dairy Show," *Motion Picture Daily* 74, no. 15 (1954): 1, 6; "How to Pre-Sell Radio/TV," *Sponsor* Oct 31, 1959: 37–38; "GM Dedicates Center on Closed-Circuit," *Motion Picture Daily,* 79, no. 95 (1956): 12.
31. Nathan L. Halpern, "The Future of Theatre TV," *International Projectionist* (July 1954): 20; "Cities Service Tries TNT," *Broadcasting/Telecasting* (October 29, 1956): 36.
32. "TNT 9-Month Gross: $2.5 Million," *Broadcasting* (October 14, 1957): 85.
33. Zipster, Jr., F1, 2. Sports of national interest were too few and far between to sustain the technological infrastructure required to carry them. "Sports No Money-Maker for Pay-Video," *The Independent Film Journal* (November 12,

1955): 11; Addiss, 10; See also "World Series of 1957 via Theatre TV to Be Sought by Television Interests," *Motion Picture Daily* 78, no. 72 (1955): 1, 8; Murray Horowitz, "Good Off-Hour Year Predicted in Theatre TV," *Motion Picture Daily* 77, no. 21 (1955): 1, 5.

34. "TNT Launching Big Closed-Circuit Slate," *Motion Picture Daily* 78, no. 109 (1955): 11; "Ten Closed-Circuit Telecasts," *Television Digest with Electronics Reports* 11, no. 50 (1955): 6. All figures in this chapter adjusted for inflation and represented in 2019 dollars via CPI Inflation Calculator.

35. "Closed-Circuit Spectaculars?," 9.

36. Ibid.

37. Addiss, 10.

38. Norman Wasserman, "Growth of Closed-Circuit TV Is Aided by Portable Projectors," *International Projectionist* (November 1955): 22.

39. Ibid. When orchestrating nontheatrical CCTV exhibition, TNT ordered AT&T long lines and local loops to be connected to its intended receiving sites and then shipped its fleet of mobile projectors to the necessary locations. RCA's service company was contracted to install (and strike) the projection equipment. Addiss, 10. Addiss was Director of Operations of TNT Tele-Sessions; Wasserman, 22.

40. Ibid.; "TNT Buys 50 Units from GPE," *Motion Picture Daily* 76, no 76 (1954): 5. Later coverage of TNT's equipment investments emphasized the equipment's applications for "meetings for business, industry, and other groups," and (in the case of color projection) emphasized its ability to showcase consumer goods (cosmetics, fashion) or informational materials (charts, maps) endemic to corporate and governmental presentations. "Larger Color Screens Available from TNT," *Broadcasting* (July 30, 1962): 44; "TNT Demonstrates First Big-Screen Color Television," *International Projectionist* (April 1964): 9, 11.

41. "Television and Business," *New York Times* (November 5, 1958): 34.

42. Robert Alden, "Advertising: G.O.P. Using Closed Circuit TV," *New York Times* (July 24, 1960): F13.

43. "Lee's to Air," 92; "Slate Bendix Theatre TV Meet Dec. 30," *Motion Picture Daily* 72, no. 104 (1952): 1.

44. Ratner, 65–66, 69. As James Carey points out, spatial control comes in large part through temporal efficiencies in "reducing signaling time" between operations. Though "radically extended" by computing, "the penetration of time, the use of time as a mechanism of control, the opening of time to commerce and politics" was an understanding of time, efficiency, and empire made possible by the telegraph and, I argue, enlivened and extended by proponents of industrial television. James W. Carey, *Communication as Culture: Essays on Media and Society* (New York: Routledge, 1989), 228.

45. "Bendix," 1; "Television and Business," 34.

46. Zipster, Jr., F1: 2.

47. Halpern, "The Future," 46.

48. Douglas W. Cray, "Television Watches and Teaches: Closed-Circuit TV Turns Its Volume Up," *New York Times* (August 7, 1966): 1, 7.

49. They were also billed as private "as a telephone call." "70,000 Take Part in G.O.P. TV Rally," *New York Times* (January 21, 1956): 12; "More Firms Switching," 61; Alden, F13.

50. Ratner, 70. Reprising modes of talking about the tight constellation of materials handling, automation, and communications technology that reshaped modern manufacturing, one article prefaced its discussion of business by television by

noting, "Modern invention has speeded up the movement of men and goods extraordinarily, of course, but the progress pales before the way in which distance has been annihilated when it comes to the sending of information. . . . Probably most revolutionary is closed-circuit communication." "Television and Business," 34.

51. Ratner, 69. Emphasis mine.

52. Robert Vianello, "The Power Politics of 'Live' Television," *Journal of Film and Video* 37, no. 3 (1985): 27–29.

53. Mary Ann Doane in particular suggests that liveness is a temporal category. However, as noted in the following, the emphasis on place and access within her writing suggests that space is perhaps just as important to her formulation. Mary Ann Doane, "Information, Crisis, Catastrophe," in *Logics of Television*, ed. Patricia Mellencamp (Bloomington: Indiana University Press, 1990), 251–264. Mimi White, in turn, suggests a de-centering of time in favor of increased appreciation of spectacle, banality, connection and space. Mimi White, "The Attractions of Television: Reconsidering Liveness," in *MediaSpace: Place, Scale and Culture in a Media Age*, eds. Nick Couldry and Anna McCarthy (London: Routledge, 2004), 75–92.

54. Jane Feuer, "The Concept of Live Television: Ontology as Ideology," in *Regarding Television: Critical Approaches*, ed. E. Ann Kaplan (Frederick, MD: University Publications of America, 1983), 18–20; Vianello, 36–39.

55. White, 85.

56. Feuer, 14 (emphasis mine); Vianello, 39. Indebted to radio, this "presence" effect (initially) resulted from audiences' understanding of networks' drive (and authority) to blanket the country with an increasingly inescapable (and sometimes threatening) "simultaneous electronic community." Jeffrey Sconce, *Haunted Media: Electronic Presence from Telegraphy to Television* (Durham, NC: Duke University Press, 2000), 113.

57. Doane 251, 262, emphasis mine.

58. Feuer, 20, emphasis mine.

59. "Business Screen International," *Business Screen* 27, no. 6 (1966): 28; "Warner-Lambert Annual Meeting Spans the Ocean," *New York Times* (May 11, 1966): 86. (TNT itself offers a through-line between these two uses. Soon after the 1965 launch of Early Bird, the company orchestrated an annual meeting-by-satellite for Warner-Lambert International that allowed American shareholders to ask questions of the company's general managers from Italy, Germany, France, and England who had gathered in London for a 30-minute "discussion." TNT also developed satellite communications for AT&T. TNT changed its name to TNT Communications, Inc., in 1966. Stacy V. Jones, "Wide Variety of Ideas," *New York Times* (April 4, 1970): 41; Cray, 1, 7.

60. Ratner, 64.

61. Ibid.

62. Ibid., 66, This language is especially common in promotions of ETV. See, for example, Steve Lefkowitz, "Good Training + Television = Comprehension + Accuracy," *Educational Television* 3, no. 9 (1971): 27.

63. Ratner, 64.

64. "Closed-Circuit TV Set for Ike Dinners," *Broadcasting Telecasting* (November 28 1955): 74; "TNT 100th Closed Circuit," *Broadcasting/Telecasting* (May 7, 1956): 102; "GM Plans TNT Celebration," *Broadcasting/Telecasting* (November 15, 1954): 103.

65. Paddy Scannell, *Television and the meaning of "live,"* (Los Angeles: Polity Press, 2014), 26, 66.

66. Vianello, 33.

67. "Companies Facing Sticky Issues as Meeting Season Approaches," *New York Times* (February 5, 1961): F1, 11. The article's subtitle emphasized the care function of these meetings, calling them stockholders' "moment of glory." These meetings were becoming increasingly important as the New York Stock Exchange began courting individual shareholders at mid-century in order to confront negative public opinion and low trading volume. Janice M. Traflet, *A Nation of Small Shareholders: Marketing Wall Street after World War II* (Baltimore, MD: Johns Hopkins Press, 2013), 7, 39, 50.

68. "Sticky Issues," 12.

69. Ibid., F1; Verne Burnett, "Annual Meetings and Stockholder Relations: A Review of Company Practices," *Management Review* 49, no. 4 (1960): 16–17.

70. Preceding quotations all from Burnett, 12–15.

71. Ratner, 69; Alden, F13. These properties would become "even more essential to public confidence" as companies grew and internationalized. "Business Screen International," 28. See also "Warner-Lambert," 86.

72. "Television and Business," 34.

73. White, 87.

74. Albert Abramson, *The History of Television, 1941–2000* (Jefferson, NC: McFarland, 2003), 73.

75. Ibid., 71.

76. Brian Winston, *Media Technology and Society: A History: From the Telegraph to the Internet* (London: Routledge, 1998), 265, 267, 269; Jeff Martin, "The Dawn of Tape: Transmission Device as Preservation Medium," *The Moving Image*, 5, no. 1 (2005): 55.

77. Christopher H. Sterling and John Michael Kittross, *Stay Tuned: A History of American Broadcasting*, 3rd edn. (Mahwah, NJ: Lawrence Erlbaum Associates, 2002), 348–349; Martin, 55, 57–58.

78. The Army may have used video for self-confrontation (improving speech delivery) as early as 1962, though it's not widely cited as a precedent. J. M. Stormes and J. P. Crumpler, *Television Communications Systems for Business and Industry* (Hoboken, NJ: John Wiley & Sons, 1971), 15.

79. The original aim of T groups thus shares bonds with the televised role play discussed by Anna McCarthy as a means of connecting with the Other to ameliorate racism. *The Citizen Machine: Governing by Television in 1950s America* (New York: The New Press, 2010), 97–101. On the development of T groups and their influence on organizational social theory and training, see David A. Kolb, *Experiential Learning: Experience as the Source of Learning and Development*, 2nd edn. (Upper Saddle River, NJ: Pearson Education, 2015), 8–12.

80. These terms were sometimes used interchangeably. Here they are distinguished to provide a sense of how the purpose of such groups shifted in the 1960s and 1970s as they became more widely adopted.

81. Richard A. Swanson, "Industrial Training," in *5th Encyclopedia of Educational Research*, ed. W. H. Mitzel (New York: Macmillian, 1982), 867.

82. Frederick H. Stoller, "Group Psychotherapy on Television: An Innovation with Hospitalized Patients," *American Psychologist* 22, no. 2 (1967): 160.

83. For a film precedent, see Stephen Groening, "'We Can See Ourselves as Others See Us': Women Workers and Western Union's Training Films in the 1920s," in *Useful Cinema*, eds. Charles R. Acland and Haidee Wasson (Durham, NC: Duke University Press, 2011), 40.

84. Betty Lee Conrad, *An Exploration of Nonbroadcast Television*. Master's thesis, Western Kentucky University, 1984, 41.

85. This use was even positioned as a kindness to employees who, paid at piece rate, could produce and earn more with the preferred methods. Ibid., 42.

86. This formulation is repeated nearly verbatim across training literature. Roy Foster, *Communications, Control, Decision Making and Training with Television* (Bearsden, Glasgow: Department of Industrial Administration, The University of Strathclyde, 1968), 78. Stormes and Crumpler, 132; "Videotape Recording in Industry," *Educational/Instructional Broadcasting* 3, no. 3 (1970): 36; Edward Stasheff and Aryeh Lavi, *Instructional Television in Industry (ITVI): A Survey* (Office of Research Administration, Ann Arbor: The University of Michigan), 31.

87. See, for example, the emphasis on emotional interaction (that cites Stoller's work directly) in William N. Dehon, "Self-Confrontation Via TV: Videotaped Feedback for Training at Sandia Laboratory," *Training and Development Journal* (October 1967): 42–46.

88. William R. Johnston, "Closed Circuit TV in Sales Training," *Training and Development Journal* (August 1967): 16–17; "VTRs in California Business," *Educational/Instructional Broadcasting* 5, no. 3 (1972): 33; James Robert Spencer, *Closed Circuit Television in Industrial Training Programs: A Study of Three Companies That Have Utilized TV For Training*. Master's thesis, San Diego State University, 1974, 56; Anthony Wiggins, "Television in Industry," *Education & Training* 12, no. 9 (1970): 335; "Audio-Visual Techniques for Industry," No. 6 (New York: United Nations Industrial Development Organization, 1978): 72; Stormes and Crumpler, 131.

89. L. U. Lawrence, "Coffee, Tea, and Me on CCTV: Stewardess Training with VTRs," *Educational and Industrial Television* (May 5, 1972): 29.

90. Ibid.

91. "Videotape Recording in Industry," 39.

92. McCarthy, 98.

93. Rosalind Krauss, "Video: The Aesthetics of Narcissism," *October* 1 (1976): 50, 55.

94. Kris Paulsen convincingly revises Krauss's argument, asserting that early video artists' work (especially that of Acconci and Joan Jonas) was *also* relational insofar as it interpellated the museum viewer into a present-tense relationship with the recording. Corporate uses of video may thus represent the apotheosis of the narcissistic mode, since no Other exists to interrupt the feedback loop between the recorded and viewing subject. Kris Paulsen, *Here/There: Telepresence, Touch, and Art at the Interface* (Cambridge, MA: MIT Press, 2017), 45–52.

95. Stoller, 160; "Videotape Recording in Industry," 36.

96. Skillings, 8; Dehon, 44.

97. Foster, 77.

98. As Jay David Bolter notes, the promise of transparency (a more perfect immediacy) was a common selling point of new technlogies. "Remediation and the Desire for Immediacy," *Convergence* 6, no. 1 (2000): 69. Lawrence, 27; Johnston, 16; Foster, 82; Dehon, 42–43; Skillings, 27; Sharon Stea, "CCTV— The Potential and the Challenge," *Educational Television* 2, no. 5 (1970): 18; M.

Fauquet, "Orientation of Research on the Use of Closed-Circuit Television for Teacher Training," *Educational Media International* 8, no. 2 (1971): 11.

99. Vianello, 39.

100. Hyett, 491; Dehon, 43; Foster, 79.

101. Dehon, 43; Foster, 82. Emphasis mine.

102. Johnston, 15.

103. Quote from Stormes and Crumpler, 132. Johnston, 15; Ralph Chipling, "Are You Getting Value from Your CCTV?" *Journal of European Industrial Training* 3, no. 4 (1979): 18–20; Stoller, 158; Stea, 18; Stasheff and Lavi, 37.

104. Stasheff and Lavi, 35; Ken Hyett, "Video Recording in Management Training," *Industrial and Commercial Training* 8, no. 12 (1976): 493; Dehon, 42–46; Johnston, 16; David Katz, "Videotape Programming for Social Agencies," *Social Casework* 56 (1975): 48.

105. Preceeding citations from Johnston, 16–17.

106. Johnston, 17. Dehon, 42.

107. Johnston, 16.

108. Lawrence, 27.

109. "California Business," 33.

110. Stea, 18; Fauquet, 11.

111. Lu Bartlow, "CCTV at Illinois Bell," *Educational Television* 2, no. 8 (1970): 18–20.

112. Michael Owen, "Seeing Clear through the Video Maze," *Public Relations Quarterly*, (Winter 1975): 18.

113. Dehon, 43; Lorraine L. Hedman and Elaine Mansfield, "Hospital to Hospital via TV," *The American Journal of Nursing* 67, no. 4 (April 1967): 808–810; Campbell, 15, 17.

114. Katz, 44–51; "Videotape Recording in Industry," 35.

115. Skillings, 7, 8; Stormes and Crumpler, 15; Some studies, however, found little positive long-term learning correlated to this mode of video use. John P. Campbell, "Personnel Training and Development," Minnesota University Report sponsored by Personnel and Training Research Programs, Psychological Sciences Division, Office of Naval Research, June 1970, 41.

116. Paul W. Lowry, "Where Television Belongs within the Corporate Structure," talk delivered to New York Chapter of the ITVA, October 13, 1976, 5.

117. This quote in Buck, 18, reflects sentiments found throughout AT&T's promotional materials and house organs.

118. Buck, 18. For an in-depth examination of the Hagerstown experiment as well as a similar experiment in the Chelsea neighborhood of New York, see Amanda Keeler, "Old New Media: Closed-Circuit Television and the Classroom," *Convergence* 24, no. 6 (December 2018): 538–553.

119. William S. Brown, Jr. "ETV—A Progress Report," *Bell Telephone Labs Magazine* (Summer 1961): 12. Brown was the Product Marketing Supervisor in the Marketing Department.

120. "News Features," *Bell Labs* (April 1962): 5, 6. 140 10 01 13. AA.

121. Keeler, "Old New Media," np. The language of "service" is pervasive in AT&T's house organs and promotional material for ETV. See, for example, note 9. *Ford Foundation Activities in Noncommercial Broadcasting, 1951–1976* (New York: The Foundation): 1976, 8–9. "Bell System Files Tariff for Educational TV Service," *Information Bulletin, Bell Telephone Laboratories, Inc.* 12, no. 61 (1961): 1. AA.

122. "The All-Purpose Picture Network," *Bell Telephone Magazine* 46, no. 2 (1967): 33.

123. This influence is discussed in "Industrial TV in the Bell System," c. 1976, 1, 3. Papers from John D. Sheahan's personal collection. Sheahan was an AT&T TV producer/director, 1977–1979. He later moved to Johnson & Johnson as director of its Worldwide Video Network. Henceforth SC.

124. Foster, 50, 79; Quote in Gerald Gronau, "CCTV at Kaiser Foundation," 3, no. 6 (1970): 29, emphasis in original; "In the Bell System," SC. As Gregory Waller points out, advertisements for 16mm classroom film likewise emphasized ease of use for "anyone," namely female teachers and male schoolchildren. Gregory A. Waller, "Projecting the Promise of 16mm, 1935–45," in Useful Cinema, eds. Charles R. Acland and Haidee Wasson (Durham, NC: Duke University Press, 2011), 129.

125. On magnification in business and ETV, see John R. Martin, "Two-Way Closed-Circuit Educational Television," Research Report 948-4, Case Institute of Technology, Cleveland, Ohio. August 1, 1957: 3; "California Business," 34; Walter V. Hardy, 20; Ray Blain, "The Telephone Industry's Part in Educational Television (ETV)," Telephony (May 11, 1963): 54; Allison Perlman, "Television Up in the Air: The Midwest Program on Airborne Television Instruction, 1959–1971," Critical Studies in Media Communication 27, no. 5 (2010): 480–481. On "guaranteeing uniform control of content," see Gronau, 27; Stasheff and Lavi, 89, 105; Hedman and Mansfield, 810; Raymond V. Lesikar, Kenneth R. Van Voorhis, and Ellen B. Jordan, "Lights . . . Cameras . . . Action . . . Progress: An Encouraging Perspective on TV Teaching," The Journal of Business Communication 8, no. 4 (1971): 8; "Earliest Ref. to TV," c. 1967, 1, SC.

126. Paul W. Lowry, "Where Television Belongs within the Corporate Structure," talk delivered to New York Chapter of the ITVA, October 13, 1976; Lowry was staff supervisor of CCTV at AT&T; 3–4.

127. "Omaha Bank Puts in TV Now—and for Tomorrow," 70.

128. Hedman and Mansfield, 808–810; Blain, 21, 52–54; "Cutting Administrative Expenses with Closed-Circuit TV," Management Review (Condensed from Business Week, January 30, 1971) (April 1971), 49–50, 52.

129. On ETV as a means to meet the educational demands of the post-war era, see Keeler, np; Perlman, 480; "The Booming World of Education," 195 Magazine 38, no. 10 (1965): 16.

130. Lefkowitz, 23–24, 26–27, 34.

131. "Cutting," 52. Citation from "California Business," 34–35. See also Kenny, 47–50; Bartlow, 18. Shooting script for "First of . . . a series of video reports . . . concerning the future management of television in the Bell System," Bob Quickstad to Ed Block, March 29, 1977: 5. SC. (Henceforth "Shooting Script"); "In the Bell System," 1; Andrew M. McCosh, "The Case Method of Accounting Instruction and Microwave Television," The Accounting Review (January 1972): 162; Gronau, 127; Quickstad noted that "tapes avoided the necessity for at least five regional meetings with the three different segments" for a single ad program introduction (6). Training industrial workers to follow standardized (rather than idiosyncratic) production methods was likewise seen as a crucial means of approaching maximum efficiency. Mayer and Chipp, 74; H. F. Schneider, "How Can Industry Use Television?" Paper presented at the 3rd annual Conference of the Professional Group on Industrial Electronics (September 5, 1955): 26.

132. "Shooting Script," 4. By 1977, the ability of TV to "[extend] the influence of" or make "available" the precious expertise of "busy public officials, outstanding

scholars and leading authorities" was one of the most oft-repeated promises of instructional television (not least in AT&T's own ETV publicity materials). Citations from Blain, 21; Hedman and Mansfield, 810; "Tele-Lecture" Promotional Pamphlet, AT&T, c. 1963. 458 02 02 07. AA.; Dan Rusthoi, "Using VTR to Develop Your Training Program," *Training and Development Journal* (May 1977): 3; Peter E. Kneedler, "Noon Hour ITV in Industry—Can It work?" *Educational Broadcasting* 4, no. 7 (1971): 22; Hardy, 20; "New Focus on ETV: A Progress Report on Classroom Television" c. early 1960s. AT&T Public Relations Pamphlet. AA; Buck, 23; "ETV . . . " 195 (January 1953): 6. AA.; "Answer-Back TV" 17 (1965): 12. Western Electric Collection. AA. On ETV's parallel emphasis on enabling the "expanded reach" of expert teachers elsewhere, see Perlman, 480–484.

133. Blain, 54.

134. "California Business," 34. Walter V. Hardy, "Ten Years of CCTV at Autonetics," *Educational/Instructional Broadcasting* 2, no. 8 (1969): 23. Reportedly, "with the addition of several monitors in the company auditorium and two cafeterias, as many as 18,000 employees have viewed special television presentations during a single 3-shift day" (21).

135. This and the preceding citation from "In the Bell System," 1.

136. Halpern, "The Future," 20. Similarly, Ford directed star-studded CCTV programs to its dealers "to stimulate the people who make it possible for consumers to buy." "Pre-Sell," 37.

137. This practice reached its logical conclusion when a company filled the second half of its CCTV sales meeting with a live boxing match theatrically distributed by their CCTV producer (TelePrompTer, a TNT competitor). Alden, F13.

138. "In the Bell System," 4; Robert H. M. Smallwood, "Using CCTV in Management Training," *Journal of European Industrial Training* 1, no. 2 (1977): 15; Lefkowitz, 26.

139. "Shooting Script," 9; Kenny, 48; Lefkowitz, 26; Gronau, 29.

140. Caranicas, 1-3-1-8; Buck, 15. On attention and ETV, see also Brown, 5. "TV That Competes with the Office Grapevine," *Business Week* (March 14, 1977): 50–51; Lefkowitz, 24; Stasheff and Lavi, 216; Patricia Tierney Wilson, "International Video Operations," in Sambul, 26-6; Henry W. Latsch, "Closed Circuit Television Requirements," *Training Development Journal* 23, no. 1 (1969): 40. On the implicit relationship between production values and narrowing "the gap . . . between the home office and the field," see Conrad, 20.

141. Stasheff and Lavi, 146.

142. Kneedler, 28. "Shooting Script," 1; "Management In Practice," *Management Review* 61, no. 2 (1972): 33. See also Stasheff and Lavi, 16.

143. Andrew Stoddard quoted in "New Focus on ETV," 4.

144. "In the Bell System," 1, 3; Rusthoi, 5; "Shooting Script," 5.

145. Stuart Hyde, "College in Crisis: The Legacy of Poor Communications," *Edu/Instructional Broadcasting* 2, no. 6 (1969): 22.

146. Lassor A. Blumenthal, "The Soft Sell in Sales Meetings," *Management Review* (January 1966): 27.

147. Television was used, for example, to introduce potentially threatening changes (e.g., increasing automation) to the white-collar workplace. "In the Bell System," 1, 3. Lefkowitz, 23; Kneedler, 29; Hardy, 29; Blumenthal 27.

148. Jerry Marlow, letter to G. B. Santos, May 20, 1977. Reproduced in AT&T Media Center Kit, 4. SC.

149. Ibid., 3. For the quantification of these returns, see Richard I. Tumin, "Accountability at Autonetics," *Educational Television* 2, no. 10 (1970): 26. By their count, Autonetics saved $1.9 million per week due to a training and motivation series that cost $178,000 to produce—"a small investment for the dramatic savings involved."

150. Caranicas, 1–3. David R. Simmons, "Visual Aids in Insurance Teaching," *The Journal of Risk and Insurance* 34, no. 4 (1967): 606–610; On criticisms of the expense (and vanity) of CCTV versus "a well-edited, concise film" and a blackboard, see "Hook-Ups for National Sales Meetings—Film vs. TV," *The Management Review* (1956): 450.

151. John P. Wiliszowski, "The Future of Private Television," in Sambul, 29-3; Robert C. Kemper, "Industrial Applications of CCTV," *Training and Development Journal* (December 1974): 9; "Videotape Recording in Industry," 35; Caranicas, 1–4.

152. "In the Bell System," 1; "Earliest Ref.," 1–2.

153. "In the Bell System," 1.

154. "Earliest Ref.," 2. On cartridges, see Chapter 4.

155. Ibid.; "In the Bell System," 1.

156. "Earliest Ref.," 3.

157. A list of other early experimenters reads like a who's who of American industry: Ford, GE, GM, US Steel, IBM, Xerox, Hewlett-Packard, Lockheed, North American Aviation, RCA, and Texas Instruments. Caranicas, 1–4; Kenneth S. Teel and Robert G. Kinkade, "Attitudes of Production Workers Toward Closed-Circuit Television," *Personnel Psychology* 17, no. 1 (1964): 1; Foster, 1, 16; Stasheff and Lavi, 96, 129; Stormes and Crumpler, 227.

158. "Earliest Ref.," 4.

159. These might range from training, photographic or film, HR, and marketing and sales. Robert Passaro, "An Organizational Perspective of Corporate Television," in Sambul, 2-1–2-3.

160. Positioning television within PR guaranteed the fledgling project more resources than it would have likely received had it been placed elsewhere, e.g., in training and education, where budgets were more sensitive to the ups and downs of the market. "In the Bell System," 1. AT&T's emphasis on proximity to certain parts of the organization is cited only in retrospective talks. It is unclear if this was simply a convenient truth after the fact. Paul W. Lowry, "Industrial Television—An Awakening Giant," speech written for ITVA conference, c. 1976. SC; Lowry, "Belongs," 7.

161. "In the Bell System," 3.

162. "Shooting Script," 4.

163. Alvin von Auw, letter to all Public Relations Vice Presidents, March 31, 1967: 1–2. 141 03 03 08. AA.

164. von Auw, 1; "AT&T's A-V Center: Videotape in Action," *Business Screen* 30, no. 11 (1969): 36.

165. "AT&T's A-V Center," 36–37.

166. Ibid., 36.

167. "In the Bell System," 4; "Shooting Script, 14."

168. "Grapevine," 51.

169. "Management In Practice," 33. With a wider purview, another lunchtime program—*The Management Forum Series*—distributed live telecasts, including

lectures, panel discussions, and conferences, to audiences across New Jersey and New York. "CCTV Notes," AT&T Media Center Kit, June 1977: 4. SC.

170. Bartlow, 18.

171. Lowry, "Giant," 7.

172. In the mid-1970s, as the fateful *United States v. AT&T Co.* anti-trust trial was getting underway, one such big-budget series explained the issue of discovery—a lawsuit's pre-trial phase when both sides are gathering evidence—via an elaborate mock trial. Interview with the author. John Sheahan, producer, AT&T and Johnson and Johnson, University of Wisconsin Madison, October 25, 2014.

173. *Viewpoints*, for example, aired four programs over two consecutive days during hour-long blocks in the morning and afternoon. Bartlow, 18.

174. "Shooting Script," 5–6.

175. "In the Bell System," 3–4.

176. Ibid., 3.

177. von Auw, 1.

178. "CCTV Notes," 4.

179. H. I. Romnes, "CCTV Program: Final Used," July 6, 1967: 1–2. 191-11-01-15. AA.

180. The company estimated an additional $9 million would be necessary over 1981–1983 for an updated studio to replace the facilities at 195. "Shooting Script," 12–13.

181. Robert Mason, Jr., Speech to PRVP Conference, September 17, 1979, 1, 2.

182. "Interview with John Walsh, September 20, 1978," 1; "Interview with Jerry Hargitt, September 26, 1978," 3; "Interview with Don Sharp, September 25, 1978," 5, 11 04 03 07, AA.

183. "Interview with Frank R. Zimmerman, October 3, 1978," 3, 11 04 03 07, AA.

184. By one count, 150 companies had such programs in 1977. "Grapevine," 49.

185. Robert N. Ford, "The Obstinate Employee," *Public Opinion Quarterly* (delivered as the Presidential Address at the annual meeting of the American Association for Public Opinion Research, Lake George, NY, May 18, 1969): 302.

186. Ibid.

187. Ibid., 309.

188. Mason, 5, 8–9.

189. The organization changed its name once again in 2001 to Media Communication Association (MCA-I) to represent the widening technological purviews of many of its employees. The organization went defunct in 2016, due to the declining ability of members to pay dues as poorly paying contract work (rather than permanent staff positions) became the norm. Interview with the author. Dick Van Deusen, founder, National Industrial Television Association. Telephone, August 25, 2014. Connie Terwilliger, "MCA-I (formerly ITVA) Fades to Black," *LinkedIn* (August 21, 2016). Terwilliger served in several positions at MCA-I, including president. https://www. linkedin.com/pulse/mca-i-formerly-itva-fades-black-connie-terwilliger/ (retrieved September 13, 2016). Like many trade organizations, ITVA provided opportunities for networking, sharing field- specific knowledge, and carving out professional identities that legitimized their work.

190. See, for example, Nathan J. Sambul, ed., *The Handbook of Private Television: A Complete Guide for Video Facilities and Networks within Corporations, Nonprofit Institutions, and Government Agencies* (New York: McGraw Hill, 1982).

191. Brush, Judith M. and Douglas P. Brush. *Private Television Communications: A Report to Management*. White Plaines, NY: Knowledge Industry Publications, 1974;

Brush, Judith M. and Douglas P. Brush. *Private Television Communications: An Awakening Giant*. Stockholm: Esselte Video, 1978; Brush, Judith M. and Douglas P. Brush. *Private Television Communications: Into the Eighties*. Berkeley Heights, NJ: International Television Association, 1981; Brush, Judith M. and Douglas P. Brush. *Private Television Communications: the new directions: The Fourth Report*. Cold Spring, NY: HI Press, 1986; Brush, Judith M. and Douglas P. Brush. *The Fifth Brush Report: User-Driven Communication Systems*. LaGrangeville, NY: HI Press, 1992.

192. This was the case even in ETV discourse, where the logic of selling might not have the same salience: Lesikar et al., 13. Stasheff and Lavi, 150; Sambul, "Guidelines for Success," in Sambul, 10-3; Linc Shirley, "Rolling!' An Era Passes," *Back Stage* (July 8, 1977). Reprinted in AT&T Media Center Kit: 18. SC.

193. Ron Whittaker, "The Pitfalls of Private Television," in Sambul, 3-4.

194. Another strategy was the "charge-back" system of accounting, which charged company departments with covering some portion of production, distribution, and overhead costs, thus quantifying the value television provided company departments and (ostensible) savings from not working with an outside producer. "Shooting Script," 16.

195. Lowry, "Giant," 5. A *Back Stage* article circulated by AT&T's CCTV group reinforced this approach when it chastised media producers for "thinking in fragments not systems." Instead, readers were compelled to see TV as "their own private television 'network' to reach every audience segment involved in its operation." Shirley, 14.

196. Lowry, "Giant," 9.

197. "Block CCTV Circuit Presentation," 8.

198. "Shooting Script," 4.

199. A handwritten note scrawled on the front page of the speech identifies it as "The Philosophy." Lowry, "Belongs," 3.

200. Lowry, "Belongs," 5–6. Emphasis mine.

201. H. I. Romnes, "Managing Change through Communications," speech delivered to Industrial Communications Association via CCTV. May 4, 1965. 191 11 01 14. AA.

202. Above also from Lowry, "Belongs," 6.

203. The preceding also from Lowry, "Giant," 5, 7

204. Lowry, "Belongs," 2.

205. Lowry, "Giant," 9.

206. "Projects for 'Ma Bell' are Many and Diverse," *Wilke Report* (Winter 1977): 1. Reproduced in *The Wilke Papers*, ed. Richard E. Van Deusen, 92, 95.

207. "Projects for 'Ma Bell,'" 1, 4 [page 95 in *The Wilke Papers*].

208. In my discussions with former professionals, "Fortune 500"—or, more often, "Fortune 100" or "Fortune 50"—was used as a shorthand label of value to indicate the importance, size, and resources of a mediated company (and therefore the sophistication and complexity of their communication needs).

209. "Hubert Wilke, Inc.: History and Modus Operandi," reproduced in *The Wilke Papers*, ed. Richard E. Van Deusen, 6–8.

210. "'Ma Bell,'" 4.

211. In describing the new form of these "control societies," Deleuze suggests "the corporation is a spirit, a gas"—an evocative way of picturing the intensified mediation enabled by televisual technologies. Gilles Deleuze, "Postscript on the Societies of Control," *October* 59 (Winter 1992), 4–5.

212. "All-Purpose," 33.

CHAPTER 4

1. "Pepsi-Cola Bottlers Standardize on Video Cassettes," *Business Screen* 34, no. 3 (1973): 10.
2. Ibid, 10, 15; "Video Is Versatile at Foxboro," *Business Screen* 33, no. 1 (1972): 26.
3. James P. Smith, "Tape? Film? Both!" *Business Screen* 35, no. 3 (1974): 33; Clay Felker, quoted in "Tape, 16mm and Super 8 Live Together at New York Magazine," *Business Screen* 34, no. 6 (1973): 23.
4. John A. Bunyan, James C. Crimmins, and N. Kyri Watson, *Practical Video: The Manager's Guide to Applications* (White Plains, NY: Knowledge Industry Publications, 1978), 3, 34, "When Pepsi Went Video, They Selected the Sony Videocassette System," *Business Screen* 34, no. 5 (1973): 12–13; "Telemation Places Large Order: Sony Looks to Manufacture 1 Million Units," *Billboard* 84, no. 12 (March 8, 1972): 40.
5. Bunyan et al., 193; "1974 Industrial A/V Survey," *Business Screen* 35, no. 4 (1974): 30; Hope Reports, Inc., "An Evaluation . . . Video Communication System of Bank of America," 1977, 21. Box 4, Folder 5. Hope Reports Collection. Rare Books, Special Collections & Preservation Department, University of Rochester (henceforth HRC).
6. Ed Block, "Block CCTV Circuit Presentation," March 29, 1977: 7. John Sheahan Collection (SC) Lent to the author. "AV Man: James G Damon Jr.," *Business Screen* 33, no. 3 (1972): 22.
7. Those interested in corporate dynamics may reach back six years earlier when Sony partnered with Matsushita and Japan Victor Company (JVC) to collaborate on the standard for the ¾-inch U-matic. According to Wasser, due to Sony's dominance in sales of the shared format, JVC and Matsushita became dissatisfied with the alliance and went their own ways on later cassette development projects. Frederick Wasser, *Veni, Vidi, Video: The Hollywood Empire and the VCR* (Austin: University of Texas Press, 2002), 71.
8. The Betamax initially offered one hour of recording while the VHS offered two. James Lardner, *Fast Forward: Hollywood, the Japanese and the Onslaught of the VCR* (New York: Norton, 1987), 151–152.
9. Wasser, 73.
10. Wasser, 72–73. 75; S. J. Liebowitz and Stephen E. Margolis, "Path Dependence, Lock-In, and History," *Journal of Law, Economics, & Organization* 11, no. 1 (1995): 205–226; Kalyan Chatterjee and Robert Evans, "Rivals' Search for Buried Treasure: Competition and Duplication in R&D," *The RAND Journal of Economics* 35, no. 1 (2004): 160–183.
11. On Hollywood and the home, see Michael Z. Newman, *Video Revolutions: On the History of a Medium* (New York: Columbia University Press, 2014); Ann Gray, *Video Playtime: The Gendering of a Leisure Technology* (New York: Routledge, 1992); and Eugene Marlow and Eugene Secunda, *Shifting Time and Space: The Story of Videotape* (Santa Barbara, CA: Praeger, 1991). On the format wars, see Joshua Greenberg, *From Betamax to Blockbuster: Video Stores and the Invention of Movies on Video* (Cambridge, MA: MIT Press, 2008) and James Lardner, *Fast Forward*, 1987. On regulation, recording, and renting as cultural practice, as well as video aesthetics, see Lucas Hilderbrand, *Inherent Vice: Bootleg Histories of Video and Copyright* (Durham, NC: Duke University Press, 2009); Daniel Herbert, *Videoland: Movie Culture at the American Video Store* (Oakland: University of California Press, 2014); Dennis Redmond, *The World Is Watching: Video as Multinational Aesthetics, 1968–1995* (Carbondale: Southern Illinois University

Press, 2004); and Gladys D. Ganley and Oswald H. Ganley, *Global Political Fallout: The VCR's First Decade* (Cambridge, MA: Program on Information Resources Policy, Harvard University, 1987); Caetlin Benson-Allott, *Killer Tapes and Shattered Screens: Video Spectatorship from VHS to File Sharing* (Berkeley: University of California Press, 2013). On video art and activism, see Sean Cubitt, *Videography: Video Media as Art and Culture* (Hampshire, UK: Palgrave MacMillian, 1993); Michael Renov and Erika Suderburg, eds., *Resolutions: Contemporary Video Practices*. (Minneapolis: Minessota Press, 1996). Within mainstream broadcasting histories, cartridges appear briefly in discussions of the transition to faster-paced music-heavy broadcast formats. Christopher H. Sterling and John Michael Kittross, *Stay Tuned: A History of American Broadcasting*, 3rd edn. (Mahwah, NJ: Lawrence Erlbaum Associates, 2002), 409.

12. Wasser, 60–70. Max Dawson's discussion of video as a high-brow alternative to broadcasting likewise touches on several often-forgotten devices, but only in the context of home media consumption. Max Dawson, "Home Video and the 'TV Problem': Cultural Critics and Technological Change," *Technology and Culture* 48, no. 3 (2007): 524–549.

13. Janet Abbate, *Inventing the Internet* (Cambridge, MA: MIT Press, 1999), 179.

14. Jonathan Sterne, *MP3: The Meaning of a Format* (Durham, NC: Duke University Press, 2012), 11; Kit Hughes, "Record/Film/Book/Interactive TV: EVR as a Threshold Format," *Television and New Media* 17, no. 1 (2016): 45.

15. "Make Your Own TV Schedule," *New York Times* (August 27, 1977), "This Amazing Machine Can Add Hours to Your Day," reprinted in Marlow and Secunda, 125.

16. Nikki Porter, *Isn't It about Time? American Television Networks in the Face of Temporal and Institutional Challenges 1970–1985*. Master's thesis, Concordia University, March 2011, 161–164.

17. Carolyn A. Lin, "The VCR, Home Video Culture and New Video Technologies," in *Television and the American Family*, eds. Jennings Bryant and J. Alison Bryant. (London: Lawrence Erlbaum Associates, 2001), 93.

18. Porter, 163–164.

19. "Thanks to Our Novel Idea," *New York Times* (October 12, 1976), 19.

20. Ibid., "Make Your Own TV Schedule," *New York Times* (August 27, 1977).

21. Nick Browne, "The Political Economy of the Television (Super) Text," in *American Television: New Directions in History and Theory*, ed. Nick Browne (New York: Routledge, 1994), 71.

22. Ibid.

23. Jefferson R. Cowie, *Stayin' Alive: The 1970s and the Last Days of the Working Class* (New York: The New Press), 2012.

24. Michael Hardt and Antonio Negri, *Multitude: War and Democracy in the Age of Empire* (New York: Penguin Books, 2004), 114.

25. Frederick Harry Pitts, "Labour-Time in the Dot.Com Bubble: Marxist Approaches," *Fast Capitalism* 10, no. 1 (2013): np.; Paolo Virno, "General Intellect," in *Lessico Postfordista*, eds. Adelino Zanini and Ubaldo Fadini (Milan: Feltrinelli, 2001), 146–152. English translation by Arianna Bove available online at www.generation-online.org/p/fpvirno10.htm.

26. Virno, np.

27. Ibid.

28. For a discussion of why *labor time* is the primary target of profit-seeking in the current economy of downsized workforces, see Pitts, np.

29. Lardner, 73.

30. Lardner, 51. The possibility that endless-loop and reel-rewind cartridges set the conditions for videotape's adoption has also eluded scholars. Wasser notes briefly that Noel Bloom found U-matic tapes easier to use in pornography arcades than the by-then conventional 8mm cartridges—foreshadowing Bloom's role in the development of the video industry (Wasser, 71). Peter Alilunus only recently took up this buried thread to explore the role that X-rated film cartridges in motels played in the pornography industry's transition to video and private home exhibition. Peter Alilunus, *Smutty Little Movies: The Creation and Regulation of Adult Video* (Berkeley: University of California Press, 2016), 40–83.

31. "New Equipment: Technicolor's 'Instant 8,'" *Educational Screen and Audiovisual Guide* (April 1962): 223; J. L. Anderson, "Looking Back for the Single Concept Film," *Journal of the University Film Producers Association* 17, no. 2 (1965): 30.

32. Everett Hall, "Audiovisuals of the 1970s," *Business Screen* 31, no. 6 (1970): 27.

33. For a discussion of competing sound cartridge formats, see Richard Kahlenberg and Chloe Aaron, "The Cartridges Are Coming," *Cinema Journal* 9, no. 2 (1970): 2–12.

34. James L. Page, "Closing the Film-Projector Availability Gap," *Journal of the University Film Producers Association* 17, no. 2 (1965): 20.

35. Bunyan et al., "Practical Video," 11–12; Roland J. Zavada, "The Standardization of Super 8," *Journal of the University Film Association* 22, no. 2 (1970): 41.

36. "Technicolor's 'Instant 8,'" *Educational Screen and Audiovisual Guide* (April 1962): 223.

37. Curtis E. Avery, "Eights, Sixteens, and Satellites," *The Family Life Coordinator* 14, no. 3 (1965): 123.

38. Charles "Cap" Palmer, "Single Concept Comes of Age," *Business Screen* 32, no. 3 (1971): 27.

39. Ibid., 26.

40. Palmer, 27. Underlining the temporal flexibility of truncated messaging, some suggested avoiding content (e.g., stylized exposition) "that repetitive viewing may make annoyingly uninteresting." L. B. Happé, "The Silent Single Concept Film," *Journal of the University Film Producers Association* 17, no. 2 (1965): 4; John P. Vergis, "Home-Made Films at Arizona State University," *Journal of the University Film Producers Association* 17, no. 2 (1965): 26.

41. "Training, Selling with Single Concept Loops," *Business Screen* 30, no. 6 (1969): 18.

42. "Technicolor: Sound Plus Super 8," *Business Screen* 28, no. 2 (1967): 67.

43. "'Instant Meetings' Speed Sales, Customer Education," *Business Screen* 30, no. 7 (1969): 20.

44. There was strategic benefit for manufacturers and cartridge film publishers in promoting individualized audiovisual programming. As Cap Palmer put it, individuals are the "ultimate big market," since, "God made a lot more of them than group audiences." Charles "Cap" Palmer, "We Gotta Stop Pitching to Second Base," *Business Screen* 34, no. 5 (1973): 29–31, 48.

45. Happé, 7; Frank L. Moore, "Films in Music Education: Visual Cues for an Aural Art," *Music Educators Journal* 57, no. 5 (1971): 58.

46. Moore, 59.

47. "Technicolor's 'Instant 8,'" 223; Happé, 3.

48. Avery, "Eights, Sixteens, and Satellites," 127–128.

49. Ibid., 128.

50. Ibid., 125; Curtis E. Avery, "Some Thoughts on the Fourth 'R,'" *The Family Life Coordinator* 15, no. 2 (1966): 37.

51. R. L. Uttley, "American Oil Films Encourage Driver Safety; Build Company's Image among Teen-Agers," *Business Screen* 28, no. 1 (1967): 122.

52. "Chrysler/Plymouth-Dodge Dealers Switch to Super 8," *Business Screen* 33, no. 4 (1972): 10.

53. This use of cartridges recalls Haidee Wasson's analysis of the "small film screen" at the 1939 World's Fair and offers a clear continuance of the corporatist project of building "an everyday consumer ecology, one that shows the easy integration of film projectors and films into a culture of buying and selling, of individual ownership, self-operated display and mobile, electrical entertainment." Haidee Wasson, "The Other Small Screen: Moving Images at New York's World Fair, 1939," *Canadian Journal of Film Studies* 21, no. 1 (2012): 83.

54. "This Is a Best Seller," *Business Screen* 28, no. 5 (1962): 3.

55. "Meeting of the Minds," *Business Screen* 28, no. 3 (1962): 32–34.

56. This may also be a software issue. Whereas the first ad asks users to generate their own films for the machine, the second one boasts "thousands of films, covering hundreds of subjects."

57. Palmer, "Single Concept Comes of Age," 27. Here we might consider Anna McCarthy's work on how point-of-purchase television in retail spaces was designed to act on the viewer in precise (temporal and) spatially-motivated ways: "video on the sales floor must intervene in the space and time of the shopping trip, increase our interaction with merchandise, and generally make customers' time in the store more 'productive' (i.e., produce more purchases)." Anna McCarthy, *Ambient Television: Visual Culture and Public Space* (Durham, NC: Duke University Press, 2001), 156.

58. "Technicolor: Sound Plus Super 8," 67; "This Is a Best Seller," 3; "Technicolor's 8mm 'Instant:' Projector," 61; "The Perfect Audio Visual System," 41. See also Haidee Wasson, "Suitcase Cinema," *Cinema Journal* 51, no. 2 (2012): 151. Fairchild's "Agent" projector—a briefcase that unfolded into a projector—represents the most fully realized vision of portable work communications. Reinforcing its globe-trotting potential, the ad copy playfully invokes espionage via spy-comics font and "secret 'agent'" copy. "It's No Secret!" *Business Screen* 33, no. 2 (1972): 37.

59. "Servis Demonstrates with Film," *Business Screen* 30, no. 4 (1969): 191.

60. "'Instant Meetings' Speed Sales, Customer Education," 20; "The Survival of the Fittest," *Business Screen* 30, no. 7 (1969): 19.

61. Palmer, "We Gotta Stop Pitching to Second Base," 31.

62. Ibid., 27.

63. Haidee Wasson, "Protocols of Portability," *Film History* 25, no. 1 (2013): 243; Wasson, "Suitcase Cinema," 151.

64. "The Survival of the Fittest," 19.

65. O. H. Coelin, "A-V for Trade & Training," *Business Screen* 26, no. 9 (1968): 10; "'Instant Meetings' Speed Sales, Customer Education," 20.

66. "I Talked for Two Hours But They Still Didn't Understand," *Business Screen* 33, no. 2 (1972): 47.

67. Coelin, "A-V for Trade & Training," 10.

68. "I talked for two hours. But they still didn't understand," 47.

69. Jeorg Agin, "Super 8? Stronger than Ever," *Business Screen* (January/February 1975): 31; similar language was already in use by Sony to position the U-matic as "the new concept in communications." "So Simple. So reliable. So effective. So successful. Sony," *Broadcast Management Engineering* 10, no. 9 (1974): 9.

70. Devin Orgeron, Marsha Orgeron, and Dan Streible, "A History of Learning with the Lights Off," in *Learning with the Lights Off*, eds. Devin Orgeron, Marsha Orgeron, and Dan Streible (New York: Oxford University Press, 2012), 41. The legislation funded other educational initiatives; I focus on media here.

71. On the impact of the NDEA on the incorporation of new media technologies into Cold War classrooms and pedagogies, see Charles R. Acland, *Swift Viewing: The Popular Life of Subliminal Influence* (Durham: Duke University Press, 2012), 165–191.

72. Robert L. Shoemaker, "The Filmstrip Future," *Business Screen* 31, no. 6 (1970): 33–34.

73. Ott Coelin, "Sight and Sound at the Crossroad," *Business Screen* 28, no. 4 (1967): 4.

74. CBS Electronic Video Recording Demonstration Film, c. 1970: https://www.youtube.com/watch?v=pB8zQWs89wU; Peter C. Goldmark, "Color EVR." *IEEE Spectrum* (September 22, 1970), 22–33.

75. For a lengthier discussion of the technological development of the machine and its affordances, see Hughes, "Record/Film/Book/Interactive TV," 2016.

76. Brockway, "EVR Moves from Promise to Reality," 28; "EVR—Promise of the Future?," 22; "How Equitable Salesmen Learn the Facts of Life," *Business Screen* 32, no. 4 (1971): 12.

77. On home study and self-instruction via EVR, as well as the tendency to link self-instruction to more efficient use of professionals' time, see "EVR—Promise of the Future?," 23; "The Cassettes Are Coming," 23; Robert E. Brockway, "EVR Moves from Promise to Reality," *Business Screen* (February 1971): 28; Samuel C. Gale, "What about Software?," *Business Screen* 32, no. 2 (1971): 29–30; Benjamin DeMott, "EVR: Teacher in a Cartridge," *Change* 3, no. 1 (1971): 41. Goldmark would later pursue this ambition in his "New Rural Society" project, a Housing and Urban Development–funded project that positioned telecommunication technologies as a tool of population redistribution from crowded urban areas to failing rural towns. Technology—the likes of the EVR, but also CCTV, satellite, and other media—were positioned as the infrastructure that could reconfigure where people lived, worked, healed, schooled, and socialized (not to mention save gasoline in the midst of an energy crisis). Peter C. Goldmark, "New Directions: Toward a New Rural Society," *Management Review* 63, no. 10 (1974): 52–54.

78. Lee Coyle, "Cassettes and Beyond—User Leaders Speak Out," *Business Screen* 32, no. 2 (1971): 31.

79. "How Equitable Salesmen Learn," 12; Brockway, "EVR Moves from Promise to Reality," 28.

80. "The Cassettes Are Coming," *Business Screen* 32, no. 2 (1971): 23.

81. "How Equitable Salesmen Learn," 12.

82. Countries included the United Kingdom, France, Italy, Germany, Austria, Switzerland, Scandinavia, and Japan. The EVR Partnership that backed the machine's development and expansion was comprised of CBS (50% ownership), Imperial Chemical Industries Ltd. (30%), and CIBA Ltd. (20%). Brockway, "EVR Moves from Promise to Reality," 28–29.

83. Gale, 29.

84. Hedden, "From the Laboratories—Even Better Quality," *Business Screen* 8, no. 31 (1970): 24; Brockway, "EVR Moves from Promise to Reality," 29; DeMott, 40–41.

85. Robert Finehout, "Please . . . Don't Say Distribution!" *Business Screen* 30, no. 8 (1969): 28.

86. Gale, 29, 30.

87. Thomas F. Hatcher, "Cassettes and Beyond—User Leaders Speak Out," *Business Screen* 32, no. 2 (1971): 30. Hatcher was concerned with circuits of corporate communication, e.g., "from a headquarters location to many detached offices, or from a central location to individuals working in the field."

88. "EVR—Promise of the Future?," 22. Positioning the EVR as an alternative to broadcast rather than industrial film undergirds the review's elision of EVR's continuity with film cartridges.

89. An early review of the machine noted that the first model would be "an industrial-educational unit of 'ruggedized' design." "Motorola to Make EVR Player," *Business Screen* 30, no. 2 (1969): 23. Although it's possible this was due to engineering difficulties in offering a miniaturized consumer model, CBS maintained the plan for separate industrial/consumer models through 1971, indicating an understanding of the two markets as distinct—in their price points, if nothing else. "Comparative Analysis of Video Cartridge Systems," *Business Screen* 32, no. 2 (1971): 26. Elmer H. Wavering, president of Motorola Inc., described the dual stages of their strategy in a 1968 press release, noting that hospitals and schools "are not in any sense the outside limitation. Rather, they represent the most obvious needs to be served on a priority basis. These are markets in which we now provide other communications equipment and for which we have on board fully qualified engineering, production, and marketing people." Motorola Information Service Press Release, October 12, 1968, Motorola Solutions, Inc., Legacy Archives Collection, Consumer Products, Teleplayer, and Electronic Video Recording System series (MSLAC): 2.

90. Wasser, 60.

91. Frank Stanton, quoted in "Motorola to Make EVR Player," 23. Motorola Information Service Press Release, October 12, 1968, 2. MSLAC.

92. "Modern to Offer Sponsored Films in EVR Format," *Business Screen* 30, no. 5 (1969): 6; "Motorola to Market EVR Programs, Player," *Business Screen* 31, no. 6 (1970): 49.

93. Richard E. Kobak, "Motorola Systems, American Program Bureau Announce Plans to Bring Leading Personalities to Campuses via Cartridge TV" (August 1970); Lawrence R. Thorpe, "Polk Brothers First Motorola Distributor to Order EVR Teleplayer for Training and Education" (June 1970); Robert E. Bouzek, "ABA Names Motorola to Distribute EVR Programs" (January 1972); all in MSLAC.

94. "Motorola to Market EVR Programs, Player," 49.

95. Lawrence R. Thorpe, "Motorola Distributor Organization First to Use EVR Teleplayers for Training and Education," News Releases, MSLAC (June 9, 1970): 1–3.

96. Brockway, "EVR Moves from Promise to Reality," 29.

97. Ibid. This emphasis on the home market as a guarantee of success across markets was taken up again three years later by Motorola president Elmer H. Wavering to promote another round of software agreements. Jesse Rotman, "Wavering Sees Rapid Growth of Cassette TV for Home Use" (April 16, 1971), MSLAC.

98. Provided they adopt their employer's video format. "EVR—Promise of the Future?" 23; Gale, 29–30. Certainly, employers sent workers home with print materials; my focus here is electronic communication.

99. Hatcher, 32.

100. "IAVA: Industry a Guinea Pig for Manufacturers?" *Business Screen* 33, no. 1 (1972): 19.

101. Hall, 28. "EVR—Promise of the Future?," 23.

102. Max Dawson, "Home Video and the 'TV Problem'," 539.

103. Ibid.

104. Bob Chandler, "Where the TV Elite Don't Meet," *Variety* (March 29, 1961): 1. Qtd. in Dawson, "Home Video and the 'TV Problem,'" 538.

105. "Motorola Introduces Closed-Circuit Hospital TV Network for Entertainment and Training" (September 14, 1970); Lawrence R. Thorpe, "STP Racing Films to be Converted to EVR Format by Motorola" (June 9, 1970), MSLAC. "Memphis Memorial Gets Largest Hospital Teleplayer System," *Voice of Motorola* XXVI, no. 1 (January 1, 1971): 2.

106. Charles A. Sengstock, Jr., "Motorola Signs Rowan and Martin Company to Produce Shows for Its EVR Teleplayer Series. Jack Benny, George Burns to Appear" (1970), MSLAC.

107. Lawrence R. Thorpe, "STP Racing Films to Be Converted to EVR Format by Motorola" (June 9, 1970), MSLAC.

108. "Motorola Introduces Closed-Circuit Hospital TV Network for Entertainment and Training" (September 14, 1970), MSLAC. Although they don't discuss the EVR, Joy V. Fuqua's *Prescription TV: Therapeutic Discourse in the Hospital and at Home* (Durham, NC: Duke University Press, 2012), 71–92, covers similar dynamics in detail.

109. "Motorola Introduces Closed-Circuit Hospital TV Network for Entertainment and Training" (September 14, 1970); Daniel E. Lees, "Ayerst Lanoratories Plans First Medical Use of Cassette TV with Motorola EVR Teleplayer Units" (May 5, 1971); both in MSLAC.

110. "Motorola Executive Sees 1971 as 'Year of Decision' in clarifying 'Cassette TV' Confusion," MSLAC. Motorola had never before entered software production. The EVR was also targeted to hotels as in-room entertainment *for traveling salesmen*. Even when entertainment was the focus of software, discussion of viewers' professional identities was not far behind. Hatcher, 30.

111. Daniel E. Lees, "Statement of Purpose by Motorola Systems, Inc. Regarding Involvement in the Law Enforcement Training Field" (1971); Daniel E. Lees, "Motorola Introduces a Professional Police TV Network for Use by Law Enforcement Agencies in Training and Community Relations"; Daniel E. Lees, "New EVR Training Package Unveiled for Police Chiefs by Motorola Systems, Inc." (September 28, 1971); all in MSLAC.

112. Wasser, 61.

113. Revolutionary, according to Sony. Quotation in preceding heading from "The Sony U-Matic" [Display Ad 52] *Wall Street Journal* (August 28, 1972): 11. Coelin, "Who Speaks for the USERS," 14; "The Cassettes are Coming," 23.

114. Larder, 70.

115. "Ampex Instavideo Cartridge Meets EIAJ Standards," *Business Screen* no. 4 (1971): 10; Lardner, 80; Jeffrey A. Hart, *Technology, Television, and Competition: The Politics of Digital TV* (Cambridge: Cambridge University Press, 2004): 79–80; Richard Gilkey, "Instructional Media: Video Cassettes: Problem or

Solution?" *The Clearing House* 45, no. 5 (1971): 319; Richard A. Donnelly, "Blank
Cartridges? Video Cassettes May Be Way Ahead of Their Time," *Barron's National
Business and Financial Weekly* (September 4, 1972), 5; "Comparative Analysis of
Video Cartridge Systems," 26.

116. Wasser dates the U-matic to 1969, though it's unclear what event this signifies
(70). Lardner places the release at 1971 (73). A news report places the date at
1972. Eliot Tiegel, "Sony's Many Actions Keep It Progressing," *Billboard* 84, no.
13 (March 25, 1972): 33. The 1971 date is substantiated in "Sony—New York,"
Business Screen 32, no. 5 (1971): 31.

117. "Sony—New York," 31.

118. "Sony Corporation," *Business Screen* 34, no. 1 (1973): 41. The industrial market alone
purchased 80% of videoplayers (of any format) sold in 1972 and 1973. Thomas W.
Hope *AV-USA, 1973–1974* (Rochester, NY: Hope Reports, 1975), 34. HRC.

119. "Telemation Places Large Order: Sony Looks to Manufacture 1 Million Units,"
Billboard 84, no. 12 (March 8, 1972): 40.

120. Judith M. Brush and Douglas P. Brush, *Private Television Communications: A Report
to Management* (White Plains, NY: Knowledge Industry Publications, 1974), 62.
According to HR, videocassette sales rose 78% in 1973, more than any other medium
(though other media, like super 8mm non-cartridge projectors, sold more units).
Hope, *AV-USA 1973–74*, 62. Hope also indicates that U-Matic use rose rapidly
between 1972 and 1976 before exhibiting the slowed growth of "a maturing system."
Hope Reports, "Potential for Entry into the Video Field," 1978 Box 4, Folder 5. HRC.

121. Judith M. Brush and Douglas P. Brush, *Private Television Communications: An
Awakening Giant* (Stockholm: Esselte Video, 1978), 30.

122. Hope Reports, "Analysis of Audiovisual Activities in 97 Major Corporations,"
1975, 5. Box 4, Folder 6. HRC.

123. Bunyan et al, 34.

124. Lawrence R. Thorpe, "Motorola Distributor Organization First to Use EVR
Teleplayers for Training and Education" (June 9, 1970), MSLAC.

125. Ibid.

126. "2 Firms Aim for 'Totality'," *Billboard* 84, no. 12 (March 18, 1972): 40.

127. "The Sony U-matic" [Display Ad 52], 11.

128. "Pepsi-Cola Bottlers Standardize," *Business Screen* 34, no. 3 (1973): 10.

129. Donnelly, 15; Howard Geltzer, "A Retail Video Fashion Network," *Training and
Development Journal* 27, no. 11 (1973): 35.

130. Guy Cephas Gentry, Jr., *Videotape in Manpower Development and Training: A Study
of the Use of Videotape in Business and Industry*. Master's thesis, Florida Atlantic
University, 1974, 58.

131. "Audio-visual Equipment Helps Make Sales," *Agency Sales Magazine* (December
1988): 25.

132. Ibid.

133. Ibid, 26.

134. Challenging common wisdom, Jennifer Delton argues that historians downplay the
extent to which employers and the National Association of Manufacturers supported
workplace integration efforts via a series of experiments and negotiations over the
form that race-based equal opportunity would take. *Racial Integration in Corporate
America, 1940–1990* (Cambridge: Cambridge University Press, 2009), 191–195.

135. Firms with over 100 employees were targeted first, with companies comprising over
25 employees not bound by the act until 1968. Terry H. Anderson, *The Pursuit of
Fairness: A History of Affirmative Action* (Oxford: Oxford University Press, 2004), 83.

136. David L. Rose, "Twenty-Five Years Later: Where Do We Stand on Equal Employment Opportunity Law Enforcement?" in *Equal Employment Opportunity: Labor Market Discrimination and Public Policy*, ed. Paul Burstein (New York: Aldine de Gruyter, 1994), 45.

137. Anderson, 97.

138. Ibid., 125.

139. Rose, 45.

140. Anderson, 100.

141. Ibid., 124, 133.

142. Katherine Turk, *Equality on Trial: Gender and Rights in the Modern American Workplace* (Philadelphia: University of Pennsylvania Press, 2016), 26–31.

143. Ibid., 34.

144. Ibid., 59–60.

145. Anderson, 140.

146. Rose, 46; Turk, 81–83,

147. Alfred W. Blumrosen, "The Law Transmission System and the Southern Jurisprudence of Employment Discrimination," in *Equal Employment Opportunity*, 232.

148. Rose, 51.

149. Norman C. Amaker, *Civil Rights and the Reagan Administration* (Washington, DC: The Urban Institute, 1988), 110–112.

150. Rose, 49.

151. Amaker, 129; Blumrosen, 242.

152. Cowie, 235. There is a distinction to be made between private and public sector unions. Public sector unions, e.g., AFSCME—which would embrace the cause of comparable pay for women workers in the 1980s—grew in the 1960s and 1970s in large part due to women members working in booming clerical and health industries. Turk, 109.

153. Cowie, 239. On the move away from class-based solidarity to individualized victories under EEOC determinations, see Turk, 43–71.

154. Hope Reports, "Communicating, Media and Training," 1983, 4–6. Box 4, Folder 3. HRC.

155. Hope Reports, "Analysis of the Training Market," 1972, 8. Box 4, Folder 7. HRC.

156. Hope Reports, "Communicating, Media and Training," 1983, 4–6. Box 4, Folder 3. HRC.

157. Hope Reports, "Communicating, Media and Training," 1983, 5, 8. Box 4, Folder 3. HRC. All figures in this chapter adjusted for inflation and represented in 2019 dollars via CPI Inflation Calculator.

158. Anderson, 91; Ameker 114. GM, for example, agreed to devote $15 million to training and education for minority workers to settle a 1983 class-action lawsuit.

159. Hope Reports, "Analysis of the Training Market," 1972, 4. Box 4, Folder 7. HRC. Xerox, also included in this list, would be found liable in the 1990s. Rather than suggest a direct relationship between EEOC complaints and media use, it is likely that larger companies also set the "best practices" for the industry.

160. Hope, AV-USA 1973–1974, 62. Other popular topics for training included automotive mechanics, supervisory training, health science, math and engineering, industrial skills, accounting, motivation, and management-related data processing. Hope Reports, "MTI Teleprograms Incorporation," 1973, Box 18, Folder 4. HRC; Hope Reports, "Communicating, Media and Training," 7.

161. Brush and Brush, 1974, 47, 32.

162. Although the U-Matic boasted a two-thirds market share in 1982, it was starting to lose significant ground to ½-inch formats like Betamax and VHS in the mid-1980s, comprising only a third of these expenditures. Brush and Brush, 1978, 31. See Brush and Brush, 1986, 63, and Hope Reports, "US Training Business 1977–1982, Preliminary Findings," 1984, 17. Box 37, Folder 9. HRC. Chris Murray, "Corporate Video" *Corporate Television* 1, no. 1 (1986): 37. Hope often pointed out the primary training medium for decades was the oft-overlooked 2" x 2" slide.

163. Brush and Brush, 1978, 2–3. The Brushes were fond of invoking an alphabet soup of changing workplace regulations to demonstrate video's ability to respond quickly to changing conditions. The Occupational Safety and Health Administration (OSHA) was founded in 1971 to address workplace safety. Invoked elsewhere, the Employee Retirement Income Security Act (ERISA) was passed in 1974, setting standards for private industry retirement plans. Brush and Brush, 1978, 34.

164. Connoly, 30; Bunyan et al., "Practical Video," 3, 88.

165. Judith M. Brush and Douglas P. Brush, *Private Television Communications: Into the Eighties* (Berkeley Heights, NJ: International Television Association, 1981), 90.

166. Howard Gross, "The A to Z of Corporate Television," *BusinessTV* (January 1992), 81.

167. Brush and Brush, 1981, 90. The Brushes referred to this as "selective networking." By their count, most firms (58%) used selective networking by the mid-1980s. This number grew to 65% by the early 1990s. Brush and Brush, 1986, 98, 104; Judith M. Brush and Douglas P. Brush, *The Fifth Brush Report: User-Driven Communication Systems* (LaGrangeville, NY: HI Press, 1992), 71. Hope Reports, "An Evaluation: Video Communication System of Bank of America," 21. HRC.

168. Judith M. Brush and Douglas P. Brush, *Private Television Communications: The New Directions: The Fourth Report* (Cold Spring, NY: HI Press, 1986), 58.

169. Ibid., 3.

170. Barbara Ladd, "Interactive Training Growing Steadily in Larger Companies," *Interactive Technologies* supplement to *Training* (September 19, 1989), 8. Fittingly, Ladd's example is the car industry.

171. Hope Reports, "An Evaluation: Video Communication System of Bank of America," 9. HRC.

172. Brush and Brush, 1974, 92–93; Brush and Brush, 1986, 25.

173. Dr. Stafford L. Hopwood, Jr., "Videocassettes: How Far and How Soon," *AudioVisual Communications* (December 1972): 16.

174. Brush and Brush, 1981, 81; Brush and Brush, 1992, 21; Hope Reports, "A Report on Television Commercial, Nontheatrical Film & Videotape Production in the USA," 1977, 4. Box 4, Folder 6. Kirk quote in "Audio-visual Equipment Helps Make Sales," 26. This particular "final frontier" is buying committees who might be otherwise unlikely to allow in-person pitches.

175. Brush and Brush, 1992, 21; Hope Reports, "Media Effectiveness Case Studies," 1989, 2. Box 8, Folder 9. HRC.

176. "Audio-visual Equipment Helps Make Sales," 27. Brush and Brush, 1986, 104.

177. "Network" also invokes telephony's possibility of interactivity and precisely directed action (and control) at a distance. See Sony's marketing materials, which elide the asynchronicity of taped programs and use telephonic language

("long-distance"). Brush and Brush, 1992, 14. "The Sony U-matic" [Display Ad 52]," 11.

178. Brush and Brush, 1974, 82; Brush and Brush, 1978, 75; Brush and Brush, 1981, 81.
179. Brush and Brush, 1974, 82, 56. For more on the size and shape of these networks, see "Pepsi-Cola Bottlers Standardize," 10. Bunyan et al., *Practical Video*, 88–89, 98, 109, 110, 115; "Datsun Distrib Buys 24 Sony Units as Aide," *Billboard* 84, no. 17 (April 22, 1972): 43.
180. Brush and Brush, 1981, 81; The median number of locations would double by 1986—an indication, perhaps, of the corporate environment of mergers, acquisitions and expansions in the 1980s. Brush and Brush, 1986, 104.
181. Brush and Brush, 1981, 166.
182. Brush and Brush, 1978, 59.
183. Brush and Brush, 1986, 27.
184. Ibid., 96, 98; Geltzer, "A Retail Video Fashion Network," 34. Bunyan et al. "Practical Video," 10, 193.
185. Brush and Brush, 1978, 15, 39; Murray, 81; Connoly, 30; Bunyan et al., 87. On the use of film to manage distributed organizations, namely franchises, see Kit Hughes, "For Pete's Sake, I'm Not Trying to Entertain These People": Film and Franchising at International Harvester," *Film History* 27, no. 3 (2015): 41–72.
186. Brush and Brush, 1974, 56; Trudye Connoly, "Audio-Visuals in the Hosiery Industry," *Business Screen* 37, no. 1 (1976): 29; "The Sony U-matic" [Display Ad 52]," 11.
187. On international networks, see Brush and Brush, 1986, 104. It should be noted that even into the 1980s, Hope was championing 16mm precisely because it was "the only small-format motion medium that can be used in any country in the world." Hope Reports, "Analysis of 16mm Sound Motion Picture Projector Sales 1975–1988," 1980, 12. Box 4, Folder 4. HRC. "Audio-visual Equipment Helps Make Sales," 25.
188. Much like VHF or UHF waves, cassettes supposedly allowed for saturated coverage of these otherwise unwieldy spaces. Furthermore, as the 1980s wore on and smaller organizations and community groups purchased consumer-grade equipment designed for home television sets, video became a means to increase the penetration of corporate information networks even further. Brush and Brush, 1986, 104.
189. David Lachenbruch, quoted in Brush and Brush, 1978, xi.
190. Brush and Brush, 1986, 58. Evidence suggests that industrial media makers were increasingly thinking of the home/work markets not as distinct markets, but as a "continuous spectrum." Brush and Brush, 1981, 18. Users were allegedly "furious" when Beta 1—promoted as industrial model—was incompatible with the consumer market model (Brush and Brush, 1981, 88). This collapse was also reinforced by a joke made by the Brushes: if you're not getting your tapes back, "They're probably being used to record 'Sunday Night at the Movies'" (Brush and Brush, 1986, 4).
191. Barbara Ladd, "Interactive Training Growing Steadily in Larger Companies," *Interactive Technologies, Supplement to Training* (September 19, 1989): 10. This was certainly the goal for Texas Instruments, which contextualized their adoption of video cassettes by telling the story of their predecessor— a training program broadcast at 6:00 AM on local television stations. "Employees took workbooks home from work, set their alarms an hour early,

and took the classes at home." Notably, the temporal cost is to the workers' full night's sleep—the "eight hours of rest" historically demanded to protect workers' rights and lives. "A Texan's view of business television," *BusinessTV* (May 1988): 43.

192. Nona Y. Glazer, *Women's Paid and Unpaid Labor: The Work Transfer in Health Care and Retailing* (Philadelphia: Temple University Press, 1993), 6.

193. Ibid.

194. Ibid., 205.

195. Sarah Sharma, *In the Meantime: Temporality and Cultural Politics* (Durham: Duke University Press, 2014), 14.

196. Brush and Brush, 1992, 74; Ladd, 10.

197. Sarah Sharma, *In the Meantime: Temporality and Cultural Politics* (Durham: Duke University Press, 2014), 14.

198. "Pepsi-Cola Bottlers Standardize," 15.

199. Gentry, *Videotape in Manpower Development*, 8; Howard Geltzer, "A Retail Video Fashion Network," *Training and Development Journal* (November 1973): 34.

200. Gentry, *Videotape in Manpower Development*, 36.

201. Geltzer, 34.

202. Connoly, "Audio-Visuals in the Hosiery Industry," 30.

203. Brush Reports, 1986, 65.

204. Sidney Holtz, "A Glimpse into the A/V Crystal Ball," *Public Relations Journal*, 44–45.

205. Brush and Brush, 1986, 51. The union likewise sent tapes home to maintain solidarity.

206. "Business" Use of AV," *Hope Reports Perspective* 3, no. 1 (1977): 17. HRC.

207. Brush and Brush, 1992, 48; Holtz, 44–45; Brush and Brush, 1978, 59; Brush and Brush, 1992, 48.

208. Ibid., 30; Bunyan et al. 189; Geltzer, 34. On television's deep imbrication in domestic power relations, see Lynn Spigel, *Make Room for TV: Television and the Family Ideal in Postwar America* (Chicago: University of Chicago Press, 1992).

209. Clarence Petersen, "TV Today: Sony Unveils Videocassette for Home Use," *Chicago Tribune* (November 24, 1970): A13.

210. "Cartridge TV: Sony Plans Full Dealer Net, Ads for Its System," *Billboard* 84, no. 7 (February 12, 1972): 23; "Second Major Chain Shows Sony TVC Unit," *Billboard* 84, no. 39 (September 16, 1972): 57.

211. "When Pepsi Went Video," 12–13; "The Sony Videocassette System Proves," 6–7.

212. "The Sony U-matic" [Display Ad 52], 11.

213. Anne Douglas, "Consumer-wise: Home Video Tape Ready—Again," *Chicago Tribune* (November 8, 1975): N_B10; "Sony to Market Lower-Priced Model of Recorder Player," *Wall Street Journal* (April 17, 1975), 24; "Facts Trends Ideas," *Hope Reports Briefing* 1, no. 1 (September 1986): 10.

214. Ray Oviatt, "Goodyear Relies Heavily on A/V for Training, Sales," *Back Stage/Business Screen* (May 1977): S-10.

CHAPTER 5

1. Chistopher Liu, quoted in Steve Lohr, "Don't Get Too Comfortable at That Desk," *New York Times* (October 6, 2017): https://www.nytimes.com/2017/10/06/business/the-office-gets-remade-again.html.

2. Recalling just-in-time production, these practices—and their forebears like hot-desking—apply the principles of tight inventory control (ordering inputs only when they are imminently needed) to avoid overhead and ensure that infrastructural resources are continually consumed at maximum rates.

3. Ross Love, quoted in Lohr, np.

4. Mark Blyth, *Great Transformations: Economic Ideas and Institutional Change in the Twentieth Century* (New York: Cambridge, 2002), 138.

5. Lewis F. Powell, Jr., to Eugene B. Sydnor, Jr., "Attack on the American Free Enterprise System," August 23, 1971. Shortly after the memo was written, Powell joined Nixon's Supreme Court, where he wrote his political leanings into his court opinions.

6. David Harvey, *A Brief History of Neoliberalism* (Oxford: Oxford University Press, 2005), 43.

7. On the project of securing intellectual legitimacy for neoconservative ideas (in part through these organizations), see Andrew Hartman, *A War for the Soul of America: A History of the Culture Wars* (Chicago: University of Chicago Press, 2015), especially 38–69.

8. Daniel T. Rodgers, *Age of Fracture* (Cambridge, MA: Harvard University Press, 2011), 49–50.

9. Blyth, 142.

10. Rodgers, 75; Harvey, 22–24. Funded by a bank celebrating its tercentary in 1968 rather than the estate of Alfred Nobel, The Sveriges Riksbank Prize in Economic Sciences in Memory of Alfred Nobel is not technically a Nobel Prize, though it is casually referred to as such.

11. Rodgers, 31; Harvey, 52–53.

12. Rodgers, 196.

13. Blyth, 182–183.

14. Kenichi Ohmae, *The Borderless World: Power and Strategy in the Interlinked Economy* (New York: Harper Business, 1990): 3–9.

15. Arne L. Kalleberg, *Good Jobs, Bad Jobs: The Rise of Polarized Employment Systems in the United States, 1970s to 2000s* (New York: Russell Sage Foundation, 2011), 28.

16. Ibid., 39.

17. Terrance E. Deal and Allan A. Kennedy, *The New Corporate Cultures: Revitalizing the Workplace after Downsizing, Mergers, and Reengineering* (Reading, MA: Perseus Books, 1999), 69.

18. Joan M. Greenbaum, *Windows on the Workplace: Computers, Jobs, and the Organization of Office Work*, 2nd edn. (New York: Monthly Review Press, 2004), 87.

19. Ibid., 95.

20. Kalleberg, 13, 29.

21. Ibid., 9–10.

22. Ibid., 84–85.

23. Deal and Kennedy, 2.

24. Kalleberg, 40–57.

25. Ohmae, 9.

26. Term borrowed (and reformulated) from Harry Braverman's *Labor and Monopoly Capital: The Degradation of Work in the Twentieth Century* (New York: Monthly Review Press, 1974).

27. John Thornton Caldwell, *Production Culture: Industrial Reflexivity and Critical Practice in Film and Television* (Durham, NC: Duke University Press, 2008), 5.

28. The contradiction noted by Harvey—"a seductive but alienating possessive individualism" and "a desire for a meaningful collective life"—is resolved by companies who nominate themselves as the site of meaningful connection amid individual striving (69).

29. R. T. Pascale and A. G. Athos, *The Art of Japanese Management* (New York: Schuster, 1981), 81, 202–204.

30. Ibid., 83, 86.

31. William G. Ouchi, *Theory Z: How American Business Can Meet the Japanese Challenge* (Reading, MA: Addison-Welsley, 1981), 72.

32. Douglas McGregor, *The Human Side of Enterprise*, annotated edn. (New York: McGraw-Hill, 2006), 45–58, 63–78.

33. James C. Collins and Jerry I. Porras, *Built to Last: Successful Habits of Visionary Companies* (New York: HarperBusiness, 1994), 48.

34. Christopher A. Bartlett and Sumantra Ghoshal, *Managing across Borders: The Transnational Solution* (Boston: Harvard Business School Press, 1989), 289.

35. Ohmae, 91. Emphasis mine.

36. Pascale and Athos, 86.

37. On "family feeling" see, for example, Rosabeth Moss Kanter, *The Change Masters: Innovation and Entrepreneurship in the American Corporation* (New York: Simon & Schuster, 1984), 33, 370. On clans, see Ouchi, 84–85. *Built to Last* features an entire chapter on cults: Collins and Porras, 115–139. On religion, see Gordon F. Shea, *Company Loyalty: Earning It, Keeping It* (New York: AMA Management Briefing, 1987), 71–73.

38. Kanter, 149.

39. Arjun Appadurai, *Modernity at Large: Cultural Dimensions of Globalization* (Minneapolis: University of Minnesota Press, 1996), 22. Zygmunt Bauman, *Liquid Modernity* (Cambridge: Polity, 2000), 90.

40. Collins and Porras, 115.

41. Office redesign also emphasized collaboration and "family feeling" through open planning and by making the office seem "homier" with the addition of washing machines and workout rooms. Greenbaum, 64, 128. On nicknames (Nordstrom's "Nordies"), songs, cheers, pledges, and other activities that "reinforce psychological commitment," see Collins and Porras, 136.

42. Pascale and Athos, 160, and Deal and Kennedy, 9–11; William Bridges, *Managing Transitions* (Reading, MA: Addison-Welsel, 1991), 23–24, 35, 41, 52; John P. Kotter, "Leading Change: Why Transformation Efforts Fail," *Harvard Business Review* (March–April 1995): 67; Katherine I. Miller and Peter R. Monge, "Social Information and Employee Anxiety about Organizational Change," *Human Communication Research* 11, no. 3 (1985): 381–382. Although authors prized in-person, "flesh-to-flesh, eyeball-to-eyeball" communication, BTV capitalized on leadership literature stressing "symbolic management"—using "images, metaphors, and models" to "frame the collective reality inside the organization" and engender commitment. Quotes in Deal and Kennedy, 235, and Per-Olof Berg, "Symbolic Management of Human Resources," *Human Resource Management* 25, no. 4 (1986): 559, 567. Bridges, 52; Kotter, 63; Kanter, 160. On substituting videotape for in-person communication, see, for example, Bridges, 14, 111; Warren Bennis and Burt Nanus, *Leaders: The Strategies for Taking Charge* (New York: Harper & Row, 1985), 39.

43. Benedict Anderson, *Imagined Communities: Reflections on the Origin and Spread of Nationalism* (London: Verso, 1983).

44. Peters in particular championed the medium, arguing that it "revolutionized" Hewlett Packard's business practice. "A Day with Peter F. Drucker," *BusinessTV* (September–October 1988): 27; Mary E. Boone, "The Silicon Valley Cooperative: A Creative Approach to Training," *BusinessTV* (March 1988): 42; Mary Boone, "Tom Peters: Bullish on business television," *BusinessTV* (November 1987): 36–37.

45. Ohmae, 91–92.

46. Anna Lowenhaupt Tsing, *Friction: An Ethnography of Global Connection* (Princeton, NJ: Princeton University Press, 2004), 57–58.

47. David Morley, *Home Territories: Media, Mobility and Identity* (New York: Routledge, 2000), 14; John Tomlinson, *Globalization and Culture* (Chicago: University of Chicago Press, 1999), 2.

48. Arjun Appadurai, "Disjuncture and Difference in the Global Cultural Economy," *Theory, Culture, and Society* 7 (1990): 296.

49. Michael Hardt and Antonio Negri, *Empire* (Cambridge, MA: Harvard University Press, 2000), 11, 327.

50. Bauman, 11. Emphasis in original.

51. On the power of the "colonial sublime" based in infrastructures of modernization (factories, rail transportation, bridges, and, I would add, satellites), see Brian Larkin, *Signal and Noise: Media, Infrastructure, and Urban Culture in Nigeria* (Durham, NC: Duke University Press, 2008), 11. We might also consider satellites' contributions to an "imperial imaginary" constituted through infrastructure and media that build pleasure in identifying with colonizers while exoticizing margins. Ella Shohat and Robert Stam, *Unthinking Eurocentrism: Multiculturalism and the Media* (New York: Routledge, 1994), 104–119.

52. Daya Kishan Thussu, "Mapping Global Media Flow and Contra-Flow," in *Media on the Move: Global Flow and Contra-Flow*, ed. Daya Kishan Thussu (London: Routledge, 2007), 12.

53. Michael Curtin, "On Edge: Culture Industries in the Neo-Network Era," in *Making and Selling Culture*, ed. Richard Ohmann with Gage Averill, Michael Curtin, David Shumway, and Elizabeth G. Traube (Hanover, NH: Weslyan University Press, 1996), 181–202.

54. Timothy Havens, *Global Television Marketplace* (London: BFI, 2008), 158.

55. David Morley and Kevin Robins, *Spaces of Identity: Global Media, Electronic Landscapes and Cultural Boundaries* (New York: Routledge, 1995), 68.

56. Morley and Robins, 68–69, 226–228; Sara Fletcher Luther, *The United States and the Direct Broadcast Satellite: The Politics of International Broadcasting in Space* (New York: Oxford University Press, 1988), 7; Edward W. Ploman, *Space, Earth and Communication* (Westport, CT: Quorum Books, 1984).

57. Brian Winston, *Media Technology and Society: A History: From the Telegraph to the Internet* (New York: Routledge, 1998), 304; Thomas Streeter, "Blue Skies and Strange Bedfellows: the Discourse of Cable Television," in *The Revolution Wasn't Televised: Sixties Television and Social Conflict*, eds. Lynn Spigel and Michael Curtin (New York: Routledge, 1997), 225; George A. Codding, Jr., *The Future of Satellite Communications* (Boulder, CO: Westview Press, 1990). Practical manuals on satellite law likewise proliferated. See Stephen de B. Bate, ed., *Television by Satellite—Legal Aspects* (Oxford: ESC, 1987).

58. Heather Hudson, *Communication Satellites: Their Development and Impact* (New York: Free Press, 1990); Patrick R. Parsons and Robert M. Frieden, *The*

Cable and Satellite Television Industries (Boston: Allyn and Bacon, 1998); Edward Binkowski, *Satellite Information Systems* (Boston: G. K. Hall, 1988).

59. Shaun Moores, "Satellite TV as Cultural Sign: Consumption, Embedding and Articulation," *Media, Culture and Society* 15 no. 4 (1993): 621–639; Charlotte Brunsdon, "Satellite Dishes and the Landscapes of Taste," *New Formations* (Winter 1991): 23–42.

60. Lisa Parks, *Cultures in Orbit: Satellites and the Televisual* (Durham, NC: Duke University Press, 2005).

61. Hudson, 80–81. On "specialized services" provided by satellites, see Hudson's chapter 6, 72–90.

62. Jody Berland, "Mapping Space: Imaging Technologies and the Planetary Body," in *North of Empire: Essays on the Cultural Technologies of Space*, ed. Jody Berland (Durham: Duke University Press, 2009), 242–272.

63. Heather Hudson, 13.

64. Allen Dulles, National Security Council, "Discussion at the 347th Meeting of the National Security Council, Thursday, December 5, 1957," December 6, 1957, NSC Series, Box 9, Eisenhower Papers, 1953–1961 (Ann Whitman File), Dwight D. Eisenhower Library, Abilene, Kansas. https://history.nasa.gov/sputnik/dec57.html

65. The National Defense Education Act of 1958 alone devoted hundreds of millions of dollars to mathematics and science education to produce future defense workers. See Ploman, 4.

66. See the SITE project, for which two countries partnered to share the burden of infrastructure costs. UNESCO, *Communication in the Space Age* (Amsterdam: UNESCO, 1968), 61. Fletcher Luther, 7; Binkowski, 69–84.

67. Fletcher Luther, 7.

68. United States Information Service, "Worldnet: Putting Satellite Technology to Work for Global Understanding," Washington, DC: USIA-TV, 2 (Pamphlet).

69. Ibid., 3.

70. Ibid., 2.

71. Arthur C. Clarke, "Prediction, Realization, and Forecast," in *Communication in the Space Age: The Use of Satellites by the Mass Media*, ed. UNESCO (Paris: UNESCO, 1968), 38.

72. Kenneth A. Polcyn, *An Educator's Guide to Communication Satellite Technology* (Washington, DC: Andromeda Books, 1975), 39–41, 47, 51–99. See also National Education Association (NEA), *Appalaska Intercom: Report of the NEA's Satellite Experiment-1977* (Washington, DC: National Education Association, 1977). Delbert D. Smith, *The Use of Satellite Communication for National Development, Education and Cultural Exchange* (Madison: EDSAT Center, c. 1971), 126, 138–153; Prakash M. Shingi, Gurinder Kaur, and Ravi Prakash Rai, *Village Affluence, Knowledge-Gap and Satellite Television* (Ahmedabad: Centre for Management in Agriculture, 1977), 1.

73. John Middleton, "Educational Needs in the Developing World," in *Toward International Tele-Education*, eds Wilbur T. Blume and Paul Schneller (Boulder, CO: Westview Press, 1984), 16. See also Herschelle S. Challenor, "Current International Plans and Programs to Address Educational Needs in Developing Countries" in the same anthology, 29–42.

74. NEA, *Man-Made Moons: Satellite Communications for Schools* (Washington, DC: National Education Association, 1972), 13, emphasis in original; Mary Kay Platte, *The Beginning of Satellite Communication: Airborne ITV, MPATI, and*

the *Ohio Story* (Dubuque, IA: Kendall/Hunt, 1982), 86; Polcyn, 51–52; NEA, *Appalaska*, 35–36; Smith, 138, 163.

75. NEA, *Man-Made Moons*, 8.

76. Ibid., 28; Grayson, 1378; NEA, *Appalaska Intercom*, 117–118. This appendix suggested satellites would provide savings of $11,359 (almost $50,000 in 2019) per meeting. James M. Janky, "Low-Cost Receivers and the Use of Direct Broadcast Satellites for Instructional Television," *Stanford Journal of International Studies* V (June 1970): 139; Wilbur Schramm, "Instructional Television: Promise and Opportunity," *Monograph Service Issue 4*, Instruction Division of the National Association of Educational Broadcasters (January, 1967): 15.

77. Philip H. Coombs, *The World Educational Crisis: A Systems Analysis* (New York: Oxford University Press, 1968), 129. Quoted in Janky, 139.

78. Hudson, 16–17.

79. Almost 10 years lapsed between a private company's proposal for a domestic commercial satellite (ABC) and the 1974 launch of Westar 1 (owned by Western Union). Hudson, 40, 52, 64.

80. "Teaching and Selling via Outer Space," *Management Review* (June 1978): 4–5.

81. Jeff Charles, "Some Firms Use 'Business TV' to Reach Their Employees," *Marketing News* (May 8, 1987): 9–10.

82. Stephen Day, quoted in Russell Miller, "What's Up in the Satellite Business?" *Management Review* 74, no. 7 (1985): 22. Slippage occurred between the terms "teleconferencing," "video conferencing," and "BTV." See also John Marcom, Jr., "Satellites Search for Business as Demand Misses Predications," *Wall Street Journal* (January 11, 1985): 1.

83. Ken Leddick, "Business Television: A Strategic Resource," *Management in Practice* (September 1988): 53–54; James C. Totten, "Satellite Technology Comes to the Workplace," *North Force Magazine* 4, no. 4 (1991): 5.

84. Usage was "expected to top 12,000 hours" in 1988. Virginia A. Ostendorf, "Applying Business Television," *Satellite Communications* 12, no. 9 (1988): 19–20, 22–23; "Wang to Link Its Offices with Own TV Network," *Marketing News* (March 14, 1986): 27; Leddick, 53–54; "The BEST Companies in the Country Use Business Television," special insert to *BusinessTV* (March 1988): I-2, I-6.

85. John Bell, "Industrials: American Business Theatre in the '80s," *The Drama Review* 31, no. 4 (1987): 36–38, 43, 49–50.

86. Ostendorf, 20; Grace Leone, "Business TV Growing Up," *Satellite Communications* 13, no. 12 (1989): 9A.

87. Deidre Sullivan, "Texas Farm Credit Bank Links Remote Units by Satellite," *American Banker* 157, no. 14 (1992): 3.

88. James N. Budwey, Satellite Communication: A Status Report," *Telecommunications* 25, no. 12 (1991): 19.

89. "Hughes Network Systems Introduces World's First Hybrid VSAT Frame Relay Node," *News Release* (March 22, 1995); Sofia McFarland, "Supermarket Chains Turn to Satellites to Address Their Everyday Problems," *Wall Street Journal* (June 5, 1992): np.; "The Global VSAT Market: Retail VSAT Network," *Research Studies-Mega Tech Resources* (January 1, 1994): 27.

90. Chris O'Leary, "Satellite Feed New Applications Are Helping Satellite Networks Pay for Themselves," *Supermarket News* (June 19, 1995): 17.

91. While 1998 numbers were remarkably consistent with 1992, it is unclear whether these are the *same* companies (likely they are not). In 1998, about 150 North American and 40 non-US companies had BTV networks. Sullivan, 3.

92. "U.S. Private Satellite Network Markets," *Research Studies-Frost & Sullivan* (March 1, 1996): 1. The United States accounted for 75% of private satellite networks in this period. Carolyn Leitch, "Telesat Canada to Offer TV Stock Talk by Satellite," *The Globe and Mail* (April 27, 1990): B4; Jane Becker, "Telsat Gets Aggressive with Sales," *The Globe and Mail* (May 2, 1988): B7. Figures in this chapter adjusted for inflation and represented in 2019 dollars via CPI Inflation Calculator unless otherwise noted.

93. Peter Lloyd, "AV at 40: Corporate Video—From Film to Facebook," *AV* (April 2012): 31–35. Becker, B7.

94. Binkowski, 24–25, 84; R. Michael Feazel, "The Birds Fly Low," *Channels '89 Field Guide to the Electronic Environment* (December 1988): 123; Miller, 22. For as little as $140,000, a company could contract with a hotel and a BTV coordinating company, which would arrange program production, distribution, and even coffee and Danish. In 1981, Ford spent about $500,000 for what was then one of the largest programs ever produced: a live sales meeting connecting Detroit to 17,000 managers and representatives in 38 "first class hotels from Miami to Seattle." At this time, installing a system might cost $5 million. "Teleport Minnesota: Business TV Networks," *Via Satellite* (July 1, 1997): np; Markus B. Zimmer, "A Practical Guide to Videoconferencing," *Training and Development Journal* (May 1988): 84–89. Stephen J. Shaw, "No Full House for Public Networks," *Business TV* (March 1988): 5–6; "Teleconferencing: New Prospects for HRD," *Training and Development Journal* (May 1982): 10; "Ford Motor Company Selects General Instrument's Digicipher System for 'Fordstar' Satellite Service," *PR Newswire* (June 8 1994): np.

95. Leddick, 53–54. Shaw, "No Full House for Public Networks," 6.

96. John J. Albert, "The World of Satellites: Your Global Voice," *Public Relations Quarterly* (Spring 1987): 22.

97. Marjorie Hudson, "Mastering the Market," *BusinessTV* (May 1988): 52. Carole King, "Satellite Seminars Draw Consumers to Agents," *National Underwriter Life & Health Financial Services* (April 24, 1995): np.

98. Leddick, 53–54; "EDS Named by Readgat Subsidiary to Build Interactive Satellite Network," *Business Wire* (May 28, 1992): np.; Stephen J. Shaw, "Video PR," *BusinessTV* (July 1988): 25–26; "Distribution and Evaluation," *BusinessTV* (July 1988): 29.

99. See the three-part series by Richard Neustadt and Amy Rosmarin, "Program Netowrks for Business Television—Patterns Emerge," in *BusinessTV* (July 1988): 5–6, (September 1988): 8–9, and (November–December 1988): 15–16.

100. "Who Are the Networks?" *BusinessTV* (Fall 1986): 11–14, 16, 18; "Who Are the Networks?" *BusinessTV* (November 1987): 14–15; "Alphabetical Program Listings," *BusinessTV* (September–October 1988): 33; Stephen J. Shaw, "Associations Slow to Adopt Business Television," *BusinessTV* (March 1988): 14–15.

101. Richard Neustadt and Amy Rosmarin, "Program Networks for Business Television—Patterns Emerge," *BusinessTV* (July 1988): 5–6. In the former case, organizations might lease time on an existing network like ALN (and use their studio facilities) for a special program or two. Brian Cox, "Savings in Costs and Time Boost Video Conferencing," *National Underwriter Life & Health-Financial Services* (January 24, 1994): np. Two hours of programming does not a network make; it is the signifying power of "network" as a claim to spatialized control rather than the accuracy of the term that is important to users.

102. Leitch, B4.

103. Cox, np.; Roger B. Cooper, "New Ways to Cruise the Information Highway," *American Gas* 79, no. 7 (1997): 2; "TV Network for MIS Pros Planned in Fall," *Marketing News* (May 8, 1987): 7.

104. This impulse to carve audiences into professional communities creeped into public service satellites as they jumped into the fray of unwieldy institutional collaborations. Facing Reagan budget cuts, PBS sought additional revenue streams in the form of the National Narrowcast Service (NNS), piloted in 1986. Supported by microwave relay, the NNS offered multiple channels of satellite-delivered programming to selectively chosen, nationally distributed networks simultaneously. William Reed, Sr., VP of PBS educational services, described NNS's specialized programming, reorganizing PBS's public into a series of narrowcast audiences disembedded from local communities served by member stations, and bound instead (primarily) by employment:

> While stations are serving their broadcast audience with television courses and regular general audience programming, they can simultaneously de- liver live programming from Cape Canaveral with astronauts talking to K–12 schools; a seminar on office automation to business leaders at work; the latest techniques in emergency preparedness for firefighters and po- lice officers at city buildings; and a review of current research for health professionals in hospitals. That's five different programs at the same time—to different audiences with clearly different interests.

NNS promoters naturalized audience fragmentation as a way to meet their public service mandate via a "something for everyone" approach that offered "a (program) menu . . . attractive to many individuals." While this focus on individual choice and engagement paralleled commercial media strategy of the multichannel era, it also elided the fact that much NNS programming supported the narrow needs of workplaces. The seminars chosen to launch the service—on "AIDS, product liability, 'right-to-know' legislation, mergers and acquisitions, and the financing of small to mid-size businesses"—imagined an audience whose primary informational needs concerned corporate management. (NNS also leased its publicly funded infrastructure to companies for ad hoc private nationwide videoconferences.) Sally Bedell Smith, "Public TV—Still Poor but Newly Hopeful," *New York Times* (July 3, 1983): H1; Zerita S. Walther, "PBS Offering Credits for College on TV," *New York Times* (November 15, 1981): EDUC62; Shaw, "Associations Slow," 15; Reed quoted in Arthur Unger, Arthur Unger, "PBS Entertains, Educates with Wide Range of Programming," *The Christian Science Monitor* (August 19, 1983), www.csmonitor.com/1983/0819/081951. "Menu" quotation and program description from Greg Johnson, "PBS Ready to Beam Business Expertise across the Nation," *LA Times* (February 4, 1986): http://articles.latimes.com/1986-02-04/business/fi-4275_1_narrowcast-signals. See also David W. Shively, "National Narrowcast: Business Television from PBS," *BusinessTV* (November–December 1988): 12.

105. George W. Chane, "The Coming Role of Administrative Management," *Management Review* 49, no. 12 (1960): 19, 24. Published by Elliot Gold's Telespan, the magazine founded in 1986 featured contributions from market researchers (including Douglas and Judith Brush), blue chip users (HP, IBM, FedEx), and management gurus (Tom Peters). *BusinessTV* boasted 11,000 subscribers by

the conclusion of its first year, and 16,000 the year after. Sometimes referred to as *Telespan's BusinessTV*, the magazine built on a newsletter Gold published starting in 1981 to support his consulting business. The magazine went through several titles and shifts in focus, eventually recentering on two-way videoconferencing. http://www.telespan.com/consultation.html.

106. "U.S. Private Satellite," 1; Elliot M. Gold, "Happy Anniversary to *BusinessTV* Magazine!" *BusinessTV* (November 1987): 38.
107. Budwey, 19; Geoffrey Kurtzman, "Business Television: The Competitive Edge," *BusinessTV* (September–October 1988): 39.
108. "Penney Adds Satellite Service," *New York Times* (June 13, 1981): 2.
109. Hank Gilman, "J.C. Penney Decentralized Its Purchasing," *Wall Street Journal* (May 8, 1986): J; Leone, 9a.
110. "U.S. Private Satellite," 1; Bruce Marshall, "A Training Success Story," *Training & Development* (September 1991): 63–65; Raymond Snoddy, "Survey of World Telecommunications: The US Leads the Way," *Financial Times* (October 19, 1987): 29; Sullivan, 3; Ostendorf, 19–20, 22–23; Joan Stableford, "Advances in Technology Boost Corporate Use of Satellite TV," *Fairfield County Business Journal* 37, no. 10 (1998): 5; "Wang tolLink," 27; Stephen J. Shaw, "Boarding the Bandwagon: Franchise Business Network," *BusinessTV* (March 1988): 35; "U.S. Private Satellite," 1; David Churbuck and Jeffrey Young, "Who Needs an Office in These Days of Miracles and Wonders," *BRW* (May 14, 1993): 66; Zimmer, 85; Jerri Stroud, "New Business Routine," *St. Louis Post-Dispatch* (July 14, 1991): 1E.
111. Bernd Stauss and Frank Hoffmann, "Minimizing Internal Communication Gaps by Using Business Television," in *Internal Marketing: Directions for Management*, eds. Richard J. Varey and Barbara R. Lewis (New York: Routledge, 2000), 141; "Echelon," *BusinessTV* (Fall 1986): 17; "Scientific-Atlanta Begins Shipments for World's largest Business TV Network," *PR Newswire* (May 3, 1991): np.
112. Stephen J. Shaw, "IBM's Field Television Network," *BusinessTV* (Winter 1988): 39–41.
113. "U.S. Private Satellite," 1; Stableford, 5; Stauss and Hoffman, 153; Zimmer, 85; Budwey, 19.
114. "U.S. Private Satellite," 1; Crisp, "UK News: Speeding Up Transatlantic Business," *Financial Times* (January 28, 1982): 7; Totten, 5; "Teleconferencing: New Prospects," 10; John Penrose, "Telecommunications, Teleconferencing, and Business Communications," *The Journal of Business Communication* 21, no. 1 (1983): 100–101; Raymond P. Fisk, "Videoconferencing: Tips for Business Users," *Marketing News* (November 9, 1984): 34; "A Panoply of Applications," *Via Satellite* (February 1, 1997): np.; Stephen J. Shaw, "Training Is Tops with Business Networks," *BusinessTV* (September–October 1988): 10–11; Sherry Keene-Osborn, "Cost Controls Hit Corporate Travel," *Colorado Business* 18, no. 1 (1991): 14.
115. "U.S. Private Satellite," 1; Stauss and Hoffman, 152.
116. "A New Company Offering 'Business Television' via Satellite Was Launched This Week," *Broadcast* (March 4, 1988): 12; Richard Neustadt and Amy Rosmarin, "Program Networks for Business Television," *BusinessTV* (September–October 1988): 15.
117. Stauss and Hoffman, 143, 154–55; "Channel Home Center Announces, as Part of Continuing Expansion, Launching of Its New Business Television Network," *Business Wire* (September 30, 1993): np.; Crisp, 7; Charles, 9;

Joan C. Szabo, "Training Workers for Tomorrow," *Nation's Business* (March 1, 1993): 22; "Scientific-Atlanta Begins," np.; "U.S. Private Satellite," 1; "Teaching and Selling," 4–5; "Audio-visual: Putting Your Event in the Global Spotlight," *Marketing Event* (September 1, 1997): np; John Tyson, "The New Promises of Video Teleconferencing," *FE Manual* (June 1985): 44; Leddick, 54; G9.

118. Zimmer, 85; "Teaching and Selling," 4–5; Marjorie Hudson, "Kodak Develops Training & Marketing over KBTV," *BusinessTV* (May 1988): 51.

119. Stephen J. Shaw, "Business Television in Crisis (Communications, That Is)," *BusinessTV* (September–October 1988): 42. This was also mentioned unprompted in one of my interviews with a former BTV professional.

120. Leddick, 53–54; "Business Television Use Not Confined to High Tech Companies," *BusinessTV* (Fall 1986): 10; Charles, 9–10; Szabo, 22.

121. Charles, 9.

122. Ibid., 10; Stauss and Hoffman, 144. BTV's ability to engender unity and commitment was oft-repeated in news coverage. Leddick, 53–54.

123. Stableford, 5; F11; Stauss and Hoffman, 150.

124. Ostendorf, 22; "AT&T Business Video Puts Time on Your Side and the Future in Your Hands," *BusinessTV* (November 1987): special insert, I-2.

125. King, np.; Miller, 20; Michael G. Elliot, "Managing the Sales Force," *BusinessTV* (November–December 1988): 33–34; Gil E. Gordon, "Lights, Camera, Laughter: Taking Time Out of a Zany Look at Corporate Life," *BusinessTV* (September–October 1988): 17; Marjorie Corbett-Hudson, "Tandem Television Network Recipe for Success," *BusinessTV* (Winter 1988): 43.

126. Ostendorf, 20; Daniel G. Masanov, "Video Magazines," *BusinessTV* (November–December 1988): 9; Hudson, "Kodak," 51. Workers were also understood to be more open to learning from peers. Ostendorf, 22; Masanov, 9–10; Gwenn Kelly, "Who's Watching Business TV?" *BusinessTV* (March 1988): 10.

127. Scott Chase, "On the Road with DPSN," *BusinessTV* (March 1988): 36.

128. "CMD Management Highlights: Human Resources," *Forum* 68, no. 1 (1979): 34; Mary Young and James E. Post: "Managing to Communicate, Communicating to Manage: How Leading Companies Communicate with Employees," *Organizational Dynamics* 22, no. 1 (1993): 31.

129. Susan J. Ashford, "Individual Strategies for Coping with Stress during Organizational Transitions," *The Journal of Applied Behavioral Science* 24, no. 1 (1988): 22, 30–31; Laurie K. Lewis, "Disseminating Information and Soliciting Input during Planned Organizational Change: Implementers' Targets, Sources, and Channels for Communicating," *Management Communication Quarterly* 13, no. 1 (1999): 43–75; "Executive Insights: Council Debate Shifts in Business-Government Roles," *Management Review* 80, no. 6 (1991): 55–56.

130. James Ott, "Videoconferencing Use Expands to Meet Rising Business Needs," *Aviation Week & Space Technology* (July 22, 1985): 157; Stauss and Hoffman, 154.

131. "Executive Insights," 56; Anonymous executive quoted in Young and Post, 37. The same authors refer to "interactive television broadcasts" on 36.

132. Ibid., 32. It's possible that FedEx at one time boasted the largest permanent BTV system. Founded in 1987, it was used for training and daily logistical information. As of 1995—two years after this particular merger—the network reached 1,450 locations in North America and Europe and a total of 114,000

employees. "Federal Express's Timely Techniques," *Via Satellite* (December 1, 1995): 40; Shaw, "Training Is Tops," 11.

133. Young and Post, 31–32.

134. Ibid., 32. This same speed and constancy was central to providing reassurance during emergencies. See "'Mother Merrill' Hits the Airwaves," *BusinessTV* (September–October 1988): 47.

135. Young and Post, 41.

136. Joseph Turow, *Breaking Up America: Advertisers and the New Media World* (Chicago: University of Chicago Press, 1997), 5, 44.

137. Turow, 55.

138. Quotation from Turow, 3 (see also 104–105). Heather Hundley, "The Evolution of Gendercasting: The Lifetime Television Network- 'Television for Women,'" *Journal of Popular Film and Television* 29, no. 4 (2002): 178, 180. Hamid Naficy, "From Broadcasting to Narrowcasting: Middle Eastern Diaspora in Los Angeles," *Middle East Report* 180 (January–February 1993): 31–34; Beretta E. Smith-Shomade, "Narrowcasting in the New World Information Order: A Space for the Audience?" *Television & New Media* 5, no. 1 (2004): 69–81; Ron Becker, *Gay TV and Straight America* (New Brunswick, NJ: Rutgers University Press, 2006); Evan Elkins, "Cultural Identity and Subcultural Forums: The Post-network Politics of Adult Swim," *Television & New Media* 15, no. 7 (2014): 595–610.

139. Megan Mullen, "The Fall and Rise of Cable Narrowcasting," *Convergence* 8, no. 1 (2002): 64.

140. Turow, 2.

141. Ibid., 126.

142. Smith-Shomade, 74, 78.

143. Mullen, 75.

144. Ibid., 79. See also Amanda Lotz's discussion of the work of Arlene Dávila and Néstor García Canclini in *The Television Will Be Revolutionized* (New York: New York University Press, 2007), 180.

145. Vincent Mosco and Andrew Herman argue that although capitalism seems to promise a divided life—alienated labor during the day in exchange for evening leisure—this system structures leisure (reinforcing passivity and consumption) for its own benefit. I argue here that the feelings workers generate toward television during leisure activities are the target of corporate media strategies that seek to channel these feelings into soft management practices. "Critical Theory and Electronic Media," *Theory and Society* 10, no. 6 (1981): 889–891. See Becker's chapter on "The Affordable, Multicultural Politics of Gay Chic," which explores how NBC took up discourses of multiculturalism to appeal to a class of viewers (slumpys, or socially liberal, urban-minded professionals) that would have already adopted these ideals in professional and higher-education contexts.

146. Johnson Controls, *125 Years: Honoring Our Past. Inspired by Our Future* (Milwaukee: Johnson Controls, 2010), 43.

147. Ibid., 45–46.

148. Ibid., 48.

149. Ann Abshier, "Stuck in the Eighties . . . (the 1880s): How the Communication Profession Evolved from the House Organ," *Communication World* 7, no. 6 (1990): 23.

150. Ibid., 23; Peter Francis O'Shea, *Employees' Magazines for Factories, Offices, and Business Organizations* (New York: H. W. Wilson, 1920), 13.

151. O'Shea, 8.

152. Paul Arvidson, "Manager's Journal: House Organ Will Play Your Company's Song," *Wall Street Journal* (November 2, 1987): 1.

153. Ibid.

154. Marie Gottschalk, "Operation Desert Cloud: The Media and the Gulf War," *World Policy Journal* 9, no. 3 (1992): 472–473.

155. John Thornton Caldwell, *Televisuality: Style, Crisis, and Authority in American Television* (New Brunswick, NJ: Rutgers University Press, 1995), 125.

156. See, for comparison, Caldwell's discussion of broadcast news flows (*Televisuality*, 120–125).

157. According to Dave Sobczak, JCI *did* use videoconferencing for multi-continent communication on rare occasions, but the difficulty of coordination meant that such truly "global" uses for JCI were uncommon. On news, liveness, and presence, see Mary Ann Doane, "Information, Crisis, Catastrophe," in *Logics of Television: Essays in Cultural Criticism*, ed. Patricia Mellancamp (Bloomington: Indiana University Press, 1990): 222–239.

158. Interview with the author (July 21, 2014), Johnson Controls Headquarters, Milwaukee, WI.

159. Faking liveness was common, especially for seminars aired separately for East and West Coast audiences. After producers aired a recording of the main presentation, performers appeared live for the question-and-answer session.

160. Parks, 24.

161. As Vianello notes, even in commercial news, the sheer "display of the networks' web of correspondents 'around the world'" sometimes outweighed a focus on delivering "hard news" (39). As the years wore on and, perhaps, as satellite networks became less novel in the context of business communications, JCI began dropping its claims to liveness, turning instead to a more traditional video format with shot-reverse shots and other noticeable editing.

162. "Cultural interlopers" borrowed from Lotz, who uses the term to describe both a practice (watching programming not targeted for one's demographic) and an industrial set of conditions that make this practice more or less possible (41).

163. All quotes taken from the inaugural episode of JCI Reports.

164. Shows would be scheduled between 10:00 a.m. and 2:00 p.m., when they knew the entire country would be at work and available to see their programming.

165. Deal and Kennedy, 234.

166. This emphasis on teamwork, empowerment, unity, intimacy, interactivity, recognition, motivation, care, and support (and global power) can be seen throughout the JCI collection.

167. Interview with the author. Johnson Controls Headquarters, July 21, 2014.

168. According to Sobczak, one of his former employees who still worked in JCI production (as of 2014) was trying to recapture the aesthetics of their earlier satellite broadcasts due to their exciting and personal appeal. Figures mentioned by Sobczak are presumably not adjusted for inflation, though I did not confirm. In any case, they reveal a dramatic increase in the price of satellite time.

169. Steelcase also features in Sarah Sharma's discussion of "sedentary time" experienced by (and enforced on) office workers. Her book reproduces an image of Steelcase's Walkstation—a treadmill with an affixed desk—which extends the white collar worker's endurance for uninterrupted work. Sarah Sharma, *In the Meantime: Temporality and Cultural Politics* (Durham: Duke University Press, 2014), 97.

170. J. A. Andrews, "Steelcase Sets Up Dealer Distribution System in Six Mid-East Countries," 1977. Steelcase Centennial Timeline Exhibit: http://timeline.steelcase.com/timeline/#/e/middle-east-dealer-expansion.

171. Ibid.

172. Stauss and Hoffman, 153. Adam Shell, "Reaching Out to the TV Generation," *Public Relations Journal* 46, no. 11 (1990): 29.

173. Stableford, 5; Zimmer 87; Masanov 10; Shell, 28, 32.

174. Linda Evans (head of AT&T Corporate Video) quoted in Warren Berger, "TV for the Boardroom and the Factory Floor," *New York Times* (August 21, 1988): F13.

175. Masanov, 9.

176. Caldwell, 12–13.

177. Steelcase was not alone in its explicit pursuit of MTV's cachet. Dow Plastics also invoked the teen channel when describing the model for its educational programming for schools, while the editor of *Public Relations Journal* identified the channel as worthy of emulation for more effectively targeting younger audiences with management communications. Shell, 30.

178. Quoted from "Message."

179. William Bridges, *Managing Transitions* (Reading, MA: Addison-Wesley, 1991), 111.

180. Shell, 32.

181. Karen Smith, quoted in Masanov, 10.

182. John McGlothlin III, "In Good Company: Corporate Personhood, Labor, and the Management of Affect in *Undercover Boss*," *Biography* 37, no. 1 (2014): 125–126.

183. Lucas Hilderbrand, *Inherent Vice: Bootleg Histories of Video and Copyright* (Durham, NC: Duke University Press, 2009), 6.

184. Bridges, 111.

185. Described in its contemporary form in the introduction of this chapter, this efficiency practice ensures that workers have no assigned office resources, like desks, phones, or printers, and instead "check in" to use equipment from a general bank.

186. Marshall, 63.

187. Whatever Domino's claims, video artists explicitly pushed back against satellites' illusionary power to suggest multi-way intercommunication serving "the people." As Kris Paulsen notes, even when multipoint-to-multipoint communication was technically possible, it remained "structurally" impossible—that is, controlled by corporate and government interests. Kris Paulsen, *Here/There: Telepresence, Touch, and Art at the Interface* (Cambridge, MA: MIT Press, 2017), 105.

188. Carey and Elton trace a genealogy of videoconferencing directly from teleconferencing. However, videoconferencing was also shaped by BTV. John Sheahan, the person primarily responsible for installing global videoconferencing facilities for Johnson and Johnson, for example, also led J&J's video production. If we understand videoconferencing as stemming at least in part from the same desires that animate business television—not least of which is the development of a strong corporate identity—we can recognize the false equivalence drawn between teleconferencing and videoconferencing, and reinvestigate established explanations of videoconferencing as a failed version of teleconferencing that offered users too little for the added trouble. John Carey and Martin C. J. Elton, *When Media Are New: Understanding the*

Dynamics of New Media Adoption and Use (Ann Arbor: University of Michigan Press, 2011), 184, 193–194, 201.

189. See, for example, John J. Albert, "The World of Satellites: Your Global Voice," *Public Relations Quarterly* (Spring 1987): 22.

190. Paddy Scannell, *Television and the meaning of "live"* (Cambridge, UK: Polity, 2014), 99.

191. In this particular instance, the loose and playful nature of the program—the host invokes inside jokes with callers, refers to himself as (soporific) Ted Koppel, reminds a caller to not say the service is "too good" to avoid being charged more—likewise builds a sense of community and intimacy among Steelcase locations.

192. Gwenn Kelly, "Hello? Are We On?" *BusinessTV* (September–October 1988): 6.

193. Mary E. Boone, "Texas Instruments Broadcast Solution to Artifical Intelligence Equation," *BusinessTV* (Fall 1986): 42; "Live . . . from Anywhere to Anywhere," *BusinessTV* (Fall 1986): 35. For ads, see, for example, "Somebody Up There Likes Us," *BusinessTV* (Fall 1986): 15; "Leading Supplier," *BusinessTV* (March 1988): 1; "Lost in the Complex Jungle," *BusinessTV* (May 1988): 1; "Some of the Most Advanced," *BusinessTV* (November 1987): 16.

194. "The Latest Fight: Roof Space," *New York Times* (November 10, 1985): F6; Stephen J. Shaw, "BizNet Looks at Cable Television," *BusinessTV* (March 1988): 16; Ott, 157; Ostendorf 23; Albert, 22–23. On Wang Laboratories' failed system, see Kathleen J. Hansell, "International Business Television," *BusinessTV* (Winter 1988): 5.

195. James Royal, "Television in the Workplace: Ford and FCN TV," *Communication and Critical/Cultural Studies* 6, no. 4 (2009): 353.

196. Ibid., 359–360.

197. Anonymous IBM employee quoted in Stableford, 5; "Teleconferencing Effective for Certain Training Aspects," *Training and Development Journal* (February 1983): 8; "The VSAT Industry Fights Back," *Via Satellite* (February 1, 1997): np.

198. "Amateurish Production Portrays Execs as 'Telenerds,' so They Shun Videoconferences," *Marketing News* (November 25, 1983): 23. An additional stumbling block: the inability to send pheremones. The article predicted "at least 10 years before 'telesmell' equipment could be designed to detect the pheremones at one end of a videoconference and then release equivalent odors at the other end."

199. Warren Berger, "TV for the Boardroom and the Factory Floor," *New York Times* (August 21, 1988): F13.

200. Don Labriola, "Here's Looking at You," *Computer Shopper* 17, no. 9 (1997): 334; David D. Busch, "Multimedia Adventures on the Intranet," *Net Guide* (September 1, 1996): 129; Nick Mitsis, "The Migration to the Desktop Continues," *Via Satellite* 16, no. 8 (2001): 16–19. Some "dozens" of networks persisted in the early 2000s. P. Brown, "The Changing Scene for Corporate Communications," *Via Satellite* 15, no. 11 (2000): 30–37.

201. Kenneth Lipartito, "Picturephone and the Information Age: The Social Meaning of Failure," *Technology and Culture* 44, no. 1 (2003): 57.

202. Ibid., 77.

203. Discussions of videoconferencing and cable can be found alongside reports of BTV across sources cited in this chapter. On supersonic flight, see Marion Cotter, "A Pounds 3,000 Ticket for Fast Talkers," *The Sunday Times* (November 6, 1988): np.

CONCLUSION

1. "acknowledgement | acknowledgment, n.." OED Online, March 2018, Oxford University Press. http://www.oed.com.ezproxy2.library.colostate.edu/view/Entry/1614?redirectedFrom=acknowledgement (accessed April 12, 2018).

2. Jacques Derrida, *Archive Fever: A Freudian Impression*, trans. Eric Prenowitz (Chicago: University of Chicago Press, 1995), 1–3, 17, 91.

3. Michel Foucault, *The Archeology of Knowledge*, trans. A. M. Sheridan-Smith (London: Tavistock Publications, 1979), 129.

4. Michelle Caswell, "'The Archive' Is Not an Archives: On Acknowledging the Intellectual Contributions of Archival Studies," *Reconstruction: Studies in Contemporary Culture* 16, no. 1 (2016), np. https://escholarship.org/uc/item/7bn4v1fk; Francis X. Blouin, Jr., and William G. Rosenberg, *Processing the Past: Contesting Authority in History and the Archives* (New York: Oxford University Press, 2011), 31. On authority, archives, and the historian, see Carolyn Steedman, *Dust: The Archive and Cultural History* (New Brunswick, NJ: Rutgers University Press, 2002).

5. Derrida, 17. This is an understanding shared by theorists of the archives as well. See Blouin and Rosenberg, 47–49.

6. The lack of the academy's interest in pursuing non-commercial, non-entertainment directions is well illustrated by the 1982 essay by Daniel J. Perkins that attempts to draw scholarly attention to sponsored films using many of the same arguments for their historical and cultural significance that would be taken up almost 25 years later with the turn to nontheatrical and useful cinema in well-received anthologies and major conferences. Despite his compelling reasons for why sponsored film should be central to our understanding of film history (and his very clear plan for going about and doing the actual research—recommended trades, extant collections, etc.), he would have to wait for decades for his call to arms to be heeded. Daniel J. Perkins, "The Sponsored Film: A New Dimension in American Film Research?" *Historical Journal of Film, Radio and Television* 2, no. 2 (1982), 133–140.

7. Again, I use the definition of precarity offered in Michael Hardt and Antonio Negri, *Commonwealth* (Cambridge, MA: Harvard University Press, 2009), 146.

8. Shannon Lausch, "Dispatches from the Void," presented at Society of American Archivists (August 9, 2012): 8. See also Rebecca Goldman and Shannon M. Lausch, "Job Search Experiences and Career Satisfaction among Recent Archives Program Graduates," August 8, 2012, Professional presentations. 4. http://digitalcommons.lasalle.edu/libraryconf/4; Myron G. Myron, "On Precarity," Bibliocracy, January 1, 2014, http://bibliocracy-now.tumblr.com/post/72506786815/on-precarity; "Do We Eat Our Young," message board thread started by Tom Tiballi, January 21, 2012, parts one and two, http://forums.archivists.org/read/messages?id=118375, http://forums.archivists.org/read/messages?id=118501, http://forums.archivists.org/read/messages?id=118594; Samantha Winn, "Are We a Profession or Aren't We?" Archivasaurus, January 27, 2014, https://archivasaurus.wordpress.com/2014/01/27/are-we-a-profession-or-arent-we/; Progressive Librarian's Bulletin, CFP for third annual symposium on the theme of "Precarious Labour," 2.7, July 2013, http://www.progressivelibrariansguild.org/content/pdf/PLG_Bulletin_July2013.pdf.

9. Even networks took some time to recognize the value of taped programs. W. Barksdale Maynard, "Rescuers Rush to Preserve TV Shows Shot on Fragile Videotape," *The Washington Post* (July 15, 2013): http://www.washingtonpost.com/national/health-science/rescuers-rush-to-preserve-tv-shows-shot-on-fragile-videotape/2013/07/15/ef6e2ee4-cd3c-11e2-8845-d970ccb04497_story.html (accessed September 12, 2013).

10. Formats include: Ampex's 2" open reel Quadraplex, which was produced in both low band and high band formats, 2" open reel helical, produced by Ampex and Sony, EIAJ-1" open reel, 1" Type B and 1" Type C videotape, ¾" U-matic cassettes, S-VHS, VHS, Betacam-SP, Ed-Beta, Hi8, and Cartrivision.

11. Library of Congress, *Television and Video Preservation 1997: A Report of the Current State of American Television and Video Preservation*, 3 vols. (Washington, DC: Library of Congress, 1997), 42.

12. Ron Brown, in conversation with the author. Telephone. September 22, 2014.

13. John Sheahan, in conversation with the author, University of Wisconsin Madison, October 25, 2014.

INDEX

For the benefit of digital users, indexed terms that span two pages (e.g., 52–53) may, on occasion, appear on only one of those pages.
Figures are indicated by f following the page number

deskilling, 8–9, 37–38, 52, 96, 167–68
Detroit Police Department, radio at, 41
Dewar's Scotch, 49–50, 51–52
Diamond Power Specialty
    Corporation, 68
dictating machines, 37, 232n81
    division of labor and, 37–38
distribution. *See also* home, as
        distribution site
    of audiovisual content, 44–45, 46,
        54–55, 98–100, 119–20, 130, 145,
        151–52, 157, 175–76, 192–93
    of data, 30–31, 84–85, 111–12,
        174, 177–78
    of goods, 28–29, 74–75, 79–80, 94
    television, via long lines, 96–97, 98–
        100, 119–20, 214–15
    vertical integration in, 24–25
    of workers, 41, 102–3, 159, 176
diversity
    of workers and workforce, 8–9, 36–37,
        96, 137, 153, 169, 268n134
division of labor, 37–38, 121
Doane, Mary Ann, 104, 252n53
Dodge, 250n26
domestic medium, television as
        the, 18–19
    borrowing the efficacy of, 7–8, 112–13,
        137, 144, 165
    as foil, 60, 91
    U-matic and, 160–61
Domino's Pizza, 181
Douglas, Kirk, 94
downsizing, 79, 157–58, 167–68, 209
Drucker, Peter, 145–46, 171–72, 215–16
dual-earner households, 168–69
DuMont, 63–64, 65–67
Dunlop, Robert G., 102–3

Eastman Kodak, 142–43, 178
E. C. Brown Trust Foundation, 137–38
edge, 173, 181, 193
Ediphone, 37–38
Edison, Thomas, 35–36, 38
Edison Company, 67
education
    consumer, 136–37
    8mm cartridges and, 137–38
    labor and, 176
    satellite technology in, 175–76

educational television (ETV), 95–96
    AT&T and, 111, 113–14
    corporate television and, 112
EEOC. *See* Equal Employment
        Opportunity Commission
efficiency
    BTV and, 165, 169–70, 171–72, 176
    fax and, 47
    ITV and, 69–70, 74–75, 79–80,
        84–85, 91
    radio and, 43
    Taylorism and, 37–38
    training and, 107–8, 112
    video cassettes and, 152, 158–59
8mm cartridges, 134
    in Cold War, 143
    colonizing capacities of, 141–42
    education and, 137–38
    flexibility of, 136–37
    standardization of, 143
    temporality of, 136–37
elasticity, 64–65
electronic communication
    meaning of, 30–31
    problem of, 4–5
Electronic Industry Association, 67
Electronic Video Recording (EVR), 127–
        29, 128f, 130–31, 144
    convenience of, 144–45
    flexibility of, 145–46
    targeting capacity of, 145
    Wasser on, 150–51
    work and leisure boundaries blurred
        by, 149
Elton, Martin C. J., 284–85n188
emergent media, 16
    intermediality and, 16
emotional valence
    of BTV, 200
    of CCTV, 109, 129–30
    of U-matic, 160–61
    of videocassettes, 129–30
    of videotape, 109, 129–30
empire, 28–29, 122, 123, 165,
        172–73, 189–90
Empire of America Federal Savings
        Bank, 176–77
employee newsletters, 184
    at AT&T, 98, 117–19
    goals of, 186

liveness of, 189, 201–2
productivity and, 202f
quasi-collaborative nature of, 190
visible management and, 191
job security, 7, 132–33, 168, 209
John Hancock Mutual Life, 178
Johnson Controls Conference Network
(JCCN), 185, 186–88, 208–9
Johnson Controls Inc. (JCI), 184–85
BTV at, 185
labor at, 192–93
Johnson & Johnson, 180, 210, 214–15
Jones, Simon C., 234n130
just-in-time manufacturing,
79–80, 273n2
JVC. See Japan Victor Company

Kalleberg, Arne L., 168
Kanter, Rosabeth Moss, 171–72, 215–16
Kay Labs, 68
Kennedy, Allan A., 168
Keynesianism, 166
kinetoscope, 35–36
KIPI. See Knowledge Industry
Publications, Inc.
Kline, Nathan, 88–90
knowledge industries
corporate expansion and, 19, 122
market for, 144–45, 147, 148–49
Knowledge Industry Publications, Inc.
(KIPI), 121–22
Kolashefski, Rich, 190
Koppel, Ted, 285n191
Kosxarski, Richard, 63
Krauss, Rosalind, 108
Ku Brand, 185

labor
alienated, 11, 62–63
anti-labor reforms, 166
the body and, 5, 62
BTV and, 206
childbirth as, 5
consumers and, 126 (see also audience
commodity)
cultural, 11–12
defining, 5
of dictating machines, 37–38
division of, 37–38, 121, 132–33,
152–53, 223n40

education and, 9, 176 (see also
employee training)
gender and, 132–33
globalization and, 167
immaterial, 133
intensification of, 7–8, 126, 164–65
job security, 7, 132–33, 168, 209
leisure bound to, 9–10, 149, 165, 184
(see also entertainment, commercial,
exploiting affective resonance of)
machines appropriating, 90
narrowcasting and, 184
organization of, 5–6
as play, 10
self-service as, 6–7
shifts in paid, 8–9, 96, 153–54, 165–
66, 182–83 (see also work transfer)
temporality of, 132–33 (see also
coordination functions)
work distinguished from, 5
Lardner, James, 134–35
large-scale firms, telegraph and
development of, 29–30
Large Screen Theatre Television, 60
Latour, Bruno, 16
Laugh In (television), 149–50
leadership, 171
Leete, Larry, 197–98, 199
Leggett-Gruen Corporation, 55–56
legibility, of new media
practices, 227n71
leisure
blurring boundaries of work and,
1, 6–7, 9–10, 11, 46, 74, 129–30,
149, 165, 182–83 (see also agnostic
media; entertainment, commercial,
exploiting affective resonance of)
narrowcasting and, 184
use value of, 10–11, 133
Leonardi, Paul M., 14–15
Levey, Harry, 54–55
Lewin, Kurt, 106–7
Lewis, Joe, 191, 192
licensing systems, 40–41
Lipartito, Kenneth, 205–6
Lippincott, Jesse, 232n79
liveness, 86, 103–4, 203–4, 252n53
immediacy and, 95, 108–9, 200 (see
also immediacy)
of JCI Report, 189, 201–2

whenever-whomever-wherever triad, 131–34, 162–63
  the home and, 146
  U-matic and, 152
Wilding Productions, 55–56
Wilke, Hubert, 124–25, 210
Williams, Raymond, 15–16, 64
  on flow, 64, 81
Wilson, Jim, 190–91
wireless, 39–40. *See also* radio
work, 1, 3. *See also* labor
  audience at, 9 (*see also* audience commodity)
  blurring boundaries of leisure and, 1, 5, 9, 46, 74, 129–30, 149, 165, 182–83 (*see also* agnostic media; entertainment, commercial, exploiting affective resonance of)
  defining, 5
  labor distinguished from, 5
  media at, 12
  nonwork and, 6–7, 10, 20–21, 129–30, 133, 205
  transformations of, 5, 8–9, 96, 153–54, 165–66, 182–83 (*see also* work transfer)
workday, extension of, 5, 146. *See also* whenever-whomever-wherever triad
workers and workforce
  demographics and diversity of, 8–9, 65, 96, 154–55, 167–68

empowerment and, 191 (*see also* self-skilling)
  flexibility of, 91–92, 106 (*see also* post-Fordism)
  flow and experience of, 79, 245n108
  productivity of (*see* productivity)
  socialization of, 8–9, (*see also* cultural turn, of management; employee training)
workplace. *See also* coordination functions; home; logistical media culture, 15 (*see also* cultural turn, of management)
work systems, socialization in, 64–65. *See also* socialization
work transfer, 6–7
  Glazer on, 159–60
World's Fair 1939, 264n53
World War I, 37
World War II, 56–57, 167, 239n200
  applied radio in, 41
  radio in, 38–39

Xerox, 184–85

Yates, JoAnne, 14–15
Yellow Book, 102

Zanuck, Darryl F., 147–48
Zworykin, Vladimir, 63–64, 90–91